A THEORY OF TEXTUALITY

D1557977

A Theory of
TEXTUALITY

The Logic and Epistemology

JORGE J. E. GRACIA

State University of New York Press

Published by
State University of New York Press, Albany

© 1995 State University of New York

For infomation, address State University of New York Press,
State University Plaza, Albany, N.Y. 12246

Production by M.R. Mulholland
Marketing by Nancy Farrell

Library of Congress Cataloging-in-Publication Data
Gracia, Jorge J. E.
A theory of textuality : the logic and epistemology / Jorge J. E. Gracia.
p.   cm.
Includes bibliographical references and indexes.
ISBN 0-7914-2467-7 (alk. paper). — ISBN 0-7914-2468-5 (pbk. : alk. paper)
1. Meaning (Philosophy)   2. Criticism (philosophy)   3. Theory
(Philosophy)   I. Title.
B105.M4G73   1995
121'.68—dc20
94-3613
CIP

10 9 8 7 6 5 4 3 2 1

To Norma

———

"Habet nescio quid latentis energie vive vocis actus,
et in aures discipuli de auctoris ore fortius sonat."

—Attributed to Jerome

"Paintings look alive, but if you question them,
they maintain a solemn silence;
the same is true of written words...."

—Socrates, *Phaedrus*

CONTENTS

Preface   xiii

Introduction: The Issues   xix

   I. General Character of the Issues   xxii
   II. Overall Outline   xxv
     A. The Logic of Texts   xxv
     B. The Epistemology of Texts   xxvii

Part I. The Logic of Texts

1. Intension   3
   I. Elements in the Definition of Texts   4
     A. Entities that Constitute Texts (ECTs)   4
     B. Signs   7
     C. Specific Meaning   14
     D. Intention   23
     E. Selection and Arrangement   24
     F. Context   26
   II. Conventionality of Texts   30
   III. Conclusion   36

2. Extension   41
   I. Texts and Language   42
   II. Texts and Artifacts   44
   III. Texts and Art Objects   52
   IV. Texts and Works   59
   V. Conclusion   70

3. Taxonomy   73
   I. Modal Classification   74
     A. Actual Text   74
       1. Historical Text   74
       2. Contemporary Text   75

3. Intermediary Text   76
B. Intended Text   76
C. Ideal Text   83
II. Functional Classification   86
  A. Linguistic Functions   87
    1. Informative Texts   87
    2. Directive Texts   87
    3. Expressive Texts   88
    4. Evaluative Texts   88
    5. Performative Texts   88
  B. Cultural Functions   89
    1. Legal Texts   89
    2. Literary Texts   90
    3. Philosophical Texts   90
    4. Scientific Texts   91
    5. Religious Texts   92
    6. Historical Texts   93
    7. Political Texts   94
    8. Pedagogical Texts   94
    9. Confessional Texts   94
    10. Entertaining Texts   95
    11. Inspirational Texts   95
    12. Pneumonic Texts   95
    13. Other Functional Categories of Texts 95
III. Conclusion   97

Part II. The Epistemology of Texts

4. Understanding   101
  I.   Understanding versus Meaning   103
  II. Number of Understandings   104
  III. Understanding and Textual Identity   106
  IV. Limits of Understanding   107
    A. Limits of Meaning   108
     1. Essential and Accidental Differences in Meaning   110
     2. Meaning and the Implications of Meaning   111
     3. Meaning and Intentions   112
    B. Factors that Establish the Limits of Meaning   114
     1. Author   114
     2. Audience   116
     3. Context   117
     4. Society   118

5. Language   118
6. Text   119
7. Cultural Function   123
C. Limits of Textual Understanding   127
D. Legitimacy of Understanding Texts Differently
   than their Historical Authors   136
V. Truth Value and Objectivity of Understanding   141
VI. Conclusion   143

5. Interpretation   147
I.   Nature and Ontological Status of Interpretations   147
II. Interpreter's Dilemma and Function of Interpretations 152
     A. Historical Function   155
     B. Meaning Function   160
     C. Implicative Function   161
III. Types of Interpretations: Textual vs. Nontextual   164
IV. Number, Truth Value, and Objectivity of Interpretations 168
     A. Of Textual Interpretations   168
        1. Number   168
        2. Truth Value   171
        3. Objectivity and Subjectivity   173
     B. Of Nontextual Interpretations   175
V.   Understanding, Meaning, and Interpretation of Interpretations 176
VI. Conclusion   177

6. Discernibility   181
I.   How Do I Know that Something Is a Text?   182
II. How Do I Learn the Meaning of a Text?   189
III. How Can I Be Certain that I Know the Meaning of a Text? 193
     A. Expected Behavior and Certainty in Textual Understanding 193
     B. Objections   196
     C. The Role of Tradition in the Discernibility of Texts 207
IV. Conclusion   212

Conclusion: A Theory of Texuality — Logic and Epistemology 215

Notes   235

Select Bibliography   269

Index of Authors   301

Index of Subjects   305

PREFACE

Texts are one of the most common objects of human experience. Indeed, they constitute the very foundations of cultures and civilizations. Cultures include everything that human societies develop to adapt themselves to and cope with their environment. Religion, art, science, philosophy, morality, values, laws, organizations, technology, language and so on are all part of culture. Civilizations are complex cultures in which a reliable means for preserving and transferring knowledge and information to future generations has been developed. Both cultures and civilizations rely on texts, for texts constitute the means whereby most knowledge and information are communicated and stored. But cultures may rely on oral texts alone, whereas civilizations almost always rely also on written texts. The use of written texts facilitates a greater and more precise transference of knowledge and information than is possible through oral texts alone and over longer periods of time, thus allowing civilizations to grow in sophistication and complexity. Written texts have been until now the very stuff out of which civilizations are made. Whether they will continue to be so in the future in the light of new developments in technology, it is still too early to tell. One way or another, however, it is clear that texts have played and will continue to play a key role in cultures and civilizations.

The importance of texts has not gone unnoticed by philosophers particularly in the West; the interest in texts goes back to the very roots of Western civilization. Concern with texts can be easily found in Greek antiquity and at the beginning of the Christian era, and in our time considerable attention has been paid to language by philosophers. It is in literary circles, however, that texts and textuality have been discussed more vigorously. Literary critics have raised important questions concerning interpretation, authorship, and the role that audiences play in the determination of the meaning and function of texts. Indeed, it is largely as a result of these concerns that some philosophers, particularly in the Continental tradition, have begun to notice the puzzling issues raised by texts.

My interest in texts arose from a concern with the relation of philosophy to its history. This concern forced me to consider the object of study of the history of philosophy. This object, I realized soon enough, reduced to texts; for the access to the views the history of philosophy studies is mediated through texts. This led me in turn to questions concerning the nature of texts, their understanding and interpretation, and the role they play in the recovery of the past. I raised and tried to answer some of these questions in a chapter of *Philosophy and Its History*

(1991), but found that many more questions remained unanswered. So I set out to rethink the philosophical issues posed by texts and to provide an overall, coherent and systematic view of their nature and function; that is, a theory of textuality.

Theory building has not been very popular in Anglo-American or Continental philosophy in recent years. Post-Wittgenstenian Anglo-American philosophy tends to be suspicious of any sort of system building. It favors a piecemeal approach marked by a generally skeptical attitude toward the development of theoretical schemes. Philosophers in this tradition are more comfortable criticizing than proposing theories; and when they venture to advance theoretical positions, those positions are restricted to narrow parameters or presented as something other than theories.[1]

Postmodernist Continental philosophers differ from Anglo-American philosophers in that their efforts are more general and often devoid of the sharp critical spirit that permeates Anglo-American philosophy. But theory building is not popular among them either, for they see their task primarily as working through the ideas and texts of historical figures rather than as developing new theoretical schemes. Indeed, many of them explicitly reject the possibility of theory, particularly in a hermeneutical context.[2]

In this climate of opinion, one may ask why anyone would try to develop a theory of textuality, as I am attempting to do. Is that task not an old-fashioned modernistic approach that goes contrary to the thrust of contemporary philosophy? Why waste time and energy in such an enterprise?

There are three reasons that support the attempt to develop a theory of textuality. One is philosophical; another, we might say, aesthetic; and the third, pragmatic. The first is based on a conception of philosophy as the articulation of our fundamental beliefs about the world into a consistent, comprehensive and systematic view. Thus, philosophy involves the formulation of theories, because it seeks to make consistent what we already believe, to complete the picture we have about the world by drawing out the implications of those beliefs, and to submit those beliefs to critical scrutiny. This is required because our views about the world are fragmentary and contain inconsistencies and imprecissions, which frequently result from our lack of awareness of the limits and implications of our beliefs and the uncritical acceptance of those beliefs.

The job of philosophy, then, is both constructive and critical. It is constructive insofar as philosophers seek to put together a systematic view of the world or any of its parts that is consistent and comprehensive. It is critical insofar as in doing so philosophers must examine critically the various views they hold, rejecting those that fail to stand up to rational scrutiny. Indeed, in many ways the history of philosophy is the history of the dialectical process between those who try to build theories and those who try to tear them down. To argue that one is possible without the other is to miss the nature of the process. The critic cannot criticize without an object, and the theory builder cannot effectively build without the critic's watchful eye.

The second reason that supports the attempt to develop a theory of textuality is aesthetic, for there is a certain aesthetic pleasure that derives from trying to develop theoretical schemes. This task appeals to the artisan in us; it is akin to the craft of building something and, thus, yields the satisfaction derived from both the accomplishment of something tangible and from the contemplation of a finished product. A theory is something we can objectify and regard as a completed product.

Finally, there is a pragmatic reason why theory building may be justified, for the building of a theory reveals and deepens one's understanding of the issues the theory is meant to solve. Even if the theory is ultimately untenable, the process of developing it often leads to greater understanding. After we have worked through a problem and formulated a theory as to how to solve it, we may still be puzzled and ignorant as to its ultimate solution, but our puzzlement and ignorance are enlightened insofar as we may know better and in greater detail where we have failed and the directions we might take were we to make another attempt at a solution.

Having said this much, I should add that the theory of textuality I defend is not intended as a closed position regarded by me as "the truth." The truth is not very easy to come by, and the older I get, the more difficult I find it to believe that I am certain of any part of it. The theory of textuality I have developed, rather, is intended as a model whose understanding should lead to a deeper comprehension of the difficult issues textuality poses. Nor is the theory to be regarded as complete by any means. It is to be considered, rather, as a starting point, for many questions concerning the subject matter it addresses are still left unanswered. It is for others to continue at the point where I leave off, or even to begin anew if they think that they must discard everything I have proposed. The theory I propose is not intended to end discussion but to promote it, and I will consider myself satisfied if it does so.[3]

Concerning the substance of the theory, I should note that it is guided by the conviction, based on my experience and the arguments I examine, that texts are semantically significant artifacts in relation to which authors, audiences, and contexts play interesting and idiosyncratic roles. Thus, it is essential to my view that proper distinctions be mantanied among the notions of texts, the entities that constitute texts, meanings, understandings, and interpretations. It is also important to distinguish texts from works and establish how texts and their meanings are related to authors, audiences, and contexts. It is part of my claim that a clear understanding of textuality requires the understanding of such distinctions and the aforementioned relations.

In general, I am convinced that most of the confusion surrounding textuality nowadays is a result of three factors: The first is a too narrow understanding of it, which is in turn a result of the piecemeal and unsystematic approach to texts characteristic of the literature. Contemporary authors tend to see texts within narrow parameters, in the light of certain types of texts, ignoring other types and thus missing the richness of the category. As a consequence, their views appear onesided and puzzling when considered in relation to other texts. This is particularly evident in those who view literary texts as paradigms of textuality and thus indiscriminately impose the categories that apply to them to texts of very different sorts, such as scientific and philosophical texts.

A second factor is a lack of a proper distinction among logical, metaphysical, and epistemological issues. It is frequent to find, in the recent literature, logical and metaphysical questions treated as if they were epistemological, thus undermining the value of the answers given to them. A common example of the confusion between logic and epistemology occurs when logical questions concerning the concept of a text are treated as if they were epistemological questions about discernibility of the concept.

Finally, a good portion of the confusion present in the literature is a result of a lack of proper grounding of epistemological questions on logical analyses. It is, indeed, frequent to find discussions of textual interpretations, for example, that rely on no clear conception of textuality.

Thus, to avoid the confusion resulting from the three factors mentioned, I have tried, first, to develop a broad and comprehensive view of textuality that can account for most of our ordinary experiences of texts without doing violence to the idiosyncrasies of particular species of texts. Second, I have introduced clear distinctions among the logical, epistemological, and metaphysical, questions that most concern contemporary philosophers.

The logical and epistemological dimensions of my theory will be presented in this book; the metaphysical dimensions of the theory will be expounded in a subsequent volume. The advantages of a single volume are obvious: It would have presented the theory as the whole it is intended to be and made clear the interrelations among its logical, epistemological, and metaphysical dimensions. But the size and cost of such a volume would have been forbidding.

Some readers will no doubt be surprised at the lack of references in the body of the book to other contemporary or historical authors. Indeed, it appears odd that someone like me, who has devoted considerable energy to the history of philosophy, should have produced what is, considered by any standard, a historically sanitized text. But the reasons for the procedure I followed have to do precisely with my respect for historical work and also with the need for economy. The development of a theory involves considerable breadth and depth, and such a task could not have been carried out in the space in which I have tried to do it if in addition I had had to worry about historical accuracy. I have, therefore, banished references to the Notes, where those readers interested in the background of the discussion will be able to find further information.

This procedure has allowed me not only sufficient space to present, even if in broad outlines, an overall theory of textuality, but has also saved me from having to offer detailed arguments against views with which I disagree. To have attempted to do that would have been beyond the scope of this book and would have necessarily ended in superficiality.

Another feature of this study that may strike readers as peculiar in the context of the division between Analysis and Continental philosophy which characterizes the current philosophical community, is my use of both analytic and Continental sources. The reason for this is, first, that, as I have made clear elsewhere, I find the schizophrenic state of the contemporary philosophical community unproductive.[4] Second, I have found much that is challenging and useful even in authors who are foreign to me and to the traditions with which I am most familiar. I have worked my way through widely different materials and, I believe, profited from it, even though it often cost me considerable pain. There are limits to what I was able to look at and digest, of course — a fact that will be obvious to anyone familiar with the extensive literature relevant to textuality — but I hope I have taken into account most of the signposts in the field. This does not mean, however, that I have tried to produce a stylistically eclectic text or one in which no philosophical tradition is evident. This book is the product of my training and intellectual heritage and therefore it does, as it should, reveal them. But this does not stop it from trying to take seriously the views of authors whose philosophical culture is different from nime.

Let me finish by thanking those who have contributed to the realization of this project in one way or another, for I have received considerable help in the composition of this book from many persons. Moreover, in it I have used materials from several previous publications, although in each case only sections of them have been used and in every case subst antial modifications have been introduced in them. The first attempt I made to develop a theory of textuality appeared as an article, entitled "Texts and Their Interpretation," published in *Review of Metaphysics* 43 (1990): 495–542. A modified version of this article appeared as Chapter 4 of the book already mentioned, *Philosophy and Its History: Issues in Philosophical Historiography* (Albany: SUNY Press, 1991). There is also the articles, "Can There Be Definitive Interpretations?: An Interpretation of Foucault in Response to Engel," in B. Smith, ed., *European Philosophy and the American Academy* (La Salle, Ill.: Hegeler Institute, 1994), pp. 41–51; "Las interpretaciones definitivas," *Revista Latinoamericana de Filosofía* 19 (1993): 203–212; and "'La legitimidad en la interpretación," in a volume in honor of Ricardo Maliandi (Buenos Aires: Universidad de Río Cuarto, 1995). The materials borrowed from these publications are scattered throughout the book. I am grateful to the editors of the journals and to SUNY Press for their permission to use the materials in question. Three other articles serve as background and support for this volume and will be used in the second installment of this project: "Can There Be Texts Without Audiences? The Identity and Function of Audiences," *Review of Metaphysics* 47, n.4 (1994): 711–34; "Can There Be Texts Without Historical Authors?" *American Philosophical Quarterly* 31, n.3 (1994): 248–53; and "Autor y represión," *Cuadernos de Etica* forthcoming. I should also mention that some parts of the book have been presented as papers in various forums. In particular, parts of Chapters 4, 5, and 6 were delivered as lectures at the University of Puerto Rico, the University of St. Thomas, Pennsylvania State University, St. John's University, Geneseo State College, the University of Notre Dame and at a conference on the influence of European ideas on the American academy hosted by the Hegeler Institute. On all occasions, I profited considerably from questions posed by the audience.

Among those who have helped me think through the ideas presented here are the students who took graduate seminars I taught in the spring of 1990 and the autumn of 1992 on the topic of this book. I am also grateful to six students who were my research assistants at various times during the period in which I was working on the book: Michael Gorman, Ky Herreid, Jeremy Fantl, Gordon Snow, William Irwin, and Jane Bristol. They helped me with the research, the preparation of the notes, proofreading, and the critical analysis of the ideas presented. I am particularly grateful to the first three for the time they took to think of counterexamples and objections to my views. Indeed, some portion of the counterexamples and objections I discuss were originally raised by them. In addition, Elizabeth Millán took a tutorial with me in the Fall semester of 1991 in which we discussed the book in ways that proved beneficial. Finally, I am also grateful to several of my colleagues at the State University of Buffalo and to various other friends who obliged me by reading and criticizing parts of the book or by offering bibliographical suggestions. I would like to mention especially John Kearns, Kenneth Barber, Rudolf Makkreel, Bruce Reichenbach, James Brady, James Bunn, Randall Dipert, and Timothy Madigan.

INTRODUCTION: THE ISSUES

Perhaps the most dramatic example of the type of issue raised by the consideration of texts and textuality can be expressed in the question: How do I know the meaning of a text? This issue arises because very often what we understand when we say we understand a text appears to have little to do with the nature of the object that functions as the text.[1] Consider a text such as '2 + 2 = 4.' What I see are certain marks made on paper that have a certain color and certain shapes. But what I understand when I say I understand the meaning of the text is that two and two make four, a fact that has no color or shape. When I turn on the radio or pay attention to what one of my daughters is saying, I am again perceiving certain sounds that produce in me certain understandings. These understandings presumably correspond to the understandings that the utterers of the sounds experienced themselves and want me to experience. When later I recall those sounds or the marks on the paper, again I find myself thinking thoughts similar to the ones I had when I first perceived those sounds and marks. However, seldom does the object of understanding, that is, the meaning of the text, consist in what I perceive or remember when I perceive or remember the objects that function as the text, be they visible shapes or audible sounds.

How can understanding take place, then? What is it in the marks, sounds, or images that produces understanding in those who are exposed to them? It seems almost miraculous that something like this should happen. And it appears to be even more miraculous when the texts I perceive originated long ago. How can it be possible that I understand the text of Cicero's *De amicitia*, for example? Can I be sure that I understand it correctly? Can I be certain that what I understand is what Cicero and his contemporaneous audience understood by it? How do I know that it concerns friendship?

Even more than this, how do I know that the text of Cicero's *De amicitia* is a text and not just a design on paper that has no meaning and is intended to convey none? Someone might wish to say that it is not difficult to determine that Cicero's *De amicitia* is a text, for it is composed of signs easily recognized by those who know Latin. But even if we were to accept this, what do we make of some designs recently found in an excavation from an ancient culture about which we know nothing beyond what the excavation has uncovered? How do we determine whether those designs are texts or not? And if they are texts, how can we discover their meaning and be certain that we have discovered it?

These questions provide a stark example of the sorts of questions that may be asked concerning texts, but they represent just a very small number of the many issues that can be raised. Indeed, the very nature of these questions points to the need to raise questions concerning the nature of textuality itself; for any attempt to answer these questions must begin with an attempt to identify the conditions that make texts what they are. But this is by no means easy. For one thing, we speak of texts in conflicting ways, indicating that we think of them as having what appear to be incompatible characteristics. To illustrate this point, let us look at five sentences that are paradigmatic of some of the ways in which we speak about texts:

1.   The text we shall discuss today is a novel.
2.   Give me the text that is in front of you.
3.   Do not throw away the text.
4.   That text is ungrammatical.
5.   The text we have been discussing is logically incoherent.

    This list could easily be extended to include hundreds or even thousands of sentences regularly used in ordinary discourse. Such an abundance would seem to suggest that we know, at least implicitly, what texts are and that there are no particular problems with the notion of a text. Yet, even a superficial perusal of these sentences reveals potential conflicts and problems, for the sentences speak about texts in ways that prima facie appear to be incompatible. Indeed, they suggest that we think about texts in terms of categories that could not be expected to apply to the same thing. For example, 1 implies that at least some texts are literary works that can be classified as falling into particular literary genres. Sentences 2 and 3 refer to texts as if they were physical objects that can occupy space, be passed from hand to hand, and be discarded. In 4, the text is understood as a grammatical unit, and 5 applies to the text a logical criterion that one would only expect to be applied to concepts or views. Thus, even in this small sample of the ways we speak about texts, it is evident we think of them in terms of literary, grammatical, physical, and logical categories; and, of course, there are many others.

    In particular, it is worrisome to find both physical and nonphysical categories applied to texts, for if texts are physical objects, how can we speak of them as being logically incoherent? Yes, we could say that they are illegible, meaning that they cannot be read, for illegibility may apply to physical objects.[2] But logical incoherence does not apply to physical objects. I do not think anyone would wish to say that a pencil is logically incoherent, even if what I write with it turns out to be so. And the same could be said about other physical objects. It is concepts or views that can be logically incoherent. If texts are physical objects, we can perceive them, physically destroy them, or move them from place to place, but we cannot think about them in the same way as we do concepts, nor can we apply to them other logical categories that we regularly apply to concepts.

On the other hand, if texts are concepts or conceptlike, as suggested by 5, how are we to interpret the physical-object language we frequently use in connection with them? For concepts cannot be physically long or short, legible or illegible, and so on. Take, for example, the concept of goodness. Would anyone be willing to argue that such a concept is physically very long, as we might say a text is, or that the concept is illegible? We could say that a concept is difficult to grasp, or complex, or even unintelligible, but it is not easy to argue that it has physical characteristics such as dimensions. Indeed, even the concepts of physical objects, such as the concept of a piece of marble, do not appear to have physical characteristics. Although a piece of marble has dimensions and color, the concept of a piece of marble does not appear to have dimensions or color.

One may want to argue, nonetheless, that when we think about concepts, there are physical characteristics that accompany them even if those physical characteristics do not characterize the concepts themselves. For example, when I think about the concept of a particular piece of marble, there are certain electrical currents in my brain and also certain chemical reactions that can be described in physical terms. But even if thinking about concepts were always accompanied by certain processes that can be characterized in physical terms, one would still want to distinguish between the concepts on the one hand and the processes whereby we think about them on the other. Indeed, common sense would seem to dictate that the physical characteristics in question would not be predicated of the concepts, but of the physical processes in the brain. In short, the predication of physical and nonphysical characteristics of texts creates a problem that requires solution, and this is so even if one were to reject the characterization of the entities I have cited as examples. Indeed, even if one were to accept, for example, that some physical objects can be described in terms of nonphysical characteristics and that some nonphysical entities can be described in terms of physical characteristics, the problem remains as to how to do it in a consistent and sensible way, particularly in the case of texts.

The initial problem that one faces concerning the physical or nonphysical nature of texts is not limited to the parameters indicated. Leaving the physical-nonphysical issue unresolved affects other questions related to texts, such as their classification, the identification of their causes, their ontological status, and so on. Consider, for example, the question concerned with the causes of texts. The causal analysis of texts will differ drastically, depending on whether texts are conceived of as physical or nonphysical. For physical objects have physical causes, but it is not clear how physical causes affect nonphysical objects. And the same could be said, for example, if we were to take up the matter of the composition of texts. A physical text might be composed of, say, ink or paint, but a nonphysical text would be composed of, say, mental images. The solution to the problem posed by the physical or nonphysical nature of texts is, therefore, important not only for its own sake, but also because it affects the solutions to other problems and issues.

The questions I have raised so far constitute just a sample of the sorts of questions that may be raised concerning texts. There are, as noted earlier, many others. I shall postpone their consideration, however, until we get to the various chapters set aside to deal specifically with them. For the moment, my purpose is not to formulate all the issues that can or should be raised concerning texts, let alone to do so in a precise and clear way, but only to present some samples of those issues to give an indication of what is to come and to emphasize the fact that the various chapters of this book aim to deal with clusters of problems that require solutions. Before I present an overall outline of those issues, I would like to say something about the general character of those issues to avoid possible misunderstandings.

I. General Character of the Issues

Of the cluster of philosophical issues that surround texts, some are logical, others are epistemological, and still others are metaphysical.[3] The differences among these are not often observed and as a result confusion develops. Let me begin, then, by illustrating the distinctions among these three types of issues.

The distinctions among logical, epistemological, and metaphysical issues may be illustrated by referring to a sentence such as, 'A human being is a rational animal.' This sentence may be understood logically, epistemologically, or metaphysically:

Logically:	The necessary and sufficient conditions of the *intension* of 'human being' are given by the *intensions* of 'rational' and 'animal.'
Epistemologically:	The necessary and sufficient conditions of *knowing* a human being are *knowing* a human being as rational and as animal.
Metaphysically:	The necessary and sufficient conditions of *being* a human being are *being* rational and animal.

The first way of understanding the sentence is logical insofar as it involves the intensional analysis of "human being" into its components, "rational" and "animal." Understood in this way, the sentence makes no reference to things, objects, or realities on the one hand, or the knowledge of those things, objects, or realities on the other; it is concerned only with the intensions of the terms.

The second way of understanding the sentence is epistemological, because it is taken as giving the criteria that may be used to identify something as a human being. As epistemological criteria, the conditions in question may be taken as causes, not of the thing for whose identification they are to be used, but rather of the knowledge of the thing in question. Their function is to serve to identify the thing correctly.

The third way of understanding the sentence is metaphysical because the conditions it identifies concern the way the thing described by the sentence *is* and not the relations that exist between it, considered as an intension, and other intensions, or the conditions of knowing it. Thus rationality and animality in this context are not taken either as the intensions into which the intension of 'human being' is to be analyzed or as conditions of our knowing human beings as such; they are the very conditions in human beings that make them *be* such.

The logical understanding of the sentence, then, yields an analysis of the intension of its subject-term; that is, of the conceptual content associated with it. By contrast, the epistemological understanding of the sentence provides criteria of identification of the thing and, thus, about how it can be known. Finally, a metaphysical understanding of it yields information about the nature of the thing to which the subject-term refers, that is, about what that thing is.

As is clear from the example used, it is not necessary that the conditions identified in each of these three ways of understanding the sentence in question be different. It is possible for them to be, in fact, the same. For example, the reasons why a human being is a human being and why we know a human being as a human being may be the same; namely, that a human being is rational and animal. But they do not need to be so. Consider another example: It is possible that the conditions we use to know that something is a fish (epistemological understanding) and what makes something a fish (metaphysical understanding) are not the same. The reason is that such conditions, which we call criteria, are always related to particular observers and their circumstances. Someone who lives in a place where the only animals that swim are fish could very well use swimming as a criterion for identifying fish even though swimming is not peculiar to fish. Dolphins, whales, dogs, and even human beings swim, and they are not fish. But the conditions that make something what it is are not necessarily related to an observer. That does not mean that they are never related to an observer or that they are not related to anything, however. They may be relational in various ways. For example, the conditions that make something necessary for something else must depend on the relation between the things in question. Having eyes is necessary for seeing, but the relation between eyes and seeing is not dependent on an observer in the way criteria are.

These examples illustrate the distinction and relations between epistemological and metaphysical understandings. Something similar could be said about the distinction and relations between logical and epistemological understandings. That the intension of 'human being' is to be unpacked logically into the intensions of 'rational' and 'animal' does not entail that the criteria we use to identify something as a human being need be rationality and animality. On the other hand, when we come to the metaphysical understanding, it looks as if it would make no sense to say that the conditions identified in a logical analysis could be different from the conditions identified in a metaphysical one. Would it make sense, for example, to say that the nature of human beings consists in being rational and animal and at the same time say that the intensional analysis of 'human being' does not yield the intensions of 'rational' and 'animal'?

The reason for this anomaly is that ultimately we all expect, as most pre-Kantians firmly believed, that thought be a reflection of reality and thus that logic mirror metaphysics.[4] Accordingly, the conditions identified in logical analyses are expected to coincide with the conditions identified in metaphysical ones. And, indeed, the confusions between logic and metaphysics so frequently found in the history of philosophy, not only before Kant but also after him, are probably the result of this ingrained belief. Notice, however, that in presenting this position, I speak about "expectations," for this coincidence is not obvious by any means. Since Kant, it has become difficult to continue holding uncritically the assumption that thought follows being and logic mirrors reality.[5]

Another point that should be made before we continue is that a lack of co-incidence between the conditions identified in metaphysical and epistemological understandings should not be accepted uncritically either. Indeed, if the epistemological field is not identified with a particular world or set of circumstances, but is extended to all possible worlds, it may be reasonable to argue that in such a case epistemological criteria must coincide with metaphysical and logical conditions. The further investigation of this point is certainly worthwhile, but it would take us far afield, and so I will not pursue it here.

The three understandings of the sentence given previously illustrate, then, the distinctions among logic, epistemology, and metaphysics. They also illustrate the importance of understanding the diverse nature of the issues they comprise, for the value of the answers to those issues will depend to some extent on that nature. It will not do, as we already saw, to confuse a metaphysical with an epistemological issue, for the answer to the former may not fit the latter and vice versa. Nor would it do to confuse a logical with an epistemological issue or a metaphysical with a logical one for the most part for similar reasons. Keeping a perspective on the nature of the issues to be addressed, then, should help prevent confusions and mistakes.[6] The first thing that we must keep in mind concerning the various issues we are going to discuss about texts is, therefore, their logical, epistemological, or metaphysical nature. From what has been said, we should expect that at least in some cases their nature will have important repercussions. One word of caution, however: Logic, epistemology and metaphysics are closely related. Therefore, although the discussion in this book tries to preserve the distinction among questions pertaining to each of these branches of philosophy, it should not be expected that questions pertaining to each branch can be treated in complete isolation from questions pertaining to the other branches.

II. Overall Outline

To facilitate the discussion of the logical and epistemological issues that can be raised concerning texts I have divided them into six different clusters, dealing respectively with intension, extension, taxonomy, understanding, interpretation, and discernibility. Each of these clusters is discussed within a chapter. The six resulting chapters are, in turn, gathered into two parts that signal the general nature of the issues in question. The first part is concerned with the logic of texts and includes the chapters on intension, extension, and taxonomy. The second part concerns the epistemology of texts and contains the chapters on understanding, interpretation, and discernibility. The order I follow—logic first, epistemology second—is not casual. It reflects my conviction that streightening out the logic of a concept is essential for finding solutions to the epistemological questions it poses. It is also a requirement of good metaphysics. Hence, Part I of this book should function propaedeutically not only to Part II of this book, but also to the volume to follow which deals with the metaphysics of texts.

A. The Logic of Texts: Intension, Extension, and Taxonomy

What has been said so far is partly relevant to the problem involved in determining the intension of 'text,' for to determine the intension of that term is to formulate a definition of it that provides an analysis of its intensional content. As already noted, this is not the same as presenting a metaphysical understanding of it, where the necessary and sufficient conditions of being a text are identified. For our immediate purpose, however, to present a logical analysis will be sufficient, because it will satisfy the audience for which it is intended. That audience is composed of three types of philosophers. First, there are those who make a distinction between logic and metaphysics but, following in the pre-Kantian tradition, maintain that logic mirrors metaphysics.[7] If logic mirrors metaphysics, then the result of a logical analysis should coincide with a metaphysical one and its logical or metaphysical character makes no difference in the end. Second, there are those who make a distinction between logic and metaphysics, but regard metaphysics as impossible.[8] And, third, there are those who do not make a distinction between logic and metaphysics, thus identifying them.[9] In the second case, the logical analysis is the only possible one, and in the third, it is the same as the metaphysical one. Therefore, in providing a logical analysis we can satisfy all three groups, although for some the implications of the analysis will also be metaphysical and for others it will not. Later, when I present the metaphysical dimension of my theory, however, it will become clear that the logical analysis provided in Part I of this book is not sufficient for a complete metaphysical understanding of textuality.

Our first task, then, is to provide an intensional analysis of the term 'text.'

Such an analysis should identify the conceptual content of the term and be formulated as a definition. This task comes first because a clear definition is fundamental for the discussion of the other problems involved in textuality and constitutes the centerpiece of a theory of textuality. It involves, first, the analysis of the terms that compose the definition and, second, the distinction of the notion of a text from other notions that, because of their close connections with it, may be confused with it. Accordingly, Chapter 1 is taken up with the discussion of such notions as the entities that constitute texts, signs, meaning, the selection and arrangement of signs, intention, and context, which explicitly or implicitly enter into the definition of a text. There is also a discussion of the conventional nature of texts and their epistemic character. Chapter 2 explores the notions of language, artifact, art object, and work, which are closely related to the notion of a text but should not be confused with it. The intensional distinctions among these notions have extensional implications, which is the reason why the chapter purports to deal with the extension of 'text.'

Once these tasks are carried out, I turn to the classification of various types of texts in Chapter 3. This inquiry falls within the province of logical analysis insofar as it involves fleshing out some of the implications of the formulated definition. It differs from the first task in that it goes beyond the formulation of a definition to explore the implications of the definition in relation to other notions. Although there are many ways in which texts may be classified, I concentrate on two such ways for two reasons: economy and the greater relevance they have for the issues discussed in this book. The two classifications in question have to do with modality and function.

Within the modal classification, I take up the actual, intended, and ideal texts. Actual texts are further subdivided into historical, contemporary, and intermediary. Within the functional classification, I distinguish between the linguistic and cultural functions of texts. The classification according to linguistic function yields informative, directive, expressive, evaluative and performative texts. The classification according to cultural function yields legal, literary, philosophical, scientific, religious, political, pedagogical, confessional, entertaining, inspirational, pneumonic, and a miscellaneous category of texts.

Although some of these categories may have strong claims to exhaustiveness and mutual exclusivity, other classifications do not. Functional categories in particular are notorious for overlapping, because in most cases texts carry out multiple functions at once. The value of these classifications has to do with the light they shed on the notion of a text and the help they render in preventing conceptual confusions concerning it. This is the reason why this classificatory scheme should be considered as part of the logical analysis of the intension of 'text' and why it should precede the discussion of epistemological issues which concern textuality. Its implications and usefulness will become evident in the second part of the book.

B. The Epistemology of Texts: Understanding, Interpretation, and Discernibility

The understanding, interpretation, and discernibility of texts have to do with epistemology rather than logic or metaphysics; they concern our knowledge of texts and not the logical categories to which texts belong or the way texts are. The issues involved in understanding are not parochial to texts. Understanding extends to all sorts of things. We speak of understanding persons, emotions, facts, views, and so on. In this context, however, we are concerned with only the understanding of texts. The main issues that will be discussed have to do with the distinction between the understanding and the meaning of texts, the number of understandings that may be had of a text, the relation of understanding to textual identity, and the limits of the understanding of texts. The last topic is a complex one that requires a discussion of the limits of meaning, the factors that establish such limits, and the legitimacy of understanding texts in ways different from the ways in which their historical authors understood them.

When compared with the issues involved in understanding, the issues involved in interpretation appear to be more closely related to texts. It is true that we speak about interpreting things other than texts. For example, we speak of interpreting events.[10] But in such cases what is usually meant is that we have put together some conjectures as to what are the causes or consequences of those events. For example, when we say that X gave the wrong interpretation of Y's action (where Y's action is the event under interpretation), we might be noting that X misunderstood Y's motives or, alternatively, that X did not foresee correctly the consequences of Y's action. X may have thought, wrongly, that Y killed his wife because of jealousy, whereas, in fact, her death may have been an accidental occurrence. Or X may have conjectured that, after the death of Y's wife, Y would become a playboy, whereas, in fact, he became depressed and eventually committed suicide.

Most often, when we speak of interpretation, however, we are speaking about the interpretation of texts. This sort of interpretation raises many important and challenging questions, some of which have been discussed in great detail by philosophers, particularly in this century. I concentrate, however, only on those questions that seem to be especially crucial, questions that concern the nature, ontological status, function, classification, number, truth value, and objectivity of interpretations. With respect to the nature and ontological status of interpretations, I discuss various issues that are of a metaphysical character but must be discussed at this point because this is the only place where interpretation is discussed in the book.

With respect to the function of interpretations, I inquire as to the purpose that interpretations serve. In other words, I identify what interpretations are for and what they are meant to do. This is a particularly important section of the inquiry, for in it I answer questions related to the effectiveness of interpretations as well as to the bases on which that effectiveness, if there is such, rests, and the criteria that can be used to measure it. Following this, I provide a discussion of various types of interpretations that are frequently confused in the literature, such as textual and nontextual interpretations. Finally, I explore the possible number, truth value, and objectivity of interpretations.

As in the cases of understanding and interpretation, the issues concerning the discernibility of texts are not parochial to texts. Similar questions may be raised concerning all sorts of other things, although in the case of texts there are peculiarities that complicate matters to some degree. Three issues of discernibility are of particular interest. I have framed them in terms of three questions: (1) How do I know that something is a text? (2) How do I learn the meaning of a text? And (3) how can I be certain that I know the meaning of a text? The first question seeks an answer that will identify the necessary and sufficient conditions under which a knower can effectively identify something as a text. The second applies to the conditions that make it possible for a knower to learn the meaning of a text. And the third seeks an answer that will identify criteria under which one can be certain of the meaning of a text. All three are clearly epistemological in nature because they are concerned with the conditions that make it possible for knowledge to occur; in this they differ from logical and metaphysical issues.

With the general direction indicated by these preliminaries in mind, we can now turn to the more substantive and detailed part of the book. I begin with the intension of 'text.'

PART I

THE LOGIC OF TEXTS

1

INTENSION

The aim of this chapter is to answer the question: What are texts? It aims to do so by proposing a definition of texts that provides an intensional analysis of the notion of textuality. The definition of texts is the cornerstone of any theory of textuality, for such a definition not only elucidates the notion of textuality itself, but also helps to clarify other philosophical questions that pertain to it. The definition I propose will help indicate, moreover, the way to resolve some of the issues raised in the Introduction. In particular, it will point a way to the solution of the problems arising from the incompatible ways in which we think about texts. Thus, we will uncover the reasons why texts are referred to in terms of predicates that imply that they are, for example, both physical and nonphysical entities and show that such predications do not imply an incompatibility in the nature of texts or an inconsistency in the way we think about them.

Finding an appropriate definition of texts is by no means easy both because of the complex and peculiar nature of texts and because of the many different conceptions of texts that have been proposed, particularly in recent years.[1] Two ways of proceeding suggest themselves: One is to present a definition at the outset and follow it with an analysis of its meaning and implications; the other is to begin by discussing the problems that proposing a definition involves, examining various possibilities along the way, until an acceptable definition is reached. The main advantage of the first procedure is clarity —because it gives the favored definition upfront, it provides a signpost to guide subsequent discussion. Its main disadvantages are two: First, it hides the problematic nature of the procedure whereby the definition has been reached, giving the mistaken impression that it is the result of some fundamental and clear intuition; and, second, it suggests that the definition is to be taken dogmatically as precise and unmodifiable.

The advantage of the second procedure is that, in contrast with the first procedure, it accurately reproduces the difficult, complicated, and at times confusing process whereby the definition has been reached, thus presenting the issue in its true problematic character. Moreover, precisely because of the difficulties it makes evident in the process of formulating the definition, it leaves the distinct impression that the result is not to be considered final. Its main disadvantage is the lack of clarity that results, for the path eventually leading to the definition can be tortuous, cumbersome, and confusing.

I have chosen the first procedure both for the sake of clarity and because it makes it possible to sidestep the discussions of the many views of textuality that have been proposed. Thus, the discussion can be pointed, analytic, and clear, avoiding historical entanglements and difficult questions of exegesis that could not be resolved just in passing. To avoid the negative consequences of this procedure, however, it must be kept in mind that the development of a definition of texts is a complicated and problematic issue which the discussion in this chapter does not aim to reproduce, and that the definition itself must be taken as provisional and thus modifiable. Moreover, it is not only in the rest of the chapter, but also in the rest of the book, that its full understanding and implications are developed.

Let me begin, then, by providing the definition of texts whose viability and implications will be explored subsequently:

> A text is a group of entities, used as signs, which are selected, arranged, and intended by an author in a certain context to convey some specific meaning to an audience.

The elements of this definition are the group of entities used as signs, the signs, the selection and arrangement of those signs, the intention, the context, the author, the audience, and the specific meaning that is intended to be conveyed. The author and the audience will be discussed in part in Chapters 4 and 5 respectively, because of the epistemic character of some of the issues that can be raised in connection with them, and in part in the volume devoted to metaphysics.[2] This chapter concentrates on the remaining six elements. The discussion of all these takes place in Section I. Section II of the chapter deals with the conventional nature of texts and their epistemic character. The chapter concludes with a summary.

I. Elements in the Definition of Texts

As noted, apart from the author and the audience, the elements present in the definition of texts are the entities that constitute the signs of which a text is composed, the signs themselves, the specific meanings texts are intended to convey, the intention, the selection and arrangement of the signs, and the context. I deal with these in the order given.

A. Entities that Constitute Texts (ECTs)

A proper understanding of textuality requires that we distinguish texts from the entities used as the signs that compose texts.[3] This is important because, as we shall see later, the distinction between texts and the entities that constitute them may account for the seemingly incompatible predicates that are often predicated of texts. Hence, this distinction may solve some of the problems concerning texts raised in the Introduction.

As noted earlier, I have proposed that texts be conceived as groups of entities, used as signs, which are selected, arranged, and intended by an author in a certain context to convey some specific meaning to an audience. But the signs that make up texts are themselves constituted by entities. This is not different than the case of a horse that is constituted not only by its head, body, and legs, but also by the parts that constitute its head, body, and legs, such as the eyes, the belly, the hoofs, and so on. Consider the text, "No smoking is permitted here." In one sense it may be taken to be composed of several signs such as the words of which it is composed, the punctuation—in this case the period at the end which marks the end of the sentence—and so on. But in another sense the text is constituted, at least in part, by the lines, points, ink marks, and such, which constitute the signs that compose the text.

The distinction between the entities that constitute a sign and the sign may be illustrated with an example. Consider the case of a circle drawn on the sand. The circle is by itself nothing but a circle. But if the circle is used to convey meaning it becomes a sign, and all sorts of things may be communicated through it. It could be intended as a letter, or a secret symbol that should trigger a particular action by some of those who observe it, and so on. In these cases, the circle taken by itself is a mere object of perception, but the circle used as a letter or a secret signal is something else. The identity conditions for the circle and the identity conditions for the circle considered as a letter, say, are quite different. Of course, the relationship between the two is quite close, ontologically speaking. If the circle is destroyed, the letter is destroyed, and if the letter is destroyed the circle is destroyed. Indeed, if one were to ask how many things one sees when looking at the circle and the letter, it would be incorrect to answer that one sees two things. Yet, that does not mean that the circle is the letter and the letter is the circle. This relationship is in some ways like that of the animal and the rational individual in a rational animal. In a rational animal, if the rational individual is destroyed, the animal is destroyed; if the animal is destroyed, the rational individual is destroyed; and the animal and the rational individual are not two numerically distinct things. But to be a rational individual and to be an animal are two different things, for it is possible that there can be animals that are not rational and rational individuals that are not animals.

For the sake of simplicity, I shall refer to the entities that are used as signs as entities that constitute the signs and I shall refer to the signs as being constituted by these entities. Thus, in the earlier example, the circle drawn on the sand constitutes the letter that results from using it in certain ways. Now, because texts are composed of signs, the entities that constitute those signs may also be said to constitute the texts composed of those signs.

The character of the entities that constitute texts and signs may vary a great deal. In written texts they are visual as the example provided earlier illustrates, but they can also be sounds emitted orally that are perceived through hearing. Still, in other cases they may be mental images rather than physical entities, and thus subject to imagination rather than perception. When I form a mental picture of the text "No smoking is allowed here," for example, the text or the signs of which it is composed are not constituted by external objects of perceptions. The text and its signs are constituted by images not present to the eye.

It is important to distinguish texts from the entities that constitute them, for their respective functions and features are quite different. Indeed, the identity conditions for a text and for the entities that constitute it are quite different, and as we shall see later keeping these two categories separate prevents a number of the confusions frequently found in the literature.

The differences between the identity conditions of texts and the identity conditions of the entities that constitute them depend on the nature of the entities in question on one side and on the nature of texts on the other. The conditions of textuality were stipulated in the definition given earlier, its certerpiece being that they are entities with meaning. But the identity conditions of the entities that constitute texts considered apart from their function as texts may vary a great deal, depending on the entities in question, for these entities have meaning only if they are used as texts. Indeed, as we saw earlier, some of those entities may be physical, whereas others may be mental. In no case, however, do those conditions include all the conditions identified in the definition of texts, unless they are used as texts.

One point that needs to be kept in mind is that, because the entities that constitute texts are complex, not all features of those entities are semantically significant, that is, not all of them are used to convey meaning. In a written text, for example, constituted by lines and figures of a certain color, the color may be semantically irrelevant—for the meaning of the text it may not matter whether it is red, blue, or any other color for that matter. Not all features and parts of the entities that are used as texts need be semantically significant. Strictly speaking, only the entities or features of entities that function semantically should be considered constitutive of a text.

In all this we can see the beginning of the solution to some of the problems raised in the Introduction. There we saw, for example, that incompatible predicates are frequently predicated of texts, suggesting that they are, say, physical and nonphysical. But now there is a way out, for when incompatible predicates are predicated of a text it may be that the predicates in question are not being predicated of the same thing. A physical description may apply to the entities that constitute a text, whereas a nonphysical one may apply to the meaning of the text. I may ask a student, for example, to hand me a text and then remark that what she has handed to me is logically incoherent. In this case what I mean is for the student to hand me a physical object and that the views expressed by that object when used as a text are logically incoherent. The same confusion may result from taking semantically nonsignificant features of an object, some of whose features are semantically significant and thus constitutive of the text, as constitutive of the text.

Let me finish, then, by saying that from now on I shall understand texts and signs as entities used to convey meaning and thus distinguishable from those entities considered apart from meaning.[4] The entities that constitute texts and signs considered apart from the meaning that turns them into texts and signs will be referred to as ECTs, short for "entities that constitute texts (or signs)."

B. Signs

I have identified texts with groups of entities used as signs that fulfill various conditions. That texts are composed of signs implies that texts are complex. Indeed, the etymology of the word 'text' suggests that they are always complex and, therefore, composed of more than one thing. 'Text' comes from the Latin *textus*, which means texture, tissue, structure and, in relation to language, construction, combination, and connection. *Textus* comes in turn from the verb *texo*, which means to weave, compose. Finally, the English term is related to such other terms as 'textile' and 'texture,' all of which have the connotation of some sort of composition and complexity.

Because texts are closely related to signs and composed of them, one might be led to believe that texts are fundamentally signs and differ from them only in degree of complexity. Yet, the fact is that texts and signs differ in many ways and therefore we should distinguish between them.[5] Indeed, the failure to distinguish between texts and signs may be the source of adscribing features of the former to the latter, and vice versa, creating confusions about both and leading to various errors. I shall return briefly to this point after I introduce the distinction between texts and signs, although the implications of a failure to observe it will become clear only later in the book, particularly in Chapters 4 and 5.

Several ways to establish the distinction suggest themselves. Based on what has been said, a most obvious way of distingushing the two is to argue that texts are somehow complex composites, whereas signs are not. Let us call this the *Complex-Composite View*.

The Complex-Composite View is easily assailed, for most signs are not simple. Words, for example, are always complex, being composed of letters, shapes and so on. Indeed, even periods, when they are only dots, have a certain shape and width in addition to other features, without which they would not be considered significant, and thus would have to be considered composites of those features. Of course, one can always conceive a certain color as a sign. Say that red means danger. In cases like this it may be possible to argue that we have simple signs, for a color does not appear to be complex.[6] But the existence of simple signs is not sufficient to establish a distinction between signs and texts, because most signs are complex. To say that signs, in contrast with texts, can be simple, whereas texts cannot, does not tell us enough about texts and signs, and therefore, it does not sufficiently elucidate textuality.

A second possibility is to argue that the composition essential to texts is a composition of signs and not just any type of composition. Let us call this the *Complex-Composite-of-Signs View*. This position rests on a distinction between two types of composition. One is a composition in which the components are signs; the other is a composition in which the components are entities that are not themselves signs. The sentence 'My cat eats only Fancy Feast cat food,' is composed of signs and thus it is an example of the first type of composition. By contrast, the letter 'M' in the word 'My' is an example of the second type of composition for it is composed of four lines that are not themselves signs. Now, according to this view, texts are not composites just in the second sense, but, more important, also in the first sense; namely, they are always and necessarily composed of signs. This distinguishes them from signs, for signs may be composites only in the second sense. In this way, even though 'M' is a sign standing for the letter M, 'M' is not a text, because it is composed only of elements, namely four lines, which are not signs themselves.

Although this way of distinguishing texts from signs appears at first to be quite sensible, upon closer scrutiny it becomes clear that it will not do. Two reasons may be given for this failure: one from the side of texts, and another from the side of signs. The first, which turns out to be questionable, argues that, although generally texts may be composed of signs, it is possible to have texts that are composed of things that are not signs. This is the case of 'P,' which stands for the order to print in my word processing program. Indeed, when one looks around, one finds many such examples. Therefore, it becomes very difficult, if not impossible, so the argument goes, to maintain that texts are always composed of signs.

This reason, taken from the side of texts, may be questioned on the basis of ordinary use, for the ordinary use of 'text' seems to confirm the view that texts are always composed of signs. We speak of signs that are not themselves composed of signs, but we do not call them "texts." The term 'text' is generally reserved for compositions of signs. This may be illustrated by the very example given earlier, 'P,' for computer commands are referred to as "signs" but not as "texts."[7]

The reason from the side of signs, why texts cannot be distinguished from signs merely on the basis that the first are composed of signs and the second are not, is that signs are frequently composed of signs themselves. So is the case of most words in English. The word 'cat,' for example, is composed of three signs, 'c,' 'a,' and 't,' and few would argue that in virtue of that it is a text and not a sign.[8]

Although the first reason given against the Complex-Composite-of-Signs View may be doubted, the second reason is sufficient by itself to undermine the view. One could still try to save it by weakening it, however. Instead of claiming that signs are never composed of signs, one could argue that what distinguishes texts from signs is that texts are always and necessarily composed of more than one sign, whereas signs may be composed of no more than one sign. Thus, we may have signs such as the letter 'M' that consists in only one sign and whose components are not themselves signs. But there are other signs, such as 'cat,' that are composites of signs. This version of the view may be called the *Modified-Complex-Composite-of-Signs View*.

But even this modified position is not satisfactory. Although it does provide a way of distinguishing some signs from texts and vice versa, it is not helpful in distinguishing others. According to it, such things as 'M' and 'P' are signs and not texts. And we also know that such things as 'My' is a sign, but we cannot determine whether it is also a text and whether there are texts that are not signs. In short, complexity of composition in the sense understood earlier is not sufficient to distinguish texts from signs, even if it appears to be a necessary condition of textuality. We must look, therefore, for another candidate to establish the distinction.

One such candidate that readily suggests itself is complexity of meaning. Is complexity of meaning a necessary or sufficient condition of textuality, and does it also distinguish texts from signs? Can it be argued that texts have complex meanings whereas signs do not, and therefore, that such complexity of meaning distinguishes between the two? This position, which may be called the *Complex-Meaning View*, seems to receive some support, first, from the etymology of the term 'text.' As we saw earlier, the etymology of 'text' seems to imply a certain degree of complexity and composition that could be easily transferred to the meaning. Second, there is some support from experience, for most texts seem to convey complex meanings whereas signs do not; indeed, the complexity of the meanings of texts is generally reflected in turn by their own complexity. This degree of complexity is lacking in signs; signs tend to express simple meanings that are generally accessible and not difficult to grasp. Texts, by contrast, are more intricate complexes whose import is not so clear and that require attention and a certain conceptual sophistication and analysis.

Yet, one can easily find objections to this line of reasoning, first, from the side of signs and, second, from the side of texts. Beginning with an objection from the side of signs, there are cases where relatively simple signs are used to convey complex meanings, and so the question arises as to whether the signs used in this way are texts or not. Consider the case of the word 'fire' uttered in a crowded theater.[9] The reaction of the audience gives us a clue as to the complexity of its meaning. In one situation, for example, those present in the theater try to get out, whereas in other situations they laugh. In both cases a complex meaning seems to have been communicated. The first might be something like this: "There is a fire in the theater and we should all leave because otherwise we might perish." The second would be even more complex than that, for it appeals to the audience's sense of humor and humor depends on complex understanding. So, what do we make of words like 'fire' when used in situations such as the one described? Are they merely signs or are they also texts?

This question could be answered in two ways. One may wish to argue that when signs with relatively simple meanings are used to express complex meanings, the context in which they are used supplies the complexity missing in the meaning of the sign. The utterance of 'fire' in a crowded theater elicits a certain response from the audience because the context provides the complexity of meaning missing in the utterance. The point, then, is that in some cases signs with relatively simple meanings can function as texts because of the context in which they are used; the context provides the complexity of the meaning which they appear to lack.

The second answer is that often what appear to be signs with relatively simple meanings turn out to be more complex upon analysis. In the case we have been discussing, for example, the way the word 'fire' is uttered has much to do with what it means. If shouted in a certain way, it means a warning, but said in another way it may mean something quite different. Hence, just as an exclamation mark placed next to a written word is part of the text of which the word is also a part, so the intonation of the voice in an oral text is to be considered part of the text, thus providing a complexity that may at first go unnoticed.

Even if the objection from the side of signs fails, other objections from the side of texts can be formulated against the Complex-Meaning View. One may argue that there are texts whose meaning is relatively simple and signs whose meaning is relatively complex. For example, the text 'The cat spilled the milk' seems to have a relatively simple meaning. Indeed, its meaning seems much more simple than the meaning of the sign 'essence.' Can it really be argued, then, that what distinguishes texts and signs is complexity of meaning? Perhaps one could insist, but it is doubtful that the issue can be brought to closure. The reason is that complexity of meaning is too vague a notion to serve to demarcate clearly between texts and signs. A more precise and clearcut criterion is required.

The way I propose to distinguish between texts and signs is by noting that, in texts, meaning is in part the result of the meaning of the signs of which the texts are composed and the arrangement in which they are placed, whereas in signs this is not so, even in cases where the sign is composed of other signs.[10] Thus, the meaning of the text, 'My cat eats only Fancy Feast cat food,' is in part the result of the meanings of 'My,' 'cat,' 'eats,' etc., and of the way in which those signs are put together. By contrast, the meaning of a sign, such as 'cat' is not in any way the result of the meaning of the signs of which it is composed, 'c,' 'a,' and 't,' and their arrangement. The meaning of 'cat' has nothing to do with the meaning of 'c,' whose meaning is the letter c, for example. Of course, the existence of the sign 'cat' depends on the existence and meaning of the letters of which it is composed, namely, 'c,' 'a,' and 't,' but that is not the same as saying that the meaning of 'cat' results from the meaning of 'c,' 'a,' and 't.'

Prima facie, then, this way of distinguishing signs and texts appears effective, because it allows us to know whether something is a sign or a text and prevent any overlap between the categories. If something is a sign, it cannot be a text and vice versa. I call this view the *Causal View*.

This way of distinguishing signs and texts is not devoid of difficulties, however.[11] For example, it appears that some signs are composed of other signs whose meaning is at least in part the result of the meaning of the signs of which they are composed and of the arrangement of those signs. One such case is 'No smoking,' where its meaning clearly has to do with the meaning of 'No,' 'smoking,' and their arrangement.

This and similar counterexamples, however, do not undermine the view, for they arise from an ambiguity in the use of the term 'sign' in ordinary English discourse. Indeed, this term is used for a variety of things, but I am interested only in the two meanings with which it is used that undermine the Causal View. In one way, call it S^1, 'sign' is used to mean one or more entities, which may or may not be signs themselves, and whose meaning, if the entities are signs, is not the result of the meaning of those signs and their arrangement. This is the sense in which a sign has been understood in the preceding. In another way, call it S^2, 'sign' is used to mean a publicly displayed notice which can be a sign in sense S^1 or can be a text. The 'No smoking' notice posted in the classroom where I teach on Thursdays is a sign in sense S^2, although it is a text and thus not a sign in sense S^1. It is not a sign in sense S^1 because its meaning is in part the result of the meaning of the signs of which it is composed and of the arrangement of those signs. Thus it turns out that the examples given do not count as counterexamples to the Causal View.

Still, some problematic cases remain that may challenge the suggested way of distinguishing between texts and signs. Consider, for example, the earlier mentioned case of 'fire' shouted in a crowded theater or written with an exclamation mark next to it. Could it not be argued that the meaning of the shouted word, or of the written word, is not the result of the meaning of the signs of which they are composed and thus that they are not texts? After all, the meaning of 'Fire!' has nothing to do with the meaning of 'f,' 'i,' 'r', 'e,' and '!.' What has been written is a word composed of four letters next to an exclamation mark and the meaning of the word is not the result of the meanings of the letters and exclamation mark of which the word is composed. And if this is so, the Causal View is undermined, for 'Fire!' appears to be a text and yet it cannot be distinguished from a sign.

This reading of the example, however, is not the only one possible. Another reading is possible that makes room for the textuality of 'Fire!' without undermining its distinction from a sign. 'Fire!' is composed of two signs, 'Fire' and '!,' and the meaning of 'Fire!' is in fact the result of the meanings of 'Fire' and '!.' 'Fire,' of course, is not a text, even though it is composed of signs, because its meaning is not the result of the meaning of the signs of which it is composed. But 'Fire!'

is a text, for its meaning is the result, at least in part, of the two signs of which it is composed and of their arrangement.

A final problematic example needs to be considered. It is the case of words composed of other words, such as 'mailman,' whose meanings appear to be the result of the meanings of the signs which compose them. The meaning of 'mailman' appears to be the result of the meaning of 'mail' and 'man,' just as the meaning of 'Fire!' appears to be traceable to the meaning of 'Fire' and '!.' Thus, it would seem that words composed of other words meet the criterion of both texts and signs.

Upon reflection, however, the difficulty with this kind of word disappears, for it becomes clear that their meanings are not in part the result, as is the case of texts, of the meanings of the words that compose them. The reason is that the words which compose them do not function semantically and thus cannot be considered to be signs. It may be true that originally, when the word 'mailman,' say, developed, it was a shorthand version of 'the man who delivers the mail' and thus that perhaps at that point its components, 'mail' and 'man,' may have been put together into the sign 'mailman' precisely because they had meanings which added up to the meaning of 'mailman.' But once the two words were put together into the word 'mailman,' the word became a sign whose meaning is "mailman" but whose parts have no independent meanings in the sign which contribute to the meaning of 'mailman.' Such signs as 'mailman' function as simple signs with meanings which are independent of the meanings of the signs that compose them.

Three points support this conclusion. First, often those who use signs such as these have no knowledge of the meanings of the signs that compose them. Second, with time many of these signs change so that the signs which originally composed them become so different that only experts can tell they were once signs with meanings related to the meanings of the signs they compose. Third, the signs that compose such composite signs are not chosen by authors and arranged by them to convey the meanings of the composite signs to audiences in certain contexts.[12] These three points indicate that the meanings of signs such as 'mailman' are not the result, even in part, of the meanings of the signs that compose them and, therefore, that they are signs and not texts.

The Causal View allows us, then, to distinguish between texts and signs. Of course, there may still be other contestable cases, but those would have to be examined and argued on a case by case basis as has been done with the case of 'Fire!.' I should also add that the position presented here concerning the distinction between texts and signs is not essential to many of the views I defend in the rest of this book. For many of them, it is quite immaterial, first, whether the meanings of texts are in part traceable to the meanings of the signs of which they are composed and to the arrangement of those signs, and second, how texts differ from signs. Nevertheless, the position described has several important implications for some of my views, as will become evident later. For the present let me indicate just a couple of these implications.

First among these is that the identity conditions of signs and texts are different. The meaning of a sign is not the result of the meanings of the entities of which the sign is constituted. But the meaning of texts is in part the result of the meanings of the signs of which they are composed. This changes things considerably. Whereas the meaning of signs depends directly on the use made of the entities that constitute the sign considered as one, the meaning of texts depends in part on the established meanings of the signs of which they are composed and the arrangement of those signs. This has important implications for the understanding and interpretation of texts, as we shall see in Chapters 4 and 5. It entails, among other things, that a text imposes certain limitations on both its author and its audience with respect to understanding and interpretation that are lacking in the case of signs. A text takes for granted much that is not taken for granted by a sign, thus limiting the interpretative freedom of authors and audiences.

Also important is that the context of signs is generally a text, for signs are most often used as signs within texts.[13] There are cases, of course, in which texts are not the context of signs. As mentioned earlier, 'P,' which is used as the command to print in my word processing system, can be used by itself and not as part of a text. And the same can be said about pointing, when this act is not accompanied by any other sign or text. In these cases, the sign's context is not a text. But most often in our experience the contexts of signs are texts, whereas the situation is different in the case of texts. For many texts, their contexts are not texts. Indeed, the context of texts can vary enormously, thus influencing the understanding of texts in ways in which the understanding of signs is seldom, if ever, influenced, for in most cases such contexts influence signs only through the texts that they compose.

Finally, the discussion of the distinction between texts and signs has allowed me to explore the ambiguity in the use of 'sign' in ordinary English discourse mentioned earlier and to make clear the sense I shall give the term in this book. It is important to keep in mind that when I speak of signs I do not have in mind the sense of public notices discussed earlier, that is not S^2, but rather S^1. Likewise, when I speak of texts, I have in mind groups of signs whose meanings are in part the result of the meanings of the signs that compose the group and their arrangement. Note, of course, that the meaning of a text depends on other factors as well, which I shall discuss later, and that there are other conditions of textuality as indicated in the definition given at the beginning of this chapter.

I should also mention that, as we shall see later at greater length and as should be already obvious from what has been said so far, by 'sign' I do not mean only letters or words belonging to certain alphabets and languages. Anything that is both part of a text and has meaning or contributes to the establishment of the meaning of the text is a sign. Punctuation, emphases, spaces (or silences), headings, underlinings, and so on may be considered signs.

Finally, let me indicate that the fact that texts are composed of signs does not preclude texts from being composed of other texts. Indeed, a long text, such as a novel, may be composed of shorter texts, such as chapters, paragraphs, sentences, and so on.[14] But that does not undermine the fact that it is itself composed of signs, for each of the texts of which it is composed is itself composed of signs.

C. Specific Meaning

Another element in the definition of a text given earlier is specific meaning. I shall, however, begin by discussing meaning before I turn to its specificity.

From the definition of a text I gave earlier and what has been said concerning ECTs, it follows that, although having some meaning is a necessary condition of textuality, texts are not to be identified with the meanings they are intended to convey.[15] The nature of meaning has received substantial attention in contemporary philosophy. To consider it in any satisfactory manner would require the kind of analysis that would take us far from the subject matter of the present investigation. Fortunately, we do not need to dwell on the intricacies of contemporary semantic theory to establish the distinction between a text and its meaning. (I shall have something more to say about meaning in Chapter 4.) For present purposes, the discussion that follows should suffice. Let me begin with some examples.

Written texts are some of the most, if not the most, obvious cases of texts with which we are acquainted, and so they should serve us well as examples. The sentences written on this page or displayed on the screen of my word processor, this chapter of the book, and the book itself, are all examples of written texts. Consider the following:

1. $2 + 2 = 4$
2. $2 + 2 = 4$
3.   Two and two make four.
4.   Two plus two equals four.
5.   Dos y dos son cuatro.

Examples 1–5 should help us see the distinction between texts and their meaning, for in them we have five texts and only one meaning. Texts 1 and 2 are the same, but all the rest are quite different. Here, 1 and 2 are rendered in the language of mathematics; 3 and 4 are in English; and 5 is in Spanish. But, as noted, they all mean the same thing.[16] The distinction between a text and its meaning, then, can be supported by the fact that different texts can have the same meaning. Consider written text 1. This written text is constituted by the semantically significant marks which are actually made on the paper; the text is the actual picture given there, composed of ink marks drawn and arranged in a certain way to convey some specific meaning. But the meaning of that text is something that is neither material nor composed of marks made by ink on that particular page. Indeed, the meaning of texts 1–5 is the same. Thus, sameness of meaning cannot be a sufficient condition of being the same text; if it were so, 1–5 would be the same text, which is not the case.

So far I have been arguing that texts are not to be identified with their meanings. But that does not entail the opposite, namely, that texts are to be conceived as completely independent of their meanings and, thus, that they should be identified with their ECTs. If that were the case, then there would be no difference between a mere object, even when that object is the product of human activity and design, and a text. Yet, the distinction between the two is not difficult to illustrate extensionally. A tool, for example, which is the product of human activity and design, is not a text, because it is not produced and intended by an author to convey some specific meaning to an audience. A hammer is an object intended to be used to build other objects, but it is not intended to convey meaning. Like a hammer, a text is the product of human activity and intention, but it has a semantic function that a hammer, qua hammer, does not have. Texts are products of human action made for specific ends, but not all products of human action made for specific ends are texts. It is a mistake, therefore, to consider texts as being in any way independent of the meanings they are intended to convey.

A text is a group of entities used to convey meaning, but precisely because of that, a text is not to be identified either with the entities that constitute it apart from the meaning, what I call *ECTs*, or with the meaning alone to the exclusion of those entities.

Some philosophers like to identify the meaning of a text with its reference.[17] This referential view of meaning appears to work well when one is dealing with signs such as proper names, for it does indeed make sense to say that the meaning of 'Socrates' is Socrates. And something similar could be said about definite descriptions, such as 'the teacher of Plato,' whose meaning is supposedly Socrates.[18] It is more difficult to maintain that the meanings of abstract nouns such as 'goodness,' constitute the reference of those nouns, because it is not at all clear that abstract nouns have any reference. Of course, there have been philosophers who have argued that they have.[19] But such a view is very controversial and plagued with difficulties. And the same could be said concerning the reference of texts in which all terms are universal, such as 'Water boils at 100° C.'[20]

Moreover, it is also not evident that the meanings of texts, particularly long and complex texts, can be accounted for in terms of reference, for what would be the reference of the text of Gibbon's *History of the Decline and Fall of the Roman Empire*? The history of the decline and fall of the Roman Empire? The Roman Empire? A particular set of events through which the Roman Empire passed? Gibbon's view of the history of the decline and fall of the Roman Empire? Obviously, the answer is not clear. And the case of the texts of fictional works, such as Cervantes's *Don Quijote*, pose special problems, because the characters dealt with in these texts never existed. None of these difficulties, however, have deterred proponents of this view from defending it, for they have found ways to get around these problems, although not to the satisfaction of their critics.

Finally, there are cases where two different signs or texts have the same reference but different meaning. Consider the expressions 'animal capable of reasoning' and 'featherless biped.' Assuming that everyone who is an animal capable of reasoning is also a featherless biped, and vice versa, the reference of these expressions is the same, but still their meanings are quite different. Thus it makes no sense to say that meaning is always the same as reference.[21]

To avoid the problems faced by the referential view, some philosophers propose an ideational theory of textual meaning that understands meaning as the idea or ideas a text expresses.[22] Thus the meaning of 1 earlier is the idea that two plus two equals four. But again there are difficulties with this theory. Some of these difficulties are related to the view (held by some supporters of this position) that ideas are independent of the mind, whereas others have to do with the experience that the use of texts is seldom, if ever, preceded by a clear set of ideas in the mind of the author or user. These difficulties concern the status of ideas. For, on the one hand, if ideas are independent of the mind, as Plato thought they were, their ontological status creates all sorts of problems and the view amounts to a referential position of sorts that applies only to abstract nouns. And, on the other hand, if ideas are not independent of the mind, it would seem to be necessary for them to exist in the mind clearly and distinctly prior to the existence of the texts of which they are the meanings.[23] But this does not in fact seem to be the case; authors and users of texts do not always have in their minds clear and distinct ideas before they compose or use the texts of which such ideas are supposed to be the meaning. So, where do ideas exist?

Another difficulty of the ideational view has to do with the fact that it makes no sense that the meaning of 'cat,' for example, be 'the idea of cat,' for the idea of cat is something quite unlike a cat. If I am asked to define 'cat' I will say something like "feline with fur, etc." But if I am asked to define 'idea of cat' I might say something like "mental notion about a feline with fur and so on."[24] The meaning of 'cat' cannot, therefore, be the idea of cat; it has to be cat, because the idea of cat is the meaning of 'the idea of cat.'

Finally, there is also the question of such texts as biographies, that deal with individual persons. The application of the ideational view of meaning to them would seem to imply that when we understand texts that describe individuals what we understand are ideas about the individuals rather than the individuals themselves and that does not seem appropriate. As in the case of the referential theory, supporters of this position have suggested various ways of getting around this and the other difficulties mentioned, but their critics remain unconvinced.[25]

These and other difficulties with both referential and ideational theories of meaning lead some philosophers to speak of meaning as "use." In this sense, meaning is conceived as the role that a text plays within a cultural context. This approach, which may be characterized as "functional," can be best illustrated by reference to the notion of an illocutionary act.[26] What an illocutionary act is may be gathered from an example. When I say to Peter, "Peter, open the door," I utter a sentence. The act of *uttering* the sentence is called locutionary. Apart from my act of uttering the sentence, the act may produce certain effects, such as *getting Peter to open the door*, which is also an act I perform. This is called the *perlocutionary act*. Finally, I also perform another act; namely, that of *ordering* Peter to open the door. This last act is called *illocutionary*. Note that not all illocutionary acts are acts of ordering, of course. Illocutionary acts vary a great deal and comprise such acts as stating, questioning, apologizing, and so on.

For our purposes, what is important to note is that textual meaning may be expressed in terms of the notion of an illocutionary act as follows: The meaning of X is that in virtue of which one who performs a locutionary act also performs a certain illocutionary act.[27] This understanding of meaning concerns primarily oral texts, but for our purposes it could be expanded to any type of text, including written ones. In that case, the locutionary act would not consist in the act of uttering but in the acts of writing, printing, and so on.[28]

In spite of various advantages, the functional theory of meaning also faces difficulties. Indeed, as is the case with the referential theory, it seems to work best for short and somewhat simple texts. It would be difficult to think of the illocutionary act or acts that take place upon the locution of the text of, say, Aristotle's *Metaphysics*. But again, it is also clear that in some cases this theory seems to be the one that works best, as with performatives such as 'I apologize.'[29]

For our purposes it is particularly important that none of the three views of meaning presented implies that the meaning of a text is to be identified with the text. In the case of the referential theory, the meaning is in fact the things or states of affairs that we understand when we are said to understand the text; in the ideational view, it is the ideas expressed by the text; and in the functional view it is that in virtue of which locutionary acts bring about certain illocutionary acts. Thus, for the purpose of distinguishing between a text and its meaning all three theories are equally effective.

All the same, it may be pertinent to ask whether we need or are going to adopt one of these theories of meaning to the exclusion of the others. As noted earlier, what I propose at this point is to adopt a theory of the meaning of texts concordant with all three theories just discussed, but that avoids the difficulties each of them faces. Three points need to be made clear. The first is that this theory is not presented as a theory of meaning as such, but only as a theory of *textual* meaning; it is therefore not intended to cover all cases of meaning. Second, this view is not to be taken as an alternative to the views discussed, but as a working formulation that will help us proceed without having to choose and defend one of the theories of meaning discussed previously to the exclusion of the others. If this investigation were concerned with meaning primarily, such a procedure would be inadequate. But our object of inquiry is not meaning but texts, and this allows us to leave open the question of what meaning is ultimately, provided our working hypothesis about meaning covers the most obvious cases and is neutral enough not to raise serious objections from the three views of meaning mentioned.

The view I propose to adopt holds that the meaning of a text is what is understood when a text produces understanding. This does not entail, as already noted, that all that texts produce or are intended to produce is understanding. As we shall see later, the texts of works that are artistic, such as Shakespeare's *Hamlet*, produce and are intended to produce in audiences much more than understanding. The view I present here entails only that for something to be a text it must be able to produce, or be intended to produce, understanding, not that this is all it produces.[30] Nor does this view entail that only texts produce understanding; all sorts of other things may also produce understanding, but that is of no concern to us here.

Note, moreover, that the three theories of meaning mentioned earlier could be accommodated by this view. Indeed, one may hold the meaning of a text to be both what is understood when a text produces understanding and also that to which the text refers, and, moreover, that a text is understood precisely because its meaning is that to which the text refers. The meaning of 'Socrates is a philosopher,' namely, the philosopher Socrates, is both what is understood when the text is said to be understood and also Socrates, the philosopher. Likewise, one may hold the meaning of a text to be what is understood when a text produces understanding and also that the meaning of the text consists of ideas; indeed, one may hold that "the idea the whole is greater than the parts," is what we understand when we are said to understand that the whole is greater than the parts. Finally, one may hold that the meaning of a text is both what is understood when a text produces understanding and also that in virtue of which it produces an illocutionary act, because for a text to have meaning is in fact to be able to produce an illocutionary act. Hence, the meaning of 'Paul, open the door' is what Paul and the utterer of the sentence understand when they understand that Paul is to open the door and thus what makes the illocutionary act of ordering Paul to open the door effective.

Meaning, conceived in the way I have proposed here, should be distinguished from significance.[31] The verbs 'to mean' and 'to signify' are frequently interchanged in ordinary language, so that what X means is also what X signifies. But when one speaks about "the significance of X," a broader concept is usually at play. Significance involves relevance, importance, and consequence. The significance of a text has to do with the relevance, importance, and consequences of it, and this relevance, importance, and consequences, although in part affected by and resulting from its meaning, may be related to factors other than the meaning of the text. For example, a text may be significant because it was available at a particularly propitious juncture in history which made possible for it to play a key role in subsequent events. Significance, then, is a relational notion that involves a text and its meaning on one side and other events, texts, phenomena, and so on, on the other. Of course, as will become clear shortly, the meaning of texts also depends on their context and thus may be considered relational. But the elements in the relation in question are different, for in the case of significance the text's meaning is one of the relata that determine the significance of a text. Significance, moreover, is a broader and less determinate notion, whereas meaning, as conceived here, is a more restricted notion, referring only to what is understood when one is said to have understood a text.

Note, again, that I do not need, nor wish, to hold that the only function of texts is to produce understanding, nor that their only meaning is what is understood when they produce understanding. Texts may, and often do, do other things than produce understanding, as is clear from the example just given concerning the illocutionary act of ordering. And a text may have more than textual meaning. For something to be a text, however and this is my point, it must be able to produce, or be intended to produce, understanding.[32] My thesis may be formulated in two parts: (1) the meaning of a text pertains to the understanding, and (2) a text is always intended to convey some meaning in addition to whatever else it may be intended to do. Admittedly, both of these parts of the thesis may be challenged, but they are not without support. Indeed, if what we are talking about are philosophical texts, I imagine a good number of philosophers would agree their meaning is cognitive and their purpose is to make someone understand such meaning.

The case with nonphilosophical texts, however, does not seem as straight-forward. Many of the nonphilosophical texts we encounter do not seem to produce, or be intended to produce, understanding, but rather to direct action or elicit some kind of emotion. One could say, indeed, that at least part of the purpose of so-called poetic texts is to create a mood or produce an emotion in the audience. Moreover, commands and the like are meant either to prevent or produce an action. In either case texts function as causes of certain events (emotions, actions, inactions) that are not causes of understanding.[33]

Still another case should be considered, namely; the case of texts used simply to vent emotion or give pleasure to those who use them. The logical positivist view developed earlier in this century was indeed that many ethical texts have no meaning if by meaning something cognitive is understood.[34] Texts such as 'Killing is wrong' do not mean anything; they simply vent the emotion of those who produce them and who, in this case, "disapprove" of the action of killing. This view was later extended to religious language, so that statements such as 'God is good' were considered to express nothing more than certain emotions or attitudes on the part of those who use them. More recently it has become fashionable among some postmodernists to argue that texts have nothing to do with the understanding of cognitive material, but have as their primary function the experience of, say, pleasure or release in those who produce them. Along these lines we find authors arguing that texts neither need nor are intended for audiences.[35]

I do not wish to dispute that the purpose of texts is manifold and that in many cases their primary function is to cause or prevent actions or emotions in someone other than the authors or users or to vent the feelings of and give pleasure to their authors or users rather than to produce understanding.[36] The primary purpose of the 'No smoking' text posted above the blackboard in the classroom where I teach on Thursdays is not to inform me that smoking is not permitted in the room, but to prevent anyone in the room from smoking. Likewise, in the case of performative texts, such as 'I apologize,' the primary function of the text is not to produce understanding but to perform a certain act—in the example given, the act of apologizing. The same could be said about certain poetic texts, whose reading produces the sort of aesthetic experience that goes well beyond understanding. Indeed, I am even willing to accept that the production of some texts may be intended primarily, or even solely, for the experience of an emotional release in their authors. This is not as frequent as the other phenomena, but there are cases of writers, particularly poets, who feel an internal compulsion to write and others who use their writing to reconcile themselves to adverse circumstances. A lover who lost her beloved might cope with the situation by writing a poem, for example.

All this seems quite sensible. However, I do not think it is correct to argue that texts can have purposes other than understanding, and achieve the results established by those purposes, without in fact producing understanding, for in order for texts to cause or prevent action and emotions, for example, it is necessary that they first be understood to some degree.[37] Those who argue against the view that texts are intended to produce understanding frequently confuse the primary purpose of the author with the meaning of the text. Because they see that the primary purpose of an author is to produce certain actions or emotions, they conclude that the text through which the author tries to do so conveys no cognitive meaning.[38] Thus, they argue, 'No smoking' and 'I apologize' convey no cognitive meaning because the function of the first as determined by the author is to prevent an action and of the second to carry out an action. This confusion is emphasized, unfortunately, by the fact that the term 'meaning' in English is frequently interchanged with 'intention' and its synonyms, so that "to mean something" is "to intend something."[39] Under these circumstances, it is easy to see that if the meaning of a text, in the sense of what it is "intended to do," is to cause, prevent, or carry out an action, for example, its meaning cannot be what is understood. But that is because 'meaning' is used *only* in the sense of purpose. However, if meaning is understood both as purpose and as what is understood, then there is no difficulty for a text to be meant to carry out an action in the sense of having that purpose and at the same time for its meaning to be an object of understanding. (More on intention, meaning, and understanding in Chapter 4.)

If one looks at the examples provided, it becomes clear that, for those texts to cause, prevent, or carry out actions, they must be understood. Thus the conveyance of meaning is a necessary condition of fulfilling their intended primary function. Take 'I apologize.' The utterance of this text is effective only when the audience for which it is intended understands it. I can go red in the face repeating my apologies in Spanish to an audience that knows no Spanish, and will not achieve my goal.[40] The same applies to texts whose primary function is to direct or prevent action and to cause or vent emotions. In all cases, some meaning is expressed and understood that, in turn, triggers the intended effect. Even when someone is clearly using language to vent emotion, we frequently say that we "understand" them, which means both that we think we have grasped correctly what the person has said and are aware of the emotion being vented. (We may also mean that we see the reasons why the person is doing what he or she is doing or even that we agree or sympathize with her.) The primary aim of authors when they produce texts, then, does not have to be to produce understanding, but producing understanding is a prerequisite of effectively fulfilling any other aim that is to be carried out through the use of texts.

The fact that the meaning of a text pertains to the understanding is particularly evident in the case of long and complicated texts. Whereas some short texts may appear to be primarily performative in nature or meant to vent emotion rather than convey cognitive meaning, in cases of long and complex texts such functions become less obvious. Even in the case of poems, which are often cited as the epitome of texts whose function is other than to produce understanding, it is difficult, when they are long, to deny that they have a cognitive meaning. But even with short texts, we can always ask whether they have been understood. For example, when I say, "Open the door," it is clear that the primary and intended function of this text is to order someone to open the door and, thus, to perform that particular illocutionary act of ordering someone to open the door so that the door be opened. But once I have performed the illocutionary act, I can always ask of the person to whom I gave the order whether she has understood me, say if she did not act quickly to open the door or did not act at all. This implies that, although the primary and intended function of my utterance may be the performance of the illocutionary act of ordering, or even the perlocutionary act of having the door opened, the production of understanding is also involved; indeed, it is a requirement of the illocutionary act effectively causing the action it is intended to cause. For in order for the perlocutionary act to take place as a result of the locutionary and illocutionary acts, the person who responds to the illocutionary act has to be aware of the locutionary act, of the illocutionary force of that act, or put differently, of the illocutionary act, grasping the meaning of the text. An act of understanding, then, mediates between the locutionary act and an effective perlocutionary act. The cause of the effective perlocutionary act is the locutionary act through the act of understanding the locutionary act's meaning on the part of the audience. I cannot get Peter to open the door unless he hears and understands me.

What has been said underlines the point made earlier about the distinction between a text and its meaning, but it does not explain exactly how meaning is related to texts. For the moment I need only to say that the confusion of a text with its meaning has serious philosophical implications. Indeed, the identification of a text with its meaning has led some postmodernists to the extraordinary conclusion that there are no texts, only meanings.[41] This conclusion in turn leads to a kind of subjective relativism in which meanings are not anchored on any objective grounds, giving free reign to interpretative license. These excesses are prevented, however, if texts are not confused with meanings.

Second, I would like to note explicitly a consequence of the way I conceive understanding, namely, that what we understand when we are said to understand a text is not, strictly speaking, the ECTs that constitute the text, but their collective meaning. The understanding of a text is the mental act whereby we grasp the meaning of a text. What we understand when we understand a text, then, is the meaning of the text; that is, the meaning conveyed by the group of signs arranged in a certain way and so on. This becomes obvious when we consider the text constituted by the marks written on this page. What the reader qua reader understands when she is said to understand the text constituted by those marks is the meaning of the marks. If what one understood were the marks themselves, one would understand that the marks are marks, they have a certain shape, they are physical, composed of a certain type of ink, and so on. But that is not what is meant by "understanding a text." True, those marks have a causal relation to the understanding insofar as, without seeing the marks and understanding what they are and their relation to a certain meaning, there would be no act of understanding *their* meaning. But it is the meaning of the marks that is ultimately at stake. In Aristotelian jargon one would say that the meaning is the formal cause of understanding a text whereas the marks, that is, the ECTs, are the material cause. Whether we adopt Aristotle's terminology or not is irrelevant for my purpose. What I wish to make clear is that a consequence of my view of meaning is that meaning is what is understood when one is said to understand a text; meaning plays the same role as the object known in the process of knowledge.

We have established that texts have meanings, that the meaning of a text is not to be identified with the text, and that the meaning of a text is what is understood when the text is understood. But in the definition of texts presented above, the expression used was "specific meaning," so we must ask what specific meaning is. To say that a meaning is specific and not general indicates that there are limits to it. But those limits are not established by the author in all cases. I shall leave the discussion of how they are established and questions related to the exact meaning and understanding of texts and their relations to authors and audiences for Chapter 4. I shall, however, say something about intention here to prevent misunderstandings at a later stage of the argument.

D. Intention

The notion of intention is one that has received considerable attention in contemporary philosophy. For my purposes, however, it is not necessary to delve into it too deeply. Generally, we intend two sorts of things: We intend X or we intend to X. In the latter case sometimes the action has an object toward which it is directed, as when I intend to drink water, and at other times it does not, as when I intend to run. The case with which we are concerned is the intention by an author to convey a specific meaning to an audience. Our object of study, then, is an activity, to X, that is the goal or end intented. Moreover, that goal or end consists in conveying a specific meaning, and the specificity of the meaning, as already noted, entails that there are limitations to that meaning. Thus, it would seem appropriate to conclude that the intention is directed to the conveyance of a meaning that is determinate.

These considerations prompt an important question, namely, whether authors of texts need to be fully aware of the determinate meanings they intend to convey in virtue of the fact that they intend to convey them. The answer to this question in turn depends on a more general question concerned with whether intentions imply full awareness of what is intended on the part of those who have the intentions.

The answer to this question is hotly debated in ethics for understandable reasons. Full awareness of what one intends would seem to be a necessary condition of moral responsibility: One cannot be held accountable for that of which one is not fully aware. Our concern here, however, is not with moral responsibility, and therefore, the issue we are addressing should not be confused with that of establishing it. Our concern is much more limited. What we wish to determine is whether it is possible to have intentions that lack full awareness of what is intended; in our specific case, whether authors can be said to intend to convey specific meanings when they are not fully aware of the specific meanings in question. Whether the author who is not fully aware of the meaning is further to be held morally responsible for the act of conveying the specific meaning or for the consequences of that act is a different question whose answer should not affect the answer to our question.

At first sight it may appear that indeed intentions do require full awareness of the determinate meaning intended. How can it be possible, we may ask, to intend to X and not know or be aware of it? But upon inspection matters turn out differently.[42] Consider an example, such as a college sophomore who expresses her intention to one of her classmates to major in philosophy. At the time she probably knows very little about what majoring in philosophy entails. At orientation she was told something about requirements that need to be fulfilled for majors, and she has taken a course in philosophy that interested her a great deal, but this can hardly qualify as being aware of what majoring in philosophy is. Indeed, it is altogether possible that when she goes to the philosophy department to ask what is entailed by majoring in philosophy, she will change her mind and not go through with her intention. Thus, having an intention to X does not entail full awareness of it.

My conclusion is, then, that although intentions are directed toward goals, the subjects who have the intentions need not be fully aware of these goals. A fuzzy notion of the goal is sufficient for the intention. Moreover, this conclusion applies, mutatis mutandis, to the means used to achieve the goal. Consider the student about whom we have been speaking: Is she fully aware of the requirements of becoming a major in philosophy before she forms the intention to major in philosophy? Again, she may have vague ideas that they entail taking certain courses and maintaining a certain point average, but until she goes to the department office and asks, she cannot be said to be fully aware of the courses involved and the exact grade point average she has to maintain. The intending subject, then, need not have a clear idea of the means needed to achieve the goal in order to intend the goal.

Now we can apply what has been said about intentions to the case of texts and see that authors need not be fully aware of the goals or means they have to use to carry them out when authoring texts. That an author intends to convey a specific meaning to an audience does not entail that the author be fully aware of the goal he intends, that is, of the specific meaning he intends to convey, or of the means, the selection and arrangement of signs, necessary for effectively conveying it. The author may have only fuzzy notions about them and yet be said to intend them. This does not entail, of course, that the meaning the author intends to convey is not determinate. The author may not be clear about the limits of the meaning he intends to convey—indeed, he may even be mistaken about them—and still he may intend such a meaning to have determinate limits. Nor does this view entail that the author is never fully aware of the limits of the meaning he intends to convey. He may in many cases be fully aware of such limits. But, as we shall see later, that he be aware about such limits does not entail that he is exclusively responsible for the determination of those limits in all cases.

These conclusions have important implications for the relations of authors and audiences to texts and for the issues that come up concerning understanding and interpretation. I shall postpone their discussion until the appropriate chapters, for prior to that we need to discuss other propaedeutic matters. Among these are other factors, in addition to ECTs and signs, that are related to the meaning of texts. They are selection, arrangement, and context.

E. Selection and Arrangement

From what has been concluded concerning signs and texts, it follows that the meaning of a text depends on the particular meaning and function of the particular signs of which the text is composed. I say "meaning and function" of the particular signs of which the text is composed because there are signs that do not independently have meaning but rather acquire meaning only when used in conjunction with other signs that they modify.[43] In such cases, their function as modifiers consists of altering the meanings of other signs in certain ways.[44] Take, for example, syncategorematic signs like the indefinite and definite articles. Neither 'a' nor 'the' have independent meaning, but they do change the meaning of the term 'man' when used in conjunction with it. 'Man,' 'a man,' and 'the man' mean quite different things.[45]

Moreover, because the author of a text selects the signs that compose it, the author bears some responsibility for those signs. Sometimes this selection involves no more than choosing among signs that already have established meanings. This is the case, for example, when an author uses terms belonging to a so-called natural language for the composition of a text.[46] But the author may in fact make up new signs for the text. In either case, the author is at least partly responsible for the particular signs that compose the text.

A more subtle, although still rather obvious, point concerning the meaning of a text is that it does not depend only on the independent meaning and function of the signs of which it is composed, but also, as already stated, on the particular arrangement of those signs. For example, if I say, "Only men are allowed in this club," it is clear that what is meant is that all those allowed in this club must be men and, thus, women are excluded. But if I change the place of 'only' in the sentence and say "Men are allowed only in this club," what is meant is that men are allowed in no place other than in this club, leaving open the possibility that women also may be allowed in it.

This feature of texts indicates that a text is more than the sum of its components, or put differently, a text considered as a whole has characteristics that the signs composing it do not have, individually or collectively, and that are not simply the result of any random combination of the individual characteristics of those signs. A text is not like a pile of sand in which the weight of the whole is no more and no less than the sum of the weight of the grains of sand that compose it, regardless of the way in which those grains have been arranged. A text is more like an organism, in which the distribution, character, and function of its parts form a whole whose characteristics are more than the sum of the characteristics of the parts.

The metaphor of the organism should not be overextended, however, for there are important differences between texts and organisms. For example, the destruction of some parts of an organism may result in the destruction of other parts of the organism. But the destruction of some of the signs that compose a text never result in the destruction of the other signs of which the text is composed, even in cases where the identity of the text changes as a result. In a human being, for example, the destruction of the heart or liver results in the destruction of other organs. But any part of a text can be destroyed, and yet other parts remain unaffected. Consider 'No smoking is permitted.' In this text we could take out the 'No' and the other components of the text would remain unaffected, even though the overall meaning changes. If instead of taking out the 'No,' however, we were to take out the 'is,' so that the text would read 'No smoking permitted,' even the meaning would remain unchanged.

These examples make clear, again, that the features of texts—not only their physical features, in cases in which texts are constituted by physical entities, but also their meanings[47]—depend as much on the signs of which they are composed as on the arrangement of the signs of which they are composed. As far as the nature and type of arrangement is concerned, the matter will depend both on the author and the type of text in question. The type of text will determine the range of possibilities. For example, in the case of texts constituted by physical entities, the possible arrangements will necessarily have to do with physical features such as relative position. In the case of texts constituted by mental entities matters would be different. Note that in the definition of texts given earlier, the use of the word 'group' to refer to the aggregate of entities used as signs that make up a text is meant to rule out the suggestion that the signs that compose a text need to be organized in some kind of serial arrangement of the sort we follow on the printed page.[48] The components of texts need to be arranged in some fashion, but the arrangement can take practically any form. For example, there is no reason why the signs that make up texts should not be superimposed on each other after the fashion of a palimpsest, creating a new text out of preexisting ones, or should not be arranged in some nonserial way.

In all cases, the author chooses from among possible arrangements that which he thinks is best suited to the purpose of the text, although the pattern of arrangement need not be the idiosyncratic creation of the author.[49] In texts belonging to natural languages, for example, the arrangements of the signs are dictated partly by the rules of the languages in question, even if the author is ultimately responsible for the selection of particular arrangements. Selection, then, extends not only to signs but also to the arrangements of signs. It should also be clear that under the topic of arrangement come a host of possibilities, including not only order but also various types of divisions, interpolations, and so on.

F. Context

An equally important factor in the determination of the meaning of a text is its context.[50] When a mother says to her dear child, "If you touch that, I will kill you," she is using a metaphor to mean that some minor punishment will be inflicted on the child if it disobeys her. But when a bank guard says to a thief she found *in flagrante* and who is reaching for a gun, "If you touch that, I will kill you," she means that she will kill the person who touches the gun. The text used in both occasions appears to be the same, whereas the context and, consequently, the meaning, are quite different. The context, then, is extremely important in the determination of the meaning of a text.[51]

Of course, context is a determining factor not only of meaning. There are other features of texts that are also determined to some extent by, or at least depend on, context. Consider, for example, style. Although style perhaps does not characterize all texts, there is no doubt that at least some texts have style. We speak, for example, of the turgid or bombastic style of certain texts. But style depends very much on context. Take the well-known case of the text of *Don Quijote* produced by Cervantes in the seventeenth century and the one supposedly produced by Pierre Menard in the twentieth.[52] Because the ECTs that constitute the texts are exactly the same, one would expect that they would have the same style. Yet, the text produced by Pierre Menard, insofar as it uses seventeenth-century Castillian can be described as having an archaic style, whereas Cervantes's text could not be so described.[53] Style, then, like meaning, has much to do with context.

One can speak of contexts in many ways and with regard to many things. For example, we speak about historical, educational, administrative, conceptual, philosophical, and physical contexts, among many others. And we talk about the context of ideas, actions, events, and so on. In some cases the context affects whatever is in that context, but at other times, it does not. With respect to texts a similar distinction applies. There are contexts that affect texts and there are contexts that do not. It is by no means fortuitous that 'context' is a word composed of 'text' and the prefix 'con.' Literally, the word means "with (the) text" and indicates that a context is whatever accompanies a text. In this general sense, anything that surrounds a text, that is, anything that in some way is related to it but is not part of it, would be part of the context of the text, regardless of whether it does or does not affect it.

This understanding of context, however, is too broad for our purposes, because we are interested only in what may change how texts fulfill their function. When I say that a context may or may not affect how texts fulfill their function, what I mean is that it may or may not affect their conveyance of meaning, for the primary function of texts is to convey meaning. For example, whether it is 70° or 80° F in the classroom where I teach is completely irrelevant to the meaning of the 'No smoking' sign located over the blackboard. On the other hand, the shout "Fire!" in a crowded theater means something very different from what it means in a field of battle.

For our purposes the only relevant contexts are those that can affect the meanings of texts.[54] But of those, there are still many. What they are depends to a great extent on the type of text in question, and because there are many such types, as we shall see in Chapter 3, contexts vary a great deal. Given our parameters, we cannot specify the various possible types of contexts here.[55] We must be content, then, with the understanding of context as anything that may affect the meaning of a text and is not part of the text.

Although we have narrowed the notion of context in the stated sense, we have provided still a very general understanding of it. According to this understanding, both the author of a text and its audience, for example, are part of the context.[56] And, in many ways, both the author and audience are certainly part of the overall context of a text.[57] The author's intention to convey some specific meaning through the text certainly affects the meaning of the text. Indeed, an author's understanding may in some cases determine the shape a text finally takes, although an author may fail to compose a text in such a way as to convey effectively the meaning he or she wishes. This raises the question of the identity of the meaning of a text, but more on this in later chapters. To get back to the point we were pursuing, not only the authors, but also the audiences for which texts are intended and their beliefs and prejudices play important roles in the determination of the meanings of texts. The text 'No smoking' assumes an English speaking audience accustomed to supplying the missing part of the text ('is permitted').

The understanding of context presented here assumes that contexts determine to some extent the meanings of texts. This assumption, however, has been recently challenged. Many deconstructionists hold that contexts cannot determine the meanings of texts because contexts themselves are indeterminate and limitless. Texts are to be taken in themselves, apart from any context.[58]

This position, if taken in the radical form in which I have presented it, is absurd; for texts are always given in a certain language that obeys rules and whose signs denote and connote more or less established meanings. In addition, the audience cannot help but bring to the text its own cultural, psychological, and conceptual context. Indeed, the understanding of the meaning of a text can be carried out only by bringing something to the text that is not already there, and that something, not being part of the text, can be taken only as part of its context. I assume, therefore, that this is not what most deconstructionists mean. More likely, what they mean is that certain contexts can or should be ignored, such as conditions having to do with the author, the history surrounding a text, and past interpretations of it. Those who adhere to this point of view make the contemporary context the only context required to establish the meaning of a text.

Unfortunately, this more benign understanding of the deconstructionist view is also unacceptable, for it ignores the historicity of texts. It ignores the fact that the very tools, such as language, in which texts are presented, the concepts that are conveyed by those tools, and the very authors and audiences of texts are the products of history. Therefore, the understanding of texts requires historical, and thus contextual, analysis. I return to these issues in Chapters 4 and 5.

From the definition of texts that I provided at the beginning of the chapter, it should be clear that I do not believe there can be textual meaning outside context, although context is not the sole determinant of meaning. Indeed, as we shall see, the connection between a text and its meaning is conventional and, thus, depends to a certain extent on the intention of the author. (More on this in Chapter 4.) Moreover, the author intends the text to convey meaning to an audience, which is, in turn, part of the context of the text. The author makes certain assumptions about the audience—knowledge of a particular language, ability to discern certain sounds or images, and so on—without which the text would not successfully convey the meaning intended by the author. Moreover, the author does not always put into a text everything necessary for a text to convey the meaning the author wants to convey; he or she assumes the audience will supply what is not explicit in it. Most texts are elliptical, and the context supplies the missing parts required for the production of understanding. It is not, then, just that the meanings of *some* texts depend on context. That is quite clear. "Fire!" shouted in a crowded movie theater means something very different from "Fire!" shouted in the field of battle next to a loaded cannon. What needs to be stressed is that the meanings of *all* texts depend on context to some extent. This entails that there is no such thing as the "literal" meaning of a text if by 'literal meaning' is understood meaning apart from context.[59] Whether texts have literal meaning in some other sense is, of course, another question.[60] My point is only that texts always function within a context and thus context is a necessary condition of textuality.

Even though there can be no textual meaning apart from context, it is a mistake to think that all texts are equally dependent on context, that they depend on context in the same way, or that they always depend on the same type of context. Some texts depend on it more than others. Generally the shorter and less complex a text is the more different meanings it may have depending on context. 'Fire!' means two different things in the contexts mentioned earlier, but 'There is a fire' is more restrictive. The importance of context for the meaning of a text seems to be inversely proportional to its length and complexity. For the longer and more complex a text is, the more dependent it is upon internal conditions for what it expresses. This, in turn, appears to make its meaning less dependent on context. We may refer to this principle as the Principle of Contextual Relevance.

Likewise, not all texts depend on context in the same way. Some texts depend on context simply as a condition necessary for them to have meaning at all. An English text depends in this way on the English language, which functions in a way as the context that provides the signs of which it is composed and the rules of arrangement according to which it is organized to convey meaning. But some texts depend on context as a condition necessary for them to have a particular meaning and no other. This is the case of the context in which 'Fire!' means that there is a fire in a theater.

With respect to the type of context, it becomes obvious upon reflection that an extraordinary array of conditions qualify as context. Apart from the author and the audience, for example, physical conditions that affect texts constituted by physical entities. But also historical, temporal, social, spatial, and cultural factors may affect the effectiveness with which texts carry out their functions. Indeed, texts can be part of the context of texts. The meaning of 'She is guilty' may depend very much on the textual context within which this sentence appears.[61] Examples of all the types of contexts mentioned could be easily cited, but I do not believe we need to dwell further on what seems a rather obvious point.

A distinction between two basic types of context should be kept in mind, however. This is the distinction between what I call the *historical* and the *contemporary* contexts of a text. The historical context is the complete set of circumstances that affect the historical meaning of a text. I call this context *historical* because it consists of the circumstances that accompany a text at the time of its production. Thus the historical context of the text of *Hamlet* consists of all those conditions external to the text of *Hamlet* that, affecting its meaning, were contemporaneous with the text first produced. The contemporary context, on the other hand, consists of the complete set of circumstances that affect the understanding of a text by an audience that is not contemporary with the text at the time of its production. As will become clear later in this book, the contemporary context has a direct bearing on the understanding, or misunderstanding, of a text. Therefore it is important to keep this distinction in mind.

Let me finish this section by saying that the examples I have provided, first, serve to illustrate what I have tried to establish thus far; namely, that the meaning of a text depends on the meaning and function of the signs of which it is composed, on the particular way in which those signs are arranged, and on the context in which it is found. I shall return to these and other factors that have been proposed as determinants of textual meaning in Chapter 4. For the moment what has been said should suffice. Moreover, the examples in question, second, underline the fact that a text should not be confused with its meaning or with the entities that constitute it.

II. The Conventionality of Texts

Having understood texts as groups of entities, used as signs, which are selected, arranged, and intended by authors to convey specific meanings to particular audiences in certain contexts, we must next ask whether texts are natural or conventional. This is an important question not only because its answer will further reveal to us the nature of textuality, but also because, based on different available understandings of the nature of the signs that compose texts, different answers to it are in principle possible. Because texts are composed of signs arranged in particular ways, to answer this question we must establish, first, whether the signs that compose texts are themselves natural or conventional and, second, whether the arrangements of those signs into texts are also natural or conventional.

Whether signs are classified as natural or conventional depends very much on what one means by 'natural' and 'conventional' and what one has in mind when one speaks of signs. Let us suppose two things: First, let us suppose that by 'natural' one means something that occurs in the world without the input and design of persons, and by 'conventional' one means something that is the result of the input and design of persons who thus play a role in its establishment.[62] And, second, let us suppose that by 'sign' one does not mean a sign as I have understood it here, but rather the entities that are used to convey meaning considered apart from that meaning, that is, what I have called *ECTs*. If these two suppositions are adopted, it is clear that signs can be either natural or conventional. For, although many entities used to convey meaning may be the result of a person's input and design, it is perfectly possible to use natural entities that are not the result of such input and design to convey meaning.[63] For example, a certain rock naturally occurring in a place could be used to mark a turn on the road that must be taken if one wishes to reach a certain destination. Clearly, in this sense, there can be natural signs, because it is possible for a sign to be something that occurs in nature without the input and design of persons.

We can reach the same conclusion about texts, provided that: (1) by 'text' one means a group of entities used to convey meaning and the group is considered apart from that meaning (ECTs); and (2) one still accepts the first assumption mentioned earlier with respect to the understanding of 'natural' and 'conventional.' Texts, if composed of natural signs whose arrangement is the result of natural forces, could be considered natural. For example, if a meaning is assigned to each of the pebbles that compose a group of pebbles found on a beach, and the arrangement of the pebbles is also considered semantically significant, we have a text that is completely natural. In this case, each pebble would be assigned a certain meaning that, when combined with the meanings of the other pebbles that are part of the group arranged in a certain way, would yield an overall meaning resulting both from the meaning of the individual pebbles as well as from their arrangement. Of course, if either the entities that compose the group or their arrangement were the result of human intention and design, then the text would not be natural. But from what has been said it is clear that there can be natural texts, because it is not necessary for a text to be composed of entities entirely or partly created, designed, or arranged by persons.

On the other hand, we may understand a sign to be an entity considered as related to a meaning it is used to express and not the entity considered apart from such a meaning. This would be in accordance with our earlier understanding of signs. In this view, all signs are conventional, and therefore, texts can be composed only of conventional elements; for no thing, whether made by persons or not, is in fact naturally connected to a particular meaning.[64] The connection to meaning is a result of design, intention, or some kind of purposeful activity and can be subject to change according to that design, intention, or activity.

There are philosophers who have held a different point of view, however, maintaining that there are indeed natural signs in the sense that some objects have a natural connection to a particular meaning. One of the best known supporters and earliest defenders of a version of this view is Augustine, who saw the whole natural world as a sign of supernatural reality.[65] According to this position, every thing is both what it is itself and also a sign of something else, a higher and deeper truth.

I do not find Augustine's position to be contradictory or incoherent. But I do find that it relies on certain views that are unsupportable on the basis of reason unaided by faith. If this is so, then the view is weakened from the philosophical standpoint. Moreover, it is not clear that this view can be identified with the position that holds that there are natural signs because the signs in question are not signs of anything natural; they are signs of supernatural reality. For these reasons this is not a position I need to consider further.

Supporters of the natural sign view might want to reply to this objection, however, that the supernatural or religious dimension of Augustine's position is not necessary and, thus, the claim that there are natural signs in the stated sense does not necessarily rely on faith or involve meanings that are supernatural; a purely natural interpretation of the position can be given.[66] Consider, for example, the case of a leaf falling off a maple tree. Is not that a natural sign of the coming of the autumn? And is thunder not a natural sign of an impending storm?

Although the expression 'natural sign' is frequently used in ordinary discourse to refer to cases such as these, I would like to argue that even in such cases we have a conventional connection between the entity used as a sign and the meaning of the sign. Therefore, in this context, 'natural sign' does not mean that there is a natural connection between certain entities and meaning, but rather that the entities in question are related to some other entities as their causes (or in other natural ways) or that the entities used as signs are not the result of design and intention.[67] The falling of a maple leaf is called a sign of autumn, and thunder is called a sign of an impending storm because we have established a connection between them on the basis of certain observations and, therefore, use the phenomena in question to indicate something of interest to us. A different culture, for example, might see thunder or the falling of a maple leaf as signs of other events or even as indications of the divine will to punish and reward them. That there is a causal or any other kind of natural connection between natural phenomena does not entail that the phenomena in question are naturally related as sign and meaning, that is, that such a relation occurs without the intention and design of persons. That connection is made only by convention based on willful agency. Nor does the natural character of the entity used as a sign imply a necessary connection to a certain meaning.[68]

Note that I do not mean to imply by saying that signs are conventional and established by convention that it is always the case that one or more persons explicitly and consciously decided to assign a meaning to an entity in order to use it as a sign. This process is seldom deliberate and conscious. Most entities become signs in casual ways and the process of sign creation is often unconscious. Although we may be aware of what we are saying, often we are not aware of the means and processes through which we do it. Nonetheless, the connection between an entity and a meaning is always mediated through purposeful activity.

Finally, some philosophers have spoken of concepts as natural signs of the things of which they are concepts.[69] For example, the concept "cat" is, according to this view, a natural sign of cats, whereas the word 'cat' is a conventional sign used for both the concept "cat" and cats.

My reaction to this position is that I have no objection to speaking in this way, as long as it is understood that when one speaks of signs thus, one does not mean the same thing as when one speaks of things like the word 'cat' as signs. And it is things like 'cat' that I say are not natural, even if instead of 'cat' a natural entity were used to talk about cats. The same can be applied to the talk of causes and other such phenomena as natural signs. I have no objection to this language as long as it is understood that if a cause is used as a sign of something else, that connection of sign-signified is not natural; what is natural is the cause-effect connection, which nonetheless can be the reason why the cause in question was chosen to serve as a sign of the effect.

The same reasoning that has been applied to answer the question as to whether the signs that compose texts are conventional or natural can also be applied to the question concerning the conventional or natural arrangement of those signs and, therefore, need not be repeated. Let it suffice to point out that the arrangement, even in cases where it naturally occurs, is connected to a meaning only as a result of a person's activity and intention. In short, even when texts are composed of natural entities and found in a natural arrangement, the connection of those entities to a certain meaning is the result of a person's activity and intention, thereby rendering texts conventional rather than natural entities.

One may wish to object, however, that the conventionality of the arrangement of the signs composing a text is not as clear as has been claimed here. After all, if the meanings of signs are already established, do not the meanings determine the way the signs are to be arranged to convey the meaning of a text? Consider the case of the signs 'is,' 'no,' 'permitted,' and 'smoking,' and let us assume that they have the meanings that they usually have in English. Let us further assume that a particular author A wishes to convey the overall meaning that no smoking is permitted. Would it not be necessary for A to arrange the signs in the following way: No smoking is permitted? Certainly it does not seem possible to put them in any other way and still convey the intended meaning, for to do so would prevent effective communication of the meaning in question.[70] The point of the example, then, is to show that arrangement is not conventional once the signs that are to be arranged have been chosen.

This objection fails, however, because it assumes that, because the signs have to be arranged in a certain way to compose a meaningful text, the arrangement or range of arrangements available to the author is not conventional. It assumes this because the author is not responsible for the rules of such an arrangement. And, indeed, this is largely so in the case of natural languages. Someone who wants to convey the meaning that no smoking is permitted using the signs just indicated must order those signs in only one way. What this objection fails to notice is that the rules of English grammar that determine how the signs are to be arranged are not natural phenomena, but are, rather, the result of human activity and ultimately a matter of convention. Authors use the the rules of natural languages because their aim is to convey meaning to speakers of certain languages whom they know will understand what they say if they follow certain rules. But, even in the case we have been discussing, it is clear that the author could have chosen not to use those rules. She could have stipulated different rules and thus ordered the signs differently if she had wished, even though under those circumstances communication would have failed. This goes to show that the arrangement of the signs that compose a text is not determined by the meanings of those signs, but rather by the rules conventionally developed to put together those signs in order to convey meaning. The ultimate origin of the rules—whether they have been developed by the author or someone other than the author, say a small group of persons at a particular time or society at large over a longer period of time—does not make those rules any less conventional than the signs arranged according to those rules.

The conventional character of texts has an important corollary. I am referring to what I call their *epistemic character*. What I mean by this is that the semantically significant elements of the entities that constitute texts must be epistemically accessible to the authors and audiences of the texts. Texts cannot be composed of entities, or features of entities, whose semantically significant features or parts are not or cannot be epistemically accessible to the authors and audiences of the texts, because texts are intended to convey meaning through acquaintance with those semantically significant features or parts. This may be called the *Principle of Epistemic Accessibility*.

One way to explain the Principle of Epistemic Accessibility is to refer back to the entities that constitute texts. Consider, for example, a text composed of marks made on a piece of paper. In such a text, we can distinguish between the paper and the text in the following way. First, the paper is an entity whose existence and features are independent of the text, whereas the text cannot exist or function as a text without the paper. Second, the paper has many features that are not only irrelevant to the text, but of which the author is not aware. For example, the paper might have a certain weight and chemical composition. But for the text, neither the weight nor the chemical composition of the paper are relevant. (Of course, they could be relevant, provided the author had chosen to make them relevant by making them semantically significant, but they need not be relevant and in this case they are not, because the meaning of the text is tied only to the marks made on the paper and not to the weight or chemical composition of the paper.) Having made the distinction between entities or features of entities that are used to convey meaning and those which are not, we can see that only entities or features of entities that are epistemically accessible can be used to convey meaning and thus become part of a text.

This entails that whatever is semantically significant in a text must be epistemically accessible. Undiscovered elements in the composition of nature, theoretical entities not subject to acquaintance, and the like cannot be semantically significant and thus be part of texts. Texts have a fundamentally epistemic dimension; their parts must be epistemically accessible to their authors.

Notice, however, that this accessibility need not always be actually public. It is possible to have a text composed of mental images, in which case it may be that only the person who has those images is acquainted with the text. Of course, insofar as images are mental constructs that often reproduce physical objects, they can be constructed also by others. Thus, if the text is constituted by mental images that reproduce '2 + 2 = 4,' then anyone who has access to '2 + 2 = 4' can form and, thus, have access to similar images. This goes even for cases in which authors construct mental texts idiosyncratically, combining images derived from various objects. But it is in principle possible for only one person actually to have them; in which case they would be private.

Keep in mind, however, that acquaintance should not be confused with consciousness. One can be acquainted with something and not be conscious of it. For example, while I am writing these words on a piece of paper I am not conscious of the paper; I become conscious of the paper only when I direct my attention to it, as I am doing now. But all the same, I could have answered questions about it even if I never paid attention to it. If someone had asked me after I finished writing this page about the color of the paper, most likely I would have been able to answer that it was white, for example. And something similar is the case with the entities we use to make up texts. While I write a text I am not conscious of the shapes I form with the pen or even of the color of ink I use. I am conscious only of the meaning that I am aiming to convey. Yet, I am acquainted with these shapes and colors, and my acquaintance is sufficient to answer questions about them with some degree of accuracy.

Finally, the Principle of Epistemic Accessibility does not apply to the meaning of texts. It is not a consequence of this principle that authors need be acquainted with the complete meaning of the texts of which they are authors. The Principle of Epistemic Accessibility applies only to the entities that constitute texts.

By contrast, the Principle of Epistemic Accessibility does apply to the text's context. I argued earlier that context is very important for texts, for it determines to some extent their meanings and, thus, their identities. A shout, 'Fire!' next to a cannon means something different from the same shout in a crowded theater because the context of the first is different from the context of the second. Context is present and assumed, and the meaning of texts depends on it, even if the authors of texts are not conscious of it.

This brings me to the last point I want to make before concluding this chapter: Texts are historical entities. By this I mean that texts always appear at a certain time and place and are produced by authors in complex historical circumstances out of the materials that surround the authors and are prompted by the needs and desires of those authors. Texts are not independent of the cultural and personal matrices within which they are produced. This fact has important implications for their function and, therefore, must be considered in any attempt to develop a theory of textuality. We shall return to this point later in the book.

III. Conclusion

I began the Introduction to this book by indicating that texts pose some curious problems for the philosopher. The source of some of these problems is that we tend to think about texts in terms of incompatible categories. In some cases, we think of texts as works that can be classified in terms of various genres. This is most frequent in cases of literary texts, when they are talked about as novels, poems, and the like, although it also applies to nonliterary texts, as is the case with some nonliterary works of art. In other cases, we think of texts in terms of grammatical categories, which seems to imply that texts are linguistic in some sense. Moreover, we frequently think of texts as physical objects that can be perceived, touched, and moved. And, finally, we apply to texts logical categories, such as inconsistency, which suggests that texts are concepts, views, or the like. The question arises, then, as to how it is possible that the same thing be or be thought of in such different, and in some cases incompatible, ways.

One solution is to say that the ways in which we think about texts are not the ways texts are and, therefore, there is no conflict in the nature of texts but only in our conceptions of them. Perhaps texts are not at all as we think of them, or maybe they are only in some ways as we think of them, namely, those that are not incompatible.

This answer, however, is unsatisfactory, but not so much because it maintains that texts are "in-themselves" different from the way we experience them. That would certainly be an unsatisfactory solution to a pre-Kantian metaphysician, but I am not concerned with defending the pre-Kantian metaphysical program here because, for starters, the defense of that point of view would require much more than I can provide here and I am not even convinced that it can be carried out successfully. More important, such a defense is not necessary for my purposes. For, even if one accepts a Kantian position, in which the objects of knowledge are not things-in-themselves separate from experience, it is necessary that we solve the apparent inconsistencies in the way we think about texts precisely because those inconsistencies appear in the way we think about them; namely, in our experience. So, whether we adopt a pre-Kantian posture or not, we need to account for the apparent inconsistencies we fall into when thinking about texts. In other words, we need to come up with a conception of texts that resolves those inconsistencies and makes possible a sensible account of what texts are and how they function.

Such a conception is precisely what I have tried to provide and express concisely in the definition given in this chapter. The view implied by that definition explains how texts can be subsumed without contradiction under literary, grammatical, physical, and logical categories. The key to the theory is that texts are not simple, and their complexity is the root of our apparent ambivalence toward them.

The complexity of texts is rooted in the fact that they are entities conventionally connected with meanings. Their meanings are the source of the logical categories we apply to them, for what we understand (in the cognitive sense I have used here) may be subject to contradiction, inconsistency, and the like. Also, the fact that texts have meanings, and that they are composed of signs that are themselves meaningful allows us to use linguistic categories to refer to them. Grammatical predicates are applied because all languages involve grammatical rules of one sort or another, even if they are not part of the rules associated with natural languages.

At the root of the physical categories in terms of which we think of texts is the physical entities we often use as signs to compose them. Of course, those entities need not always be physical. But it is a fact of experience that a good proportion of the entities we use to make up texts are physical. Indeed, as we saw earlier, texts can be composed of any kind of thing, although their physical composition does not preclude the application of nonphysical predicates to them when we refer to some meanings they can have.

Finally, a byproduct of the contrived nature of texts is their possible classification into various types of genres, particularly literary ones. For example, we can speak of a text as a novel because it is arranged according to an established pattern.

In short, the source of the apparent inconsistencies in the way we think and speak about texts is that they are complex entities whose various dimensions warrant the use of different, and sometimes incompatible, predicates. And the solution to the problem posed by those inconsistencies is to recognize that when we speak of texts in these incompatible ways, we are thinking about different aspects of textuality and not about one thing.

So much, then, for the problems raised in the Introduction to which the discussion in this chapter is pertinent. In addition to suggesting solutions to those problems, the definition of a text proposed in this chapter has important consequences that will become evident as we go along. I would like to point out one such consequence at the outset, however, that may help keep the discussion in perspective. The consequence of which I speak is that the definition narrows down the category of texts substantially, excluding from it many categories frequently confused or interchanged with it. Indeed, in some contemporary philosophical circles it has become acceptable to extend the category in such a way that practically anything can be considered a text. One such view understands texts to be occasions for interpretation, and interpretation is, in turn, understood broadly to mean any kind of understanding.[71] Under this view, practically anything is a text because practically anything can lead to some understanding. An event, a feature of an object, any object, an activity, and so on, all would qualify as texts, for they lead to some understanding. Consider the case of a car crash. This could be a text because someone could derive an understanding from it. And the same could be said of the color of a piece of paper or of the paper itself. In each case, the event, feature, or object could become the object of understanding and, thus, interpretation.

This sort of view is not helpful for the development of a greater understanding of textuality insofar as its conception of textuality is so broad that it loses significance. Just as 'red' would lose the significance it has if we made it synonymous with 'color,' 'text' loses the significance it has if we make it synonymous with 'the occasion of an interpretation.'

The view I have presented here is, of course, very different from this. According to the definition provided earlier, only a group of entities, used as signs, which are selected, arranged, and intended by an author in a certain context to convey some specific meaning to an audience qualifies as a text. That means that events, activities, features of objects, and objects themselves, considered as such, are excluded from the category of text. A car crash is not a text even though it may give rise to understanding and interpretation. For even if it were composed of signs, which it is not, those signs have not been selected and arranged by someone with the intention of conveying some specific meaning to an audience. Obviously, if someone actually used the car crash in order to do so, say by establishing that a car crash at such and such a corner on such and such a date happening to a car of a particular make, and so on, would mean such and such, then the car crash would be a text. Indeed, as we have seen, anything, whether natural or artificial, can be used to make up a text, but it becomes a text only if it fulfills the conditions specified in the definition given earlier. There must be signs, selection, arrangement, and intention on the part of someone in a certain context in order to convey a specific meaning.

Still, even if it is effective in answering some of the problems raised in the Introduction and in delimiting the category of textuality, the view presented here does not specifically tell us how texts are to be distinguished from other things closely associated with texts and does not make explicit the various types of texts there are and how they fit the general understanding of texts provided in this chapter. To understand fully the nature of texts, a greater distinction between texts and other categories is necessary. This is provided in the next chapter. Also, a taxonomy of the category of texts is necessary, which is the business of Chapter 3.

2

EXTENSION

In the last chapter I proposed a definition of *texts* that, I claimed, provides an accurate intensional analysis of textuality. In this chapter I propose to show how the conception of textuality expressed by that definition distinguishes texts from other things that are closely related to and frequently confused with them. The title of the chapter is intended to express this program, indicating how far the category of texts extends, although it is through intensional analyses that extensional questions will be answered.[1] For this reason we may still speak of the content of this chapter as having to do with the logic of texts.

The categories I shall explore are those of language, artifacts, art objects, and works. In the previous chapter and the Introduction I referred to texts in ways that suggest that they are closely related to some of these categories, and the examples I provided indicated also a relation to the remaining ones. It is necessary, therefore, that we return to these notions now and make explicit what is meant by them and the degree to which the category of texts is related to the mentioned categories. Naturally, the understanding of the relation of texts to these categories should help with the understanding of textuality and deepen our awareness of the boundaries of the category.

Before I begin, I should point out that the discussion of textuality vis-à-vis the mentioned categories is uneven in current philosophical literature. There has been explicit and considerable discussion of the relation between texts and works, and plenty has been said, although often indirectly, about texts and art objects. However, relatively little has been said on texts and language, and practically nothing on the artifactuality of texts. The last is perhaps a result of the general lack of interest that philosophers have shown on artifacts, but there is no apparent reason why the linguistic character of texts should have been ignored, considering the extraordinary attention paid to language in contemporary philosophy.

The chapter will be divided into four parts, dealing respectively with language, artifacts, art objects, and works. A concluding section summarizes the main points made.

I. Texts and Language

Although texts are always and necessarily composed of signs, they are not always or necessarily composed of signs belonging to natural languages. Natural languages are languages produced in response to the need of social groups to communicate; they are not the product of one or more individuals who consciously set out to create them with a specific purpose other than social communication in mind. Languages that are products of such conscious processes are known as artificial languages.

The signs that compose texts are not necessarily words occurring in natural languages. A text could very well be composed of pictures that depict natural objects, as indeed some early texts are. Moreover, the meaning of the signs of which texts are composed could be established by stipulation even if the signs are taken from a natural language, as when I say that from now on I will use the term 'cow' to refer to sheep in spite of the fact that all English speakers use it to refer to cows. What is inevitable is the semantic character of texts, for signs are semantic phenomena insofar as they have meaning and texts are composed of signs arranged in semantically significant ways. Texts should not be confused with language, however. There are important differences between the two that may be made evident through the following considerations.

Both texts and languages are composed of signs. A language consists of (1) a set of signs and (2) a set of rules governing the mutual relations among those signs as well as the arrangements into which those signs may be placed. Texts are also composed of signs, but, unlike languages, texts do not contain rules, although they are arranged according to rules and knowledge of the rules according to which the signs that compose them have been arranged may be necessary to understand them. A language, therefore, is in one sense much more and in another sense much less than the texts that have been produced in that language.

Languages can and do exist without texts.[2] For example, an artificial language described in a book may never be used to compose texts. But texts exist only if signs are selected and arranged in ways to convey meaning. The signs and arrangements do not have to be part of a natural language, but they are nevertheless linguistic. Thus texts logically presuppose language even if the language has never been previously used or even described. A text, insofar as it is composed of signs and arranged in a semantically significant way logically presupposes the signs of which it is composed and the rules according to which those signs have been organized into a text. This does not mean, of course, that a text presupposes the existence of signs other than the ones it uses or rules other than the ones it follows. To that extent, texts do not presuppose complete or even extensive languages; they presuppose only the signs and rules that make them possible. If such signs and rules are not sufficient to constitute a language because languages require much more, then we can claim that texts presuppose only parts of languages rather than whole languages.[3]

The question of whether languages have some kind of ontological status prior to texts is a different issue. From practice it looks as if in the case of natural languages, the actual use of signs in a certain order antecedes the mention of the signs and rules of arrangement of which the language is composed. People talk before they talk about their talk. This applies in particular to natural languages, however. In the case of artificial languages it is frequent, or even the norm perhaps, to put together the signs and rules of the language before the language is actually used. This is evident from most logic books in which artificial languages are developed. In cases of both natural and artificial languages, however, texts presuppose the language rather than vice versa.

A text is put together by an author for a particular purpose, whereas language is an instrument authors use to produce any texts they wish.[4] As a result, a text has a fixed structure that cannot be altered without altering the text itself, and the identity conditions of a text are quite particular. Language, on the other hand, is flexible insofar as the signs of which it is composed can be used in different arrangements without changing the identity of the language. Thus the identity conditions of a language are broader and more general than those of texts. Although there are rules to which languages must adhere and that govern the arrangements of the signs of which they are composed, languages are flexible instruments that can give various results depending on the purposes of the moment. Consequently, even though languages have finite numbers of signs and rules, those signs can be combined in virtually infinite numbers of ways to create texts.[5] Texts, by contrast, have a kind of resistance to alteration that is not characteristic of language and that is the result in part of their peculiar ontological status. That status will be explored in the volume dealing with metaphysics.

The authors of texts and artificial languages are generally identifiable, because texts and artificial languages have individual authors or small groups of individual authors who are responsible for them. In this sense, texts and artificial languages have an identifiable historical origin. The authors of natural languages, by contrast, are not identifiable because natural languages have no individual authors or small groups of authors who are responsible for them; they are the products of social groups and thus are anonymous in origin. Consequently, natural languages lack an identifiable historical origin. Likewise, languages considered as such, do not have audiences. Only a text, that is, language as used by someone, has an audience for which it is intended.[6]

It should be evident that, although texts are not to be confused with language and can be composed of signs that are not part of any natural language, most texts are in fact composed of signs that are part of natural languages, and their arrangements follow the rules that operate in those languages. So, although presumably authors are free to use whatever they wish as signs and arrange them in whatever way they wish to create texts, most authors work within the narrow confines of existing linguistic sets of signs and rules. The activity of most authors does not involve the creation of new signs, the extension of the meaning of those signs beyond established limits, or the development of idiosyncratic arrangements of them. The activity of most authors involves rather the composition of new clusters of signs arranged according to certain preestablished rules, but that display some degree of novelty. Indeed, the use of signs already in existence and the adherence to established rules of arrangement facilitates communication.

The confusion of texts with language may lead to the conclusion that texts, like language, are flexible, do not have very strict identity conditions, and are independent of authors and audiences. The fact is, however, that texts are less flexible than languages, having definite structures, and generally identifiable authors and audiences. Thus, it is a mistake to conclude, as some deconstructionists do, that texts lack definition and determination.[7] This is the reason why it is important to understand the distinction between texts and language. Note, of course, that the distinction between texts and language does not imply that texts are not semantically flexible and that they are not dependent on their authors and audiences in various ways; it implies only that, if they are so, it is not because they are languages or like languages.

In short, then, texts are linguistic insofar as they are composed of signs arranged in certain definite ways, and languages supply both the signs and the rules according to which the signs that make up texts are arranged into texts. But texts do not share some characteristics of languages; there are important differences between texts and languages whose implications should not be underestimated.

II. Texts and Artifacts

If, as I have argued in Chapter 1, texts are conventional, then we must raise the question as to whether they are artifacts or not, and if they are artifacts, the sense in which they are so. The question arises because the conventional nature of texts implies that they are the result of intentional activity and design and artifacts also seem to be related to intentional activity and design. For my present purposes it is important to establish a distinction between texts and artifacts because in some contemporary discussions all artifacts are considered to function as texts and little discrimination is used in assigning characteristics proper to artifacts and texts. If, as I shall argue, all texts are artifactual, but not all artifacts are texts, then texts share in the general features of artifacts, but add to those features others that do not characterize all artifacts. To establish the distinction between artifacts and texts, we must begin, then, by saying something about artifacts.

It is by no means easy to provide a completely satisfactory analysis of the notion of artifact, and it is not my intention here to do so. Because my concern is not with artifacts but with texts, I propose instead to present a working definition of artifacts that may be of use in understanding their relation to texts and that will deepen our understanding of texts themselves without worrying too much about the precision of the definition.[8]

The notion of artifact is generally used in ordinary discourse in connection with physical objects that are either the product of intentional activity and design or have in part been modified as a result of that activity and design. We do not speak of actions, activities, events, the features of objects, and the like as artifacts; nor do we refer to nonphysical entities as artifacts. Artifacts are always physical objects, and physical objects that are durable and solid. Ice cream and orange juice, for example, are not regarded as artifacts. In ordinary language, moreover, the category of artifact is restricted to relatively small objects. Thus a hammer is considered an artifact but a building is not, even though the latter, as the former, is the product of intentional activity and design.[9] Likewise, in ordinary language, only inorganic, or organic but not living objects, are considered artifacts. Generally we would not speak of the results of genetic engineering as artifacts, even though they are the result of intentional activity and design. Whereas a stone arrow is an artifact (and so is a wooden one), a living organism is not considered an artifact. And, although artifacts may be made up of bone or other dead organic material, they cannot be made up of living organisms. Indeed, this is the way in which not only ordinary language functions, but also the way in which archeologists tend to use the term 'artifact.' Some archeologists, I might add, extend the category of artifact to physical objects that, although not the product of intentional activity and design, have been affected by such activity.

If we were to follow the lead of ordinary language in our analysis, then we would have to adopt a definition of artifact such as the following:

1. X is an artifact if and only if (1) X is an object, (2) X is durable, (3) X is small, (4) X is either (a) inorganic or (b) organic but nonliving, and (5) either (a) X is the product of intentional activity and design or (b) X is not the product of intentional activity and design but has undergone some change as a result of intentional activity and design.

Note that definition 1 is broad in an important sense: By speaking about intentional activity and design without reference to human beings, it allows for the inclusion of products of animal activity in it. Whether these products should or should not ultimately be included in the category depends, however, on whether they fit the other criteria specified in the definition. But they should not be ruled out merely because they are produced by animals. Note also that conditions (3) and (4) imply the conditions of physicality and solidity, present in our ordinary intuitions about artifacts mentioned earlier. So there is no need to list these separately.

Yet, this definition is too restrictive; although it largely captures ordinary language usage, it does not seem to be supported by good reasons other than ordinary use. Indeed, none of conditions (1)–(4) seems to be essentially tied to what distinguishes artifacts from nonartifacts. Consider (4). There seems to be no good reason why living organisms should not be considered artifacts when they are the product of intentional activity and design. Why could bacteria produced in a lab and not occurring naturally outside it not be regarded as artifactual rather than natural when they are the product of the specific intent and design of a scientist? Moreover, (4) also implies that artifacts must be physical. And, indeed, in ordinary language it does seem that only such objects are regarded as artifacts.[10] However, there appears to be no compelling reason why artifacts could not be mental constructs, or modifications of mental constructs, resulting from intentional activity and design. Consider the case of someone who builds a mental image or model of an object she intends to construct. Why couldn't this image be considered as much an artifact as the object constructed after it. After all, the image is as much the product of intentional activity and design as the object.

Condition (3) is relative to a perspective or a standard, thus posing problems of demarcation. What is small according to some may be large according to others, and vice versa. Besides, at which precise size do artifacts become nonartifacts? Is a dollhouse an artifact but a life-size house not? Is a baseball bat an artifact but the giant sculpture of a bat in Chicago's Loop not an artifact? Size cannot be of any use when it comes to the determination of artifactuality. And something similar could be said about condition (2), concerned with durability.

These considerations lead to another point. I mentioned that there is no reason why mental images could not be artifacts. But if this is so, there should be no reason why a drawing of a house, for example, could not be considered an artifact. Indeed, a picture on paper and a picture in the mind do not seem to be very different as far as the content of the picture is concerned. Now, the point of these observations is to note that not only objects but the features of objects can be considered artifacts. Thus, a drawing on a piece of paper or an image in the mind, are not objects, if by object we mean something like an Aristotelian substance, but still are artifacts. Thus, condition (1) is also unacceptable.

These observations indicate that the conditions specified by (1), (2), (3), and (4) do not seem to be theoretically relevant to the understanding of artifactuality, for there seems to be no particular reason to adopt them; they do not seem appropriate to demarcate the notion of artifact. For these reasons, then, I propose to drop conditions (1)–(4), leaving the definition as follows:

2.   X is an artifact if and only if either (a) X is the product of intentional activity and design or (b) X is not the product of intentional activity and design but has undergone some change as a result of intentional activity and design.

According to definition 2 the size of an object does not enter into its artifactuality. Both an arrow head and the Empire State Building are artifacts. Nor is the organic-inorganic, living-nonliving character of the object relevant. Bacteria produced by genetic engineering as well as a pair of scissors are artifacts. Finally, the definition opens up the category to nonphysical entities and the features of objects to artifactuality.

According to 2 the determining factors in artifactuality are intentional activity and design.[11] By intentional activity is meant activity that is the product of an intention; that is, the product of an attempt to achieve a certain end. Therefore, when I move my pen to form a letter I am engaged in an intentional activity, but when I yawn because I am bored, I am not so engaged. (Because intentional activity plays a role in the production or modification of artifacts, most artifacts have well-established functions, something missing in the case of many other objects.)

Not everything that is a product of intentional activity or has been modified as a result of intentional activity is an artifact, however. A baby, for example, whose parents engaged in sexual intercourse with the view to its production and did everything they could to facilitate its growth is the product of the intentional activity of the parents. Yet, no baby is an artifact, for a baby is not the result of the parents's design. Design is a necessary condition of artifacts. This is the reason why not all human modifications of the environment produced as a result of an activity directed toward an end are artifacts. The leaf I crush while I build a hut in the woods appears not to be an artifact not because I crush it unintentionally, although that could also be reason for it not to be an artifact, but because it follows no established pattern of design.

So far I have been speaking largely as if for something to be an artifact it would have to be completely the result of intentional activity and design, although the conditions specified in 2 clearly indicate that a change in it resulting from intentional activity and design is sufficient for it being considered an artifact. This must include changes in context, for such changes, provided they result from intentional activity in such a way that the product is a specific design, are sufficient for artifactuality. A precious stone, cut and mounted on a ring, is an artifact partly because its context has been changed (mounted on a ring), although it has also undergone modification (cut) in itself. The jawbone that Samson used to fight the Philistines was neither the product of intentional activity and design nor modified by intentional activity and design, but its context was changed by intentional activity and design so that it became an artifact—a weapon. Other examples similar to the last one are easy to find—a piece of driftwood used as decoration on a mantelpiece or a rock used as a paperweight are such. In the last three cases the change has occurred in the context rather than the object itself. To take into account these cases, we may modify the definition of artifact further in the following way:

3.   X is an artifact if and only if either (a) X is the product of intentional activity and design or (b) X is not the product of intentional activity and design

but has undergone some change and/or its context has undergone some change and the change in either case is the product of intentional activity and design.

Of course, an object does not in itself become an artifact when its context is changed; the object becomes an artifact only when it is considered in the context in question.[12] A tiger does not in itself, as a tiger, become an artifact when it is moved from its natural environment in the wild into a cage in a zoo, although a zoo is an artifact and the tiger insofar as it is displayed in a zoo may also be considered an artifact. This brings out another interesting point about artifacts, namely, that they can be composed of natural objects that remain natural objects in themselves even if, in context, they may be artifactual. A tree that happens to be in a garden is as natural, qua tree, as a tree in the forest, even though the garden is not natural but artifactual. On the other hand, the tree considered as part of the garden is, like the garden, artifactual. Moreover, if the tree is trimmed in a certain shape, and considered as having that shape, it is no longer just a tree and thus a natural object, but rather a tree shaped in a particular way, and that shape adds to it an artifactual dimension. The same could be said of a rock used as a paperweight. The rock is a natural object, but the rock used as a paperweight, or even better, the paperweight, which happens to be a rock, is an artifact. Thus, 3 needs to be further modified to take into account these points:

4.   X is an artifact if and only if either (a) X is the product of intentional activity and design or (b) X is not the product of intentional activity and design but has undergone some change and/or its context has undergone some change, the change in either case is the product of intentional activity and design, and X is considered in the context where the change has occurred rather than apart from it.

What has been said about changes in context applies also to changes in the attention or perspective of a subject toward the object; a change in the attention or perspective of a subject toward an object, even if it were considered a change in context for the object—something that would be difficult to do—is not sufficient to change the character of an object in itself from natural to artifactual. Consider, for example, the case of a sunset and assume for a moment that an observer looks only at some aspect of it, disregarding the rest, very much in the way artists select a part of what they see for their paintings. Could we say that in this case the sunset or a part of it has become an artifact? I do not believe so, because there has been only selection or a change of perspective on the side of the observer. Neither the sunset nor any of its parts has been changed as a result of the activity of the observer. However, "the sunset as considered by the observer" is an artifact, for there is no such sunset in nature, apart from the consideration of the observer.

Indeed, suppose that the observer looks at the sunset through tinted glasses. In this case it is possible to argue that "the sunset as looked at through tinted glasses" is an artifact, for the sunset as seen through tinted glasses is not the same as the sunset seen with no glasses, and the sunset seen through tinted glasses is a fabrication, resulting from intention and design.

The view of artifacts that has been presented in definition 4 is by no means completely satisfactory, however. For one thing, many cases pose problems for it. What are we to make, for example, of a baby whose eye color and gender have been determined by genetic engineering? Is the whole baby an artifact or just the color of its eyes and its gender? We have accepted the artifactuality of features, but that has not committed us to the artifactuality or nonartifactuality of the entities of which they are features. And what do we make of a natural reservation where animals are allowed to roam in their natural habitat? Is enclosing an area and not changing anything else in it sufficient for artifactuality? Finally, there is the case of smog, which seems artifactual and yet neither the product of intentional activity and design nor an object whose context has undergone change. These and other cases indicate the complexity of the issues involved in coming up with a satisfactory definition of artifact. Let me take up the last of these cases in more detail to illustrate how complicated the issue can become.

I have argued that the foundation of artifactuality is to be found in intentional activity and design, yet as noted smog seems to be artifactual in nature and at the same time not to fulfill the conditions related to intentional activity and design. Smog is created by human activity but it is not designed by humans or intended by them. What do we make of smog, then? The reason that smog appears to be an artifact to us, even though it is not the result of intentional activity and design, is that most smog is an indirect product of intentional activity and design; most smog is produced because humans build machines of various sorts that burn organic fuels. Yet, it is also true that no humans set out to design and produce smog. Moreover, smog is often the result of purely natural processes initiated by humans, such as the burning of oil. In such cases smog seems very much to fall into the same category as a baby, which is the result of natural processes set in motion by human will, with the difference that in the case of the baby the processes originate in a natural inclination.

Three ways of dealing with cases such as smog suggest themselves. According to one, the problem is solved by arguing that in some cases smog is not an artifact. In cases in which the processes whereby it is produced are purely natural, even though they are initiated by humans, smog need not be considered to be an artifact. Thus, the smog produced when someone sets fire to a naturally occurring pool of oil is not an artifact. Yet, this way of dealing with the example of smog does not solve the problem it poses, for in cases in which smog is produced by processes controlled and designed by humans, even when the smog is not intended or designed by them, it could be argued that smog is an artifact.

Another way of dealing with cases such as smog is to put them in a category different from the categories of artifact and nonartifact. We could call this category the category of quasi-artifacts. The objects that would be placed in it would be objects produced or modified as a result of intentional activity and design but not what such activity and design are intended to produce. Thus smog, when it is a byproduct of intentional activity and design not intended to produce smog, is a quasi-artifact. But when it is the product of intentional activity and design—if such were so as it is with some things other than smog—then it would be an artifact.

The problem with this answer is that it complicates the taxonomy, adding a third category of objects between artifacts and nonartifacts. Moreover, this new category does not seem to be warranted by our ordinary intuitions about the world—we do not speak of quasi-artifacts. This solution lacks economy and experiential backing and thus should be avoided if at all possible.

A third way of dealing with cases such as smog is to insist that they are artifacts even when they are not intended or designed, because the conditions of artifactuality do not require of artifacts that they be intended, but only that they result from intentional activity and design even when the activity is not intended to produce or modify the artifacts in question. This point may be substantiated as follows. 'Design' is used in English in at least two different senses: (1) purpose and (2) pattern or arrangement that is not the result of natural processes. Design in the first sense involves simply having an aim or end that is sought. This is not what is meant by 'design' in the definition of artifact we are using, because it would then be redundant to include intentional activity in the definition. What is meant by 'design' in that definition is a pattern or arrangement that is not the result of natural processes; that is, sense (2). For something to be the product of design in this latter sense it must be the sort of thing whose pattern or arrangement is a byproduct of intentional activity, even if such activity did not necessarily have for its end such an object. That is why smog could be considered an artifact, for although it is not something humans intend to produce in sense (1), it is itself produced by artifacts that are the products of intentional activity and design. If this is so, then we must add to the class of artifacts those objects that are the products of other artifacts or of human activities aimed at producing artifacts, even if they are not themselves intended and designed.

This solution is not satisfactory for two reasons, however. First it would force into the category of artifact all sorts of things we normally do not classify as artifacts and for whose classification as artifacts seems to be no additional good reason. For example, a leaf I crush while building a hut in the woods would after all turn out to be an artifact, since the crushed leaf is the unintentional result of intentional activity and design. Second, it makes the definition of artifact circular, since it includes the notion of nonnatural in it.

Fortunately, for our present purposes it is not important which of these three ways of dealing with the cases of smog and the like is adopted. All three have advantages and disadvantages whose evaluation would take us away from our main purpose and therefore will be ignored. Given our present concerns, however, we need not settle the issues they raise here. Indeed, for our purposes what has already been said is sufficient to help us in the understanding of texts.

The question we do need to answer is whether texts are artifacts; namely, whether they fit the general definition given previously, even if that definition is not completely satisfactory. And, indeed, from the way we have understood texts it follows that they are artifacts. In the first place, texts are groups of entities used as signs and signs are not natural but artificial, resulting from a conventional connection between an entity and meaning. Second, for signs to make up a text they must be selected, arranged, and intended by an author to convey meaning, which indicates that texts are the product of intentional activity and design. Indeed, even when the entities used to make up the signs and texts, the ECTs, are natural, and their arrangement is also natural, the conventional connection of those entities and their arrangement with meaning reveals the artifactual nature of texts. Texts are meaningful artifacts whose meaning is the object of understanding.

Thus, texts are artifacts; but precisely because not all artifacts have meaning conventionally attached to them, it should be clear that not all artifacts are texts. Indeed, even if all artifacts had meaning, they could not be considered texts because not all artifacts are intended to convey meaning to an audience, nor are they necessarily groups of entities, used as signs, which are selected and arranged with that purpose in mind. Artifacts may both produce understanding and be understood by those who perceive and think about them, but that does not turn them into texts. The conventional character of texts, then, implies that they are artifacts, for a convention is an agreement or determination concerning the way in which something is to be regarded, interpreted, done, and so on— conventions involve intentional activity and design. But not everything that is the product of, or involves, intentional activity and design, and that is, thereby, artifactual is conventional.

An interesting fact about artifacts and natural objects is that, as noted earlier, natural objects can become artifacts through modification either of themselves or their contexts even if they do not change substantially. The jawbone used by Samson as a weapon continued to be a jawbone while and after Samson used it as a weapon. By contrast, artifacts do not appear to become natural objects unless their character is substantially changed. For example, a marble sculpture may, through time and erosion, become a rock or even a pebble on a beach. But for this to happen the erosion has to be sufficiently drastic to change the shape of the sculpture, otherwise the sculpture would continue to be a sculpture. This asymmetry between natural objects and artifacts further emphasizes their distinction.

In short, then, artifacts and texts are not the same thing for there are artifacts that are not texts even if all texts are artifacts. Qua artifacts, texts display the intentionality and design that characterizes all artifacts but they display it in ways in which most artifacts do not. Most artifacts display their intentional character and design in themselves or their context without the mediation of a subject. The artifactuality of texts, however, is founded on the conventional nature of the relation between the ECTs of which a text is constituted and the meaning it is intended to convey. Thus the artifactuality of a text is always mediated through the understanding a subject has of that meaning and depends on it. Texts, then, lack the objective, finished quality of most other artifacts and their function is much more open and diverse than that of other artifacts.

III. Texts and Art Objects

There is a marked tendency in some contemporary circles, particularly literary and postmodernist ones, to think of texts and art objects as the same or at least to subsume art objects under what is considered to be the more general category of texts or to treat texts as art objects.[13] The reasons for this tendency are quite understandable, for, as will become clear immediately, texts and art objects share or can share important characteristics. Before I turn to some of those characteristics, however, I should like to clarify what I mean by an art object.

Although a complete theory of art objects would take too much space and would be in many ways beyond the aims of the present analysis, I do need to point out that there is an important distinction between art objects and aesthetic objects.[14] It is the first and not the second sort of object that is most frequently identified with texts, although it is by no means the case that aesthetic objects are never claimed to be texts. We should begin, then, by providing a working definition of art object. I propose the following:

X is an art object if and only if (1) it is an artifact, and (2) it is capable of producing an artistic experience.

According to (1), art objects are artifacts rather than natural objects, the latter being objects that do not fulfill all the conditions of artifactuality established earlier in definition 4.[15] A sunset, a valley, a rock, and a tree are examples of objects that result from processes in which intention and design play no role. Examples of artifacts are such things as a chair, a house, a computer, and a piece of paper. None of the latter, of course, is necessarily an art object even though they are all products of intentional activity and design. That is why a second condition is necessary.

For an object to be an art object it must also be capable of producing an artistic experience. Everything, therefore, that is both an artifact and capable of producing an artistic experience is an art object. Thus, chairs, tables, and piles of bricks can be art objects provided they are capable of producing an artistic experience, a point that was dramatically made earlier in this century by Marcel Duchamp with his urinals, wine bottle racks, and other ready-mades.

Naturally, this leaves open the question of what makes an object capable of producing an artistic experience. This is an important question not only for those interested in texts, but also for the aesthetician, because an answer must be given to it if the possibility that all artifacts qualify as art objects is to be precluded. To provide a satisfactory answer here, however, will be quite impossible because of space limitations, but I shall nonetheless attempt to clarify the matter in a way sufficient for our limited aims.[16] I propose to understand an object capable of producing an artistic experience in the following way:

X is capable of producing an artistic experience if and only if it is regarded by someone both (1) as an artifact and (2) as capable of producing an aesthetic experience.

The category of artistic, then, is included within the category of aesthetic, but it is limited both by the recognition of the artifactual nature of the object that gives rise to the experience and by the historical character of the experience.[17] The object of an artistic experience must be regarded by someone as an artifact at some time and place and as capable of producing an aesthetic experience.[18] This way of unpacking the notion of the artistic allows us to exclude all sorts of artifacts from the category of art object; namely, those artifacts that have not been regarded as artifacts by someone at some time and place or have not been regarded as capable of producing an aesthetic experience. It also allows us to make room for changing historical perceptions of what an art object is. For the nineteenth century a pile of bricks, a urinal, or a crucifix dipped in urine were not considered artistic because, according to my position, they were not regarded as being capable of producing as aesthetic experience, but they certainly are considered artistic in our century. Finally, this understanding of artistic also permits us to ignore the intention, or lack thereof, of the artist. Artifacts not intended as art by their authors can become art as long as they are regarded as artifacts and as capable of producing an aesthetic experience by someone else.[19] Much folk art produced in the last century, for example, was not regarded by their authors as art, yet some of it is considered art today.[20]

I have not addressed the question of the identity and the number of the regarding persons to which I refer because it is largely irrelevant to the issue at hand. Whether one or many persons, someone mad or someone sane, regards an object as an artifact and as capable of producing an aesthetic experience is immaterial to whether the object in question is capable of producing an artistic experience. As long as the object is regarded as such, it must be considered capable of producing an artistic experience. That does not mean, of course, that it is an art object. For that it must in addition be an artifact. Nor does it mean that it is good art. For that some other conditions are required.[21]

The difference between art objects and aesthetic objects can be gathered from what has been said. Aesthetic objects do not need to fulfill either of the two conditions that art objects have to fulfill. Aesthetic objects need not fulfill the first condition; they can be products of nature.[22] That is the case, for example, with a sunset. But that does not mean that aesthetic objects cannot be the product of art. Boticelli's *The Birth of Venus* is a product of human art and yet it is certainly an aesthetic object. Furthermore, aesthetic objects need not fulfill the second condition of art objects; they need not be regarded as capable of producing an artistic experience. That is, they need not be recognized as both artifactual and as capable of producing an aesthetic experience.

The sole condition that makes an object an aesthetic object is its capacity to produce an aesthetic experience in a subject. Thus an object may be an aesthetic object whether someone actually thinks of it as such or not, and whether it has actually produced an aesthetic experience or not, and finally, whether it is an artifact or not. The only requirement that an aesthetic object need fulfill is that it have the capacity to cause an aesthetic experience in a subject. At this point the question may be raised as to what makes an experience aesthetic and what in an object can cause it, which are certainly important questions for the philosopher of art.[23] Indeed, to preclude the possibility that all objects qualify as aesthetic objects, these questions must be answered and some criteria of demarcation must be found. But I do not need not answer them for my present purposes, because my concern in this book is not with art objects or even artifacts, and therefore I am not prepared to address them here. For my limited aims, what I have said is sufficient.

From what has been said it follows, first, that art objects are aesthetic objects, because they are objects regarded as capable of producing aesthetic experiences in subjects and, second, that aesthetic objects can be art objects, if they are regarded as artifacts capable of producing aesthetic experiences, but they need not be so. This leaves open the possibility that there may be aesthetic objects that are not art objects in addition to objects that are both art objects and aesthetic objects. We have seen examples of aesthetic objects that are not art objects (a sunset) and objects that are both aesthetic objects and art objects (Boticelli's *The Birth of Venus*).[24] Whether there are objects that are neither depends, of course, on how the notion of aesthetic experience is unpacked.

Note that the notion of object I have been using in this section is to be taken broadly to include features. Much art consists of objects considered in a narrow, Aristotelian sense of substance, in which they are not features of anything else. Such is the case with sculptures, for example. But much art consists of entities that exist only parasitically in other entities, as parts or features of them. Such are, for example, drawings, dances, and the like. Art objects, like artifacts, can have diverse ontological status.

Having established a way of distinguishing between art objects and aesthetic objects, we can now turn to the question of what distinction, if any, there is between these objects and texts. From the definition of a text given previously, it follows, on the one hand, that texts can be aesthetic objects. There is no reason why a physical text, for example, either as a result of its physical appearance or of the images that its meaning may give rise to, cannot produce an aesthetic experience in a subject. Calligrams, for example, may produce an aesthetic experience even in those who do not understand the meaning of the words of which they are composed because of the peculiar shape they have. And Egyptian hieroglyphs are quite decorative. Moreover, the meaning of a text may produce an aesthetic experience in the reader resulting from the images it conjures up.

On the other hand, the production of or the capacity to produce an aesthetic experience in a subject is not one of the necessary or sufficient conditions that make something a text. I imagine that someone could argue that all texts could in principle be objects of aesthetic experience at some point and in some context, although I very much doubt that anyone could derive an aesthetic experience from reading Kant's *Critique of Pure Reason, The Chicago Manual of Style*, or the list of items I needed to buy when I went to the grocery store last Friday.[25] But that would not make texts particularly aesthetic in nature; indeed, to say that would be to say no more than what one could say about any other object, whether natural or artificial. In either case the point is that the production of or the capacity to produce an aesthetic experience in a subject is not part of what makes something a text. Aesthetic objects and texts do not necessarily share any characteristics.

The relation between art objects and texts is different, however, for they do necessarily share some fundamental characteristics. The most obvious one is that both are artifacts, that is, products of intentional activity and design. This characteristic, although essential to both, would not be sufficient to identify texts with art objects or vice versa. However, another element seems to tie them more strongly, the fact that both texts and art objects are intended to produce some changes in subjects. In the case of texts it is understanding among other things, and in the case of art objects it is the artistic experience. Indeed, the language used to talk about texts and art objects is sometimes interchanged. We frequently hear art critics speak of an art object, such as a painting or a sculpture, as subject to "reading." They ask, for example: What is your reading of that work of art? And language normally applied to art objects is also frequently associated with texts. We often talk about "seeing" something in a letter, for example.

The two characteristics common to art objects and texts that have been noted indicate also that they have something else in common; both have authors and are meant for audiences: the first, because they are products of intentional activity and design, and the second, because they are intended to produce a change in someone. All this is further supported by the existence of texts that are also generally accepted as art objects and vice versa. Indeed, entire literary genres fall into this category, such as poetry and the novel.

Bearing in mind that, first, some characteristics of art objects and texts overlap and, second, some art objects are unquestionably texts, we may ask whether all art objects are texts, whether all texts are art objects, or whether these categories simply overlap? The view that classifies all texts as art objects is neither viable nor popular.[26] Indeed, in ordinary discourse we regard many things as texts that are not art objects. As the examples already given should illustrate. I have not yet encountered anyone who would claim that the text of Kant's *Critique of Pure Reason* and *The Chicago Manual of Style* are artistic. Undoubtedly, some texts are not art objects.

But the converse position is not so clearly counterintuitive, and there are philosophers who speak as if all art objects were texts.[27] If we wish to argue that the extensions of 'art object' and 'text' do not coincide, we must find some feature common to all texts that is not necessarily shared by all art objects, or alternatively, some feature of all art objects that is not necessarily shared by all texts.

One could in principle argue that not all texts are art objects because somehow the entities that constitute texts are different sorts of entities from the entities that constitute art objects. However, that will not do, because we have accepted that any sort of entity whatever can function as a text and the same seems to apply to art objects. The reasons for distinction between texts and art objects, therefore, must be found elsewhere.

Three possibilities look promising. As we saw earlier, texts are groups of entities, used as signs, that are selected, arranged, and intended by an author in a certain context to convey some specific meaning to an audience. But signs themselves have meaning, so that texts are composed of entities that are themselves meaningful. Some art objects are, like texts, composed of signs that have meaning. Novels, poems, and even paintings can have parts endowed with meaning. The words in a poem by T. S. Eliot and the pictorial symbols in Bosch's *Garden of Delights* have meaning and function as signs. But not all art objects are composed of signs. It would be difficult to find any signs in a painting by Pollock, for example. Abstract art in general seems to be composed of shapes that by themselves do not express anything, and only the complete work of art may be said to have meaning (if it has any at all). Here, then, we have a characteristic common to texts that not all art objects have.

Moreover, a second factor separates art objects and texts: Although art objects share with texts the fact that they are intended by an author for an audience, they are intended to do different things. Texts are always intended to convey meaning, even if the author, as we saw earlier, has other and even more fundamental intentions as well. Now, we do speak of meaning in noncognitive terms as purpose, significance, relevance, and the like, but the meaning that texts qua texts aim to convey is always of the sort that results in understanding. By contrast, art objects, qua art objects, are not intended to convey meaning of this sort to audiences. Thus, although both art objects and texts are intended for audiences, art objects need not be texts. Indeed, for an object to be classified as art, it must have more than cognitive meaning—it must be regarded as capable of producing an artistic experience. Hence, it is not the cognitive aspect of an object at all that makes it art, but whatever artistic experience it is thought to be capable of producing. Many art objects produce understanding; both didactic and so-called representational art fit this bill. But even those art objects are different from texts in that, in addition to what they might cognitively say, there is also a noncognitive effect they are thought to produce, or to be able to produce, in their audiences.

It should be made clear at this point, however, that I do not mean to hold that the criterion of cognitive meaning is verifiability and least of all empirical verifiability. If verifiability were the criterion of textual meaning, commands, questions, requests, and the like would not have meaning and yet it seems difficult to argue that they do not. Moreover, if that were the case, texts composed of them would not be texts, which obviously they are. Indeed, one could very well imagine a whole text covering several pages and composed of only one sentence that ends with a question mark. Moreover, if the verifiability in question were of the empirical sort, most or perhaps all theological and metaphysical treatises would have to be excluded from the category, again something I am not prepared to do. Therefore, that meaning is cognitive does not mean that it must be empirically verifiable or even verifiable at all. For expressions to have cognitive meaning it is sufficient that they have the capacity or be intended to cause some understanding in an audience.

The third factor that distinguishes art objects and texts is that texts need not be recognized as being both artifacts and capable of producing an artistic experience. This does not mean that they may not do so. Indeed, as noted, there are ample cases of texts that are recognized both as artifacts and as capable of producing artistic experiences. But no text, qua text, is required to be so recognized, and there are many that are not. Indeed, as noted earlier, neither the text of Kant's *Critique of Pure Reason* nor *The Chicago Manual of Style* is so recognized.

From all this it follows that texts and art objects are different and, therefore, that the attempt to reduce texts to art objects or art objects to texts is misguided. The distinction between art objects and texts in terms of, first, the character of the entities that compose them; second, the intended function of texts; and, third, the recognition of the capacity of art objects to produce an artistic experience allows us to understand, moreover, how the same object can be a text and an art object without the implication that to be one is the same as to be the other.

Consider an art object that is also a text, say St. John of the Cross's *Spiritual Canticle*. This magnificent poem, among the best ever written in Spanish, is both a text and an art object. It is a text because it consists of a group of entities that function as signs, which St. John selected and arranged in a particular way to convey a specific meaning to an audience. But it is also an art object because it is regarded as affecting the reader in ways that go beyond the ways in which a nonartistic text could affect one. Indeed, St. John himself wrote an extensive commentary on the poem in which he laid down in nonpoetic language the cognitive contents of the poem. Yet the poem is much more to the attentive reader than what St. John says in his commentary; there is a world of difference between St. John's poem and his commentary. One is a work of art that never ceases to move those who read it; the other is a nonartistic presentation of what the poem meant to the author in a language that fails to move the audience in the same way.

Perhaps another, more controversial example will help clarify the view I am defending. Consider Beethoven's Fifth Symphony. Is it a text, an art object, or both? The example is controversial because what is meant by Beethoven's Fifth Symphony is complex; once its complexity is exposed, however, it can be easily fitted into the scheme I have presented.

The expression 'Beethoven's Fifth Symphony' is used to refer to two different things: a score and a group of sounds. The score is a group of entities used as signs, which were selected, arranged, and intended by Beethoven to convey two different meanings to two different audiences. One audience is composed of performers. For them the meaning of the score is a set of rules that they have to follow if they wish to perform Beethoven's Fifth. The other audience is composed of those persons who, looking at the score, can imagine in their minds the sounds that the performers are supposed to produce if they interpret the score correctly. (Naturally, there is no reason why the same persons may not be both performers and imaginers.) From this it follows that the score of Beethoven's Fifth Symphony is a text and that it has two meanings.

Apart from the score, we also talk about the set of sounds produced by performers when they correctly read the score and follow the rules it stipulates as Beethoven's Fifth's Symphony. This group of sounds can be, as noted, one of the meanings of the score, which is a text, and therefore in that capacity the group of sounds is not itself a text. However, as an artifact it could be in turn a text if the entities that compose it were used as signs by Beethoven to produce understanding.

The answer to the question posed earlier, then, is that the score of Beethoven's Fifth Symphony is without a doubt a text, but the groups of sounds that make up Beethoven's Fifth Symphony is a text only if the sounds are taken as signs intended to produce understanding. Frankly, I do not think that Beethoven had in mind to produce understanding with the group of sounds that compose the Fifth Symphony and, therefore, I believe those sounds are not a text. Herein lies the main difference between the sounds of Beethoven's Fifth Symphony and the sounds produced when someone speaks. But one may want to ask: What about singing? Are songs texts or art objects? Insofar as they are intended to produce understanding they are texts, but insofar as they are artifacts capable of producing artistic experiences, they are art objects. Songs pose no difficulties for my scheme.

On the other hand, it is clear that the group of sounds that make up Beethoven's Fifth Symphony constitute an art object when measured by the two criteria indicated earlier. But the case of the score of the symphony is not clear. It is clearly an artifact, but is it in itself capable of producing an artistic experience? More precisely, is it regarded as both an artifact and as capable of producing an aesthetic experience? It is, of course, generally accepted that the score of Beethoven's Fifth Symphony is an artifact but I doubt very much that anyone regards it as capable of producing an aesthetic experience—at least I do not know anyone who regards it as such. Thus, I do not believe it is an art object. But then someone else may have a different view, in which case it would have to be considered an art object, even by me.

In conclusion, the understanding of a text given in Chapter 1 allows us to include some art objects within the category of texts, but also allows us to maintain a distinction between art objects and texts. This distinction I believe is useful in preventing other conceptual confusions when discussing texts and art objects. In particular, it is important because the confusion of texts and art objects supports the view that, like art objects, texts do not have to do with understanding. They are primarily objects of intuition and experience rather than reason or rational scrutiny. Moreover, it also gives foundation to the position that, again like art objects, texts are open to multiple, equally valid interpretations, among which objective adjudication is neither desirable nor possible. There is no cognitive meaning to be discovered in a text, just as there is often no cognitive meaning to be discovered in an art object. Texts are to be experienced and enjoyed, not understood. Their meaning, if there is such a thing, is a matter of construction, not discovery.

This is a view I reject, as will become clear in the course of this book, and particularly in Chapter 4. Therefore, it is important for me to establish the distinction between texts and art objects at the outset. That there is such a distinction does not mean, however, that the view in question is false or that I have proven it false; it means only that part of the support for it has been taken away. For the moment that is all I need to do. I shall argue against it directly later in the book.

IV. Texts and Works

One of the most widespread views implicit in the literature about texts identifies texts with works, so that whatever is a text is also a work and vice versa.[28] Indeed, even authors who devote considerable effort to the understanding of the nature of texts frequently fail to distinguish clearly between texts and works even if they do not explicitly say that they are the same.[29] Both the explicit identification of texts with works and vice versa, or the failure to distinguish between them, have important implications for the understanding of texts, works, and their relations. If there are no differences between texts and works, they must share the same features, and this leads to some puzzling conclusions. The puzzlement arises because some of the predicates normally predicated of texts contradict some of the predicates normally predicated of works, and vice versa. We saw a similar phenomenon resulting from the failure to distinguish among texts, the entities that constitute them, and the meaning of texts. In that case, contradictory predicates were predicated of texts because texts are complex entities constituted by entities used as signs to convey meaning, and the predicates properly predicated of the entities that constitute them and the meaning of the texts were transferred to the texts in question. If one keeps in mind the subjects of these predicates and that sometimes 'text' is used for ECTs and at other times for meaning, the contradictions are dissolved, for the predicates do not apply to the same thing but to distinct elements of a complex entity.

Likewise, the failure to distinguish between texts and works leads to similar contradictions. For example, a text may be said to be physically long and logically incoherent, and similar claims may be made of a work. Moreover, as we shall see shortly, there are things we do with texts that we cannot do with works and certain phenomena, such as translation, do not make sense unless there is a clear distinction between texts and works. My way of avoiding these problems, then, is to propose a distinction between texts and works in such a way that any contradiction between their predicates can be resolved in the way contradictions between predicates predicated of texts were resolved in Chapter 1. The latter were resolved through the introduction of distinctions among texts, meaning, and the entities that constitute texts. Before I turn to my view, however, it will prove useful to look both at the origin of the view that considers texts and works as the same and at some possible, but misguided, ways of looking at the relationship between texts and works.

The origin of the view that identifies texts with works and vice versa is twofold. First, in ordinary language we frequently speak about texts and works as the same thing. Consider the following sentences:

1.   The text we shall discuss today is a novel.
2.   The text we will use in this class is Cervantes's *Don Quixote*.
3.   We are using two texts in this course: Wittgenstein's *Tractatus* and Suárez's *Disputationes metaphysicae*.

In these sentences, the term 'text' could be easily substituted by 'work' without apparent change of meaning. And there should be no difficulty in finding many other sentences common in ordinary language in which 'text' and 'work' are or can be exchanged without apparent semantic consequences.

There is a second origin of the view that identifies texts and works, moreover, for certain conceptual categories seem to apply to both. Most likely the latter reason stands behind the former, giving rise to this position. Among the categories that seem to apply to all texts and all works is the category of artifact discussed earlier. And other categories, like that of art object, although not applicable to all texts or all works do apply to some members of these categories.

The identification of texts with works and vice versa, however, is not warranted by our experience; the categories of text and work overlap in terms of extension, but do not coincide. Although some texts are works and some works are texts, there are some texts that are not works and some works that are not texts. Perhaps some examples will help make this point clear. Cases of texts that are not works are frequently found in our experience. This very paragraph of this chapter that I am now composing is a text, and the sentences of which it is composed are also texts, but neither the paragraph nor the sentences are works. Likewise we are frequently acquainted with many works that are not texts. As we saw in the last section, there are many works of art that are not textual. Moreover, we also speak of "works of nature" and "works of art" for example, which indicates that the category of "work" extends outside the category of "text." These examples show that there are works that are not texts and texts that are not works. There is no difficulty in that. The problem arises with those things that appear to be both works and texts, say, Cervantes's *Don Quixote*. On the one hand, we speak of *Don Quixote* as a text, and on the other, we also speak of it as a work. This seems to entail that at least some things fulfill the criteria for both works and texts and that, as noted earlier, the same thing may share incompatible characteristics.

Before we proceed any further, however, let me say that an overlapping of categories is not necessarily a problem. There are many things that fulfill criteria which apply to different categories and not for that reason are they considered problematic. For example, I am both the father of Leticia and the husband of Norma, and that seems to create no conceptual difficulty. So one could very well argue that there is no difficulty in *Don Quixote* being both a work and a text. And, indeed, there should be no difficulty as long as (1) we can identify the reasons why *Don Quixote* is a text and why it is a work and (2) those reasons do not coincide. The reasons why I am the father of Leticia and the husband of Norma are, of course, different, even though that I am the husband of Norma has something to do with my being the father of Leticia, because Norma is Leticia's mother. But the case is not so clear with *Don Quixote*, for it is not evident that the reasons why *Don Quixote* is a text are not also the reasons why it is a work. Moreover, it is not clear that the characteristics of *Don Quixote* as a text and of *Don Quijote* as a work are compatible.

One possible explanation of the relation between texts and works is that a work is simply a type of text. So, for example, *Don Quixote* is a work, but the "No smoking" sign posted above the blackboard in the classroom I use on Thursdays is not, even though both are texts. A recently defended view maintains that works are interpreted texts, that is, texts that have been subjected to a process of interpretation. A text is subjected to a process of interpretation when that process is necessary to get at an implicit meaning that is different from its apparent sense. Interpretations, then, generate works. They also generate authors, for authors, like works, are constructs of an interpreter who postulates the author as the agent who accounts for construing the text as a work. By contrast, the producer of a text is considered merely a writer, an efficient cause of the text but not of the hidden meaning of a text revealed in its interpretation, that is, in the work.[30]

I do not find this position viable for several reasons. In the first place, it does not seem sensible to say that the historical figure who wrote *Don Quixote* (the text) is not the author of *Don Quixote* (the work). In second place, this view makes the historical figure reponsible only for the ECTs used as a text and its "apparent meaning." But this seems dogmatic, for many writers are no doubt aware of some, even if not all, of the "deeper meanings" of the texts they produce. Indeed, the shape texts take are often the result of the conscious efforts of the authors who manipulate what they know about signs, audience, and context, to produce certain effects in audiences. Third, this view restricts works to interpretations of written texts, but there is no reason why works should be restricted in this way. There is no reason, for example, why art objects should not have corresponding works. Certainly we frequently speak of them as "works of art." Finally, it is extremely odd to say that the author of a work is a construction of the interpreter, while it is the interpreter that produces the interpretation that transforms a text into a work. If the interpreter produces the interpretation, he or she would seem to be the de facto author of the work; the writer can be the author of only the text.

For these and other reasons that will become clear in later chapters, I find this view of the distinction between a text and a work unacceptable. But, then, we may ask, how is the distinction to be understood?

Another possible explanation of the relation between texts and works is to argue that texts are a type of work. One could argue, for example, that texts are linguistic types of works. The category of work extends to nature as well as to artifacts and within artifacts to such things as art objects, chairs, and so on. A mountain is a work of nature; Velázquez's *Las Meninas* is a work of art; and a chair is the work of an artisan. It is within the category of artifacts, works produced as a result of intentional activity and design, that texts fall. What differentiates them within the category is that they are linguistic entities composed of signs and arranged according to certain rules to convey meaning.

At first sight this view seems quite reasonable, but upon further inspection it is clear that it faces some difficulties. Perhaps the most serious one is that, if this view were to be adopted, then it would be impossible to hold that the same work could be translated into different languages, for the view entails that a text is the same thing as a work even if not all works are texts.[31] Consider the Latin text of Suárez's *Disputationes metaphysicae* and its English translation. It is obvious that in this case we have two different texts composed in two different languages. But we do not want to say that the work in each case is different. Indeed, we want to say that the work is the same and that the author of the work is the same; namely, Suárez. Yet, if texts are works, then the English text and the Latin text of the *Disputationes metaphysicae* are two different works and Suárez is the author of only the Latin one, whereas the English translator is the author of the English work. But does this make any sense? No, for the translator of the text of Suárez did not compose the work, nor should he receive credit for it. Indeed, some of Suárez's translators, including myself, disagree with much of what Suárez says.

Neither the view that works are types of texts nor the view that texts are types of works is acceptable, for the categories of text and work are not extensionally included within each other and what we say when we speak of them is usually quite different.[32] So, if we wish to preserve this exclusion, we must come up with a different strategy.

Not one, but several strategies suggest themselves as ways of understanding works and, by implication, distinguishing them from texts. Three are particularly obvious.[33] The first identifies works with the acts in which authors engage when they create texts; the second identifies works with what I have called ECTs, namely, the entities that constitute texts; and the third makes works entities of a sui generis kind.

The main advantages of these three views is that they distinguish clearly between texts and works and certainly would allow us to do so even adopting the view of texts we have presented in Chapter 1. Consider the first one. According to this view, a work is the series of acts in which an author engages when composing a text, and thus it is something ontologically and logically different from the text.[34] It is ontologically different because the series of acts performed by the author of the text are causally connected to the text (the text being, say, a set of signs written on a piece of paper intended to convey a certain specific meaning, etc.). The text, then, is related to the acts as an effect, but once produced it has an ontological status of its own quite independent of the ontological status of the acts that produced it. The work, moreover, is logically different from the text because the intensions of 'text' and 'act' do not coincide. To be a text is something entirely different from being an act. Even though acts may become texts, the acts in question would only be the ECTs of those texts, not the texts themselves.[35]

Something similar can be said about the second view, which identifies works with ECTs and thus distinguishes them ontologically and logically from texts.[36] Ontologically the ECTs are closer to the texts they constitute, and vice versa, than the acts are to the texts they produce. Indeed, the destruction of the ECTs would result in the destruction of the texts, and vice versa. Moreover, this view recognizes that works are not ontologically the same things as texts because ECTs have in themselves no relation to the meaning with which they are endowed by an author when they become constitutive of texts. And texts, because they are ECTs *with* meaning, cannot be considered ontologically equivalent to ECTs. Indeed, their ontological differences make possible their different functions. With respect to logic, again, there are important differences between them, for ECTs can have different natures—they can be artifacts, natural objects, and so on—but the natures of texts are different from those of the ECTs, as is clear in their definition.

Finally, if works are considered a category unto themselves, sui generis, then they cannot be confused with texts.[37] How different works are from texts ontologically and logically will depend, of course, on how this sui generis category is understood—whether it is linguistic, mental, physical, or otherwise. What matters is that we can point out what works are not, even if we cannot point out what they are. For this is sufficient to continue writing, reading, interpreting, and so on, and to distinguish them from texts.

In spite of the advantages that these three views have, particularly insofar as they distinguish works from texts, they do encounter difficulties that make them unacceptable. Many of these could be easily pointed out, but I shall restrict myself to those that I consider most serious.

The first two views—that works are acts and ECTs respectively—face one common difficulty: Some of the most fundamental features associated with works do not appear to be the features that characterize either acts or ECTs. For example, it is characteristic of literary works to be classifiable according to certain literary genres such as novels, poems, dramas, and so on. But it would make no sense to speak of acts or ECTs as novels, poems, or dramas. And something similar could be said, for example, about style. Can one speak of the florid style of an act or the archaic style of the pebbles that constitute a text on the beach? It would be difficult to make sense of these remarks, frequently applied to works, when applied to acts and certain entities that constitute texts.[38] Indeed, in some cases they would seem to involve contradictions. This poses what I believe to be an insurmountable obstacle to the views that identify works with acts or ECTs.

The main objection against the third view, which makes works a sui generis category, is different. It springs from the difficulty any sui generis category encounters unless it is regarded as one of the primitive categories of a conceptual system, and yet there is no evidence that those who subscribe to this view intend to regard it as such. This kind of move, like the well-known view of the bare particular as principle of individuation, makes sense only when all other alternatives have been exhausted. It comes down to the position that works cannot be identified with any other category, but it is not clear why it is so. If any other view can be successfully defended, and it is my contention that it can, it is preferable to the sui generis position.

The strategy I propose is to go back to the distinction I drew earlier between a text and its meaning and identify works with the meaning of texts of a certain sort. Consider *Don Quizote*, for example. If we follow my suggestion, we have in the first place a text; namely, the group of entities, used as signs, that are selected, arranged, and intended by Cervantes to convey a certain meaning to the audience he had in mind in the context of his time. The text is, as mentioned earlier, an artifact constructed for the purpose of conveying meaning. This artifact is in fact an instance of a type of artifact that can be reproduced to convey the meaning Cervantes had in mind. Thus, different instances of the same type of artifact yield or can yield the same results. This text can be translated into other languages, that is, different artifacts can be used to produce the same understanding. But in the case of a translation we do not any longer have the same text, although we still have the same work. The work, I propose, is the meaning of the group of signs and, therefore, independent of it insofar as other groups of signs can be used to convey it.[39]

Thus, when we speak of *Don Quixote* a certain ambiguity is involved. We may be speaking of the text of *Don Quixote*, and then we are speaking of an artifact, a group of physical-type signs with a certain meaning. But we may also be speaking about the meaning of those signs; that is, about what those physical-type signs are intended to convey. My proposal is to restrict the use of the term 'text' to the first and of 'work' to the second. This allows us to speak of "the text of a work" and to distinguish between the artifact created by Cervantes to convey the meaning that constitutes *Don Quixote*, namely the text, and that meaning, for which he was also responsible. Of course, the text is not to be confused with the ECTs that constitute it because the ECTs have no meaning in themselves. Hence we have three things: the entities that constitute the text, the meaning assigned to those entities, and the entities considered as conveyors of meaning. The first is the group of ECTs, the second is the work, and the third is the text.

Note, moreover, that the work is not identified with the understanding that someone or other may have of the meaning of the text.[40] For understanding and meaning, as I shall explain in Chapter 4, are not the same.

This proposal does not appear to solve all our difficulties, however. One remaining problem concerns the fact that, if we adopt this view as presented, it may appear that we would also have to accept two undesirable consequences. The first is that even texts like "No smoking" have works corresponding to them, because they have meaning. The second is that there are works only if there are texts of which they can be meanings.

These difficulties are not real, however, because they rely on a misunderstanding of the view I have presented. Indeed, to say that the meanings of *certain texts* constitute works neither entails that the meanings of *all texts* constitute works nor that *all works* must be meanings of texts. To be a meaning of a text may be neither sufficient nor necessary for being a work. And to be a work does not imply a corresponding text. Let me take up the first point, that being the meaning of a text is not a sufficient condition for something being a work.

I have taken account of this point by adding the qualification that only the meaning of "certain texts" are works. But that qualification is too vague to be enlightening, for we do not know, based on it, which are the texts for which there are works and which are those for which there are not.

From the examples we have been considering, it might appear prima facie that whether the meaning of a text is a work or not has to do with the length of the text. The meaning of the text of *Don Quixote* is a work because the text is very long, but the meaning of the "No smoking" sign posted in my classroom is not because the sign is very short.

Upon closer inspection, however, it becomes clear that length has nothing to do with whether the meaning of a text is a work or not. A haiku composed of a few words is certainly considered a work, but a much longer text warning of the penalties for trespassing is not. Length, therefore, does not seem to be what distinguishes texts whose meanings are works and texts whose meanings are not. What, then, distinguishes a text that has a corresponding work and one that does not?

Another possibility that may be considered is suggested by the very etymology of the term 'work.' Work involves labor and it is perhaps the fact that the meaning of a text can be understood only through labor and hard effort that makes that meaning a work. Indeed, the grasp of what we call works requires reflection, that is, careful consideration of the text; and there is nothing simple or easy about reflection. Or the labor in question may refer to the act of creation—authors have to put effort into the creation of a work.

Although there may be some merit to this view, it cannot be taken seriously upon further examination. For the understanding of some works requires no labor; indeed it may be argued that they involve pleasure or play, rather than effort. This is particularly evident in short epigrams, for example. True, Mallarmé and Góngora require a great deal of effort, but perhaps fortunately, there are not many Mallarmés or Góngoras in the history of literature. And something similar can be said about the act of creation. For some authors, the creation of a work is pure delight and involves play rather than labor.

Related to this view is the position that looks at works as the meaning of texts which, because of their construction, are such that different and equally valid understandings may be derived from them. Works, then, require a certain ambiguity and latitude in texts, the impossibility of closure. Indeed, many literary critics believe that such ambiguity and latitude are the fundamental characteristics of great literature; these texts generate a doubt in the audience and are subject to diverse and even contradictory understandings.[41]

The problem with this position is that it looks at works primarily in a literary context. But why should this be so? Perhaps it is true that literary works are or should be open in the stated way so that various equally valid interpretations may be given of them. But should this apply also to nonliterary works? And if it does not apply, then are only literary pieces to qualify as works? Surely no one would like to say that Euclid's *Elements* is not a work, or to say that if it is a work it is so precisely because it is subject to diverse but equally valid interpretations even when those interpretations contradict each other. I doubt very much that Euclid was trying to be ambiguous or unclear and to leave open the way we should understand the text of the *Elements*. And the same can be said about other scientific works and works of philosophy.

Neither the length of a text, the degree of effort required to grasp its meaning, nor its openness to conflicting interpretations can be used to identify texts whose meanings are works. But what can we do, then? Must we give up the effort to try to find what kind of texts have corresponding works? One thing we could do is go through other features of texts and works, examining the merits of their candidacy for our purposes, but such an exercise would be a waste of time, because I do not believe this procedure would yield satisfactory results. For, whether the meaning of a text turns out to be a work or not seems to depend on cultural and historical circumstances rather than on nature. In other words, the notion of a work is not natural, but artificial and thus depends on human intention and design.

What makes the meaning of a text a work is that it fits a certain view of what a work is as developed by a culture at a particular point in history.[42] Consider a sonnet, for example. The meaning of a sonnet is a work because the text adheres to certain rules that are supposed to apply to sonnets. Likewise, a novel or an epic are works because the texts in question adhere to established patterns. Although these patterns and rules may be modified, however, it is essential that there be rules defining a particular type or genre. Thus, although the sign "No smoking" follows rules (the rules of the language in which it is written and so on), the rules it follows are not rules of a genre of works and that is why it is not considered a work. It is perfectly conceivable, however, that in the future such signs as the one mentioned may become works provided appropriate rules are devised or accepted for them. And the same could be said about such texts as lists of various sorts, recipes, maxims, and so on. None of these texts have corresponding works.[43]

But we may ask: What rules are the ones that count for works? The answer is that the rules in question are related to the cultural function that the text serves. As we shall see in the next chapter, texts can be divided into various categories according to the cultural function they have. Some are philosophical, whereas others are legal or literary, for example. And the cultural function determines the rules and shapes the genre. Now my point is that, as long as there are definite rules (whether they are written or unwritten is quite irrelevant) based on the cultural function texts have that establish the criteria of works and the texts fulfill them, the meaning of those texts constitute works. But if there are no such rules or there are such rules but a text does not fulfill them, then the meaning of the text is not a work. Hence, not all texts need have corresponding works. A command such as "State your purpose clearly," for example, is a text, but it is not a work because it does not adhere to the rules that govern the various genres under the diverse cultural functions according to which it could be classified as a work. That does not mean that commands could not become works. Indeed, they very well could, provided that society devised rules for them under one or more of the cultural functions texts carry out, regarding them as a separate genre of a work. This last point is important for it underlines the fact that the rules in question need not be fixed and thus can change. New genres and new cultural functions are always on the making in societies and so are new works that in previous times may not have been considered to be such.

So much then, for the reasons why being the meaning of a text is not a sufficient condition of being a work. Let me turn to the other issue, that being the meaning of a text is not a necessary condition of being a work. This is an easier issue to settle, for I have not claimed that only meanings of texts are works, not even that only meanings are works. Indeed, we often use the term 'work' for a variety of things that have not meaning, which shows that to be a work is not necessarily to be a meaning. Moreover, we also speak of works of art that are neither texts nor related to texts, and this indicates that not only the meaning of texts can be works. The meaning of an art object can also be a work even if the art object is not a text.

Let me summarize my view by saying that my proposal is to use the term 'work' technically to speak about the meaning of certain texts for which society has developed rules so they fulfill a specific cultural function that renders them works.[44] This allows us to maintain a certain precision when speaking about what is the same and what is different when a text is translated into a different language. It does not entail, however, that we may not speak of works in a looser sense according to which art objects and even the artifacts of which some texts are made up may not be works.

Before I turn to the conclusion of this chapter I must consider two possible objections to the view defended here concerning works, not only because they may undermine it, but also because the answer to them can help further in the understanding of my view. The first may be formulated as follows: The works that correspond to texts cannot be the meaning of those texts, for they often, particularly in literary texts, make reference to features of texts that are not part of their meaning. Consider, for example, a sonnet in which a lover describes the object of his love. It would appear that the work consists not only in the meaning of the words used in the sonnet, but also of the structure of the sonnet, the rhyme and so on—otherwise the sonnet would not be a sonnet, but some other type of work. Someone, for example, who wrote out in nonpoetic form what the sonnet says, as St. John of the Cross did with the *Spiritual Canticle*, would be composing a different work, not just a different text. Thus, works cannot be the meaning of texts.

The point that this objection makes is valid when it comes to works in which the form of the text of the work plays a role in the work itself. It also applies to artistic works that depend to some extent on the characteristics of the entities that constitute them. But it does not apply to texts and works devoid of artistic and literary quality. It is so for literary works because they are works of art in which the character of the work is determined in part by factors other than cognitive meaning. Consider a work of art that is not a text, such as Velázquez's *Las Meninas*. In this case the work incorporates the physical-type features of the painting *Las Meninas*. And the same must be the case for a literary work in which a certain style is part of what makes the work what it is. In this sense we cannot say that a translation of Shakespeare's *Hamlet* into Spanish is the work Shakespeare produced, for the work that Shakespeare produced cannot be separated from the language Shakespeare used. But not all texts are like Shakespeare's *Hamlet*. A text whose meaning is not essentially tied to the particular form of the ECTs that constitute it can be easily rendered into a different language while remaining the same. Euclid's *Elements* can be translated into English. The conditions of identity of works, then, depend very much on the type of work involved. In general, textual works are the meanings of texts, except in cases where the texts have an artistic dimension, for then the works are the meanings plus whatever elements are essential for the identity of the works in question.

Texts are conventional artifacts—their meaning is conventionally tied to the entities that constitute them. But in the case of literary texts some of the features of those entities are part of what distinguishes the work from other works and thus become part of the work. However, this occurs only in texts of an artistic nature. The reason is that art objects are not meant to convey cognitive meaning alone, even if they are texts—and sometimes none at all when they are not texts. Their function is other than this and thus, qua works, they must include whatever makes the object of art function in the way it does.

The second objection that can help us understand better the view I am defending may be formulated as follows: According to Chapter 1, the meaning of a text is what one understands when one is said to understand a text. Moreover, according to the view of works being defended here, a work is the meaning of a text of a certain sort, a sort determined by social conventions. Now, in principle it would be possible to argue that if we have a poem that describes a forest, the forest is the work, because what one understands when one understands the text of the poem is the forest and poetic texts are the sorts of texts that have corresponding works. Yet, we know perfectly well that it is not the forest that is the work.

This objection is useful because its answer reveals a fundamental and necessary condition of works; namely, that works are artifacts, products of intentional action and design. The answer to the objection is that the forest in question is not a work; the work is the forest considered as object of understanding via the text. As such the forest is no longer the natural object it may be, but the forest as created or modified by the author of the text and presented to the audience in that way. The forest in this sense is not a natural object, but an artifact of sorts. And here we can go back to the view considered earlier that works involve effort. As argued before, this is not a sufficient condition of works, nor is it necessary if one understands it to involve a certain degree of effort, but it applies as long as it is taken to involve artifactuality and thus intentional activity and design. Thus, a forest, qua forest, is not and cannot be a work; it is a work only insofar as it is a creation of an author of a text. I shall come back to this point in Chapter 4, where I discuss the relation of texts to their meaning.

Finally, let me add that my position is not to be confused with the view that works are interpretations of texts proposed by audiences. By 'interpretation' in this context is usually meant "understanding." Thus, an interpretation of a text turns out to be an understanding of it, or as has more properly been said in Chapter 1, an understanding of what it means by an audience. In Chapter 5 I will present a different conception of interpretation, but for the moment I shall ignore it and adopt what, I believe, is the conception used in the view that holds that works are interpretations. The differences between this view and mine should be clear. For me, works are the meanings of certain texts, and therefore they cannot be identified with the understandings of the texts that audiences may have of them. The reason is that audiences may understand texts in ways not warranted by their meaning. Moreover, audiences may understand only part of the meaning of texts. And, finally, as we shall see in Chapter 4, understandings are acts in audiences, whereas meanings can be but are often not acts of any kind. The objections that have been raised against the view that works are interpretations of texts, then, do not affect my position.[45]

V. Conclusion

The purpose of this chapter has been to explain the relation of the category of text to other categories closely associated and frequently confused with it. We have seen in the first place how texts are composed of linguistic entities, namely, signs, and follow linguistic rules in their arrangement, but that texts are not languages. The categories of language and text are mutually exclusive although related; the extension of the terms that name those categories exclude each other.

By contrast, texts fall within the category of artifacts because, even when constituted by entities (ECTs) that are the result of natural processes without the input of intention and design, their connection to specific meanings is always mediated through the intention of subjects who are also responsible for the designs, that is the selection of signs and their arrangement, of the texts. The category of artifact, then, includes the category of text, even if it does not always include the entities that constitute texts (ECTs); the extension of 'text' is included in the extension of 'artifact.'

With respect to art objects the situation is more complicated insofar as some texts are art objects but not all texts are art objects nor are all art objects texts. In this case the categories overlap but do not coincide, nor is one of them included in the other. The extension of 'text' and 'art object' coincide in some instances but not in others, depending on the object in question.

In the case of works, as in the case of language, the categories of texts and works are mutually exclusive, for to be a text and to be a work are not only different things but things that are works are not texts and vice versa. In spite of this, however, it turns out that some texts have corresponding works and thus some works have corresponding texts, but not all texts have corresponding works and vice versa. Thus the extensions of 'text' and 'work' are independent of each other and exclude each other, but at the same time there is an extensional parallelism between some instances of these categories.

Understanding the distinctions and relations between texts on the one hand and language, artifacts, art objects, and works on the other is very important for the development of a theory of textuality. For texts are frequently identified with these other types of objects and the characteristics of these objects are assigned to texts, leading to confusions as to their nature, function, ontological status, causal analyses, and significance. There are grounds, as we have seen, to assign linguistic characteristics to texts, because they are composed of linguistic entities and are arranged according to linguistic rules, but texts are not languages and thus cannot be treated as one would treat languages. Languages, except for artificial ones, do not have identifiable authors or audiences, whereas texts do, for example. And, as we saw earlier, the conditions of identity of a language allow for a kind of flexibility not available to texts. The function of language is to be used to create texts, but the function of texts is to convey meaning in a certain context. Languages are in a constant process of change, evolving and expanding at the will of those who use them, but texts have a set historical identity that does not change even if they are subject to varying understandings.

The confusion of texts with languages and the attribution of some of the characteristics of languages to texts gives support to some of the current views of textuality. For example, the flexibility of language and its constant state of evolution (except in cases in which they are dead), if attributed also to texts, helps those who wish to see texts as indeterminate in meaning and as always openended. This position, common among deconstructionists but by no means restricted to them, is weakened by the realization that texts are different from language in spite of their linguistic nature. I shall return to this issue in Chapter 4.

Because all texts are artifacts, they share in the characteristics that distinguish artifacts from nonartifacts, but they are not reducible to mere artifacts insofar as texts are a special kind of artifact, namely, meaningful artifacts. This is important for the understanding of texts, because it has serious implications for their ontological status and the relation of the entities that constitute them to their meaning. It is also important because the artifactuality of texts is one of the foundations of the view that identifies textual meaning with authorial meaning, that is, the meaning understood or intended by the author. If texts are artifacts and artifacts are the result of intentional activity and design, it makes sense prima facie to conclude that the author of the text is responsible for the design of the text and thus that the meaning of the text is whatever the author understands or intends it to be. This view, however, treats texts as mere artifacts, missing the important differences that set texts apart within the category of artifactuality. If texts are a special sort of artifacts, then other views of their meaning are possible. I shall explore some of these in Chapter 4.

The fact that the categories of text and art object overlap is the reason why many philosophers and art critics try to apply characteristics that apply only to art objects to texts as well. The conception of all texts as having some aesthetic import, the view that texts never have a precise and unambiguous meaning but must always be open to a wide range of interpretations—if not to any interpretation—the position that the meaning of texts is never cognitive or purely cognitive and the like are clear cases in which texts are seen in terms of artistic and literary categories. These perspectives forget, of course, that scientific and philosophical texts are also texts and that they do not share some of the idiosyncratic features of literary and artistic texts. The categories of text and art object overlap, but neither is to be taken as encompassing the other and thus as paradigmatic of the other. More on this in Part II of the book.

Finally, something similar to what happens with art objects and texts happens with texts and works: Characteristics peculiar to works are applied to texts and vice versa, creating confusion both about texts and about works. For example, works are seen as somehow textual and thus subject to the sort of cognitive understanding that is characteristic of texts. Moreover, when the categories of text and work are identified, such phenomena as translation become impossible, for every translation of a work, because it is a text in a different language, becomes a different work. Keeping these categories distinct, then, prevents all sorts of confusion and allows us better to understand each of them separately from each other as well as the relationships between them. The implications of this distinction will become clear as we go along in the rest of the book.

The purpose of this chapter has been to clarify some common confusions concerning texts and, thus, to prepare the way for more in-depth probing of textuality in subsequent chapters. Before we turn to them, however, something must be said about the different types of texts, because we have been giving examples of a wide variety of text types without making an attempt to present a coherent picture of their taxonomy. This issue is taken up in the next chapter.

3

Taxonomy

When we think of a text, most of us think of the written word. This might lead to
all sorts of assumptions and misunderstandings. For example, because written
texts are most often composed of words belonging to natural languages, one might
be led to believe that all texts are so composed. This in turn might lead to a conception of texts that excludes many things from the category of texts that otherwise could be included in it. Texts not composed of words belonging to natural
languages would be thus excluded. Likewise, as noted already in previous chapters, it is frequent in the literature on texts and textuality to use certain types of
texts, such as literary texts, as paradigmatic. This again gives rise to distorted
views concerning textuality, for literary texts have characteristics that some other
texts do not share.[1] For example, most literary texts are intended to produce an
aesthetic experience and to be subject to diverse, equally valid understandings, but
many nonliterary texts are not. For this reason, then, it is necessary for us to look
at various types of texts to prevent a too narrow conception of textuality.

The specific aim of the taxonomy of texts I provide here is twofold. First,
it is meant as an extension of the discussion of the intension of 'text.' As such it
is intended to reveal further what texts are through a more detailed and specific
analysis of some ways in which texts may be classified. Second, it is meant to clear
the way for the epistemic issues discussed in later chapters. This second aim
should become obvious when we get to those chapters, but all the same I will make
some reference to it in the Conclusion of this chapter.

Texts come or can come in a wide variety. This wide variety may be illustrated by presenting several ways in which texts may be classified, thus drawing
attention to the richness of the category. I would like to look in particular at two
different ways in which texts may be classified: modally and functionally. Modality has to do with the ways in which entities may exist either in themselves or in
relation to other entities, and function with the general purpose that is served.
Within modality, I discuss intended, ideal, and actual texts. And in the area of
function I identify two different types of function, linguistic and cultural, which
are in turn subdivided into several others.

I should note before going any further that in addition to the two ways of
classifying texts I provide here there are many others, and some of them are as

important and fundamental as the ones with which I deal. For example, texts may also be classified according to genres into novels, epic poems, and so on.[2] I do not discuss this and other similarly important classifications primarily for two reasons. The first is economy. In the case of genres, such classification could not be seriously undertaken without devoting to it at least an entire chapter. The second reason is that this, as well as other possible classifications, does not appear to me to be as closely related to the issues I address in this book as the ones I have chosen to discuss.

I. Modal Classification

According to their mode of existence texts may be classified as actual, intended, and ideal. The actual text is the text that presently exists or formerly existed at some point in history, whether outside the mind of the author or within it, even though it may have existed only for a short time in the past. The intended text is the text that is supposed to exist only as intended by the author. The ideal text is the text that exists only in the mind of an interpreter who thinks it is the text the author produced or should have produced whereas in fact the author never actually produced it.

A. Actual Text

The text that exists or has existed outside the mind of an interpreter is what I call the *actual text*. At least three texts may be classified as actual: the historical text, the contemporary text, and the intermediary text. This subclassification of the actual text has to do with the time at which the text exists.

1. Historical Text. The historical text is the text that the historical author actually produced.[3] It is constituted by the historical ECTs used by the historical author to convey a specific meaning to an audience in a certain context.

When we are dealing with written texts produced before the invention of the printing press, the historical text seldom survives in its original form. There are exceptions, of course. If there is an autograph or an accurate copy of it, it would appear that we do have the historical text.[4] Moreover, if we know that we have a text that was corrected by the author shortly after it was composed, even if not originally written by the author, we may be able to assume that we have the historical text. The procedure whereby an author revises notes originally taken by a student was common in the Middle Ages, for example. The revised notes were called *ordinatio* and the unrevised notes were called *reportatio*. In some cases works became known by those names, perhaps to stress the degree of their historical fidelity. This happened to Duns Scotus's *Opus oxoniense*, which came to be known as the *Ordinatio*, and to another version of his *Commentary to Peter Lombard's "Sentences"*, which came to be called *Reportata parisiensis*.

In many cases, however, the situation is not so simple, indicating that there may not be a single historical text but actually several. A case in point occurs with the texts of some of Thomas Aquinas's works. In some instances he wrote an autograph of the work, but then had the text copied by a secretary and made changes on the copy rather than on the autograph. Indeed, there is evidence that points to subsequent changes made at various times during his life. In such a situation, there is no single historical text of a particular work. What we have are several historical texts corresponding to the various times at which the author made alterations. Whether the meaning, and thus the work, of the text is actually the same is another question.

    2. Contemporary Text. By the *contemporary text,* I mean the text that is available to us in the original language in which it was produced. A translation does not qualify as the contemporary text because the identity of a text includes conditions related to the signs of which it is composed and the signs of a translation of a text are different from the signs used in the text. The contemporary text is constituted by the contemporary ECTs available at present to convey the work intended by the author as the meaning of the historical text. One of the interesting things about the contemporary text is that in many cases we do not usually have one but several different texts. This is particularly so when we are dealing with texts that originate from periods of history that preceded the invention of the printing press, although it is even the case in some texts produced subsequent to that event.

    The reason we may have several contemporary texts is usually because there are several textual traditions that go back to some original source, perhaps a lost autograph, and various editions based on those different traditions produced at different times. For example, there are today several editions of Thomas Aquinas's *Summa theologiae,* such as the Piana (1570), the Leonine (1888–1903), and the Ottawa (1941).[5] The differences among these and other available editions of the same text result because there is no available autograph of the work and there are more than 200 extant manuscripts of the complete text (except for the Supplement, of which there are only 42) and another 235 fragments of various parts of it. The task of the editor with a text of this sort, found in this state, is to produce a stemma or family tree of manuscripts and reconstruct the best possible text on that basis.

    The notion of "the best possible text," however, raises some serious questions that need to be answered. For "the best possible text" is not necessarily the one produced by the author nor the one that had the greatest historical impact. A critical edition that reconstructs "the best possible text" might be a patchwork that never existed and has no historical relevance because it never existed as such before it was reconstructed by the editor. Thus the historical value of many nineteenth century critical editions of medieval and classical texts that were put together with the methodological goal of producing the best text possible is quite limited. Many subsequent editors, to avoid this kind of problem, have produced editions that center on a good and historically important text, a so-called copy text, making on it as few corrections as possible and adding variants with other manuscripts for the benefit of historians and interpreters.[6] Nonetheless, the idea that the best possible text is an ideal selective composite of all the texts and textual traditions available is alive and well.

It is important to repeat that even the contemporary text is seldom a single text. What we usually have, rather, is a family of texts that are related in various ways and may be more or less historically accurate, depending on how close they are to the historical text, and more or less historically relevant, depending on how influential they have been, whereas their degree of historical accuracy is not necessarily and directly proportional to their historical relevance. Of course, if the historical text has survived intact, say that we have an autograph, then at least one of the texts that make up the family of contemporary texts is the historical text. But this is seldom so, even in recently produced texts, for publishers and copy editors always modify texts in the process of production, even when they have not only the autograph but also the author at their disposal.

3. Intermediary Text. By an intermediary text I mean any text that we do not actually have and is not the historical text, but that nonetheless existed at some time and functioned at that time as a contemporary text of an audience. Thus, the intermediary text is one that has been destroyed or lost. It is not contemporary because we do not have it, although at some point it was contemporary to some audience. Nor is it the historical text because it was not the one composed by the historical author.

We may or may not know anything about this text. The text may have been lost or destroyed shortly after it was produced and those who produced it may not have passed on information about its existence, so no one other than those who produced it will ever know it existed. Or, there may be a lost text about whose existence we know something because we have a record of it. In this case we know the text existed but we do not have it. Sometimes such texts are discovered, and then they become contemporary texts, but most often they remain only as mentioned in some historical record.

Intermediary texts are sometimes very important, for they explain or help to explain the differences between historical texts and contemporary texts. This happens when the contemporary texts are not the historical texts and do not depend on them directly. In reconstructing a stemma of a text, for instance, intermediary texts need often to be posited even when there is no explicit record that they ever existed.

B. Intended Text

The *intended text*, as its name suggests, is supposed to be the text the author intended to produce, but did not produce.[7] It is not supposed to be the text the author produced because such a text is the historical text. The notion of an intended text arises when one begins to consider the unintended mistakes authors make while producing a text. For example, in the case of oral or written texts authors may say or write something they may not intend; they may use words that are not exactly the ones they want because they cannot think of better ones at the time; they may omit words or phrases by mistake; they may get confused with the punctuation; and so on. There are many mechanical ways in which authors can get sidetracked and produce texts that are different from the texts they presumably intend to produce. More important still, there is always the problem of the difference between what authors want to say or write and the means they have at their disposal to do so. Once they have used a certain expression, it becomes part of the text, but authors sometimes would have preferred saying what they said differently, although at the time of composing the text the expression they were looking for did not occur to them. This is particularly evident when they use ambiguous expressions, for if one asks them later, "Did you mean P or Q, when you said R?" the author sometimes will answer P, sometimes Q, and only occasionally R. It is only when the author answers R that we may surmise the ambiguity is intended, although even then we can never be absolutely sure that the author was aware of it at the time of the text's composition; such awareness may be the result of hindsight only.

As further substantiation for the notion of an intended text one may point to the fact that authors frequently correct a text after it has been composed; they go back and change things around, sometimes altering the meaning significantly. This may be taken to signify that texts do not accurately reflect what authors intended at the time of composing them, although again one can never be sure whether authors intended something different from what they wrote or said in the first place or simply changed their minds about what they intended later.

All this sounds quite reasonable, but one may also argue that there is no such thing as the intended text for the simple reason that authors never have a clear and complete idea of the texts they intend to produce prior to the moment in which they actually produce them by writing, speaking, or thinking.[8] At most they may have more or less vague ideas of what they want to do, perhaps a mental outline of how the text should be structured, but the text is produced only at the moment of writing, speaking, or thinking it.

It is possible to argue that the intended text has no priority over the historical one for the simple reason that there is never such a thing as an intended text. And this is so in turn because a text is always a result of a process of production and does not precede such a process in any way.[9] This is the view I wish to defend.

The process whereby authors compose texts could be compared to that of artists. Consider the case of an artist who wishes to produce a sculpture. He has a general idea of what he wants to do, say to produce a composition commemorating a certain victory in battle. He also has an idea of the number of persons he wants in the sculpture, whether he wants them clothed or nude, and a general sense of the poses they should adopt. Moreover, he has decided to use marble as his material and lifesize figures. But this is all quite vague. If we were to ask him to describe the sculpture to us, he would give us only generalities. On the basis of those generalities we could perhaps, years later, pick out from a group of sculptures some among which could be the one he finally made, but we could never be sure which was the one he actually made if we were presented with somewhat similar sculptures. For the sculptor's description is too general and does not identify all the features of the sculpture that set it apart from others. Now, his description is too general because he does not have a complete and detailed idea of what the sculpture will look like when he finishes it, even if he has tentative sketches of what he wishes to produce. And he does not and cannot, because the particular sculpture that the sculptor produces is not the result of his idea alone, but involves also the materials with which he works as well as the creative process itself that produces it. Let me explain.

Once a sculptor has an idea of what he wants to do, he proceeds to see what piece of marble he can get. He has a budget, so his choices are not unlimited. Moreover, when he gets to the quarry to look for an appropriate piece of marble he finds that only five or six pieces are available, all in slightly different colors, shapes, and sizes. He wanted white marble, but marble always has veins of one sort or another and now he has to decide whether to choose the one with gray, green, or pink veins. If he chooses the grey or the green he is restricted by the size and shape of those pieces, if he chooses the pink he will have more freedom in the composition because of the size of the block. But he decides upon the gray anyway—he cannot see how a serious and sobering subject like war, even in victory, can be rendered in anything but grays and whites. Once the artist has the marble, he needs models, so he goes out to a modeling agency and asks to look at pictures of the models they have. He does not know with exactitude what he is looking for except for the fact that he needs six men. When he sees a face or a body, he sometimes discards the photograph immediately, sometimes he looks at it for a while and discards it all the same, but at other times he saves it. After a while he has accummulated a group of twenty or so possible models that he thinks he could use based on the pictures he has seen. Then he proceeds to interview the models in person and after examining them he settles for the six he thinks he needs. Eventually he gathers all six in his studio and makes them stand in the pose he envisioned, but he finds that it does not work. In the first place there seem to be too many figures and in the second place some of them are wrong for the composition. Their bodies looked appropriate when considered separately but together they do not go well. One of them is too tall and another too short, for example. Then there are the faces. In particular there is one face that he needs to express a certain emotion and none of the faces of the models he has selected expresses it well. Discouraged, the artist dismisses two of the models and asks the others to come back at some later time. He is tormented and worried about the face he needs, in particular because he cannot picture it in detail. But he gets lucky. His daughter introduces him to a new boyfriend of hers and he realizes that the boyfriend has the face he needs. Because the young man is eager to ingratiate himself with the family, he consents to pose for the sculptor and our artist has his group. But he again has doubts about the pose, and so on. Indeed, the process of rethinking and rearranging does not end until the sculpture is finished. Each decision closes certain alternatives, but also opens areas where further decisions are required.

I could go on describing the creative process but I do not believe it is necessary. The point I wish to illustrate is that an art object is the result of much more than an idea, it is the effect of many factors. There is in fact no complete intended object as such, only a more or less vague idea that slowly takes shape and is modified and transformed into an actual art object through a complex process.[10] For the artist of our example compromises were made concerning color and size; choices were made about composition, models and poses; and all these were determined in part by circumstances beyond the control of the artist and not intended prior to the time such choices were made. He did choose, but his choices were restricted and molded by the actual circumstances within which he had to make the choices.

This conclusion applies also to texts. There are no intended texts before authors produce historical texts. Authors have at first vague ideas of what they want to do, but only when they produce the texts, whether in their minds, on pieces of paper, on tape recorders, and so on, do the texts take shape. For in the process of production authors are forced to make compromises similar to those artists have to make. True, the materials with which authors and artists work are different. Artists work with such things as marble, paint, models, and they try to convey a certain plastic form; whereas most often authors work with pencils, papers, computers, and language, and they try to convey a certain meaning. All the same, the materials authors use, including language, are not significantly different from the materials at the disposal of artists. For even language is composed of elements that are very much like the marble, its color, the faces, the bodies and the expressions of the models used by sculptors. It is composed of elements some of which have meaning, as a face contorted in a certain way may suggest sadness, whereas other elements have meaning only in the context in which they are found, just as the marble acquires significance only when it is shaped in a particular form.

The point I wish to emphasize is that many factors influence authors while they compose texts, playing a causal role in various aspects of the composition. The text, just like an art object, is not caused by the author alone, but is rather a result of a causal complex that includes the author, the context where he or she works, as well as other factors.

It makes very little sense to talk, then, about the texts that authors "intended" to produce rather than the ones they "historically" produced. There are really no such intended texts. There are cases, of course, in which one might want to argue that there were plans for a text to be completed that was, however, left incomplete because of the death of the author or some such eventuality. But this does not go against the conclusion reached for two reasons. The first is that when there are outlines, notes, and plans, the production of the text has already begun. Indeed, one may want to argue, although I am not prepared to do so here without further reflexion, that notes, plans, and outlines are early versions of a text. The second is that, until texts are historically produced, extant outlines and notes as to how texts are to be completed are mere guidelines that authors feel free to modify or even discard as they go along. Thus, even when a text has been interrupted for some reason, it would be difficult to argue convincingly that a particular text is intended. The text, just like the art object, is what gets produced, the rest is only more or less vague speculation.[11]

Many examples of both texts and art objects could be cited to illustrate this point. One very dramatic instance is the plans that Gaudí left for Barcelona's *Sagrada Familia*, a church that has been under construction for about a century. Gaudi left many sketches and directions concerning the way the building was to take shape, and he even completed some parts of it before his death. But the architects that have been struggling with the building since Gaudi's death have found that they must make endless numbers of decisions about what to do as the process of construction goes on, many of which had not and perhaps could not have been anticipated by Gaudí. It is clear, then, that there was never a *Sagrada Familia* that Gaudí intended to build if by that one means a completed building. There were only ideas, plans, and sketches.

The intended text exists only as a conjecture on the part of an interpreter or the author of the historical text *after* the historical text has been produced. At that point the author himself or an interpreter may say that what the author intended to write, say, was such and such and not such and such. But that does not entail that there was an intended text before the historical text was produced; it entails only that the author may have had some ideas or intentions to which the historical text does or does not adhere.

Then, we may ask, how can we explain slips of the tongue, for example, and their subsequent correction? How can I say, referring to something I just said, "No, that is not what I intended to say?" The answer to this is that what we usually say is something like, "Oh, I'm sorry, that is not what I meant." This indicates that we are aware of producing a text that does not accurately convey the meaning we had in mind. It does not entail that there was a text we intended to use, but only that there was a meaning we intended to convey, and the signs we used to convey it do not do the job properly. Of course, we do say things like, "No, that is not what I intended to say." But in most cases this is better understood to mean precisely that what we have said does not convey the meaning we intended. If it is not, the reason is that we had already produced a historical mental text which the physical one was supposed to reproduce but did not. In either case, there is no intended text that precedes an actual one.

The distinction between the intended text and the historical text arises—like much of what has to do with hermeneutics—from various assumptions. The first has to do with scriptural exegesis, which is guided by the principle that there is a divine being who reveals his perfect views through an imperfect medium. Thus, although the text that the divinity intends to reveal is inerrant and perfect in every way, the historically produced text may be mistaken because of human instrumental agency.[12] This idea is applied to nondivinely revealed texts with the consequence that it is assumed that their authors, just like God, had an intended text in the mind before the texts were produced.

The second assumption that is behind the view of the intended text is that meanings are texts, and thus that there is a set of meanings in the mind of the author that gets translated into a text either in his or her mind or outside of it. The set of meanings is what the author intends to translate into a text, but the meanings get mangled in the process of translation. It is these meanings that are identified with the intended text.

Third, it is also believed that the cause must explicitly and actually precontain everything present in the effect. Thus, authors, to act as causes of texts, must actually have in their minds a text they intend to produce before they set out to produce one.

This third assumption becomes particularly strong when it is coupled with a fourth, which I have already disputed, that authors are the sole causes of texts. If there is only one cause and the cause must actually precontain everything present in the effect, it is obvious that authors, who are the sole causes of texts, must actually have in their minds texts they intend to produce before they produce them.

These four assumptions are quite misguided. Let me take them one by one. Concerning the first, let us assume that God did reveal the scriptures and had a text in mind that the scriptural writers took down as well as they could, although they made occasional mistakes. Even if this were the case, it would tell us nothing about how a human author proceeds and certainly does not entail that authors have an intended text in mind of the sort we have discussed before they actually produce a text. It is true that some authors (e.g., Russell), like some artists (e.g., Mozart), seem to have a completed text in their minds before they put it down in writing. But this is a misleading counterexample. For in such cases what they have in their minds is a mental text that has already been produced and consigned to their memory. They do not have to go through the process of correction and so forth, that other authors go through with their written or oral drafts because they wait until the mental text is completed before they set it down in writing. In cases like that of Russell, this is often the result of habits acquired through exposure to an educational system where one is not supposed to write or say anything that is not in good form. But none of this supports the claim that authors have an intended text before they actually produce one either mentally, orally, or through writing. And the same argument could be applied to the case of God's revelation. For one could say that the text God intends to reveal is not an intended text but a text actually produced and completed in God's mind that gets mangled and corrupted in the process of revelation.

The second assumption rests on two confusions. The first is the confusion between authors's intentions and texts. That authors have the intention to convey certain meanings when they set down to construct texts seems indisputable;[13] indeed, according to the definition of texts given in Chapter 1, such an intention is a necessary condition of texts. But that does not entail that authors have texts in mind that they intend to convey, for neither intentions in general nor intentions to produce texts need be texts. Indeed, the mental phenomena that correspond to an author's intentions do not have the characteristics associated with texts. For example, the intention to pursue a course of action is not the mental image of the text 'to pursue a course of action,' and the intention to write '$2 + 2 = 4$' is not the text '$2 + 2 = 4$.'

The second confusion blurs the distinction between meanings and texts. Even if one accepts the view that authors have meanings they intend to convey when they set out to produce texts, that does not entail that those meanings are texts. For example, the meaning of 'two' that someone may wish to convey is not a mental image of the Arabic number '2' or of any other of the signs used to convey it. As pointed out earlier, a text should not be confused with what is understood when we say the text is understood, that is, with its meaning.

This brings me to a point that is sufficiently important not to be left out even though it involves a digression. As noted earlier, it is a mistake to hold that there is ever in the mind of the author an intended text before a historical text is produced. Likewise, it is a mistake to maintain that authors always have in their minds the meanings they intend to convey with a text prior to the production of the text. I am not claiming, of course, that meanings are not independent of texts absolutely speaking—I shall leave that question for the next chapter. What I am claiming is that in the mind of the author it is not always the case—indeed some would argue that it is never the case—that there is a meaning independent of a text that is intended prior to the actual production of the text.

The status of the third assumption is again controversial, and we cannot be expected to settle its validity here. What we can do, however, is to point out that, since authors are not the single cause of texts, as the fourth assumption claims, even if we were to accept that a cause must actually precontain whatever is present in the effect, it does not follow that it is authors that have to precontain it. Whatever is present in historical texts must be actually precontained in the total set of causes of these effects and not in authors alone. Therefore, the conclusion that authors must have texts that they intend to produce before they actually produce them, is gratuitous.

With respect to the fourth assumption, I believe enough has been said. We need not dwell on it any further. Let me finish, then, by repeating that the distinction between the intended text and the historical text is unwarranted. The most that could be accepted are the following distinctions: first, a distinction between the historical text and a certain vague and fragmentary set of ideas and intentions that the author has prior to the production of the text: second, a distinction between a historical text as actually produced and the historical text purged from any mechanical or clerical mistakes that may have crept into it during the process of production; and third, a distinction between a historical text in the mind and its counterpart outside the mind. The distinction between the historical text as actually produced and the historical text purged from mistakes is in fact the distinction between a text that has been carefully composed or corrected and one that has not, and it should not serve as basis for arguing in favor of the more puzzling notion of an intended text.

An intended text, then, may be understood either (1) as a text of which the author is fully aware or (2) as a vague set of ideas and intentions concerning the text and its meaning. If (1), then it amounts to either (a) the historical physical text or (b) a historical mental text that precedes a physical one (both of which are historical texts because both were produced at a particular time by an author, although one was produced outside the mind and the other not). In either case the text turns out to be actual rather than intended, and thus, the notion of an intended text as distinct from an actual one remains unjustified. The only way to make sense of an intended text, then, is in terms of (2). But in that case the text must remain something vague and unclear.

C. Ideal Text

The *ideal text* may be understood in three different ways.[14] First, it may be understood as an inaccurate version of a historical text produced and considered by an interpreter as an accurate copy of the historical text. Taken in this sense, it may be considered ideal for two reasons: First, because the historical author of the historical text did not produce it; it is a projection speculatively posited by someone other than the author. Second, because it is not an accurate version of the historical text. Indeed, if it were an accurate version of the historical text it would be an instance of the historical text and thus would have to be considered actual. The ideal text taken in this first sense is produced by the interpreter because she is convinced of the inaccuracy of the contemporary text at her disposal.

Second, the *ideal text* may be understood as a text produced by an interpreter who considers that it expresses perfectly the view that the historical text expressed imperfectly. In this sense it is considered ideal not for the two reasons mentioned already in connection with the first understanding of the ideal text, although it may also fit those reasons, but because it is supposed to be a perfect model of the more or less imperfect copy that the historical author produced. (This last sense of 'ideal,' then, is Platonic.) This view assumes that an author's textual formulations of his views may be usually more or less imperfect copies of some perfect textual formulations of those views. According to this assumption, when an author adopts a philosophical position about justice, say, he may express it in a way that is imperfect and inadequate, although there is always a perfect and adequate way of expressing it. Note that there is an important difference between this and orthodox Platonism. For orthodox Platonism there are ideas only of what is absolutely perfect and true, whereas the notion of ideal text in question here implies that there can be perfect formulations of even false and, therefore, imperfect views. Thus, for example, although utilitarianism may be false and therefore imperfect in some sense for that reason, there is an ideal and perfect textual formulation of the position of which Mill's textual formulation fell short.

Third, the *ideal text* may be understood as a text produced by an interpreter as the text that perfectly expresses the view the historical author should have expressed, namely, the perfect or, if you like, the true view.[15] This understanding of ideal text is in accordance with orthodox Platonism. It goes beyond the idealism of the first and the second views presented, adopting a sense of ideal as the most perfect absolutely speaking.

The ideal text, considering both that it is not the historical text and that those who try to construct it accept it as such, functions in fact as a kind of regulative notion used by interpreters to understand, interpret, and evaluate a historical or contemporary text. It serves to indicate where contemporary texts might be inaccurate or the authors of texts might have gone wrong and where they have not, by comparing what they did with what they should have done. It also construes what authors may have wanted to say but failed to say adequately. The ideal text as such is a useful hermeneutical and historiographical tool, although its use can lead to abuses.

The main challenge to those who try to reconstruct an ideal text has to do with the extent to which they can legitimately depart from the contemporary text in their speculative fancy. If the modifications introduced in the contemporary text are too drastic, there is the danger that the ideal text may reveal nothing to us about the historical text and the views it sought to convey. Indeed, it may reveal more about the views of the interpreter.

This brings me to an important question concerning the criteria that are to be used for the selection of the components of the ideal text and for the modification of the contemporary text in accordance with it: Should the criteria include personal, cultural, and philosophical principles? The ideal text would look very different indeed, depending on the type of criteria used, and it is by no means obvious at the outset that one set of criteria should be used rather than another.

On the one hand, there is some point in arguing that the ideal text should be determined by taking into consideration personal and cultural elements, for example. After all, a text is always produced by a certain person in a certain cultural milieu and is itself a cultural product. So it would seem appropriate that cultural considerations enter into its determination. An ideal text produced by a certain interpreter from such and such a time and such and such a place should reflect that time, place, and interpreter. On the other hand, some will argue no doubt that personal and cultural considerations have nothing to do with the production of an ideal text. Because the function of texts is to produce understanding, the criteria to be used to construct the ideal text, and modify the contemporary text accordingly, should be strictly philosophical.

But what does 'philosophical' mean in this context? Does it mean "logical"? If that is the case, then the job involved in the production of an ideal text consists in going through the contemporary text, straightening out any logical mistakes that might have crept into the ideas it is supposed to convey. It would also involve discarding all the non sequiturs and putting in any conclusions that were carelessly left out but are logical conclusions and implications of the premises and asumptions of the views described in the text.

Philosophical may mean more than logical, however. It may mean not only cleaning up the logic and making explicit enthymematic premises and conclusions, but also clarifying the formulations that are found in the text but remain obscure. This procedure might involve substituting or expanding certain definitions to clarify various notions and views and so on. Or philosophical may be interpreted also as involving the addition of arguments that are more cogent than the ones provided in the historical or contemporary texts and even the correction of certain views expressed by these texts on the basis of our own experience and knowledge.

When we go beyond logic and include in the task of constructing the ideal text such procedures as clarification, supplementation, substitution, and correction, we are well beyond the task of constructing the perfect textual formulation of the more or less perfect views that the historical text tried to express. We are in fact trying to construct the ideal text of which all texts that deal with the specific subject matter with which a particular historical text deals are copies. In that sense we are not looking for the best formulations of imperfect views, but rather for the text that best expresses truth. In short, we have reverted to orthodox Platonism.

From all this it should be clear that, as in the previous cases of texts discussed, the ideal text turns out to be more than one. It can be the personally and culturally accurate text, it can be the logically correct text, it can be the clear and complete text, and finally, it can be the text that expresses the truth. There are, then, at least four different ideal texts, depending on the criteria applied, although in each case there is supposed to be only one text that best fulfills the criteria in question. And, indeed, there may be many more, if we were to add to the criteria mentioned other sorts of criteria. For example, there may be criteria applicable to poetic texts and so on that would alter the ideal of which a particular text is supposed to be a copy. Such criteria might include the appropriate use of analogies, metaphors, double entendres, and so on. Indeed, what the criteria in question are or include depends very much on the function the text in question fulfills. That is one of the reasons why we must turn to the functional classification of texts next.

Before we take up the functional classification, I must note, however, that the ideal text should not be confused with the meaning of the historical text. Texts and meanings, as pointed out in Chapter 1, are not the same. Now, let us assume for a moment—to make matters easier—that the meaning of a text is a set of ideas. Then we can infer that the meaning of the produced text is a set of ideas and the meaning of the ideal text is also a set of ideas. But the assumption behind the notion of an ideal text is that the ideas meant by the historical text are just more or less imperfect copies of the ideas meant by the ideal text. Even as imperfect copies, however (if one were to accept this assumption), they could be considered to be the same as the ideas meant by the ideal text. The meanings of the historical text and the ideal text *are not*, therefore, the same, insofar as the meaning of the first *should be* but is not that of the second. And this is so whether meaning is understood as ideas or not.

II. Functional Classification

Discussion of linguistic functions is commonplace in contemporary philosophy. Indeed, most introductory logic texts deal with this issue.[16] Considering the close association between language and texts, it is to be expected that the categories used to classify language in terms of function would also apply to texts. And, indeed, as will become evident immediately, it does to a great extent. But these linguistic functions are not the only ones that texts have. Based on the complex nature of texts and their correspondingly complex cultural purposes, I would like to argue that there is also a more complex classification of texts according to cultural functions. And, although this classification is to a certain extent less precise, it is nonetheless fruitful and will prove useful for the epistemic dimension of a theory of textuality, as will become clear in Part II of this book.

The difference between the linguistic and cultural functions of texts lies in the following. Linguistic functions are the most fundamental ways in which texts may be used. These functions are a byproduct of the very nature of language and do not depend on the type of language involved or the culture within which it develops. As such, these functions are presupposed by any other function for which language may be used. The cultural functions of texts, by contrast, are not as fundamental as the linguistic functions and depend not on the nature of language itself, but on various cultural phenomena. For this reason cultural functions do not apply to language as such. Cultural functions apply only to texts insofar as texts are produced to accomplish certain tasks not necessarily entailed by the nature of language but resulting from the way texts are used in particular cultural situations.

It is true, of course, that language itself is a cultural product. Thus one could argue that no distinction can be made between linguistic functions and other cultural functions because linguistic functions are cultural functions, even if they are cultural functions of a particular type. And, indeed, this objection makes sense to the extent that languages differ according to the cultures that produce them and thus one should expect their functions to differ as well. Yet, regardless of cultural differences, some basic features common to all languages derive precisely from their function as tools of communication and not as expressions of particular cultures. I do not wish to state dogmatically that this is the case, and I have no space in this book to argue for this position. I have to content myself with stating that it appears to me to be so, at least as far as natural languages is concerned. The case of artificial languages may be different to some extent because there may be some of these whose function is restricted. But any language that aims to have more than one narrow, stipulated function appears to have some basic functions that run through all cultures. To that extent, then, it is legitimate to separate the functions of language, and consequently of texts, into linguistic and cultural. I hope that the distinction between linguistic and cultural functions will become more clear in the discussion of the functions themselves.

A. Linguistic Functions

Logicians differ considerably in their views as to how language may be classified in terms of function, but at least five general categories may be identified: informative, directive, expressive, evaluative, and performative. As noted, these categories may also be applied to texts.

1. Informative Texts. Language is said to have an informative function when it is used to communicate information. The information in question may be correct or incorrect and may refer to anything whatever. I may report, for example, that so and so is mentally ill when he is not, or I may state correctly that Buffalo had more than 200 inches of snowfall in the winter of 1977. In the first case I make a false report about an internal state and in the second I make a true one about an external state of affairs. In either case I have used language for the purpose of conveying information and that language has taken the form of a text. Thus, we may speak of informative texts when their primary function is to communicate information.

2. Directive Texts. The directive function of language is involved when language is used to cause or prevent action. It may be prescriptive, as when I order someone to do or not do something. The command, "Thou shalt not kill," is a good example of the prescriptive type of directive language. But not all directive language is used prescriptively. A petitionary prayer, for example, is meant to move a divinity to act in a certain way and yet it does not prescribe such an action. And a question involves also a directive of sorts, because it seeks an answer, but is neither prescriptive in the way a command is, nor petitionary in the way a prayer is. The types of functions involved in prayers and questions may be classified as requisitive, because they both involve requests, and may be regarded as special cases of the directive function.[17] As in the case of informative language, directive language is used in texts; and the texts, accordingly, may also be classified as directive.

3. Expressive Texts. The expressive function occurs when language is used to vent or cause emotion. Expressions such as 'Wow!' are generally used to vent emotion, whereas much language used in lyric poetry is meant to create a certain mood and emotion in the reader or listener. Most expressive uses of language involve texts, although the relative brevity of some cases of the use of linguistic expressive language may work against their textuality. It is hard to see how 'Wow!' can be a text, for example.

4. Evaluative Texts. Language is also used evaluatively if it presents an evaluation of some sort. Thus, "Mother Theresa is a good person" or *"The Burial of Count Orgaz* is a great work of art" present evaluations of the person and painting to which they, respectively, refer. The evaluative use of language is frequently carried out by texts of various degrees of complexity and, thus, we may refer to those texts as evaluative.

5. Performative Texts. The performative function takes place when language is used to perform an act. For example, when I say "Excuse me!" one of the things that I am doing by saying it is precisely the act of excusing myself. The texts that are used to perform this function may, then, be classified as performative.

As noted earlier, the extension of these categories may be challenged. One may wish to argue that language seldom, or perhaps never, fits one of these functional categories to the exclusion of others. Evaluative language often contains directive, informative, and expressive functions; directive language may contain expressive and evaluative elements; and so on. Moreover, the same linguistic expression may at different times and in different contexts have different functions. What is meant as primarily directive in some contexts may turn out in others to be informative, for example. Consider the previously mentioned case of 'Fire!,' which shouted by an officer next to a cannon is an order, but shouted in a crowded theater may be taken as primarily informative or expressive.

The validity of the categories themselves may also be questioned. For example, some logical positivists rejected the evaluative category altogether, arguing that so-called evaluative expressions are to be converted into directive or expressive ones. They claimed that a sentence such as "X is good," for instance, should be translated into sentences such as "I wish X," "I like X," "I command X," or "I commend X."[18]

Finally, one may argue that it is not possible to come up with any exhaustive list of the functions of language and that certainly many others could be added to the list given here. And this, I believe, is a valid criticism. The classification of language according to the stated functions is by no means unassailable but, nonetheless, it is useful in illustrating at least that language may serve various functions. The difficulties that surround these functions of language are accentuated when they are applied to texts. The reason is that most texts are highly complex entities that have culturally complex functions and thus involve several of the functions we have discussed. It is possible to find short and simple texts, such as some of the ones given earlier, whose primary function seems to be one of the functions mentioned. But even in those cases, as with most uses of language, the function would only be one among several. When we get to texts of the magnitude of a novel, a philosophical treatise, or a scientific article, moreover, it is clear that the categories identified need supplementation. For this reason I would like to add to those categories some general cultural functions which can serve as bases of a different classification of texts.

B. Cultural Functions

Texts may carry out a great variety of cultural functions, and for that reason I will mention only the most obvious ones. Some very general categories seem to be associated with the most broad sorts of cultural functions that texts serve. I shall briefly discuss twelve basic categories of these that can be easily identified: legal, literary, philosophical, religious, scientific, historical, political, pedagogical, confessional, entertaining, inspirational, and pneumonic. Texts in each of these categories seem to share a core of characteristics related to the overall purpose they have. I shall also add a final miscellaneous category in which I mention other possibilities that I do not explore in detail. Much could be said about each of these categories, but I shall try to be brief.

1. Legal Texts. The primary function of legal texts is to formulate, preserve, clarify, and implement the rules according to which relations among members of society are to be regulated.[19] Legal texts that have to do with laws usually cover four areas: the codification, the clarification, the exemplification, and the application of laws. The first gives rise to so-called legal codes such as Justinian's or Hammurabi's, which codify a body of law. Sometimes, these laws are simply listed, but more often they are topically organized and discussed. The second produces commentaries, that is, explanations and clarifications of laws. This is the sort of thing well exemplified by Gratian's *Decretum,* where legal principles are accompanied by extensive analyses, and is also likely to appear orally in the form of lectures within and without the classroom. Third, there are compilations of legal precedents, that is, descriptions of cases that either provide examples of the application of laws or set precedents for future legal decisions, or both. This is most frequently found in places like England, where the legal tradition is based on common law. Finally, there is the kind of text produced by lawyers, prosecutors, and judges in connection with trials and legal proceedings. These are concerned primarily with the application of the law to actual cases and include such different things as arguments in a trial, depositions, statements by witnesses, confessions, warrants, and so on.

In addition to texts that have to do with the law, under the category of legal texts come also all sorts of documents that establish agreements among members of society or result from such agreements. These include such texts as contracts, wills, bills, receipts, checks, promisory notes, and so on.

2. Literary Texts. Some authors have suggested that what characterizes literary texts is that they deal with what is apparent rather than what is real; other authors claim that literary texts are characterized by being subject to multiple, equally legitimate interpretations whereas other texts are not.[20] But these views are easily contested. If the first were to be adopted, for example, biographies could not be considered literary, a consequence that would be hard to accept in all cases. With respect to the multiple interpretation view, many types of texts can be subject to more than one legitimate interpretation, as will become clear in Chapters 4 and 5, and thus this feature of texts is not restricted to literary ones.

The purpose of literary texts is a much contested issue that cannot be settled briefly. For that reason we cannot be expected to provide a convincing view of this matter here where we are dealing with it only in passing. It should suffice for the present, rather limited purposes to indicate that literary texts seem to have an artistic aim as primary. And, as we already saw, the mark of the artistic is the recognition of artifactual nature and the capacity to produce an aesthetic experience.[21]

The primary function of literary texts can be fulfilled in many ways, thus giving rise to diverse literary genres. Literary genres are the various ways in which texts and the signs of which they are composed can be organized to carry out their function. Note that there are important differences between syntactical arrangements and the sorts of arrangements that give rise to literary genres. Syntactical arrangements have to do with the ordering of signs within sentences in accordance with grammatical rules. The arrangements that give rise to literacy genres are usually larger orderings involving not only some syntactical arrangements but also the arrangement of sentences into patterns and even of paragraphs, and they may include rules about content and so on. Among the most common literary genres are poems, novels, plays, essays, dialogues, and lectures, but these by no means exhaust the category. And within each of these genres there are many others.

3. Philosophical Texts. Philosophers disagree widely on what philosophy is, so it is by no means easy to identify a noncontroversial understanding of the main function of philosophical texts. Indeed, philosophers cannot even agree on the historical or even contemporary canon of philosophical texts. Nonetheless, there are at least some texts, both historical and contemporary, that are generally regarded as philosophical. For example, I doubt anyone would exclude the texts of Aristotle's *Metaphysics* and Kant's *Critique of Pure Reason* from the category of philosophical texts, even if no agreement could be secured as to what they have in common or whether in fact they have anything in common beyond the fact that they are regarded as philosophical. This much would indicate at least that some texts fall into the category of philosophical texts and this is all we need for our present purposes.

Philosophical texts generally come in five forms which go back to ancient times; three of these became firmly established as philosophical genres within the Western tradition in the Ancient world and the Middle Ages. The first genre is the systematic treatise. Texts that fall into this category may vary in length and scope but in general aim to present an overall and systematic view of a subject matter or a concept. Thomas Aquinas's *On Being and Essence* and Francis Suárez's *Disputationes metaphysicae* are good examples of texts of this type.

A second, very popular genre of philosophical texts is the commentary. Much of what philosophers do consists in discussing and clarifying what other philosophers have written. These commentaries come in two varieties. The first, known as *ad litteram*, provides a detailed, word by word, discussion of a text. The second, having no particular name, is a looser procedure. In either case, however, the commentary follows the text, reflecting in at least some ways its structure and having as a primary aim its understanding.

Third, there is the article, which is a direct descendant of the medieval *quaestio*. This is a relatively short piece in which the author tries to settle a specific problem. In the Middle Ages the *quaestio* developed a standard organization in which a problem was posed in the form of a question (*aporia*), opinions were presented in favor and against a particular answer (*status quaestionis*), an answer (*responsio*) tried to reach a solution, and replies to objections against the view of the author followed. Today the form of an article is much more free, but in general it still reflects its medieval origin. Articles come in a variety of forms and degrees of technicality. In this category we may also include essays of a more personal nature. Thus this category contains editorials, essays, and the like.

The lecture is also a very prevalent type of philosophical genre, whether in the classroom or at a gathering of specialists (or nonspecialists). Lectures are closer to the article format than to any other of the genres mentioned, but they tend to be more informal and less technical.

Finally, philosophers also engage in oral discussions, which are frequently presented in writing as dialogues. Plato immortalized the written version of this genre in the ancient world. Today it is not a favorite genre in written form, but it is constantly used orally by philosophers.

4. Scientific Texts. The primary function of scientific texts is to develop, present, and preserve scientific knowledge. Scientists compose texts as they engage in scientific procedures and in order to communicate their discoveries to other scientists, to teach students of science, and to preserve their views for future generations.

Scientific texts are usually of five types: textbooks, articles, reports, lectures, and data banks. Textbooks are surveys of the state of scientific knowledge in a particular field. For example, in medicine, one will find works on endometriosis, cancer, heart disease, and so on. These texts keep nonspecialists up to date on the general state of a field and teach students of the discipline about it.

Scientists also compose articles and reports. Articles are short pieces that present the results of pointed discoveries and experiments or aim to inform. Reports combine some of the features of textbooks and articles. Their main characteristic is that they are quite pointed, being meant to address a specific issue that has arisen in very particular circumstances. Thus, for example, a scientist or group of scientists may prepare a report on the state of the environment in a particular region of a country. These reports are intended to analyze a situation and find a solution to the problems that characterize it. The solution is presented as a set of recommendations that society or its leaders may choose to implement. In other cases scientific reports merely inform an audience of an experiment and its results.

Lectures are also a form of scientific text where the lecturer presents essentially what one would in an article, but in a more informal and usually less technical format. Lectures are usually delivered orally, but frequently there are also written versions of them.

Finally, there are various sorts of data banks, whose function is simply to serve as sources and guides to information. The most common of these are bibliographies and indexes, but there are many others, particularly now that the computer has facilitated data storage.

Apart from these, of course, scientists engage in conversations, discussions, dialogues, and other forms of discourse while they are developing their views. But these do not generally follow established genres.

5. Religious Texts. Religious texts have a general religious intent, but the exact nature of that intent varies, giving rise to a diversity of types of religious texts. At least five types of religious texts stand out, depending on the specific function each has: sacred, theological, apologetic, instructional, and devotional. Sacred texts are supposed to contain divinely revealed truths. They come in a wide variety of genres, from epic poems, like the *Mahabharata* and the *Ramayana*, to genealogies and historical accounts like some of the books of the Old Testament. Because these texts are supposed to contain divinely revealed truths they elicit the kind of respect and reverence due to sacred objects.

Sacred texts are seldom systematic expositions of religious truths and are often written in language that is not easy to understand. The need to understand them and systematize the doctrines they contain into a coherent body of beliefs gives rise to theological texts. These often take the form of commentaries on sacred texts, but their intent is generally broader, namely, to present an overall understanding of the doctrines contained in sacred texts. Theological texts also take the form of systematic treatises and short articles. The former seek particularly the systematization of doctrine and often attempt to present an understanding of that doctrine that takes into account information derived from secular fields of learning, such as science and philosophy. The function of short articles, on the other hand, is to raise or solve problems of interpretation that arise from the attempt to understand sacred texts or to develop a systematic body of religious doctrine.

A third function of religious texts is the defense of doctrine and this is carried out in texts that may be classified as apologetic. These texts are frequently polemical in tone and take their themes from particular historical circumstances. For example, Augustine's *The City of God* is a defense of Christianity against the charge that it had been responsible for the decline of the Roman Empire. The length and structure of apologetic texts, however, can vary a great deal, going from long treatises like Thomas Aquinas's *Summa contra gentes* to short tracts and articles.

There are also many religious texts whose main function is instructional; they are meant to pass on the fundamental beliefs of a religious faith. Because of this they take the form of manuals that contain creeds, statements of dogmas, and other elements deemed essential to the faith. Catechisms, for example, are good examples of this sort of religious text. Catechisms are sanctioned instructional texts that have achieved particular status, but there can also be less authoritative instructional texts that express a person's understanding of a faith.

Finally, among religious texts there are devotional ones, such as prayers. The aim of these may vary a great deal. The purpose of some is to ask for favors from the divinity or to show proper respect and adoration. Others are used for inspirational purposes or to help develop discipline and good habits.

6. Historical Texts. There are various senses in which texts can be considered historical. In one sense a text is historical simply if it is old. In another sense, a text is historical if it is the one produced by the historical author. Finally, a text may be considered historical when it has a significant impact on history. None of these senses, however, describes the historical function of texts in the sense I wish to explore here. By *historical* in this functional sense I mean that a text provides an account of or describes the past. We might put this by saying that in this sense a text is intensionally, rather than extensionally, historical—its content is about the past.[22]

Historical texts can take a variety of forms. Some of them consist simply in the recording of certain events at certain dates. These are usually referred to as annals and chronicles, but in this category may be included notes, newspaper articles that are not editorials, records, diaries, and so on. In contrast with what are more properly called *histories*, they do not try to account for past events by explaining their causal connections and other interrelationships. Histories do try to account for the past, but they also can be classified in various ways, depending both on the elements of the past that they are intended to recount and the methodology they use to do it. Thus, biographies, for example, aim to provide an account of the life of a particular person. Autobiographies attempt the same thing, but in this case the historian is the same person whose life is the subject of the historical account. There are also histories of culture, social histories, histories of science, histories of ideas, histories of philosophy, and so on. Most of these contain methodologically distinguishing characteristics that are at least in part the result of the subject matter with which they deal. For example, the history of philosophy requires a philosophical attitude on the part of the historian that is not necessary in social histories.[23]

7. Political Texts. The primary function of political texts is to deal with the organization and function of goverment. Their range is broad. They may be concerned with the organization, administration, and conduct of government or with the ways in which groups or persons may affect and influence government.

Political texts come in a variety of genres. Among the most important are constitutions, declarations, decrees, and speeches. Constitutions are documents in which the set of principles according to which a particular society is to be ruled are laid out. Today, most countries have constitutions, although this has not always been customary in the history of humanity. Declarations are documents meant to take a stand vis-à-vis a state of affairs and notify a party or parties of such a stand. Thus the American Declaration of Independence established the wishes of the North American colonies with respect to independence and notified the British authorities of them. Decrees are laws or rules established by the government. And, finally, political speeches take various forms and have diverse aims. They may, for example, be long and formal or short and informal, plain or learned, and so on. Moreover, they may aim to inform the public or to deceive it, to promote the election of the speaker to political office, to win the audience to a cause, and so on. In all cases and in all genres, political texts have a political function, that is, they concern government in one way or another.

8. Pedagogical Texts. The primary function of pedagogical texts is to instruct. Instruction may pertain both to materials and procedure. The function of a pedagogical text may be to teach about certain phenomena of behavior or to instruct someone in how to do something or how to prevent something from happening.

The most common texts of a pedagogical nature are the lectures and other instructional procedures that take place in the classroom. But accompanying these there are also textbooks, manuals, notes, charts, maps, bibliographies, indexes, receipts, and so on, which help to instruct in a subject matter or an art. Any text used in a particular context primarily for the purpose of instruction, then, may be classsified as pedagogical.

9. Confessional Texts. Confessional texts are meant primarily to make confessions of one sort or another. A confession can be understood in two senses. In one sense it is the acknowledgment of having done something wrong, whether on purpose or not. Thus confessional texts usually provide information of a private nature previously unavailable. What a sinner tells a priest in the confessional, the documents criminals sign acknowledging what they have done, an autobiography in which the author acknowledges mistakes, and so on, are all examples of confessional texts.

In another sense a confession is a public profession of faith or a formal statement of doctrinal belief made by one or more persons. In this sense groups of believers who adhere to a particular set of beliefs are sometimes called a confession. A text is confessional in this sense if its function is to make known the beliefs of a person or groups of persons. Creeds, catechisms, and so on are standard examples of this type of text.

10. Entertaining Texts. A large number of texts function primarily as sources of entertainment. Statements made by comic strip characters, jokes, puzzles, songs, and the like, seem to have as their aim to entertain an audience. But entertainment should not be taken exclusively as the production of humorous relief. A mystery novel or a horror film have little to do in most cases with humor, yet they fit this category. Their aim is primarily to produce in an audience an experience that is valued simply because the audience enjoys it and it helps pass the time. There is seldom any other fundamental purpose here—of learning, conveying information, moral edification, aesthetic experience, and so on.

11. Inspirational Texts. This is the sort of text whose main function is to inspire its audience, sometimes by just producing in it a certain experience or feeling and sometimes by eliciting a behavioral response. Often, inspirational texts do both, they produce an emotion and through that effect changes in the way the audience behaves. To inspire, as the word suggests, is to blow or breathe in, that is, instill an active principle that changes the way we act. A good sermon, for example, will not only teach but also move the audience to follow the precepts presented in it.

12. Pneumonic Texts. Some texts seem to function primarily as pneumonic devices. I am referring to such texts as appointment books, address books, grocery and laundry lists, and instructions for the babysitter. Some of these sorts of texts contain valuable information, but they cannot be classified as scientific. Nor are they pedagogical or philosophical, and so on. They seem to occupy a category of their own that most often has to do with reminding an audience of some information it needs. A grocery list reminds us about what we have to buy, the appointment book reminds us of appointments we have to keep, and the instructions for the babysitter remind him that he should not forget to carry out certain tasks.

13. Other Functional Categories of Texts. The categories just listed are not to be regarded by any means as exhaustive. Indeed, even a brief consideration of the functions texts have in cultures will reveal many more categories that should be added to those I have listed. For example, I have said nothing about ceremonial texts. Some may wish to argue that these fit best within the category of religious but this is hardly the case because not all ceremonies are religious and thus not all texts used in ceremonies can be classified as religious. And something similar could be said about greetings, advice, congratulations, warnings, texts used in celebrations and praise, advertisements, announcements, predictions, and so on. An investigation into these and other functional categories of texts is certainly an interesting line of study to pursue but one for which we have no space here and that is only marginally related to the topics of this book.

Neither are the categories listed to be regarded as mutually exclusive. In fact, they are far from being so, and my aim in presenting them has not been by any means to suggest that they are. Indeed, if we look at some examples of religious texts, it is clear that they also fall into other categories. The Song of Songs is generally regarded both as a literary piece of very high quality and an inspirational text; Leviticus is both religious and legal; Numbers is religious and historical; the four Gospels of the Christian Church are histories and at the same time are regarded by Christians as sacred and inspirational; Paul's Epistles are historical but are also religious, inspirational, pedagogical, and so on. Indeed, the examples could be multiplied without difficulty, indicating that the mentioned categories are not mutually exclusive.

The fact that the cultural categories we have presented are not mutually exclusive also indicates that the various types of texts and the genres identified within them can also be shared by texts that fall into different categories. For example, although the most common forms of philosophical texts may be the treatise, the commentary, the article, and the lecture, there is no reason why philosophical texts might not come in other forms. And, indeed, they do; for example, they come in the form of poems or novels. Much early Greek philosophy took the form of poems, and Voltaire's *Candide* is by all accounts a philosophical novel that presents a very effective and rhetorically persuasive argument against some of Leibniz's views. There are, therefore, no hard and fast lines that separate the functional categories into which texts may be classified. Indeed, form or genre is another way according to which texts may be classified and that could be added to the four explored in this chapter. I omit separate discussion of it because it is too difficult a topic to be raised just in passing and more pertinent to studies concerned with literary form and criticism that philosophical investigations such as the present one.

Note, finally, that the cultural and linguistic functions of texts overlap with and complement each other. We need both to understand how texts function. The linguistic functions, however, are more fundamental insofar as they are based on the linguistic nature of texts and thus are easily evident in ordinary discourse, even of the most private kind. The cultural functions of texts, as products of a culture and therefore of a social group, are more easily evident in texts that have a clear social profile.

III. Conclusion

The purpose of this chapter has been to provide a somewhat rough taxonomy of texts to prevent onesided approaches to and confusions about texts and textuality. This taxonomy illustrates the richness of the category and the need to take into account radically different types of texts if a satisfactory and minimally adequate understanding of textuality is to be achieved.

The taxonomy provided in the chapter runs along two axes: modal and functional. The modal classification of texts into actual, intended, and ideal is important because references to texts are often ambiguous so that the identities of the texts in question are not always clear. Moreover, such references often hide assumptions concerning the status and identity of the texts that should be made explicit. My claim is that the actual text is the one that exists or has existed at some time. If it is the text produced by the historical author it is the historical text; if it is the text we have, it is the contemporary text; and if it is a text that is neither the historical nor the contemporary but nonetheless existed at some time, it is the intermediary text. Knowledge of these distinctions is important because it will make us modify our claims about both texts and the value and accuracy of their interpretations.

I argue against the notion of an intended text, conceived as distinct from the historical text or the vague ideas and intentions that precede the production of a historical text, pointing out that the process of textual production militates against it. In my view, there are no intended texts other than historical texts and more or less vague ideas and intentions about producing a text. As such, the intended text has no status either in the mind of the author or in reality, apart from the status of the historical text or the vague ideas and intentions of an author. Considered as something different from these, the intended text is a fiction posited by those who misunderstand the process of textual production.

The ideal text is the product of an interpreter who aims to reconstruct the historical text or to improve on it. In either case, it is not the product of the historical author and it is considered perfect, or at least as perfect as possible, by its own author; namely, the interpreter. Ideal texts are useful insofar as they fulfill a regulative function that helps us understand, evaluate, and sometimes reconstruct the historical text. But they may also distort the historical record.

The distinction of texts into actual, intended, and ideal helps to keep in perspective the roles authors and interpreters play with respect to texts. For, as we shall see in Part II of this book, there is a tendency among those who have discussed textuality to overemphasize the role of the author to the detriment of the interpreter, and vice versa. And the reason is that they fail to recognize that when one speaks of a text, one may be speaking of very different things. Thus much of the controversy concerning these roles can be traced to misunderstandings and confusions concerning the different modal types of texts.

The functional classification is intended to help us understand how texts are used. The linguistic classification makes clear that, regardless of the cultural use to which a text may be put, they fulfill some fundamental functions in virtue of their linguistic nature. But these are not enough to explain the variegated uses texts have. The picture must be completed with cultural functions and the literary genres they generate. This should also help us see how much texts are a matter of culture and therefore must be understood in the cultural matrix from which they spring.

The discussion of the cultural functions of texts is important for two reasons. The first is that I shall argue later that function is the key element in the determination of textual meaning and thus in the establishment of parameters of textual understanding and interpretation. The second is that, as mentioned in earlier chapters, much contemporary discussion of textuality focuses exclusively on specific types of texts, whether literary, scientific, or what have you, which are taken as paradigmatic of textuality, thus leading to the neglect of the very different and variegated cultural functions of texts. Once the role that cultural functions play in meaning and the great variety of textual functions are understood, it is easier to see, for example, that literary texts are not paradigmatic of textuality in general and that as a species of the most general class they display some peculiar and distinguishing characteristics that are by no means common to many other species of texts. I shall return to this point in Chapter 4 in particular.

With this I would like to close the first part of this book, devoted to the logic of texts, although it should be clear that I have merely scratched the surface of the many issues involved in it. Textuality is a complex and difficult notion that requires more analysis than I have been able to give it here. But it is my hope that what has been said in these three chapters is sufficient to demonstrate such complexity and prepare us for the questions to be raised in Part II by establishing the conceptual foundation necessary to clarify and settle the issues that have to do with the understanding, interpretation, and discernibility of texts.

PART II

THE EPISTEMOLOGY OF TEXTS

4

UNDERSTANDING

So far in this book I have been concerned to a large extent with logical issues. Part I dealt with the definition and classification of texts and with the distinction of texts from other entities which are frequently confused with them. All these matters involved the logical mapping out of our concept of texts. While discussing these issues some epistemic questions surfaced that had to be dealt with in order to proceed, but in general the discussion primarily concerned the logical analysis of concepts. Now, however, we take a new turn and the epistemological issues raised by textuality take priority while logical issues are relegated to the background, although some discussion of logical issues is appropriate and even necessary in this context as well. I begin in this chapter with the understanding of texts, and then turn in the following two to their interpretation and discernibility respectively.

The primary function of texts, considered qua texts, is to convey a specific meaning to an audience, and that entails producing an understanding in the audience. Yet, the understanding of texts seems to vary a great deal from audience to audience and in some cases we speak not of understanding, but of misunderstanding. Because most of what has been said in previous chapters has substantial implications for and raises various issues concerning the understanding of texts, we must now turn to this topic to see if we can shed some light on it.

Audiences frequently understand texts in ways different from the ways in which their historical authors understood them. However, we have not discussed, first, whether such different understandings are always to be regarded as misunderstandings or whether they can still be considered understandings properly speaking. Moreover, both of these alternatives seem at first sight undesirable. If we adopt the first alternative, it looks as if in understanding texts we are bound by what the historical authors of the texts understood, but since we have no direct access to those understandings, how are we to judge whether we in fact understand or misunderstand the texts in question? And if we adopt the second alternative, how are we to preserve a distinction between accurate and inaccurate understandings of texts, that is, between understanding and misunderstanding them?

Second, apart from the question of the limits of understanding and misunderstanding, we have not discussed whether it is legitimate for audiences to understand texts in ways that are different from the ways in which their historical authors understood them and, if it is so, under what circumstances. Again, the likely alternatives appear prima facie undesirable. If it is legitimate for audiences to understand texts differently from the ways in which their historical authors understood them, it is clear that the purpose of conveying a specific meaning those historical authors had in producing the texts may be frustrated. And if it is not legitimate for audiences to do so, how can texts be legitimately understood when audiences have no direct access to the authors's understandings?

Consider the case of the Constitution of the United States of America (including its amendments), and let us suppose that some contemporary understandings of that document are different from the understandings the framers of the Constitution had in mind. Say that the framers understood privacy in such a way that it did not include the right of women to abortion for the simple reason that they did not consider such cases, while some understand it today to include such a right. Are such contemporary understandings of the document to be considered understandings, or are they rather to be considered misunderstandings of it? Moreover, is it legitimate for the present generation of Americans to understand the Constitution in ways different from the ways in which it was understood by its authors (apart from whether those understandings are to be considered understandings properly speaking or misunderstandings)? If we answer affirmatively to this last question, then it looks as if we have given license to understand the Constitution in any way in which anyone wants. And if we answer negatively, it looks as if the Constitution can never be properly understood, since we have no direct access to how it was understood by its framers.

These issues are related to another which is equally important; namely, whether in some circumstances audiences may understand texts better than the historical authors who composed them. Teachers, for example, appear to act as if this were so when they correct the papers of their students. True, not all corrections are such that they support this conclusion. Sometimes we correct a student's paper simply because she has made a mistake, say that she has drawn a conclusion that does not follow or she has failed to follow a grammatical rule. But, at other times, by correcting we mean something like "This is not what you mean" or "This is not what you want to say." In these latter cases, we are actually telling the student that we understand the text she produced better than she did and that the text does not convey the meaning she thought it did.

To clarify and solve these issues we must deal, first, with some propaedeutic matters. We must clarify the nature of understanding and its relation to meaning, the number and different understandings about which one may speak in connection with texts, and the relation of understanding to textual identity. Let me begin with understanding and meaning.

I. Understanding versus Meaning

Let us say that to understand a text is to grasp its meaning. To understand the text '2 + 2 = 4' is to grasp that two and two equal four, and to understand the text 'Socrates was the teacher of Plato' is to grasp that Socrates was the teacher of Plato. Understanding, therefore, is closely related to meaning, because what is understood when one is said to understand a text is the meaning of the text.

Understanding is not, however, the same thing as meaning. Understanding is a kind of mental act whereby one grasps something, which in the case of texts is their meaning.[1] But the meaning of texts is nothing necessarily mental and therefore cannot be identified with understanding. It is true that in ordinary language we sometimes speak as if understanding and meaning were the same thing. For example, when we say something like, "The understanding of X as Y is incorrect," we may have in mind that the meaning of X is not Y. There is nothing wrong with usages such as this as long as the sense of understanding displayed in them is not confused with the sense we are discussing here, in which to understand is to engage in a mental activity whereby we grasp, in the case of texts, their meaning.

It must be made clear also at the outset that understanding, conceived in this way, is not a faculty of the mind, as some philosophers have proposed. That there may be a faculty of the mind whereby we understand, I am not prepared to discuss here, and so for the present I leave that question open. My point is only that by *understanding* I do not mean such a faculty, but rather the act whereby we understand.

Understanding, conceived in the way indicated, is a relational act insofar as it is directed and has a relation to what is understood. In the case of textual understanding the relation in question is to the meaning of a text. There are acts that are not relational. For example, the act of sleeping is not relational in the sense in which understanding is. And the same could be said about the act of swearing. One always understands X, but one does not swear X or sleep X; one can merely swear or sleep. But there are acts that are relational, such as the act of drinking, for one always drinks something. Understanding is likewise relational.

Although I have been speaking of understanding as a single act, it should not be concluded from this that I hold that each understanding consists in only one act of the mind. It is convenient to speak of understanding as one act, but in fact understanding is more like a series or group of acts. In this sense it is very much like such activities as running. We speak of "the act of running," but running is in fact a series of acts—raising the right foot, moving it forward, putting it down, raising the left foot, moving it forward, putting it down, and so on. The understanding of even relatively simple texts—we know from Chapters 1 and 3 that there can be no absolutely simple texts—involves the consideration of the entities that constitute the texts, the consideration of their syntactical arrangement, and the recognition of their semantic significance, and all these are acts that in some cases can themselves be analyzed into other acts. When we get to very complex texts, matters become much more complicated, for then we have to store substantial parts of the texts in our memory and consider new parts of the texts in light of them, and so on. The complexity of understanding, then, should be kept in mind throughout the discussion, even if for the sake of convenience no references to it are made.

The distinction between understanding and meaning is important because it makes clear that the understanding of texts is not reducible to the understanding of their authors or something about their authors.[2] To understand a text is not to understand something about the acts in which the author of the text engaged when he produced the text or about the author himself. Understanding concerns the meaning of the text, not the author or the author's acts of understanding that meaning. This is an important point because part of the rebellion against the whole idea that we must recapture the meaning of a text from the past, so popular in contemporary literature, is motivated by the desire to separate the text from its author.[3] This desire is based in turn in a desire to avoid the difficulties involved in knowing something about authors from the past about whom we know only what texts tell us and in a desire to set audiences free so they can understand texts in ways in which their authors may not have anticipated.

Indeed, it is a common fact of experience that audiences frequently arrive at understandings of texts that are different and even opposed to the understandings the historical authors of those texts had. There is no difficulty in coming up with many examples taken from everyday discourse. Indeed, it is frequent for different audiences to have different, and even contradictory, understandings of the same text. There is no need to give examples of this, for all of us are confronted with instances of this phenomenon daily.

Finally, because understanding has been conceived here as an act or acts of a person or persons, and both the author and the audience of a text are persons, it turns out that there are as many numerically different understandings of a text as there are persons who understand them.[4] Furthermore, because texts may have more than one author and one audience, there may be as many numerically different acts in question as numerically different authors and audiences. Let me, then, turn to the question of the number of understandings of a text.

II. Number of Understandings

To clarify this matter we might introduce a distinction between extensional and intensional conceptions of the sameness and difference of the acts of understaning. I shall consider that an act of understanding is extensionally the same as another act of understanding if and only if they are the same individual act, so that they cannot be counted as two. And I shall consider that an act of understanding is extensionally different from another act of understanding if and only if they are numerically distinct acts, that is, they can be counted as two individual acts. By contrast, I shall consider an act of understanding of a text to be intensionally the same as another if and only if, having been prompted by the same type of ECTs, the meaning understood through them is the same. And I shall consider acts of understanding of texts to be intensionally different if and only if the meanings understood through them are different, whether or not they are prompted by the same type of ECTs.

From this it follows that several persons can have the same act of understanding, taken intensionally, provided that the ECTs that prompted the act are of the same type and what the persons understand through that act is the same meaning.[5] And the same goes for the same person at different times. Thus, for example, every time someone understands the meaning of '$2 + 2 = 4$' as two and two equal four, that person shares the same act of understanding, intensionally speaking, with all other persons who understand the same meaning for that text. Extensionally speaking, however, the acts of each of the persons in question are different, for they are individual acts belonging to different individual persons. Also different in this extensional sense, of course, are acts of understanding of the same person occurring at different times.

Here, when I speak of the difference and sameness among the acts of understanding of audiences and authors, I do so intensionally rather than extensionally. As acts of individual persons, all these acts are individually, that is numerically, different, but as acts of understanding whereby persons understand a certain meaning they may be the same or different, depending on the meaning grasped and the ECTs through which it is grasped.

We have, then, a variety of possible different understandings depending on the authors and audiences involved, all of which are extensionally different, but some of which may be intensionally different and some of which may be intensionally the same. The fact that audiences may understand texts not only differently from the way the authors of the texts understood them, but even in ways opposite to them, raises many important issues, three of which seem particularly pertinent for our inquiry. The first is the question of whether, when an audience understands a text differently than its historical author, the audience can still be said to understand the same text the historical author produced. The second is the question of whether when such a different understanding occurs, it is still to be regarded as an understanding or is better regarded as a misunderstanding. The third is the question of whether it is legitimate for audiences to understand texts in ways which their historical authors did not have in mind or which are contrary to what those authors had in mind, apart from whether their understandings are to be characterized as understandings properly speaking or as misunderstandings.

III. Understanding and Textual Identity

The first question needs to be addressed because it is generally assumed, and I agree, that textual identity requires semantic identity, that is, that texts with different meanings cannot be considered the same. If semantic identity is a necessary condition of textual identity, then it would appear to follow that, when a text is understood in a way different from the way in which the historical author understood it, the text being understood is not the same text as the one the historical author produced. This seems to imply, furthermore, that textual misunderstanding is impossible, for a misunderstood text is always a different text.

This difficulty is more apparent than real, however; it concerns merely a verbal matter. To say that one misunderstands a text can be unpacked in two different ways. In one way it can be taken to mean that one text has been understood in two different ways and one of these ways is not correct. In another way, it can be taken to mean that two different texts have been identified as the same. According to the first analysis, one misunderstands a text T_1 when one takes T_1 to mean M_2 rather than what it means, say M_1. According to the second analysis, one misunderstands a text T_1 when one identifies T_1 with T_2 although T_1 is not T_2 because T_1 means M_1 and T_2 means M_2.

The first analysis is inconsistent with the view of texts presented in Chapter 1. Indeed, if such a view were to be adopted, texts would have to be identified with their ECTs and their arrangement, for their meaning would be irrelevant to their identity, and apart from their meaning and the factors that affect the meaning, the only other elements relevant to textual identity are the ECTs of which they are composed and the arrangement of those ECTs.

We are left, then, with the second analysis, which is consistent with the view of identity I favor. According to this analysis, the misunderstanding of a text is nothing but the confusion of a text with another text, which has the same ECTs (and arrangement) as the original but different meaning.

An important corollary of what has been said concerning texts and their meaning and understanding is that the identity of understandings, when these are considered intensionally, is dependent on the identity of texts. This is so because what makes an act of textual understanding intensionally what it is, and therefore intensionally the same as others, is that it is an act whereby a subject grasps a particular textual meaning based on the consideration of a particular set of ECTs. So that, if the meaning grasped is different, not only is the text whose meaning is grasped different, but also the act of understanding whereby that meaning is grasped is different. Textual identity, which includes in turn identity of meaning, is a necessary condition of the intensional sameness of textual understanding. (The extensional sameness of the act of understanding must be explained in other terms, however, such as for example, the identity of the subject who carries out the act and the existential integrity of the act.)

With respect to the relation of the identity of texts to understanding matters appear quite different, however. For understanding does not appear to be, strictly speaking, a necessary condition of textual identity. Thus, one may be tempted at first glance to conclude that there is no relation here. When one looks at the matter more carefully, however, this conclusion is in need of qualification. The reason is that texts are conventional artifacts resulting from the activity of someone who connects certain ECTs to a specific meaning, and that meaning is connected to those ECTs through the acts of understanding of that person or persons. (More on this later.) Thus, the existence of a text presupposes that someone has had certain acts of understanding that connect a specific meaning to certain ECTs. But does this mean that the conditions of textual identity require, after all, the inclusion of understanding among them?

The answer to this question is negative, for having a certain meaning is sufficient for a text to be the same, provided its ECTs and their arrangement are also the same. That understanding be necessary in order for that meaning to be connected with those ECTs does not entail that understanding is a condition of textual identity or even of meaning identity. The relation between understanding and texts is causal. But causal relations do not imply that the causes in question are parts of the identity conditions of what they cause, because different causes may bring about the same effect.

Finally, it should be clear from what has been said that the understanding of a text is not a text. If it were to be conceived as a text, then we would be led into an infinite regress, for the understanding of that text would require another text, whose understanding would require still another one, and so on to infinity. The understanding of a text, that is, the understanding of its meaning, cannot be a text. Three distinct elements are involved in the understanding of a text: first, the text to be understood, that is, ECTs and meaning; second, the audience who understands the text; and third, the act of understanding that the audience has and through which the audience grasps the meaning of the text. No further text is necessary.

Note that in this discussion I have not dealt with the part of the question raised at the beginning that has to do with the historical author. I have dealt only with understanding and textual identity. The role of the historical author in this matter will be taken up and clarified later.

IV. Limits of Understanding

The second and third questions to which reference was made in Section II reveal two different issues that should be distinguished in order to be resolved. Indeed, some of the confusion in the literature today stems from the confusion between them and the failure of those who address those issues to keep them separate. The first concerns whether there are in fact limits to the understanding of texts beyond

which there is no longer understanding but misunderstanding. This is an epistemological issue properly speaking, for it has to do with knowledge—whether an
audience has it or not and how it is to be characterized. It raises the question of the
historical accuracy of what audiences think they know, and the limits that need to
be imposed on that knowledge in order for it to qualify as accurate or even as
knowledge at all.

The second issue revealed by these questions is not epistemological but
moral, for it concerns the right of audiences to understand texts as they wish. As
such it has to do with the attitudes or actions of audiences and not with the character of what audiences know or think they know. As a moral issue, perhaps this
issue should be treated separately from those discussed in this part of this book,
which is devoted primarily to epistemological matters. However, it is convenient
to raise it at present and it does have close connections to epistemology, as will
become evident shortly, so I shall deal with it here nonetheless.

Before these two issues are addressed, however, something must be said
about meaning, for the question concerned with the limits of understanding is
parasitic on the question concerned with the limits of meaning. We saw in Chapter 1 that meaning is what is understood when one is said to understand a text. So
that, if there are no limits to the meaning of a text, there can be no limits to its
understanding. And if there are limits to the meaning of a text, then there must be
some limits to its understanding. Moreover, also in Chapter 1, I spoke of the specific meaning that an author intends to convey through a text, yet we have not
established so far the conditions of specificity in textual meaning. Finally, earlier
in this chapter we saw that sameness of meaning was the condition of sameness
of understanding; that is, of acts of understanding considered intensionally. Therefore, it is necessary for us to establish, first, whether there are or are not limits to
the meaning of texts and, if there are limits, to determine, second, the factors that
establish those limits. Only after we have dealt with these matters can we return
to understanding.

A. Limits of Meaning

Two extreme positions on the issue of whether there are limits to the meaning of
texts stand out in the contemporary literature. As should be expected from what
has been said earlier concerning understanding and meaning, those positions
roughly correspond to the two extreme positions that can be taken with respect
to the question of the limits of understanding. One position claims that there are
no limits to the meaning of texts.[6] Note that this is not taken to imply that texts
have no meaning.[7] This view accepts that texts have meaning, but rejects that
there are any limitations that can be imposed on their meaning.[8] Texts, like signs,
are polysemous, that is, they are essentially ambiguous in the sense that they do
not have a single meaning but can mean anything whatsoever.[9] So it is impossible to pinpoint a meaning, or even a range of meaning, for a particular text that

would exclude some other meanings for that text. The meaning of a text is not determinate in any sense, but openended. Indeed, no text can ever be understood in the same way, for every understanding presupposes a different point of view from which the text is seen.[10]

The strength of this position lies in its recognition that there is wide disagreement as to the meaning of certain texts and that often texts are used to mean things their authors and their historical audiences could not have guessed. Indeed, often texts are understood by different persons, or even by the same person at different times, to mean different and even contradictory things, and no determination can be reached concerning which is the correct meaning of the text. In some cases it is evident that each generation, indeed each person, identifies a different meaning for a text, depending on perspective and context.

The problem with this view is that it does not appear to reflect, at least in its extreme form, experience, for, although there is wide disagreement as to the meaning of some texts, there is little or no disagreement as to the meaning of others. The 'No smoking' sign posted on my classroom wall means that no smoking is permitted in the room and not that smoking is permitted, a fact with which everyone who knows English must agree. This and other examples that can be easily cited indicate that this view is mistaken if it claims that *all* texts and *all* signs have no limitations in their meaning.

Moreover, this position would find it hard to account for communication through texts. Communication through texts involves the conveyance of meaning and such conveyance in turn presupposes that the meaning in question is determinate in at least some ways. Communication through texts implies some limits in the meaning of the texts in question, so that, if there are no limits, there can be no communication. But communication does occur, so there must be some limits to the meaning of texts.

At the opposite end of the spectrum is the view that all texts have strict and narrow limitations on their meaning, so that there is only one, narrowly understood, meaning per text.[11] The advantage of this view is that, unlike the previous one, it accounts for the communication that we experience occurs through texts. We communicate because the texts we use have only one meaning known to the communicants.

Moreover, prima facie the very use of texts seems to imply the intent to convey some specific meaning, as noted in Chapter 1, and a specific meaning must be one and only one, with precise limitations and boundaries. So that when I say, 'Smoking is prohibited here,' I mean that smoking is prohibited here and not that, for example, smoking is allowed here or that I expect it will rain tomorrow. What could be more obvious?

Yet, this position faces problems similar to those encountered by the previous view, for it does not account for our experience of the disagreement concerning the meaning of many texts. It is true that in some cases we can agree on the meaning of texts, but frequently we cannot agree even about the meaning of very simple texts. Disagreements arise even in cases where the context is quite specific and those who participate in the exchange of texts share much in common. How can it be argued, then, that every text has one and only one meaning?

Again, there are texts, such as literary ones, which seem to be open to multiple understandings, implying that they have many meanings. Nor do their authors or the societies in which they are produced become scandalized by this phenomenon. In fact, some authors openly acknowledge it.[12] Does it make any sense, then, to hold that every text has only one meaning?

Neither of these two positions appears sound, because neither accounts adequately for all of our experiences. Both in fact take into account only some texts, using them as paradigmatic of textuality, and thus exclude from the category others that are rightfull members of it. My view is that there are limits to the meaning of all texts but that those limits depend on a variety of factors, so that we should not understand the meaning of texts narrowly. In a way, then, there is only one meaning for every text, but that meaning is to be understood broadly so as to encompass much more than particular authors or audiences have in mind when they understand the texts. This allows me to maintain conditions of textual identity while at the same time explain the disagreements that arise concerning texts.

To explain better what is involved in this view, I must introduce three distinctions concerning the meaning of texts. They involve the distinction between what is essential and accidental in meaning, between meaning and the implications of meaning, and between meaning and intentions.

1. Essential and Accidental Differences in Meaning. The first point that needs to be made is that, when speaking of differences in the meaning of texts, it is important to distinguish between major and minor differences. Not all differences in texts imply differences in identity. There are cases of changes in the ECTs of a text, such as the substitution of a period by a semicolon, that do not always imply a change in the identity of the text. And the same can be said about the meaning of a text. Some changes in meaning are so minor that it makes no sense to say that there has been a change in textual identity.

To understand this point it is helpful to introduce a distinction between what is essential and what is accidental in a text. By minor differences I mean accidental ones, that is, differences that have no relevance for the identity of a text. In a text such as that of Augustine's *City of God*, the dropping of a repetitious sentence from the text could not be taken as essentially changing the text, the ECTs of which it is composed, or its meaning. It is, then, essential differences that concern us; that is, differences sufficiently fundamental to change the identity of the text.

Of course, one may want to argue at this point that what has been said does not tell us exactly how to distinguish between differences that are accidental and essential in the meaning of texts. How do we know that one rather than another meaning is the meaning of a text? Indeed, who determines the limits of identity that in turn determine the limits of meaning, and what are the criteria of identity of texts?

The answer to this difficulty is, first, that what is essential and accidental in a text is not the same for all texts, but depends on the text in question. What is essential and what is accidental in the text of *Don Quixote* is not what is essential and accidental in the text of *Hamlet*. So no specific criteria can be given that will serve for all texts. Second, for reasons that will become clear as we go along, the exact determination of what is essential and accidental in a text depends to a great extent not only on the text in question but on the type of text in question, as determined by the cultural function that it serves. So, again, it is not possible to formulate generally applicable criteria for all texts. Third, the criteria in question are to be arrived at, if at all, through a historical process in which audiences slowly determine such criteria after much discussion, investigation, and argument. Finally, the issue for us here does not concern specific criteria, but rather the existence of criteria, for what is at stake is not the identity of the criteria but whether there are criteria at all. The important point for us is to develop a view that accurately describes and accounts for the way we think and act with respect to the understanding and use of texts, and my contention is that a view that holds that there are specific criteria that distinguish between what is essential and accidental in meaning is more accurate and accounts better for our behavior with respect to texts than other views. At the same time, to hold such a view does not entail that the same criteria apply to all texts.

The actual search for the particular criteria that would determine the limits of the meaning of particular texts, such as the text of *Don Quixote*, is not part of philosophy. Indeed, it does not fall into a single discipline, but rather is divided into the various disciplines that study the subject matter where the texts in question function. It is, for example, in religion, and in particular religions at that, that criteria for the determination of the meaning of particular religious texts are developed, and it is in law that criteria for the establishment of the meaning of particular legal texts are developed, and so on. There are, of course, common hermeneutical issues to all these which can be dealt with in general, but when it comes to particular texts, the inquiry must take place within the discipline in which the function of the texts is studied, rather than in a single discipline, and least of all in philosophy. More on this later and also in Chapter 6.

2. Meaning and the Implications of Meaning. Apart from the distinction between what is essential and accidental in the meaning of a text, we must also distinguish, second, between the meaning of a text and the implications of that meaning, for it is often the case that these two are confused. The implications of the meaning of a text are derived from the meaning on the basis of other principles, and therefore are something different from the meaning.[13] Consider, for example, the text;

1. P · Q

The meaning of this text is that both P and Q. Now, it is obvious that P follows from 1, so that P is implied by 1. But this implication relies on a principle of implication not expressed by 1; nor is the implication itself expressed by 1. The implication is in fact expressed by a different text, namely;

2. (P · Q) → P

The textual differences between 1 and 2 can be traced both to the ECTs of 1 and 2 and to their respective meanings. Indeed, the truth tables of 1 and 2 are different, indicating a fundamental difference in meaning between the two. This makes clear that the meaning of a text is not the same as the implications of that meaning. We must keep in mind, then, that the limits of the meaning of a text do not extend to, so as to include, the implications of that meaning.

3. Meaning and Intentions. A third point that needs to be kept in mind when addressing the question of the limits of textual meaning is that meanings are different from intentions.[14] We have already noted that texts are different from both their meanings and the understanding of those meanings. Texts are groups of entities used as signs that are selected, arranged, and intended by authors to convey specific meanings to audiences. Meaning is what is understood when texts are understood. (Remember that we are concerned with only textual meaning here.) And understandings are the mental acts through which the meanings of texts are understood. Now we must also add that intentions are not texts, meanings, or understandings. That they are not texts seems quite evident from the definition of texts we have adopted, for that definition contains a reference to the intention of the author, thus precluding the identification of intentions with texts. But the fact that intentions are not understandings or meanings is less obvious.

It is true that, when we speak of authorial intentions or of the intentions of authors, it is sometimes the case that we mean something like the meaning or understanding of texts, although I shall argue that this leads to confusion, for neither meanings nor understandings strictly speaking are intentions.[15] Intentions may be expressed by texts, as when I say, "I intend to write a book on textuality," but they need not be so expressed. And that they need not be so expressed entails that they need not be meanings of texts. I may have the intention to write a book on textuality and never express such an intention in a text.

Likewise, intentions are not understandings, for, although we sometimes understand our intentions and those of others, the intentions themselves are not the acts of understanding whereby we understand them.[16] The nature of intentions is too complicated to be discussed in passing, let alone be dealt with adequately here, but for our purposes it is sufficient to note that, whatever they ultimately turn out to be, they should not be confused with texts, their meaning, or the understanding of that meaning.

In discussions of textuality, what is often meant by intentions is something like an intended text, an intended meaning, or an intended understanding. In Chapter 3, we saw that the notion of an intended text is not viable unless by it one means simply the text the author actually produces. There is no such thing as an intended text in the mind of the author or anywhere else before the author actually produces the text in his mind or outside it. A text is an artifact constituted by entities through which an author tries to convey some meaning, but there is no intended text other than the produced text. If there is no intended text, however, then there can be no completely determined intended meaning before the text is actually produced. The author does not have a completely determined text in mind before producing it, nor does the author have a completely determined meaning in mind separate from the entities he or she uses before actually producing the text, that is, before selecting and arranging the signs that compose the text. The author may have some general intentions and some vague ideas he or she wants to convey, but those can hardly be regarded as a completely determined meaning, for those intentions and ideas could produce very different texts and, moreover, could change in the process of textual production.

Thus, the notion of a completely determined intended meaning considered as something other than the meaning of the actually produced text is not viable, for the meaning of a text results from the process of textual production in which the same person plays the roles of author and audience until the text is completed. There is no completely predetermined textual meaning. The most there is, is a set of vague ideas that an author wishes to convey. So, as in the case of the intended text, for most intents and purposes the intended meaning is nothing but the meaning of the produced text.

The talk of intended meaning arises as a result of the consideration of cases in which a mental text is translated into a physical text, say a written one, that has the same meaning as the mental one. In this case, there is already an understanding of a determinate meaning in the mind of the author of the mental text which he or she then proceeds to express in the written text. In this sense one could speak of an intended meaning. But note that the meaning exists because the mental text exists, so that it is not the case that authors need have, create, or understand meanings apart from texts. One can, as this case shows, think about the meaning of, say, text A and convey that meaning through text B, and in that sense speak of the intended meaning of B. But, if there is no text A, it makes no sense to talk about the intended meaning of text B as completely and determinately preexisting B in the mind of the author.

Finally, if there is no determinate intended meaning prior to the production of a text, there cannot be a determinate intended understanding, for an intended understanding is the understanding of the intended meaning. The intended understanding, then, can be taken only as the accurate understanding of the meaning of a produced text.

Now, the distinction between intentions, on the one hand, and texts, meanings, and understandings, on the other, and the rejection of the distinction between intended text, intended meaning, and intended understanding, on the one hand, and text, meaning, and understanding, on the other, are important because the issue of the limits of understanding may be posed in terms of authorial intentions. That is, it may be argued that the limits to the understanding of a text are determined not by the author's understanding but by the author's intentions. Contrary to this view, however, I shall argue that, although there are limits to the meanings of texts, such limits are not exclusively established by authors and their intentions. Moreover, I shall argue, in accordance with the definition of texts given in Chapter 1, that the meaning of a text is in fact what the author intends to convey through it. And this even though the author may not be the sole cause of that meaning or may not even be fully aware of all of it.

I would like to propose, then, that the meanings of texts have certain limits and that these limits are to be understood in terms of an essential core of meaning rather than including everything that may be understood when one says one understands a text. Moreover, I claim that the meaning is not to be confused with the implications of the meaning or with any intentions or understandings that the authors of the texts may have had in mind when they produced the text. What constitutes this core in each case varies from text to text. No rules apply across the board to all texts. But that there are no criteria across the board does not mean there are no criteria at all, as proponents of the no-limit position argue. Nor can one argue that because we do not have established or known criteria—even if this were so for all texts, which it is not—there are no limits to the meaning of texts. At the same time, and contrary to the strict one-meaning view, the meanings of texts do not always have strict and narrow limitations so that one can speak, for example, of the so-called literal meaning of a text as its meaning.[17] To understand how those limits work, we must turn to the factors that play a role in establishing them. In short, we need to know who or what determines the meaning of texts.

B. Factors That Establish the Limits of Meaning

Several possibilities suggest themselves with regard to this question: author, audience, context, society, language, and the text itself. None of these, taken by itself, seems to fit the bill, however. I shall say something about all of them but shall pay closer attention to the first and last in particular because they have attracted more attention in the recent literature, before I turn to my own position. Let me begin with the author.

1. Author. Nothing would appear more obvious, at first glance, than the author determines the meaning of a text.[18] Indeed, because the author creates the text, it must be the author who determines the boundaries of its meaning. After all, the author selects and arranges the signs of which a text is composed to convey a specific meaning to an audience. And the ECTs used as signs are not naturally tied to any meaning in particular. Thus, it appears to make sense to say that an author is responsible not only for giving meaning to the ECTs used, but also for the meaning itself of those ECTs and the text they constitute.

When one speaks of the author as responsible for the limits imposed on the meaning of a text, however, one may be referring to the author's intention to convey the meaning or to the author's understanding of the meaning. Thus we must explore both possibilities if we are going to determine whether in fact the author is to be held responsible for the semantic boundaries of the text.

The first possibility can be easily dismissed based on what has already been said about meaning and authorial intentions.[19] An author's intention is simply to convey a specific meaning, so the intention by itself does not impose limits on the meaning of a text, but the intention coupled with the specific meaning in question. And we have seen that the author's intentions, or any intentions for that matter, cannot be identified with a meaning. Moreover, as noted earlier, there is no determinate intended meaning of which an author is fully aware prior to the production of a text except in cases where the author intends to translate one text into another and thus to express the meaning of one text through some other text. But this situation cannot be applied to all cases and therefore cannot substantiate the view that the author's intention always determines the meaning of a text; indeed, an attempt to apply it to all cases would yield an infinite regress. Keep in mind that, as noted in Chapter 1, that the meaning included has limits does not entail that the author always determines such limits or is even aware of them.

Finally, even if we were to accept that authorial intentions determine meaning, it is a well-known fact that often authors use signs in their texts that do not express the meaning they are supposed to have intended. Nothing is more common than slips of the tongue, for example, that result in oral texts whose meaning is clearly not the meaning intended by those who utter the text. And the same happens in written texts. In such cases, it cannot be argued that the meaning of the texts is exclusively determined by the author's intention.

If the author's intention alone does not impose limits on the meaning of a text, then we may ask whether it is not the author's understanding that imposes such limits.[20] And, indeed, the answer appears prima facie obvious, for the author's understanding of a meaning makes possible the connection of the meaning to the ECTs of the text; there is no text if there is no authorial understanding of the meaning that is intended to be conveyed through the ECTs. Hence, it makes sense to argue that the party who sets the limits to meaning is the historical author, who is the creator of the first instance of the text by using some ECTs as signs to convey the specific meaning he or she understands.

Matters, however, do not appear so simple upon reflection. Of course, if the text produced by an author is the result of entirely new signs designed by the author, which are stipulatively used to express a specific meaning, then one may be able to claim that the author is fully and singly responsible for the text and its meaning. However, most texts produced by authors do not fall into this category, for the signs authors use in their texts are already in use and belong to natural languages; they are not created by the author of the text. Those signs have established meanings and functions within particular cultures and languages of which authors may not be completely knowledgeable. Moreover, the arrangements in which those signs are placed follow general rules well-established in particular societies; namely, the syntactical rules of natural languages. And all of this means that authors do not generally make up the conventions that connect meaning to signs and their arrangements. Indeed, as we saw in Chapter 1, authorial intention does not entail full awareness of textual meaning. Authors are responsible for the introduction of elements of novelty, but these elements are built up on much that is common, well-established, and known. Under these conditions it is not possible to argue that authors bear exclusive responsibility for the texts they produce.

Indeed, often authors may know less about the meanings of the signs they use and the ways they can be meaningfully arranged than their audiences. And this leads to the production of texts whose meaning is different from the meaning the authors think they have.[21] I shall return to this point later.

Finally, it is a well-known that authors frequently change their minds about the meanings of the texts they have created. How can one argue, then, that they determine meaning if they are not sure of what that meaning is? Perhaps the meaning in question is the one the authors understood when they first produced the text, but that surely seems an arbitrary interpretation.

2. Audience. If the author does not determine the meaning of the text, then it could be the audience that does so.[22] This makes sense insofar as it explains mutually incompatible, but equally acceptable, understandings of the same text. Moreover, as we have said earlier, often audiences know better the meaning of a text than the historical authors, and this could be explained by saying that they do because they determine that meaning.

As in the case of the author, we may distinguish between the intention and understanding of audiences.[23] The thesis that holds that the intentions of audiences alone determine the meanings of texts fails for various reasons. In the first place, as already noted, intentions are not meanings and therefore cannot by themselves alone impose limits on the meanings of texts. For them to be able to accomplish this the audiences would have to have access to meanings, and then it would not be the intentions alone but the intentions plus the meanings that together determine the limits of the meaning of the text. Second, the intentions of audiences when they approach texts are generally to understand the texts or to use them in one way or another and not to give them meaning. Indeed, even in cases where audiences have meanings in mind that they wish to project onto texts, whether consciously or unconsciously, they feel constrained by the limitations they perceive the texts impose on them. This is why, when audiences are committed to making a text have a certain meaning, they often modify and change the signs or arrangements of the signs, or add to the text.

If, instead of intentions, the audience's understanding is held to determine the meaning of texts, this also fails for two reasons. First and foremost, because to say so entails defeating the very purpose of texts. Texts are created, used, and intended to convey specific meanings, which entails certain limitations on the meaning.[24] But if it were the prerogative of audiences to establish the meanings, then communication would be thwarted, for there would be nothing specific to convey.

The second difficulty is that to say that audiences set the limits of meaning amounts to saying that the meanings of texts have no effective limits, because the number and the type of audiences texts can have is potentially infinite.[25] So this position turns into one of the already discarded views concerning this issue. Particular audiences are not the creators of the signs that compose texts or the rules according to which those signs are arranged. Indeed, particular audiences are in the same position as authors with respect to those signs and rules—they have, as it were, inherited them. Indeed, they are in a worse position than authors, for they have no option to arrange and change them at will, if they are to act as audiences—we must remember that texts lack the flexibility of language. So how can it make sense to say that audiences impose the limits on textual meanings?

3. Context. Context could also be regarded as what determines the meaning of texts. A historicist might argue, for example, that the historical location of a text determines the boundaries of its meaning.[26] And, indeed, it makes sense to bring in context, for, as is evident from the examples and discussion in Chapter 1, context is a factor in the identity of texts and their meaning. After all, the same ECTs can be endowed with quite different meanings in different contexts.[27] Borges makes the point dramatically by pointing out that the text of *Don Quixote* written by Cervantes in the seventeenth century and by Pierre Menard in the twentieth would have different meanings.[28]

However, no matter how context is taken, this position faces difficulties. If context excludes the author and audience, for example, then it clearly cannot determine meaning, for a text divorced from an author and an audience is no more than a group of entities without meaning, because no one has endowed its ECTs with meaning. But if the author and the audience are included, then it is not clear how this position would substantially differ from the two already discussed. Even if the view of context presented in Chapter 1 were stretched somehow, it would not be sufficient to yield what would be necessary for this position to work.[29]

4. Society. Society may also be considered as the determining factor of the limits of the meaning of a text. After all, society at large is responsible for the development of the signs that compose nonstipulative texts and the rules that govern the arrangements of those signs. Indeed, society is responsible for language and texts are generally expressed in language. So what better candidate to explain the limits of textual meaning?[30]

One difficulty with this position is that society is nothing but individual persons, who are related to texts as authors or audiences. There is no entity, no mind, who is society and to whom we could assign the intentions and understandings necessary for the determination of the limits of the meaning of texts. Society is nothing other than persons who function as authors and audiences or persons who function as neither. If the first, then to say that society is responsible for the limits on the meaning of texts is simply to recognize that texts have authors and audiences and that the limits of their meanings are imposed by them.[31] If the second, then there is no relation of society to the texts and thus no explanation of how society could be responsible for the limits of the meaning of texts. Indeed, although the language used in a text is the result of society, this does not entail that the meaning of the particular text is so, for society is not the one who composed the text and thus selected the particular signs and arrangements of those signs used in it. One may perhaps wish to say that society is responsible insofar as the texts, and therefore their meanings, are logical possibilities entailed by the language created by society—I shall discuss language next—but it makes no sense to say that a text and its meaning are the result of society when no one in that society has actually produced them. Texts are historical entities and thus require instantiation.

5. Language. This brings us to language, for a language seems virtually to contain in it all the possible texts and their meanings that can be expressed in that language. Therefore, one could argue that it is in a language that the limits of textual meanings are to be found. Then, no particular author or audience is responsible for determining the meaning of particular texts, for no particular author or audience is responsible for a particular meaning. The individual persons who make up the society that developed a language are responsible for the signs used in the texts composed in that language and the semantic significance of the syntactical rules according to which they are arranged, but the persons themselves are not responsible for the texts for no single person is the creator of the language.[32]

Language by itself, however, cannot be regarded as setting the limits of the meaning of texts for several reasons.[33] In the first place, because the meaning of texts, and thus of the signs and arrangements that compose a language, depend also on context, and context is not always linguistic or textual. Second, because language may contain virtually an infinite number of possible texts and meanings, but such virtual containment does not entail any actual texts or textual meanings. The situation here is similar to what we saw with a meaning and the implications of the meaning. A language, that is, a group of signs and rules of arrangements for those signs, may be arranged in many ways, thus implying many texts, but for there to be any texts decisions have to be made as to the implementation of certain rules with respect to certain signs. This means that texts and their particular meanings cannot exclusively be the result of language.

Indeed, languages by themselves are inert; they are collections of signs and rules for the arrangements of those signs, which need users to implement them and compose texts out of them. Languages are not alive, and they function only to the extent that users use them. Hence, users should be held responsible for the development of texts out of languages. The role of users is so important that languages are subject to constant changes by them. So it turns out that, except for dead languages or those that are the product of stipulation, languages are in a constant process of change as a result of the uses to which they are put. And this applies not just to the meanings of the signs that compose them, but also to the rules used to arrange those signs. This is perhaps another way of saying that languages, like texts, depend on those who use and understand them and therefore cannot be held exclusively responsible for texts and the limits of their meaning.

6. Text. One of the most prevalent views on this matter nowadays is that the limits on the meaning of texts are exclusively imposed by the texts themselves.[34] This is a clever view that aims to sidestep the problems associated with the other views already presented. Unlike language, for example, the text is not just a group of signs and rules that need to be arranged to convey textual meaning, but a concrete group of signs that display a particular organization, a series of marks and blanks.[35] This imposes certain limitations on its meaning no doubt, but such limitations are not such that the freedom of audiences to understand it in incompatible ways is ruled out.[36] Hence, this view preserves this important aspect of our experience concerning texts. By making the text the determinant of meaning, this position avoids, moreover, the difficulties associated with the recovery of the historical meaning of the text as understood by the historical author or a particular audience. Further, it also avoids the problems faced by the view that makes society the determinant of textual meaning, for the text itself and not society and the other causes that may give rise to it establish the parameters of meaning. Audiences, then, are liberated from the shackels of authorial intention and understanding, and restricted in their understanding only by the text itself. The audience can attach any meaning it wishes to a text as long as such a meaning can be consistently attached to such a text, although some authors seem to speak as if even consistency were irrelevant.[37]

There are three possible versions of this view, depending on what its proponents understand by a text.[38] According to one, the text is to be identified simply with the entities that constitute it (ECTs).[39] That is, a text is not composed of particular signs that, because they belong to a language, have determinate meanings. The advantage of this position is that it preserves consistency and allows maximum freedom of understanding in audiences. It preserves consistency because it allows no factor other than the entities that constitute the text to determine its meaning and those entities themselves have no semantic boundaries. Now, if the text were understood as composed of signs with established meanings, the source of those meanings could not be the signs themselves but rather whatever determined the meanings of the signs. So that, under these conditions, the text after all would not be the sole determinant of its meaning, but rather would depend on something outside itself for its meaning. That this view allows for maximum freedom of understanding should be obvious from the fact that it accepts no semantic limitations properly speaking, because the text is merely a group of entities open to having meaning but in themselves have no particular meaning.

Apart from the fact that this position, as we shall see immediately, faces serious difficulties, one of the problems with it is that it has not been presented clearly anywhere. But perhaps an example might help us understand it. Let us suppose that we have a text composed of five signs arranged as follows:

* - | ~ ^

Five different audiences confronted with it might regard it as having the following meanings:

1.   Cats are very smart.
2.   Cats are very dumb.
3.   Dogs are incorrigible.
4.   All liars are liars.
5.   Nature cats obvious fast here there.

If I understand the view correctly, 1 and 2 are both acceptable meanings of the text. The reasons are that they each contain five signs and they make sense. These meanings are allowed by the parameters established by the text. These parameters have to do with the number of signs and their arrangement and whatever other semantically relevant features the text may have. The parameters have nothing to do with anything outside the text, such as the present context, society, the author, or the historical circumstances within which the text was produced. Moreover, the fact that 1 and 2 contradict each other is irrelevant as long as the meanings in question can be borne by the text.

By contrast, 5 does not qualify as a legitimate meaning for two reasons: it makes no sense and meanings of texts should make sense; and it has seven meanings for only five signs. So 5 is not an appropriate meaning, then, because it is not consistent with the semantic parameters internal to the text. Of course, even here one could argue that if four signs of the text express two meanings there may be sense to 5 after all. But the burden of showing so appears daunting.

With 4 the problem is that one meaning (liars) is repeated twice, but there are no sign repetitions in the text. So it looks like 4 cannot be a legitimate meaning for the text unless an explanation can be given of this irregularity.

Finally, the problem with 3 is that it has only four meanings whereas the text has five signs. This would seem to disqualify it unless one had a reason to consolidate two signs into one, by saying, for example, the '~' and '^' go together to express "incorrigible," which is composed of "corrigible" and its negation.

There is, therefore, a great deal of latitude for the meaning of texts, but there is no complete license.[40] Moreover, the longer and more complicated texts are, the fewer are the number of meanings that can be legitimately attributed to them. Whereas a short text, like the one provided, may have a very large number of meanings arising from the relatively small number of limits it imposes on those meanings, in a long text, such as the text of *Don Quixote*, the limitations are many more and thus the possible meanings of the text are many less. Indeed, the length and complexity of a text seem to be inversely proportional to the number of meanings that can be legitimaly attributed to it.

In spite of the advantages of this view, the problems with it are very serious. Indeed, after considering them, one wonders why anyone would want to subscribe to it. A long list of criticisms have been piled up against it or its various versions.[41] I shall dispense with most of these and concentrate on what I believe are its most serious drawbacks. One of these is that if texts are, as I have noted in Chapter 1, constituted by entities conventionally endowed with meaning, those entities themselves cannot determine the meaning. The marks that were just taken as a text are by themselves only marks. They become a text only if they are endowed with meaning, but such endowment requires someone who does so, and thus the marks themselves cannot be said to impose limits on their meaning, for in themselves they have no meaning.

Strictly speaking, there is no reason, for example, why the text given earlier could not have as meaning much more than the meanings we said it legitimately could have. For, as long as we have an explanation of how the meaning is tied to its ECTs, the meaning would be legitimate. The possibilities, then, are staggering. For example, there is no reason why one could not regard the text as meaning everything the Bible means. The first sign would stand for the meanings of, say, the Pentateuch, and the second for the meaning of some other books, and so on. That this is possible shows that it is not the entities that constitute texts, then, that can determine their meaning.

This leads me to the second version of this view, in which a text is not conceived as simply a group of entities that are the locus of meaning, but as a group of signs that have determinate meanings and are arranged in syntactically significant ways.[42] This position solves some of the problems confronted by the previous position, for now there is a source of the meaning of the text: The meaning of the text is determined, and thus limited, by the meanings of the signs of which it is composed and the arrangement into which those signs are organized. But this position has difficulties of its own.

The main difficulty was already noted in the context of the previously discussed version of this position. It is its inconsistency. For the signs that constitute texts are in themselves entities without meaning that receive meaning only insofar as they are selected and arranged to do so in a certain context. This entails that their meaning is determined by factors outside, that is, external to, themselves and also to the text; indeed, the meaning is determined by nontextual factors including grammatical rules, usages, contexts, and so on.[43] Therefore, it makes no sense to say that the text is its sole determinant of meaning, or that the factors that determine the meaning of a text are only internal, unless in those factors are included all sorts of things that are neither part of the text nor textual in character. Of course, if such factors are in fact included, then the position is very different from what it portrays itself to be.

The third possibility, defended by the extreme left of the postmodernist camp, argues that there are no limits to the interpretation of texts because no text precedes its understanding by an audience. Contrary to what criticism used to think,[44] there is nothing that antecedes an understanding of a text. The text is a construction of such an understanding.[45] Under these conditions, of course, there can be no limits to the understanding of texts.

There are two criticisms I would like to make of this view. The first is that, in spite of the emphasis on freedom of understanding, this position must accept constraints on such understanding at least from the side of the audience. For texts, even if they do not exist in themselves, as antecedents of an understanding, exist as a result of or in an understanding, and such an understanding requires an audience that enacts or has it. Thus, the audience, and whatever constraints are imposed on it by its subjectivity, imposes limits on understanding. Indeed, this point of view amounts to the one explored earlier in which the audience turns out to be the sole factor of limitation in the understanding of texts.

The second criticism is that, even if there are no limits to the understanding of a text, there must be something that antecedes or at least functions as referent or point of departure for that understanding. Understanding, like discourse, refers to something even if what is understood about it is not fixed by the object in question.[46] The question is whether that something consists simply of ECTs considered independent of any meaning or of ECTs endowed with meaning. Therefore, this position ends up as one of the two previously explored.

In short, texts may be considered either as ECTs or as ECTs with a determinate meaning. If they are merely ECTs, then they cannot determine meaning, for ECTs have meaning only insofar as they are endowed with meaning on the basis of something external to them. And if texts are considered ECTs with meaning, then the meaning must result from the factors that connected that particular meaning to the ECTs in question. In neither case does the text, considered as ECTs, or as ECTs with meaning, exclusively determines its meaning.

This is evident in the way we go about determining the meaning of texts, as will become evident in Chapter 6, for such determination involves factors other than the texts themselves. It is evident in the historical nature of texts, the fact that they are artifacts, that is, products of art in which entities of various sorts are conventionally endowed with meaning. And, finally, it is evident in the very purpose of texts, which is to convey meaning. Texts are not realities of their own, floating Platonic forms that impose themselves on those who understand them. Texts are the historical creations of persons who generally use historically developed languages to communicate with other persons.

Of course, some of those who adhere to the position we have been discussing defend themselves by pointing out that they do not see a text as isolated from everything else but rather in a context that supplies constraints and a framework for understanding.[47] And there is much effort to try to show that, although meaning is constructed by audiences, this does not entail that it is arbitrary, so that no good reasons can be given for understanding in one way rather than another.[48] But these arguments are bound to fail as long as the constraints imposed on textual meaning are determined only by the text and it is not made clear what that entails.

To preserve the possibility of conflicting, but equally or nearly equally legitimate, meanings for a text it is not necessary to go to the extremes proposed by the view that the texts themselves establish the limits of their meaning, or any of the other views discussed earlier. The meaning of a text is not determined exclusively by its author, audience, context, society, language, or the text itself. The author understands the text to have a certain meaning; but by writing it in a language already in existence, the author cannot be held exclusively responsible even for the meaning he or she understands the text to have. And in many cases, the author is not fully aware of the meaning of the text. Audiences, as part of the society that uses and develops the language used in the text, again have a role to play, but it is not an exclusive role. Context is important insofar as the meaning of texts depends to a great extent on the circumstances that surround it. And, finally, the text itself imposes some limitations of its own.[49]

7. Cultural Function. Even all these factors taken together are not enough, however. A key element that has not been mentioned is the cultural function that the text has, for the function of the text as determined by the culture in which the text is produced and, added to the factors already discussed, also plays an important role in the determination of the limits of textual meaning. Let me illustrate. Some texts, such as '2 + 2 = 4' and 'No smoking,' have very strict limits of meaning. The reason for the strict limits of the first text is that it is a scientific text whose meaning, as determined by the cultural function of scientific texts, needs to be exact. The reason for the strict limits of the second is that it is a prescription for behavior, again in accordance with the cultural function of prescriptions. In both cases, the cultural function of the text—scientific in the first case and prescriptive in the second—establishes the strict limits of the meaning. The function tells both authors and audiences that texts such as the ones mentioned are narrow in meaning. But this does not mean that all texts have the same degree of limitation. Some texts may have very broad or even fuzzy limits to their meaning, and some may be such that their meaning is openended. In all these cases, the cultural function plays an important role.

One of the sources of much of the dispute concerning texts and the limits of their meaning is precisely the attempt to view all texts as having the same cultural function and thus to be subjected to the same parameters of meaning.[50] Indeed, there are those who wish to see all texts as scientific, for example, whereas others wish to view them as poetic.[51]

What has been said does not entail, however, that language, society, and context have no role to play. Indeed, language provides the signs and rules used to produce texts; society, in the form of individual persons who function as authors and audiences, maintains and develops the semantic significance of the elements of language used in texts; and contexts establish further conditions and limitations as they are considered by authors and audiences.

A culture, then, understood as a community of persons who share certain values, beliefs, and rules of behavior, determines the function of texts and those functions in turn establish the overall parameters of meaning. How the exact parameters are determined varies a great deal. In some cases, they are broad and can be determined by anyone in the community, but at other times they are narrow and up to particular groups. A particular society may establish, for example, that the limits of a text it regards as having a religious function may be determined only by certain members of the community, such as a prophet, a priest, or a group of persons who constitute a council. The meaning of texts with a scientific function is generally up to scientists; of a text with a legal function, it is up to lawyers and judges; and so on.[52] In all these cases, cultures develop rules for the determination of meaning and thus rely on expertise and authority. In many cases, credentials are required. Obviously, not everyone can determine the meaning of texts. In some cases, the function of texts is such that the author determines it, but in others it is a particular audience, or any audience for that matter. In all cases, however, the function of the text as determined by the culture establishes the rules to be applied. Note that this view of determination does not imply that the groups in question stipulatively establish the limits of meaning. The determination of meaning may indeed be stipulative in some cases. That a person or group is considered to have authority to determine the limits of meaning often entails only that such a person or group is believed to know how to go about understanding the meaning in question or that they can, more than others, approximate it.

The role of function indicates how the limits of meaning are established through the rules that govern the use of texts in particular cultures. Wittgenstein was right, then, when he introduced the metaphor of games in this context.[53] For the use and understanding of texts involves following certain rules agreed upon, and those rules are the ones that determine the limits in the meaning of texts. Insofar as they are rules of usage they are normative, for they are meant to be followed by those who engage in the games of communication within a particular society.[54]

Now we can see how it is possible to hold, as I proposed earlier, that there are limits to the meaning of texts but that such limits are not always strict and narrow.[55] For the limits on the meaning of texts depend ultimately on the cultural function texts perform, and that function may determine that the limits in question be strict, broad, vague, or even openended. Moreover, the way the cultural function determines these limits is not always directly, by determining the limits of meaning. Often the cultural function determines the meaning by identifying the person or group of persons in a society who have the responsibility of establishing those limits.

Note that, according to this view, it is a mistake to speak of different meanings of the same text, if by that one has in mind meanings that are not part of the overall meaning of the text.[56] As already explained, different meanings imply different texts. To speak, then, of an author's meaning, an audience's meaning, a literal meaning, and so on, as many do, is unnecessary. Much of this talk is based on a confusion between meaning and understanding. For those who wish to speak this way assume that intensionally different understandings of a text imply that the text has different meanings.

The view I propose is one in which the meaning of texts is determined by various factors, in accordance with the cultural function of the texts in question. In some cases, the cultural function determines that the author's understanding of the text is the determinant factor of the meaning and in other cases it is the audience, or the context, or various factors combined and so on. The meaning of texts is not always determined in the same way because texts have different functions. Thus, it makes no sense to speak of all texts as having certain types of meanings, such as literal, authorial, or contextual, for example. Or of all textual meanings as being, say, authorial. The meaning of a text generally depends on the cultural function it has, which in turn determines the factors relevant for the determination of that meaning. Attempts to establish that all texts have certain types of meanings, such as literal, authorial, or contextual, for example, fail because they do not take into account cultural function.

Nor do I want to argue that the core of meaning of a text is always the same. Texts do have a core of meaning, but what that core is and how stable it is depends again on the cultural function the text performs, that is, on how society has come to look at the text.[57] Thus, there is ample room for change as well as for continuity and stability. The point is that there cannot be uniform rules for all texts regarding these matters, because texts function differently, and it is the functions they have, as determined by the culture, that have the last word.

What has been said concerning the limits of meaning might appear to contradict the view that different meanings imply different textual identity. This applies also to signs. 'Cape,' when used to mean an article of clothing, and 'cape,' when used to mean a piece of land, are two different signs. But there is no contradiction involved because here I am not arguing that the same sign or text may have different meanings. What I am arguing is that the cultural function directly or indirectly determines the limits of textual meaning and thus establishes the identity conditions of a particular meaning. As long as the meaning is the same, the text can be the same, even if the meaning in question does not in some cases have strict boundaries. We can still hold, then, that meaning identity is a necessary condition of textual identity and also that the meaning in question may be broad or even openended.

At this point I should perhaps add that so far I have left undetermined the conditions of sameness of syntactical arrangements and type-signs vis-à-vis textual identity. But now I would like to suggest that, like the conditions of the sameness of meaning, a variety of factors determine these conditions as measured by the cultural function of the text. Thus ultimately, whether changes in syntactical arrangements and the type-signs that compose a text involve a change of textual identity will depend, as in the case of meaning, on the cultural function of the text. But now let me go back to meaning.

There are still two other objections to which I must respond if the view I propose concerning the factors that establish the limits of the meaning of texts is to be taken seriously. First, someone may argue that if the meanings of texts can be openended, then they cannot function effectively for the identification of works and thus it must be the text considered apart from that meaning that functions in this way.[58]

This objection is well taken against the view that determines the identity of works simply on the basis of the works themselves; that is, meanings. My view, however, is that works are the meanings *of texts*, and thus their identity conditions cannot ignore this fact. Textual identity includes the work, that is, meaning identity; but meaning identity depends also on its relation to other aspects of the text in cases where the culture determines that such a tie is essential. This is obviously the case with most works and particularly works of art and literature, where material features are essential to the identity of a work.[59] But this is not the case for every meaning. The meaning of '2 + 2 = 4,' for example, has conditions of identity that are not tied to the physical or syntactical features of that text.

Another objection points out that what has been said here seems to contradict the definition of texts presented in Chapter 1. There, texts were defined as involving authors who intended to convey specific meanings. But now we find not only that texts may have openended meanings but that authors may not determine them.

The answer to this objection is, first, that texts may not have a strict and narrow meaning, but include a wide range of meaning as determined by the cultural function they have does not entail that we cannot speak of the meaning of the texts. As already noted, we may still speak of a core of meaning, even if that core is more or less openended depending on cultural function.

Second, even if the author does not determine everything contained in that core of meaning, and in fact may be unaware of much contained in it, he or she can still be conceived as intending it. The reason is to be found in that the authorial role is a social one in which a person plays a part, using social conventions in a cultural context. This role implies the intention to convey a certain meaning, even when that meaning is not exhausted, because of the particular cultural function of the text in question, by the author. We can speak, then, about an author's intention to convey a specific meaning to an audience even when the author does not determine all of it or is aware of most of it.

This is not very different from what happens in a game, when one of the players makes a move the significance of which he does not quite grasp. For the player is the author of the move, and wins or loses accordingly, by virtue of the fact that he is a player engaged in the game. Likewise, an author is a player in the textual game and, in authoring a text, is to be taken as intending to convey a specific meaning, even if not fully aware of all that is contained in the specific meaning in question.

Having established, then, that there are limits to the meanings of texts, and that those limits are the result of a variety of factors whose role is determined by the cultural function particular texts have, we must now turn to the limits of the understanding of texts.

C. Limits of Textual Understanding

This is one of the most, if not perhaps the most, debated issue in hermeneutics today. Most often it is referred to as the issue concerned with "the limits of interpretation," but what is meant by *interpretation* in this context is what I have called *understanding* in this chapter. I choose a different terminology because the use of current nomenclature often results in confusions that could be easily avoided if one made a distinction between understanding and interpretation. This distinction will become clearer in Chapter 5, where I discuss interpretation in detail. For the moment it is sufficient to note that what we are concerned with are the limits of understanding, even though this is generally discussed in the literature as the limits of interpretation.[60]

Note that my concern is not with the limits of understanding when understanding is taken extensionally. That would be either a logical issue concerned with the analysis of the notion of an act of understanding or a metaphysical one concerned with the identity and ontological status of individual acts of understanding. Rather, what is at stake here is the degree to which audiences are free to understand texts without falling into misunderstanding. Can audiences understand texts in any way they wish, without any constraints imposed on them what-soever? Or are audiences limited in the way they understand texts so that, if they go beyond certain limits in their understanding, they are no longer understanding but are misunderstanding texts?

As already noted, the question of the limits of understanding is parasitic on that of the limits of meaning. For indeed, if there are no limits to the meaning of texts, there cannot be limits to their understanding and thus no misunderstanding is possible. And if there are limits to the meaning of texts, it is to be expected that there be limits to their understanding, so that, to go beyond the limit of the mean-ing of a text in understanding is to misunderstand it. Because I have argued that there are in fact limits to the meanings of texts, it stands to reason that there will also be limits to their understanding. Does this entail that it is not possible to have equally legitimate, but contradictory, understandings of the same text? Can an audience understand a text differently than its author without misunderstanding it? Indeed, can an audience understand a text better than its author? Before I turn to these questions, it might be useful to look briefly at the views under discussion in the current literature concerning this issue.

It often appears to those who survey the current literature on this topic that there are as many positions with respect to this issue as there are philosophers discussing it. In general these many views can be divided into three groups. One group holds that there are strict limits on the understanding of a text and that those limits are imposed by the author of the text, so that understanding a text in ways other than the way in which it was understood by the author at the time of com-position implies misunderstanding it.[61] After all, texts are instruments authors use to convey specific meanings. So, to understand a text differently from the way the historical author understood it is to misunderstand it and leads to historical inac-curacies that are downright pernicious and certainly unfair to the author. The author has a proprietary interest in the text, having created it, and thus audiences must submit to the author and accept his or her dominion.[62] If they want to under-stand a text differently than its author, they must accept that they are not dealing with the same text but rather with a contemporary text composed of the same ECTs as the historical text but with a different meaning. In short, audiences must under-stand historical texts as their authors understood them, otherwise audiences do not understand, but rather misunderstand them.

This view has much in common with the view that there are strict limits to the meanings of texts but should not be confused with it. Meaning is not the same thing as understanding, and not all those who believe there are strict limits to the meaning of a text identify the author's understanding as determinant of that mean-ing.

The reasons for adopting the view that audiences must understand histori-cal texts as their authors understood them appear very sensible and are rooted both in a desire to respect the wishes of historical authors and also in a concern for historical accuracy and effective communication. To look at texts and understand them, irrespective of the understanding their historical authors had in the historical context in which the texts were produced, appears to imply giving up on scientific objectivity and historical accuracy. Indeed, the consequences of this rejection go so deep that they appear to undermine the very foundations of communication, leading inevitably to a tower of Babel or to silence.

At the opposite extreme of the spectrum are those who see texts as self-contained entities independent from their historical authors, their intended and contemporaneous audiences, and the contexts in which they were produced. Texts are entities that have meaning, but the way the meaning is to be understood is open to audiences and thus audiences are free to understand texts as they see fit. Of course, this does not entail complete license. Some of the proponents of this point of view would grant that a text in English, for example, cannot be understood as a text in French would, even if the ECTs of the texts are similar or even the same. The point can be easily seen with signs, for there are some French words that look the same as English words yet they mean different things in the two languages. Most adherents to this position generally grant that there are some constraints on the understanding of texts, but those constraints are not to be found outside texts, but in them. They particularly object to constraints that involve the historical author, his or her contemporaneous audience, and the historical context in which the text was produced.[63]

Obviously, this position is closely related to the view that there are no limits to the meaning of texts, but should not be confused with it. The rationale for this is easily stated. Those who adopt this view are concerned with the excessive importance given to the historical author and the historical context in the understanding of texts. And they are also concerned with the misuse of power granted to authors, for this power may be abused and serve to perpetuate alienating social structures in which groups of persons are marginalized, not only intellectually but also economically and socially, when certain views are used ideologically to preserve an unjust status quo. To prevent such abuses, then, audiences must be granted the freedom to understand texts as they wish within the very general parameters of language and grammar.[64]

This view also tries to account for the fact that there seems to be always disagreement when it comes to the understanding of texts. Indeed, as is well documented in the literature, there appears to be no text of any consequence whose meaning cannot be the subject of a dispute. Even the words in a language are subject to different understandings and are frequently the source of disputes. The lack of closure when it comes to the understanding of texts, so the argument goes, must be recognized in hermeneutics by considering texts merely as loci of multiple understandings.[65] There can be no single, definitive, and univocal understandings of texts.[66] Indeed, some contemporary literary theorists go so far as to hold that every understanding of a text is in fact a misunderstanding of it.[67]

It is significant that the rationale for both of the extreme positions we have presented comes in part from considerations that are, as it were, external to textuality and that have a moral dimension. In the first, the moral dimension concerns the rights of the author, and in the second it is the pernicious consequences of limiting the understanding by audiences.[68] Both positions, then, adopt an answer to the question of the limits of understanding texts based in part on certain views external to the issue and not solely on an analysis of the nature of texts and their function. One might even say that in this sense these solutions are ideological, if by ideological one means those views whose adoption is based on their usefulness to carry out certain programs of action rather than a concern for truth.

Apart from the two extreme positions examined briefly here, many others fall in between, and as should be expected, these do greater justice to the facts of experience concerning texts.[69] It would not do for us, however, to discuss even a fraction of these here, for that would take more space than we have at our disposal. What I propose to do rather is to use some of the points and clarifications introduced earlier in this chapter to help us find a satisfactory answer to the question of the limits of understanding and then present the point of view I consider most satisfactory.

Let me begin by saying that, because understanding has to do with meaning and there are distinctions between essential and accidental differences in the meaning of texts, the question of the understanding or misunderstanding of texts concerns essential differences in meaning and thus in textual identity, and not accidental differences. When a text is understood in such a way that the understanding implies an essential difference in meaning and thus in identity, then the text is misunderstood. But when the understanding does not imply an essential difference in meaning and thus in identity, then the text is not misunderstood. I bring up the distinction between essential and accidental differences in meaning, then, because only essential differences need to be taken seriously when trying to determine the limits of understanding texts. If the differences of understanding concerning a text are minor, we are not justified in speaking of misunderstanding it.

Misunderstanding, then, must involve essential differences in understanding. This point is important, for the position that accidental differences in understanding do not qualify as misunderstandings lends support to the view that no differences in understanding lead to misunderstanding and thus that there are no limits to the understanding of texts. However, this generalization is not warranted if one keeps in mind the distinction between essential and accidental differences in understanding.

Next, following what was said earlier concerning the distinction between the meaning of a text and the implications of that meaning, we must say that it makes no sense to speak of understanding texts differently in terms of the implications of the meanings of the texts. The historical author of a text, or a particular audience confronted by it, may not be aware of the same implications of the meaning of a text or may be aware of different implications, but that does not entail that their understandings of the meaning of the text are different, only that they understand implications of that meaning that others do not.

Just as the distinction between essential and accidental differences in understanding, this distinction is important for the issue concerned with the limits of understanding. For the confusion between understanding the meaning of a text and understanding the implications of that meaning lends support to the view that there are more differences among the various understandings of a text than there really are and thus to the conclusion that there are no limits to that understanding. It also lends support to the view that differences among understandings of the same text are not very significant, for they are understandings of what is implied by the meaning of the text. And this in turn supports the view that there are no misderstandings of a text except for those that arise from grammatical errors. On the other hand, if the distinction between the understanding of the meaning of a text and the understanding of the implications of that meaning are maintained, the support for the view that there are no limits to the understanding of texts is undermined.

Third, texts have many different cultural functions, depending on how and for what purposes they are created and used, and these functions affect the ways in which texts are and should be understood. Consider, for example, a text of a message sent by a particular historical figure to another, and which is being examined by a historian. The historian wishes to determine exactly what the person who sent the message meant, and what the person who received the message understood by it, so that she can draw a connection among various events surrounding the message. It would do the historian no good in view of her purpose to understand the text of the message in ways different from the ways in which it was understood by the author and the receiver of the message, for that would lead to a misconstruction of history.

But not all cases are like that of historical documents. Consider, for example, the psychologist who is examining the descriptions produced by a subject who took a Rorschach test. Is the aim in this case only the understanding of what the author understood when he was writing those descriptions? Obviously not. The psychologist looks at those descriptions as clues to the unconscious workings of the mind of the subject. His understanding of the text, then, goes beyond what the author understood and is based on his knowledge of the implications of what the author said for the analysis of the mental state of that author.

This view, then, allows for the possibility that audiences may understand texts differently from authors without falling into misunderstanding; indeed, they may understand texts better than their authors.[70] For one thing, as we saw previously, it is altogether possible that an author may know less about a sign or an arrangement than does the audience. Indeed, that an author may know less about a sign or an arrangement than the audience should not be surprising at all. As noted elsewhere in this book, it is common experience that teachers understand the meaning of what their students write differently and even better than the students themselves do. The reason is that teachers generally have a better command of the tools students are trying to use to compose texts and are also more familiar with the subject matter about which students are writing. If it were not possible for audiences to understand texts differently and even better than their authors, teaching and correcting would be impossible.

But this is so only when the tools authors use to compose texts are publicly devised ones that the authors acknowledge as such. In such cases, the audience may know better than the author what the text says because the audience may know the tools the author is using better than the author. This does not entail, however, that even in such cases the audience always knows better than the author what the author means. It may turn out that, indeed, a teacher (audience) knows better than the student what the student means. But it may also happen that the audience completely misunderstands what the author means precisely because the author does not use signs and the conventions for their arrangement according to established rules. That this happens may be the result of ignorance on the part of the author or it may be the result of purposeful stipulation. I could, if I wished, use the word 'cat' from now on to mean dog. If I did that, I would be consistently misunderstood by those who hear me use the word and know English, but that does not entail that I would be confused.

Someone may object that, if what has been said is correct, then it follows that authors can be mistaken not just about the truth of what they hold, but also about what they mean. Indeed, if audiences may know better than authors the meaning of the texts the authors produce, then does not this entail that authors may be mistaken about what they mean?

Two responses may be given to this objection, and they follow easily from what has already been established. The first is that authors cannot be mistaken about what they mean; they can be mistaken only as to what a text they create means. It makes no sense to say that if I mean that $2 + 2 = 5$ I can be mistaken in the sense that I may mean that $2 + 2 = 5$. Of course, I am mistaken if I hold that $2 + 2 = 5$, but that is not at issue. At issue is whether I can be mistaken as to what I mean, and one can be mistaken as to what one means only if one does not mean it. But that makes no sense. What makes sense is that I am mistaken not as to what I mean by '$2 + 2 = 5$,' but as to what the text '$2 + 2 = 5$' means. And that is possible insofar as I am using signs from a language already in use (the language of mathematics), but I may not know the established meanings of the signs of that language I am using (or the rules according to which those signs are to be arranged). Say, for example, that what I mean by '$2 + 2 = 5$' is that $2 + 2 = 4$. In that case I am indeed mistaken as to what '$2 + 2 = 5$' means, because I take it to mean that $2 + 2 = 4$ when it in fact means that $2 + 2 = 5$ according to established usage. And, of course, the reason I am mistaken is that I take the sign '5' to mean 4 when in fact it means 5. Therefore, I am mistaken not in what I mean, but in the choice of the signs I use to convey my meaning. Strictly speaking, an author of a text who is mistaken in the stated way actually creates a text different from the one the audience identifies, thus leading to the sort of mistaken identity in which textual misunderstanding consists.

This response asumes that the author has an already complete and clear meaning in mind before choosing and arranging the ECTs for the text to convey that meaning. But, as we saw earlier, this is not generally the case. Authors do not often, if ever, have complete and clear understandings of meanings before they produce the texts that convey those meanings. The belief that they do is the result of the confusion discussed earlier between a mental text that precedes a written or spoken one and the meaning of the texts. So, even to say that an author is "mistaken" in the choice of signs and their arrangements to convey a certain meaning is misleading. What often happens is that the author is not clear as to the meaning that he or she wishes to convey—and has only vague ideas about it.[71]

In still other cases, however, one can speak about the wrong choice of signs and arrangements. To understand better what that entails we must make a distinction between two things that may be meant by saying that one is mistaken in the choice of signs (or arrangements) one uses to convey a specific meaning. In one sense this means simply that the author, as noted earlier, is not quite clear as to what he or she means and therefore produces a text whose meaning is unclear and confusing to the audience. One need only pick up any book of philosophy, including this one, to find many examples of this, in which the author was trying to grasp a point but did not quite do so and as a result produced a text confusing to the audience, whose task is to figure out the point and thus amend the text accordingly.

In another sense, however, to say that one is mistaken in the choice of signs (or arrangements) to convey a specific meaning does not mean that one is somehow confused as to the meaning of the text one has produced, even if that meaning is clear only after the text has been produced and not before. Rather, it means that one has the wrong information as to the meaning of the signs one uses in the text. This occurs very frequently when a foreign language is being learned, for in such cases the learner may simply be mistaken as to what a particular sign or set of signs may mean and consequently use them in ways which do not produce the desired effect.

Authors, then, are never mistaken as to what they mean, strictly speaking; that is, about what they understand when they act as audiences of the texts they produce. But they can be mistaken about the truth of what they mean, the meaning of the signs they use, or the meaning of the texts they create in the languages they use. Moreover, they can be confused as to the meaning they wish to convey or do in fact convey through the texts they create. All this points to the fact that authors can misunderstand the very texts they produce.

This leads to an objection, for it looks as if now we are back at the point where there are no limits to the understanding of texts. If audiences can and do in some cases understand texts better than their authors, does not that entail that there are no limits to the ways a text may be understood?

The answer to this question is negative, for that historical authors do not determine in all cases the limits of understanding of texts does not imply that there are no such limits. Indeed, there are limits to the understanding of texts, for there are certain points beyond which an understanding is no longer so, but turns rather into a misunderstanding. This occurs when an audience confuses the identity of a text by taking two texts, composed of the same ECTs but with different meanings, as the same text. Even though there are limits, however, those limits to the understanding of texts are not established by the understandings of the texts by their historical authors or by a particular audience, but by the meanings of the texts. And those meanings are not solely the responsibility of historical authors and particular audiences, but also of other factors, as we saw earlier, as determined by the cultural function of the text in question. We are, of course, speaking of nonstipulative texts; in cases of stipulative texts historical authors are responsible for meanings, but this fact does not change the situation for nonstipulative texts.

What has been said, therefore, is consistent with the earlier conclusion that the meaning of texts is not exclusively determined by the understanding of that meaning that their authors have. The boundaries of the meaning of nonstipulative texts are established not just by authors, but by authors in conjunction with the factors discussed earlier as they come together. The meaning of a particular text, then, depends on the author, the audience, the society in which it is produced, its context, the language, the text itself, and the cultural function it has. This view frees audiences from the need to adhere to the understandings of historical authors in all cases. Audiences may understand texts differently than the historical authors of those texts understood them and yet not fall into misunderstandings. Indeed, as noted, audiences can sometimes understand texts better than the historical authors of the texts and, I would venture, even understand texts in ways warranted only by meanings of the signs that compose them which developed long after the texts were produced.[72] The reasons should be obvious. In the first place, because as we said previously, there is no such thing as a completely finished and determined intended meaning that preexists a text in the mind of the author (in a sense the author of the text is related to the text once the text is completed in the same way in which the audience is), the author and the audience are both subjects who are trying to understand the text. We cannot, then, speak of the author's supposedly intended meaning of a text prior to its production as *the* meaning of the text. The meaning of the text is not something that precedes the text in the mind of the author but something of which the author becomes aware during the process of production, and even after. In some cases the author may never become aware of its full meaning.

Here we must refer back to what was said earlier with respect to what is essential and accidental in texts. It is essential to a text to have what might be called a core of meaning, whose understanding in part or as a whole, consists in true understanding, but beyond which there are misunderstandings. Authors and audiences may differ as to the understanding of the meaning they have of a text, but the misunderstanding occurs only when their understandings go beyond the limits of the core that is essential for the identity of the text.[73] That we may not easily or ever ascertain with certainty what that core may be in some texts does not entail that it is so for all texts or that there are no understandings of texts of which we can be certain. It is true that, even in science, certainty is elusive and scientific theories are always subject to revision. But that does not entail that there are no theories that are better than others.[74] Nor does it entail that every scientific statement is uncertain. One way to approach this issue is to adopt a Popperian view in which, although one can never be certain of understanding texts, one can be certain of misunderstanding them. Just as Popper argues that scientific theories are not verifiable, but that they nevertheless can be falsified, one could argue that textual understanding can never be validated but can be invalidated.[75] I shall get back to certainty in understanding in Chapter 6.

Now, from what has been said it follows that there can be many different understandings of some texts and only few or even one of others, depending on the cultural function the texts have. But one may still ask whether the limits, as established by cultural function, are stable so that, for example, a particular cultural function determines that the texts that fulfill it can always have only a certain prescribed range of understanding and no more.

The fact is that cultures are living entities in which change is an integral part, so cultural functions themselves change and thus modify the ranges and precriptions allowed for the understanding of texts. Indeed, the case of literary criticism is a good example.[76] Fifty years ago, there were certain rules of understanding literary texts beyond which critics could not go. These rules were, like all other cultural rules, the result of historical choices and activities and of the influence of groups of persons who were considered authoritative in the field. But now most of those rules have been abolished, making much more room for free understanding by critics. The rules themselves that establish limits may change, although those changes occur within the parameters that the culture allows.

Now we can see better the reason for the appeal of the two extreme positions discussed earlier, for both have some solid ground on which to stand. Those who argue for limits are on solid ground when they point to the misunderstandings to which texts may be subjected. But those who argue against the tyranny of authorial understanding are right in realizing that authorial understanding is not the only determining factor in textual meaning and thus in textual understanding. Both positions, however, neglect important aspects of the situation and do not do justice to its complexity and the role that other factors, particularly cultural function, play in the determination of the meaning and understanding of texts.

Having dealt with the epistemological aspect of the limits of understanding, we may now turn to its moral dimension.

D. Legitimacy of Understanding Texts Differently Than Their Historical Authors

This issue is moral, for it concerns the rights of audiences with respect to the understanding of texts. What has been said with respect to the limits of understanding does help us somewhat in approaching it, however. For we have concluded that to understand texts in different ways from the ways in which their historical authors understood them does not always imply misunderstanding them. Indeed, we went so far as to acknowledge that in many cases audiences other than the historical author understand a text better than the author. And this seems to suggest that it should not be illegitimate to do so. Yet, the matter may not be that simple. Let us look at an example in order to examine the issue more carefully.

The example I propose concerns the ongoing controversy about whether the Supreme Court of the United States in its understanding and application of the Constitution (including amendments to it) should go beyond what the authors of the Constitution understood by it or should be restricted by the original understanding the framers of the Constitution had in mind when they produced it. The resolution of this controversy is important, for the issue it raises affects some of the most important legal decisions of the past thirty years, particularly in the area of civil rights, including the controversial right to privacy on the basis of which abortion has been legalized.

On the one hand, some argue that the Court has no right to go beyond the understanding of the framers of the Constitution, being thus bound by the meanings understood by those framers.[77] This position allows them to challenge Supreme Court rulings that go beyond those understandings. They argue, for example, on the basis of historical analyses, that the right to abortion was not understood by the framers of the Constitution as part of privacy and, therefore, that Supreme Court decisions which read into the Constitution the right to abortion based on the right to privacy are not only historically inaccurate but legally incorrect. The result has been an attempt by some members of the present Court to reverse decisions of previous Courts that they claim were based on historically unwarranted understandings of the Constitution and that went beyond the understanding of its framers.

On the other hand, others argue that the Constitution is a public document open to interpretation by society.[78] For some, whatever understandings the framers of the Constitution had is a private matter to which we can have no access and is in any case irrelevant. For others, the understanding of the framers are relevant but it is only one of the factors to be taken into account for contemporary understandings of the Constitution.[79] As a public document, the Constitution is open to scrutiny and interpretation, and every age has the right to understand it in accordance with the circumstances prevalent at the time. Thus, the Supreme Court can understand the Constitution in ways that go beyond the understanding of its framers, as long as such understanding and application is morally defensible and concordant with established interpretative traditions. Therefore, Supreme Court decisions on abortion based on the right to privacy, for example, are not spurious simply because the framers of the Constitution did not have them in mind when they composed the document. As long as such a right is consistent with the general principles established in the Constitution as understood within the interpretative tradition that has developed through Supreme Court rulings, such a right is not only valid but rulings that establish it should not be reversed.

The case of the Constitution illustrates the fact that there is wide disagreement as to whether audiences are entitled to understand texts in ways different from the ways in which their historical authors understood them. We may formulate the alternatives with the following question: Should audiences understand texts only in the ways in which their authors understood them, or is it legitimate for audiences to have a free hand, understanding texts even in ways contrary to the ways they were understood by their authors?

There are other ways of posing this question. Two in particular stand out: (1) Is it legitimate for audiences to understand texts in ways not in accordance with the intended meaning of the historical authors? (2) Is it legitimate for audiences to understand texts in ways not in accordance with the intentions of their historical authors? But neither way of posing the question makes sense. As argued before, with few exceptions there are no intended meanings for a text other than the meanings of the produced text, so it is pointless to ask whether it is legitimate for audiences to consider such meanings. And the same applies to authorial intentions, for these are nothing clear and determinate unless they have been expressed in texts themselves. We are left, then, with only one formulation of the question: Whether it is legitimate for audiences to understand texts in ways which are different from the ways in which their historical authors understood them?

Both positions generally taken with respect to this issue are predicated on the view, rejected earlier, that the historical author somehow has a definite and complete understanding of the meaning of a text prior to the production of the text, that this understanding is independent of the text, and that the meaning of the text is determined by that understanding. But, as we have seen, neither the meaning of a text nor the understanding of that meaning by the author is something prior to and independent from the process of production of the text, nor do authors have absolute control over and knowledge of the meaning of the elements they use to compose texts. It would be unreasonable under these circumstances, then, to regard as illegitimate that audiences understand texts differently than their historical authors. Thus, there is room for freedom for the audience within the aim of understanding the meaning, for what the author intends before producing the text is still indeterminate in many ways and usually vague. The audience is free to understand the text in ways in which the author did not understand or did not understand clearly as long as such understandings are warranted by the text and its function, by the signs of which the text is composed, and by the arrangement in which they appear, taken, of course, in the set of circumstances in which the text was produced.

But this is not all, for it is in the nature and function of some texts to be understood in ways in which their authors did not understand them. We saw earlier the examples of historical and psychological texts, but the same applies to the case of literary texts, as well as to legal documents such as the Constitution. Literary texts are generally of the sort that, because of their structure and function, are intended to be understood differently by different individual persons in different circumstances.

The case of the Constitution and similar documents is different from that of literary texts insofar as the appeal here is not to individual persons but to society at large. In the first place, these documents are the product not of individual persons but of groups of persons who represent society as a whole and intend to provide documents that convey a public sense and understanding. As such, the private understandings of the authors of the documents may be superfluous, and society has the right to understand the texts in question in ways that are different from the way the authors of the documents understood them.

Note that the right of audiences to understand some texts differently from the way in which their authors understood them is not based on the intentions of the authors in question for reasons similar to those already given above in support of adhering to the intentions of authors in understanding texts. Two stand out: First, intentions are private affairs unless they are expressed textually and publicly either in a part of the document in question or in a preamble or accompanying explanatory note; second, intentions are often vague and not clearly determined, so that it is often difficult and sometimes even impossible to pin them down, even by those who have them. What counts insofar as the understanding of texts is not the intentions of the historical authors of the texts when they compose the texts, but rather the cultural function of the texts, for that function determines the limits of meaning and, thus, the degree of freedom in understanding that audiences may be given with respect to them. Neither the understanding of historical authors nor their intentions exclusively determines the limits of understanding of some texts. Such limits are to be found rather in the functions of the texts, and those functions are not determined by the historical author, but by society and culture.

This conclusion may be illustrated further by referring to the sort of text in which the cultural function determines that the author's understanding is what counts when it comes to the limits of its understanding. I am speaking of religious texts regarded by society as divinely revealed. In these cases the real author of the text is taken to be a divinity, who intends to convey a specific meaning to an audience. And it is essential for the audience to know exactly what the divinity means by the text, for the well-being of the audience depends on that knowledge. If the divinity, moreover, is conceived as all-powerful and all-knowing, in the way the God of Abraham, Isaac, and Jacob is conceived by Jews, Christians, and Muslims, then he is exclusively responsible for the text, its meaning, and the limits of that meaning.[80] Neither language, nor society, nor audiences can have a determining role to play here. Thus, what counts in the understanding of texts of this sort is the author's understanding and nothing else, and that understanding establishes the limits beyond which an audience's understanding becomes misunderstanding. These texts are different from such texts as the Constitution in that their authors are supposed to be exclusively responsible for them, and the understanding of the texts by those authors establishes the limits of understanding by audiences, for it is such understanding that audiences seek to reproduce.

Note, however, that it is the cultural function of these texts—the fact that they are to be used as "the word of God"—and not the understanding of the author that limits the right of audiences to understand them in certain ways. The understanding of the author plays the role it does because the texts in question serve a particular cultural function.

Someone might wish to object at this point that even texts supposedly divinely revealed use natural languages and are actually produced through the agency of human authors. And this entails that it is not after all the understanding of the historical authors that determine the meaning of the texts and the limits of understanding by audiences. These texts, like any others, are open to various understandings.

Conceding this point would not affect my position adversely, because the case of divinely revealed texts was cited as an example that does not look prima facie as if it fits into my scheme, but nonetheless does not, upon further analysis, create problems for it. Yet, I do not think that any ground has to be given up to the objection for two reasons. First, one must keep in mind that, when it comes to divinely revealed texts, one must make a distinction between the real author of the text, which in this case is the divinity, and the instrumental author of the text, who is the person who actually produces it. The divinity uses the instrumental author, but it is the divinity who determines the shape and meaning of the text. The instrumental author is but a tool of the divinity. Whether the instrumental author actually understands or not what he is doing, and the meaning that the text he is composing has, is immaterial, because it is the divinity who is exclusively responsible for the text. Thus, the measure of textual understanding is not to be found in the understanding by the instrumental author, but in the divine author.[81]

The second reason is that an omnipotent and omniscient author does whatever he wishes and knows exactly what he does and the implications of what he does. So, in creating a text, where he uses signs that belong to a natural language, he knows the complete meaning of those signs and their combinations in all possible situations, and he chooses the signs and combinations that are most efficacious—he is also benevolent—to convey his message. Thus, in understanding the signs from a natural language developed by a particular culture, audiences are being led to the understanding of the text as the divinity wishes it.[82]

This point also illuminates another source of worry; namely, that divinities may have different and greater understandings than human audiences because of their superior nature. How can humans understand the revelation of the God of Abraham as he does, when he is infinite and humans are finite? But, from what has been said earlier, humans need not understand the meaning of texts as God understands them, but as God intends them to be understood; that is, as a human audience understands them.

In short, then, the specific conditions of textual identity may vary, depending on the type of text as determined by its cultural function, and so vary the limits of its understanding, for the general conditions that apply to all texts may be modified by that function. Meaning, one of the general conditions of textual identity, may not be understood as narrowly in some types of texts as in others.

I should add, perhaps, that documents such as the Constitution, are usually very general and abstract, precisely because their aim is to convey fundamental principles that should govern social behavior. This feature is what makes possible their variegated understandings and flexible application. Indeed, framers of constitutions and similar documents seem to know this quite well. So in a sense it is not contrary to their general intention for future audiences to go beyond what may appear to be the meanings they had in mind when they produced the texts. Indeed, authors of such documents are so clearly aware of the need for openness that they generally establish the possibility of future amendments.

I realize that the possibility of amendment could be the basis for arguing that understandings of constitutions and similar documents by audiences should adhere to historical understandings. If society needs (1) to extend the principles understood by the framers of a document to cases they did not envisage, or (2) to add new principles not contemplated by those authors, this should be done through amendment and not through the development of new understandings. But this argument can be turned around, for the possibility of amendment can be seen precisely, as I have done, as the recognition by the authors of a need for flexibility and development in the documents they create and thus as opening the door to the development of some new understandings.

Our conclusion, then, is that the legitimacy or illegitimacy of understanding texts differently from the way their historical authors understood them depends very much on cultural function. A mathematical equation such as '2 + 2 = 4' is supposed to be understood in a rather limited way, but the text of the Constitution of the United States bears a much broader range of understandings.

Note that what is at stake here is much more than simply the extension of universals to individuals not thought about by the historical authors of texts. Consider a sign such as 'human being.' When I understand 'human being' I understand that a human being is a rational animal and I may imagine some examples of individuals who fall into the category. Now, if someone else comes along and, upon being confronted with the sign, imagines some human beings I did not imagine when I thought of the meaning of 'human being,' they might say that she is understanding the meaning of 'human being' differently. But this is not very significant—indeed, individual instances of the category are not essential to the meaning of 'human being.' For, when someone thinks of human beings differently than I think about them, they think not just of instances I did not think about, but of features of human beings I had not thought of.

To make sense of the question we have been addressing we must conceive the meaning of certain texts as having very broad boundaries, or even as openended, so that many different understandings of the texts are possible. This is so because in these cases the author is not taken as the determiner of meaning but as the creator of a locus of understanding. In such cases the responsibility for determining the meaning rests not with the author alone, but includes other factors as established by the cultural function of the text. Most literary critics think of all texts in this way and thus miss an important aspect of textuality.[83] But others think of texts in just the opposite way, making the author the sole determiner of meaning, and they also miss important aspects of textuality. The source of the mistake of both groups is that they look at texts by using as paradigms certain cultural types of texts rather than accepting the luxuriant variety of the category.

A text is a complex entity whose meaning and significance depend on a variety of factors. The author has a key role among these, and in some cases is the determining factor, but the author and what he or she does in turn depend on context, society, audience, the text, and the cultural function of the text.

V. Truth Value and Objectivity of Understandings

Having concluded that texts may be understood in different ways by their historical authors and their audiences, we must now turn to the question of the truth value and objectivity of such understandings. With respect to truth value, the answer appears simple enough: We might say that understandings are true if and only if they accurately grasp the meaning of texts, and they are false if and only if they do not. Consider an example. If subject S looks at the text, 'No se permite fumar aquí',' and understands it to mean that no smoking is permitted here, the subject has a true understanding of the text because she understands what the text means. But if S understands the text to mean that smoking is permitted here, then S has a false understanding of the text because her understanding does not correspond to the meaning of the text. In either case the understanding has truth value.[84]

Note that truth value is not determined by authorial understanding. That could not be the case for all texts, because I have argued that some texts may be understood in ways different from the ways their historical authors understood them. Truth value, then, is determined by the meaning of the text, which may be fully or partially understood, or not understood at all.[85]

One further point needs to be made clear concerning the truth value of understandings: such a truth value is not always as simple as what I have said may suggest. The reason is that texts are often composed of many signs and sentences and the sentences of which they are composed are often complex. Thus one may understand only part of a text truthfully. There is most often, then, no simple answer to the question: Is the understanding of text T by audience A true or false? Most often the truth and falsity of the understanding of a text, except in cases of very simple texts, is a matter of degree and proportion. Yet, in principle and *in abstracto*, there is nothing wrong with speaking about the truth value of an understanding.

Concerning the objectivity or subjectivity of understandings, we must resist the temptation to use this distinction to refer to the degree of similarity between acts of understanding of a contemporary audience and the acts of understanding of a historical author for two reasons. First, because, as just noted, the acts of understanding of the author are not necessarily paradigmatic of understanding. Second, because I propose conceiving objectivity and subjectivity in a different way. Subjectivity can be understood in various ways. In the case of understandings in general, however, I will take the degree of subjectivity of an understanding to refer to the degree to which an understanding is a product of the subject independent of the object of understanding; that is, the text and whatever else determines its meaning. Naturally, because the understandings we are discussing are understandings of texts, the text will always be taken into account to some extent, and the subjectivity of understandings will always be tempered by that consideration.

Objectivity is the counterpart of subjectivity, and in the case of understandings I will take the degree of objectivity to refer to the degree to which an understanding is a product of the subject's consideration of the object and thus as dependent on that object, namely the text and the factors outside the understanding subject that determine its meaning. As in the case of the subjectivity of understandings, the objectivity of understandings is a matter of degree, because all understandings of texts are to some extent products of subjects and thus depend on them. The objectivity or subjectivity of understandings depends, then, on the causal complex that gives rise to them and on the extent to which that causal complex excludes or includes elements external to the understanding subject that play a role in the determination of a text's meaning. They do not depend, as is frequently held, on the degree of similarity between the acts of understanding of an audience and the acts of understanding of the historical author or on the accuracy with which the audience grasps the meaning of a text.

VI. Conclusion

Let me now summarize briefly what has been accomplished in this chapter. I began by posing the controversial questions of whether there are limits to the understanding of texts and whether it is legitimate for audiences to understand texts differently than the historical authors of the texts. To deal with these questions, however, we had to discuss some propaedeutic matters. The first of these involved the distinction between understanding and meaning. The view I proposed in this matter is that understandings are mental acts whereby the meanings of texts are grasped and therefore must be understood as distinct from meanings. Meanings are not necessarily mental or acts.

The second of the propaedeutic issues discussed concerned the number of understandings of a text. The most obvious response to this issue results from the conception of texts as mental acts occurring in the minds of those who understand texts. For, if that is the case, then there are as many understandings as there are authors and audiences who engage in mental acts whereby they understand them. This way of answering the question is at least ambiguous and perhaps misleading, for we do want to speak of understandings as being the same as well as being different. To account for this way of speaking, a distinction between intensional and extensional conceptions of the sameness and difference of the acts of understanding of texts was introduced. Extensional conceptions concern individual acts of understanding, whereas intensional conceptions concern the meaning understood through these acts. Thus one may speak of acts of understanding that are intensionally the same because what is understood through them is the same meaning, but extensionally different because they are individually different acts of understanding.

The third propaedeutic matter had to do with understanding and textual identity. For the conditions of textual identity adopted in this book seem to preclude the possibility that a text can be misunderstood. I argued that this is merely a verbal matter, for misunderstanding may be taken in either of two ways. According to one, it means that the same text has been understood in two different ways, one of which is mistaken. According to the other, it means that one text has been confused with another. The first way expresses more closely the way we speak and think about texts, but leads to problems. The second, although less intuitive, avoids those problems.

Having dealt with the three propaedeutic matters, I turned to the question concerned with the limits of understanding. And here we encountered two issues, one epistemological and the other moral. The first has to do with whether there are in fact limits to the understanding of texts beyond which there is no longer understanding but rather misunderstanding. The second concerns the right of audiences to understand texts differently than their historical authors.

To deal with these issues, two other questions were introduced. The first concerned the limits of meaning; the other, the factors that enter into the determination of the meaning of texts. With respect to the first, two positions were discussed. The first position argues that there are no limits on the meaning of texts; the second proposes strict limits on the meaning of texts. Both positions were found wanting for several reasons, but most important because they do not do justice to our experience.

To clear the way for the position I propose, distinctions were introduced between essential and accidental differences in meaning, meaning and the implications of meaning, and meaning and intentions. I argued that the limits of meaning apply neither to implications nor intentions, but refer to an essential core necessary to maintain textual identity. This naturally took us to the question of what or who determines this core; that is, the limits of the meaning of texts. Several possibilities were explored: author, audience, context, society, language, and the text itself. But none of these by itself and exclusively seemed to work. The reason is that the most important element is missing; namely, the cultural function of the text. For the cultural function ultimately determines the factors that do determine it. And these factors include the ones mentioned in various proportions.

Having established that the meanings of texts have limits and the factors that enter into the determination of those limits, I turned next to the limits of understanding properly speaking. And here we found again two extreme positions. One argues that any understanding that does not conform to the understanding of the historical author is a misunderstanding. The other holds that there are no limits to the understanding of texts, so that it is absurd to speak of misunderstanding them. Both positions were found to be at fault for various reasons and a third position was proposed. In accordance with what had been said about meaning and its limits, it holds that there are limits to the understanding of texts and that those limits depend on the limits of the meaning. Moreover, because the limits of meaning depend on cultural function, the limits of understanding depend ultimately on cultural function. Therefore, it is misguided to try to apply the same limits or criteria of limits to all texts, because their functions differ. From this it follows not only that there may be contradictory understandings of some texts, neither of which are misunderstandings, but also that audiences may understand texts differently and even better than their authors.

Next I turned to the moral dimension of this issue, concerned with the legitimacy of audiences understanding texts differently than their historical authors. And here again there are some who categorically deny such legitimacy whereas others extend it to every text. Following what had already been established concerning the limits of meaning and the epistemological limits of understanding, I argued that morality follows function and thus the legitimacy of understanding texts differently than their historical authors depends on the cultural function of the texts in question, not on authorial intention or understanding. What determines the legitimate limits of understanding texts is ultimately the function of the texts in a particular culture, for that function specifies the immediate factors that set those limits.

The chapter ends with a discussion of the truth value and objectivity of understandings. I take understandings to be true if they accurately grasp the meaning of texts and false if they do not. But, because meaning is not necessarily determined by authorial understanding, true understandings do not necessarily have to adhere to the understandings of historical authors.

With respect to objectivity I take it that an understanding is more or less objective to the degree that it is a product of the subject's consideration of the object and thus dependent on the object; that is, the text and the factors external to the subject. The subjectivity of an understanding is just the reverse of its objectivity. Subjectivity and objectivity are inversely proportional, but because understanding occurs in a subject and concerns an object, there is never pure objective or subjective understandings of a text.

So much, then, for understanding. Now we must turn to interpretation, for this notion is closely related to understanding and, indeed, as noted earlier, frequently confused with it.

5

INTERPRETATION

The interpretation of texts poses serious and interesting problems for the philosopher and the historian. The problems generally occur because we often do not and cannot have direct access to the meaning that texts are supposed to convey. Usually we have direct access only to the ECTs authors use to convey that meaning. How are we, then, to get at that meaning, and what is the role that interpretations play in the process that leads to getting at it? These general questions constitute the background of the more specific questions discussed in this chapter.

The specific questions concerning interpretations that give rise to more disagreements among philosophers have to do with their nature, ontological status, function, types, number, truth value, and objectivity. Because some of these topics are closely related to each other, I have combined them. Accordingly, the chapter is divided into four parts, dealing respectively with (I) the nature and ontological status of interpretations, (II) their function, (III) their types, and (IV) their number, truth value, and objectivity.

I. Nature and Ontological Status of Interpretations

The term 'interpretation' is the English translation of the Latin *interpretatio*, from *interpres*, which etymologically meant "to spread abroad." Accordingly, *interpres* came to mean an agent between two parties, a broker or negotiator and, by extension an explainer, expounder, and translator. The Latin term *interpretatio* developed at least three different meanings. Sometimes it meant "meaning," so that to give an interpretation was equivalent to give the meaning of whatever was being interpreted. *Interpretatio* was also taken to mean "translation"; the translation of a text into a different language was called an *interpretation*. Finally, the term was used to mean "explanation," and by this an interpretation was meant to bring out what was hidden and unclear, to make plain what was irregular, and to provide an account of something or other.

All these meanings point to the fact that three different factors play a role in an interpretation: whatever is being interpreted, something other than what is being interpreted that is added to it, and an interpreter who produces the interpretation. Because our concern here is with the interpretation of texts, I shall identify what is being interpreted with a text, although interpretations are by no means restricted to texts. We frequently speak of interpreting facts, behavior, people, and even the world. All these and other meanings of the term are well recorded and there is no need to reject them as spurious or inappropriate. For our purposes, however, it is the interpretation of texts that is pertinent and to which the discussion will be restricted.

Today, there are three main ways in which the term 'interpretation' is used in connection with texts, giving rise to three different sorts of things that can be discussed when dealing with interpretations.[1] In one way, an interpretation is the same thing as an understanding one has of the meaning of a text.[2] In this sense, for example, when two different but correct answers are given to the same question, we speak of two different interpretations of the question. Obviously, what is meant here are two different understandings of what the question means that give rise to the two answers. This example brings out an important subdivision within this view of interpretations. For sometimes 'interpretation' is used as any kind of understanding one may have. Thus an interpretation of '$2 + 2 = 4$' is that two and two equal four. But more frequently 'interpretation' is restricted to a certain type of understanding that is characterized by two aspects: It is not the only possible valid understanding of the text in question; and a subjective element plays a key role in it.[3] This is the sort of interpretation illustrated by the example of the two correct answers given to the same question. Since I have devoted Chapter 4 to understandings, there is no need for us to dwell on this view of interpretation here.

'Interpretation' is also frequently used to refer to a process or activity whereby one develops an understanding of a text.[4] Therefore, the procedure I follow to grasp the meaning of the sentence, 'Minina is on the mat,' is called an interpretation. In this sense, an interpretation involves decoding the text to understand its message, and it is not to be identified with the message itself. This meaning is frequently interchanged with the other two I mention here, leading to imprecisions and ambiguities in the literature. Interpretation, understood thus, has more to do with the methodology of developing understanding and thus is not directly relevant to our topic. For this reason, I shall leave its discussion for some other occasion.

The term 'interpretation' is also used in a third way, to refer to texts, and this is the sort of interpretation that I shall discuss in this chapter.[5] In this sense we speak of an interpretation as a text T_3 composed of a text T_2 and another text T_1, to which T_2 is added. Thus, for example, the text of Averroes's commentaries on Aristotle, composed of the text of Aristotle with Averroes's comments and glosses, are called *Averroes's interpretation* of Aristotle.

In accordance with what has been said concerning the factors that play a role in interpretations, an interpretation of a text understood in the third sense indicated involves three factors: first, the text being interpreted; second, the interpreter; and third, a text added to the text that is being interpreted.[6] Note that the interpretation is not just the added text, for, as we shall see, for an interpretation to do the job required of it, it presupposes the text that is being interpreted. Thus, an interpretation includes, at least intentionally, the text under interpretation, being composed of both the text under interpretation and the text that is added to it in the interpretation. In the case of Averroes's commentaries on Aristotle's texts, it is not Averroes's textual additions and comments to Aristotle's texts, but rather Aristotle's texts *together with* Averroes's textual additions and comments that constitute the interpretation. If this were not so, it would not be clear to which text the added textual comments would refer. That does not mean, however, that what is added to the text under interpretation is always placed next to it. For the sake of economy it is frequent to omit the text under interpretation and even to speak of the added text as the interpretation. But this way of speaking leads to misunderstandings. Therefore, I shall stick with a technical sense of 'interpretation' according to which an interpretation includes both the text under interpretation and the text added to it.

A comparison may be helpful here. An interpretation as I have presented it is very much like a definition. A definition is composed of a *definiendum*, the term to be defined, and a *definiens*, the defining expression. 'Man is a rational animal' is a definition in which 'man' is the *definiendum* and 'rational animal' is the *definiens*. Likewise, an interpretation is composed of the text to be interpreted, call it the *interpretandum*, and the commentary added to it, call it the *interpretans*. The text being interpreted (*interpretandum*), then, is ontologically part of the interpretation, just as the *definiendum* is part of the definition.

What is added to a text under interpretation, namely, the *interpretans*, is something *other* and therefore an interpretation is something *more* than the text under interpretation. The text under interpretation itself, whether written somewhere, spoken at some time, or mentally present in some mind, is not an interpretation. The interpretation comes in when the interpreter begins to analyze the text and its elements into terms and concepts that are not explicit in the text. For example, merely to reproduce Boethius's statement, "Atque ideo sunt numero plures, quoniam accidentibus plures fiunt," is not an interpretation.[7] To translate it into "Wherefore, it is because they are plural by their accidents that they are plural in number" is a kind of interpretation, because it changes the original into a different set of linguistic terms whose denotations and connotations may not be the same as those of the original Latin sentence, but that are meant to be equivalent in meaning, considered as a whole, to the original text, even if the translation is not accompanied by the original text. A translation taken by itself is only an *interpretans*, but if presented as a translation of a text, then it is an interpretation properly speaking. Moreover, if we go further and say, for example, that what Boethius had in mind in that text is to say that the principle of individuation is a bundle of accidents, we are without a doubt providing an interpretation of Boethius's text, for the text contains no such formulation of Boethius's doctrine.

What an interpretation adds to a text is in fact another text. The added text, that is, the *interpretans*, as well as the interpretation and the text under interpretation can be mental, spoken, or written. Nor do they have to be all of the same sort. There can be a written *interpretandum* and a mental *interpretans*, a mental *interpretandum* and a written *interpretans*, a spoken *interpretandum* and a mental *interpretans*, and so on. In Chapter 3, however, we saw that there are at least five different texts with which interpreters can deal, so we must determine (1) which of these is the *interpretandum* and (2) which is the interpretation. The texts in question are the actual text—which can be in turn historical, intermediary, or contemporary—, the intended text, and the ideal text. Let me begin with (1), concerned with the object of interpretation.

The answer to (1) is that the text toward which the efforts of interpreters are directed is the historical text. However, because what they have is not necessarily that text, but only a contemporary text, their interpretations are often based on the contemporary text, although they keep in mind that the overall aim is to provide interpretations of the historical text. There is nothing unusual about this. Interpreters often have bad editions of a text that depart in substantial ways from the historical text, but that they must use as long as the historical text is not available. Indeed, in many cases there is no hope of ever recovering the historical text, as is the case with the works of most pre-Socratic philosophers, and we must do with what we have. Moreover, in cases where there are several historical texts that reflect the evolution of an author's thought through a period of time, interpreters must take them all into consideration, keeping in mind the evolutionary processes that they reflect, if they are to provide accurate historical interpretations. Strictly speaking, then, interpreters often work with texts that are not the historical text they wish to interpret—that is, the identity of the historical text and the contemporary text is not the same, either because the ECTs of the historical text have not survived or because the meaning of the historical text has been misunderstood; that is, understood in ways essentially different from the way warranted by its meaning.

The function of the intended and the ideal texts in the process of interpretation, on the other hand, should be primarily regulative and instrumental. The aim of interpreters is not the reconstruction of an ideal text regardless of its perfection, for that would be outside their task, as we shall see. Nor should interpreters aim to reconstruct the text that the author presumably intended to produce but never did, for, as we saw, that text never existed, even in the mind of the author. The concern of interpreters is with the text that was actually produced, the historical text. However, insofar as the historical text is not always available, interpreters can profit from considering what they can surmise about both the intended and the ideal texts. These texts are reconstructions of what interpreters believe the historical author was trying to do or should have been trying to do. As such, these texts allow interpreters to correct what appear to be mistakes and supply missing elements that help in the understanding of a historical text. But interpreters must keep in mind that their task involves the development of an interpretation of the historical text and must resist the temptation to see that task as the reconstruction of the intended or ideal texts. To fall into the latter trap leads surely to distortions in the meaning of texts and thus of history. But that need not happen if the interpreter is aware of the merely regulative and instrumental function of the intended and ideal texts. These remarks have to be tempered by what has been said concerning the legitimacy of providing interpretations that go beyond the intention of the authors or the understandings of a text that intended and historical audiences may have of it. As noted, the functions of texts have much to do with the range of legitimate interpretations that may be given of them.

In contrast with the contemporary, historical, intended, and ideal, the intermediary text has no direct function to play in the epistemological process of interpretation. For a text to have such a function it must be present to the contemporary audience that seeks to interpret the text. But the intermediary text is one that was destroyed or has been lost and thus cannot be the direct object of investigation. Nonetheless, if there is some notice of its past existence, it may serve the purpose of explaining gaps among various contemporary texts produced at various times and thus have an indirect influence on the development of interpretations.

Knowledge of the audience should be particularly helpful to interpreters because of the elliptical character of most texts. With rare exceptions, texts are meant to be read or heard by an audience and they, thus, presuppose a certain context that allows for shortcuts and *lacunae* intended to be filled by the assumptions and views of the audience in question. Knowledge of the intended audience may be especially useful to an interpreter insofar as it may reveal, as already stated, some of the assumptions made by the historical author in the composition of the text.[8] Knowledge of the historical audience may also be helpful because it may, in an indirect fashion, reveal something about the historical author himself and may put in perspective whatever contemporaneous interpretations of the text were produced. This last point also applies to the knowledge of the intermediary audience. Finally, no less important than the others is the knowledge of the contemporary audience, particularly the selfknowledge of interpreters, for such information may help in two ways. First, it may help to make explicit the assumptions and prejudices of interpreters and, thus, prevent them from distorting their understanding of the historical text. Second, it could help them develop the proper additions to a text under interpretation to make it better understood.

Concerning question (2), raised earlier (Which text is the interpretation?), we must begin by noting again that an interpretation is composed of the *interpretandum* and the *interpretans*. Moreover, as we have seen, the *interpretandum*, or object of interpretation, is the historical text. So an interpretation is a composite of the historical text—in cases where that is available, in other cases it is the contemporary text—and the *interpretans*. The *interpretans* is a new text added by the interpreter to the contemporary (or historical, depending on what is available) text to help a contemporary audience develop an understanding in relation to it, by providing a translation, an explanation, or a commentary on it. Nor should an interpretation be confused with the intended text or the ideal text. Indeed, even if the interpretation in question were presented as a reconstruction of the ideal text or the intended text, it would not be either one of them. It could not be the ideal text because the ideal text is supposed merely to take the place of the historical or contemporary texts in places where such texts are corrupt or make no good sense; it is not supposed to make them understandable to an audience, as an interpretation ought to do. Nor could it be the intended text for, like the ideal text, the intended text is supposed to take the place of the historical text and therefore is not meant to clarify it—remember that the intended text is a construction of an interpreter. The actual function of intended and ideal texts is purely regulative. Those texts help the interpreter to come up with an interpretation in cases where there are doubts concerning the meaning of a text and the evidence available is inconclusive, but they are neither the interpretation nor the text that is added to the text under interpretation, that is, the *interpretans*. An interpretation of a text amounts, then, to a historical text with a textual commentary. And the textual commentary is not the historical text under interpretation, but a new historical text.

That interpretations are texts has the implication that interpreters act as historical authors of their interpretations, although not as historical authors of the texts under interpretation. The difference between these two authors comes from the fact that both produce texts but the texts are different and the aims of their activities are also different. The general aim of both is to convey specific meanings to audiences, but in the case of the authors of interpretations, those meanings are restricted by the functions of interpretations.

Thus far I have described the function of interpretations in various ways as the translation or explanation of a text, but these descriptions are not clear enough. Indeed, the addition of a text to another text raises what looks like a serious difficulty. Let us turn, then, to the function of interpretations.

II. Interpreter's Dilemma and Function of Interpretations

The difficulty concerning the addition of a text (*interpretans*) to a text under interpretation (*interpretandum*) arises because it would appear that such an addition changes the text under interpretation and, therefore, precludes the possibility of understanding its historical meaning. Can an interpreter really add anything to a text and still have the contemporary audience understand the text as it was historically understood? Can we go beyond the historical text and add to it anything without actually changing it? Indeed, some might argue, the only way we have of understanding a text without distorting it is that of reproducing the text—becoming Pierre Menards and nothing more—for any addition would transform the text, thereby eliminating the possibility of understanding it in its historical dimension.[9] But if no additions are made to a text from another period, how can a contemporary audience hope to bridge the cultural and temporal gap that separates it from the text? How can a twentieth century executive from New York City understand a text meant for a tenth century monk from Monte Casino?

This brings me to what I have called elsewhere the *Interpreter's Dilemma*: Either the interpreter simply reproduces a text, adding nothing whatever to it, or he or she glosses it.[10] If one adds nothing to it, as antiquarians would wish, one cannot really say one has made it possible for the contemporary audience to understand the text in its purely historical dimension, because that audience is neither the author of the text nor the members of the historical audience of the text who, because they were acquainted with the meaning of the signs used in the text and the ways the signs could be arranged in the context in which the text was produced, knew what to supply to understand it. But the interpreter who adds to the text, as anachronists favor, clearly changes the text and again would seem to prevent the contemporary audience from having access to its historical meaning. Can the interpreter escape this dilemma and avoid both antiquarianism and anachronism?[11] I believe one can because the dilemma is based on a misunderstanding of the function of interpretations.

To explain how the Interpreter's Dilemma can be escaped, let me begin by pointing out that interpretations have different functions, and thus that interpreters have different aims. The overall, generic function of interpretations is to produce understandings in a contemporary audience in relation to a particular text.[12] In other words, an interpretation is supposed to act causally on an audience, producing in it acts of understanding in relation to the historical text that is the object of the interpretation. The interpreter of the text of *Don Quixote*, for example, will add a text to it so that a contemporary audience may experience acts of understanding related to the text of *Don Quixote*. As noted earlier, interpretations are texts, and therefore, it should not be surprising that their primary function is to produce understanding. But not all texts are interpretations. What differentiates interpretations within the generic function common to texts is that their function is to produce acts of understanding related to the part of the interpretation I have called *interpretandum*.

Note, however, that I have not put any specific constraints on the acts of understanding intended to be produced in the audience as a result of an interpretation. The reason is that, apart from the generic overall function indicated, interpretations may have at least three different specific functions that affect the constraints to be put on the acts of understanding they are supposed to cause. One function, which I shall call the *Historical Function*, aims to re-create in the contemporary audience the acts of understanding of the historical author and the historical audience of the historical text. The aim of the interpreter in this case is to try to have an audience understand a text as its historical author and historical audience understood it. The task is to make a contemporary audience understand the meaning of a text that its author and contemporary audience thought it had. This is obviously a purely historical aim, whose purpose is not to go beyond the parameters of understanding experienced by the historical author and the historical audience. Indeed, if the effect of the interpretation is to create in the contemporary audience acts of understanding that neither the historical author nor the historical audience experienced, then the interpretation is a bad one. For those acts of understanding would imply a meaning that is essentially different from the meaning implied by the acts of understanding the historical author and the historical audience had. And in such a case the interpretation fails to produce understanding and produces misunderstanding instead.

A second specific function of interpretations, also concordant with their overall generic function, I shall call the *Meaning Function*. This function is to produce in contemporary audiences acts of understanding that may go beyond the acts of understanding of the historical author and the historical audience of the text, revealing aspects of the meaning of the text with which their historical authors and historical audiences were not acquainted. Obviously, the aim of this kind of interpretation is not the historical re-creation of the understandings of the historical author and the historical audience, and the measure of the success or failure of the interpretation has nothing to do with such understandings. Moreover, it assumes that, as noted in Chapter 4, the text in question has a meaning that is broader, and perhaps deeper, than the meaning the historical author and historical audience of the text thought it had.

Finally, a third specific function of interpretations, which I shall call *Implicative Function*, is to produce in contemporary audiences acts of understanding whereby those audiences understand the implications of the meaning of texts, regardless of whether the historical authors and the historical audiences were or were not aware of those implications. Again, the aim of the interpreter in this case is not historical in the sense implied by the first function, and the success or failure of the interpretation cannot be measured by how closely it reproduces in a contemporary audience the acts of understanding which the historical author and the historical audience of the text had.

Three points follow from what has been said. The first is that the three functions mentioned are not mutually exclusive. An interpretation may have all these functions simultaneously, although in practice interpretations that try to do so usually create more confusion than understanding. Indeed, the unconscious mixing of these functions by interpreters is one of the main flaws of most interpretations of texts. Interpreters who are not aware of the differences among these functions mix them in such a way that they leave their audiences thoroughly confused as to what they understand the historical author and historical audience understood, what the meaning of the text is, or what the implications of that meaning are. It is essential to the production of successful interpretations to distinguish among these functions, although the functions are not incompatible in principle.

The second point is that the preeminence of one of these functions with respect to a particular text depends very much on the type of text in question as determined by the cultural function it is supposed to carry out. In a divinely revealed text, where the author's understanding determines its meaning and the aim of the audience is to find out that meaning, the first function is most important even if unlikely to be carried out successfully.[13] But in a legal text, where the aim is to serve as a guide for action, the second and third functions may be more important.

The third point is that the Interpreter's Dilemma applies only to the first function. It would make no sense at all to speak of the dilemma in cases where the function of the interpretation is to get at dimensions of the meaning of a text, or the implications of that meaning, with which neither the historical author nor the historical audience were acquainted. Let me now turn, then, to the first function and the Interpreter's Dilemma.

A. Historical Function

To explain how the Interpreter's Dilemma can be escaped, let me begin by pointing out that the historical function implies that the aim of the interpreter is to re-create in the contemporary audience, first, the mental acts of the historical author of the text, not as creator of the text, but as audience.[14] In other words, the aim of the interpreter taken in this sense is to produce an understanding in the contemporary audience that is intensionally the same to the understanding the author had of the text.

The interpreter, second, has in mind the re-creation in the contemporary audience of the acts of understanding through which the historical audience of the text or the audience for which the work was intended went or were expected to go. Remember that the historical author usually has in mind an audience and it is that audience, composed of the author or other contemporaries, that the interpreter needs to become to re–create in the interpreter's contemporary audience an understanding of the text in its historicity.

In trying to re-create the acts of understanding of the historical author and the historical audience of the text in one's contemporary audience, an interpreter needs to create a causal complex that will produce in the audience of the interpretation acts of understanding that are intensionally the same as the acts the historical author and the historical audience underwent when they came into contact with the text in their historical context. But to do this, it is necessary to add to the historical text elements that will make it possible to re-create those acts. For the distance in time and culture and so forth, that is, in context, that separates the contemporary audience from the historical text would ensure that, even if the interpreter's audience had access to the text as it was given historically, it would develop acts of understanding that would surely be intensionally different from those of the historical author and his historical audience. This is similar to what would happen if the historical author and audience had access to a text contemporary to the interpreter, for in that case they would most likely understand it differently than the interpreter's contemporary audience would unless a gloss of it were provided. The function of the additions that the interpreter supplies is, then, to ensure that intensionally the same acts of understanding expected of those who were contemporaneous with historical texts would be reproduced in the contemporary audience.[15]

The view I have stated can be summarized in what I call the *Principle of Proportional Understanding*.[16] According to this principle;

> An interpretation of a text (composed of a historical text and the interpretative textual additions of an interpreter) taken in a contemporary context, should be to the contemporary audience with respect to the production of their contemporary acts of understanding as the historical text, taken in the historical context, is to the historical author and the historical audience with respect to the acts of understanding of the historical author and the historical audience.

Perhaps this principle will be more easily understood if we present it schematically as follows:

1. $\dfrac{\text{historical text in the historical context}}{\text{historical author} + \text{historical audience}} = \begin{array}{l}\text{acts of understanding of historical}\\ \text{author and historical audience}\end{array}$

2. $\dfrac{\begin{array}{l}\text{interpretation (i.e., historical text} +\\ \text{interpretative additions) in the}\\ \text{contemporary context}\end{array}}{\text{contemporary audience}} = \begin{array}{l}\text{acts of understanding of}\\ \text{contemporary audience}\end{array}$

3. $\begin{array}{l}\text{acts of understanding of historical}\\ \text{author and historical audience}\end{array} = \begin{array}{l}\text{acts of understanding of}\\ \text{contemporary audience}\end{array}$

What the principle of proportional understanding claims is that, for an interpretation of a historical text to function as it should in a contemporary context, the ratio of the interpretation to the contemporary audience, that is, the acts of understanding it produces in such an audience, must be the same as the ratio that holds between the historical text, taken in the historical context, and the historical author and the historical audience, that is, the acts of understanding it produces in the historical author, considered qua audience, and in the historical audience.

The aim of an interpreter, then, is to create a text that produces in the audience (the contemporary audience) acts of understanding that are intensionally the same to those produced by the historical text in the historical author and the historical audience of the historical text. The interpreter creates the text that will produce the kind of thoughts and judgments in the contemporary audience that the historical author and audience had.

This view of interpretation presupposes, of course, that different causes can produce the same effect. In our case, a historical text can produce the same acts of understanding in the historical author and the historical audience as the interpretation of the text produces in the contemporary audience. But I do not believe that this presupposition is unreasonable, because it is supported by our experience. There are, indeed, various ways to skin a cat, as the saying goes.

Now we can see more clearly why interpretation is an integral part of the historical task of understanding texts, for its aim is to bridge the conceptual, cultural, and other contextual gaps that separate the historical text from a later time at which it is being read, heard, or even remembered. It also explains why interpretations need not be considered anachronistic simply in virtue of the fact that they add to the historical text, because the function of the additions they contain is precisely to produce acts of understanding in the contemporary audience that are intensionally the same as those the historical text produced or would have produced in the historical author of the text and the historical audience.

In spite of the advantages that the view of the function of interpretations presented seems to have, it faces two serious difficulties. The first is that interpretations still appear somehow distorting, for the acts of understanding produced by an interpretation could never be exactly like the acts of understanding the historical author and historical audience had. Consider the following text:

1. Dos y dos son cuatro.

And consider the following interpretation of 1:

2. 'Dos y dos son cuatro' means that two and two equal four.

The point of the objection is that what the historical author and the contemporaneous audience understood by 1 is that two and two equal four, but what the English speaker for whom I have provided 2 understands is that 'Dos y dos son cuatro' means that two and two equal four, *not* that two and two equal four. Indeed, the truth-value conditions of 1 and 2 are different, which seems to imply that, after all, the contemporary audience does not understand the same meaning as the historical author and the historical audience.

This difficulty appears very serious at first, but I believe it can be resolved if we take into account an important fact; namely, that interpretations are not presented as the historical texts (the *interpretanda*) of which they are interpretations. The audience of the interpretation knows that the function of interpretations is to help them understand the *interpretanda*, a fact that is clear from the language used in the *interpretans*. The term 'means' used in the example given, for example, indicates to the audience that the meaning of the expression that follows it is to be taken as equivalent to the meaning of the *interpretandum*, and not that the meaning of the whole interpretation is to be taken as equivalent to the meaning of the *interpretandum*. Remember, the function of the sort of interpretation about which we have been speaking is not to produce meaning equivalence, but rather equivalent acts of understanding, and those acts are the result of the addition of the *interpretans* to the *interpretandum* and the audience's understanding of the relation between *interpretandum* and *interpretans*.

The second serious difficulty may be formulated as a dilemma: the interpreter either understands a text or does not. If he or she does, then there is no need for an interpretation. But if he or she does not, how can the interpreter know that the interpretation is accurate? Put this way, it would seem that interpretations turn out to be either unnecessary or necessary but impossible.

In response to this objection we must grant that, under most circumstances, interpretations that have a historical function presuppose an understanding of the historical text by the interpreter similar to the understanding of it the historical author and the historical audience had and in that sense they are superfluous to that understanding. (Note that I say "under most circumstances," for there is no logical necessity here. It is possible, although unlikely, for an interpretation based on the misunderstanding of a text to produce an understanding of the text. More on this in Section III.) Nevertheless, it is still possible to hold that such an understanding does not make interpretations superfluous. The reason is that the purpose of interpretations is to produce understanding not in the interpreters but in their contemporary audiences. Although an interpretation is not what produces an understanding of the text in the interpreter, it does produce, or is supposed to produce, an understanding in the audience for which the interpretation is given.

The task of the interpreter is similar in many ways to the task of the translator. What the translator does is to change the signs (or their arrangements) of which a text is composed to convey the meaning he or she understands the original signs and their arrangements to have.[17] The translator's audience is one that does not understand the significance of those original signs and arrangements, but understands other signs and arrangements that can be combined to produce in the audience understandings similar to those produced by the historical text in its author and historical audience.

This does not mean that translations and interpretations are the same thing. There are some obvious differences between translations and interpretations. For example, a translation is always composed of signs and arrangements in a language different from the language in which the historical text was rendered, whereas an interpretation may be, but seldom is, so composed. A translation takes the place of the historical text, whereas an interpretation is a composite of the historical text (*interpretandum*) and the textual additions to it (*interpretans*). Finally, translations follow texts carefully and aim to preserve as much of the order and structure of the original as possible, but interpretations generally are quite free to change order and structure. Indeed, in many translations it is important to try to reproduce the form of texts—a procedure common in the translation of poetry, for example—whereas in most interpretations this is not important. In short, there are significant differences between translations and interpretations that stem from the fact that translations are a peculiar type of interpretations, but do not always function as interpretations.

Let me go back now to the point I was making; namely, that the similarities between translations and interpretations illustrate the role of interpreters. For just like translators, interpreters prepare the causal framework that makes possible the conveyance of meaning to an audience unfamiliar with the semantic significance of the components of a historical text.

I have, then, granted that interpretations are superfluous for interpreters, but I have indicated that they are still important for contemporary audiences insofar as, without interpretations, audiences could not bridge the temporal, cultural, and other contextual gaps that separate them from the circumstances surrounding the genesis of the historical text. Moreover, the reason that interpretations are superfluous for interpreters is that, as noted, interpreters are required in most cases to understand the historical texts to produce interpretations. This brings us to an important and difficult question: How can an interpreter, or anyone for that matter, come to know the meaning of a text he or she has not produced, particularly when temporally and culturally distant from the historical period in which the text was produced, and how can he or she be certain of knowing it? This is an important issue in hermeneutics that requires further attention, but I shall postpone its consideration until the next chapter. I shall return later in this chapter to the requirement of understanding on the part of the interpreter whose task involves a historical function.

Now let me turn to the other two functions of interpretations mentioned earlier. As stated, the generic function of interpretations is to produce acts of understanding in contemporary audiences in relation to a text, but whether those acts are supposed to re-create the acts of the historical author and the historical audience or not depends very much on the type of text and the cultural function it has. As we saw in Chapter 4, some texts tolerate and in some cases even require understandings on the part of contemporary audiences that are different from the understandings their authors and historical audiences had. The reason is that their meaning is not determined by their authors and historical audiences alone, but by other factors as well, such as society and language. It is a mistake, then, to restrict the function of interpretations to the re-creation in the contemporary audience of the acts of understanding of the author and historical audience of the text.

B. Meaning Function

The first of the two other functions of interpretations mentioned earlier, the Meaning Function, is to create in contemporary audiences acts of understanding warranted by the meaning of the text, whether such acts were or were not had either by the author or the historical audience of the text.[18] In short, an interpreter might, through the interpretation, provide a glimpse of the meaning of a text for an audience that neither the historical author nor the historical audience of the text had. Note that the understanding in question has to be warranted by the meaning; it is not a matter for the interpreter simply to provide an understanding of a meaning that is not the meaning of the text. If that were so, then the text would not be the same, even if its ECTs were the same. To preserve understanding and not fall into misunderstanding, the acts of understanding produced by the interpretation must presuppose that those acts have as their object a meaning that is not substantially different from the meaning of the text. In other words, they must presuppose textual identity.

Our experience often vouches for this sort of thing. Authors frequently say and write things that subsequent generations interpret as meaning much more or much less than the authors and their audiences thought the texts meant.[19] And yet we would not want to say that those interpretations lead to misunderstandings or do not refer to the same texts. Indeed, many of the Supreme Court's commentaries on the Constitution of the United States can be seen precisely as involving this sort of thing.

But, as noted elsewhere in this book, the function of the audience is not creative in the sense that its job is always, and for all texts, to create new meanings.[20] If that were so, then the job of the audience would be to create new texts, because essential differences in meaning imply changes in textual identity, converting the audience into an author. There must be creativity in audiences, but the creativity of the audience and that of the author are of different sorts. The audience may discover meanings for texts of which no one, including the historical author, was aware before, but those meanings must be part of the overall meaning of the text as warranted by the cultural function that the text in question has.

Note, finally, that in this function it is even more clear that the task of the interpreter, generally, even if not logically, presupposes an understanding of the meaning of a text. For to create a text that together with the historical text will produce acts of understanding of the meaning of the historical text in a contemporary audience, one must oneself, under most circumstances, understand that meaning.

C. Implicative Function

The other function interpretations have that is consistent with the overall aim of producing acts of understanding in contemporary audiences in relation to a text is to uncover the implications of the meaning of historical texts. In this sense, an interpretation is no longer concerned merely with understanding the meaning of the historical text, but with much more. The distinction between the meaning of a text and the implications of that meaning, introduced in Chapter 4, helps us here. For the function of an interpretation in this third sense is to provide an understanding of those implications.

Again, this function of interpretations is common in our experience, for our critics frequently point to implications of our expressed views that had escaped us and that, if we had been aware of them at the time we were developing those views, would have led us to change them and thus the way we express them. There is no need to give examples of this phenomenon, for most readers of this book are probably quite familiar with it.

Finally, so as not to leave any loose ends, it should be clear that understanding the meaning of the historical text by the interpreter generally is a requirement to the fulfillment of this function. An interpreter could in principle produce acts of understanding of the implications of the meaning of a text in a contemporary audience without personally understanding the meaning of the text, but this is very unlikely. One expects that an interpreter will not be able to produce such acts of understanding unless the interpreter understands the meaning of the text the understanding of whose implications are in question.

Let me finish this section, then, by drawing attention, first, to the distinction made earlier among three things that are frequently identified as interpretation: (1) an interpretation conceived as a composite of the text to be interpreted (*interpretandum*) and the textual additions (*interpretans*) required to understand it, (2) the acts of understanding of a subject, and (3) the process or activity whereby someone develops an understanding. It is commonplace to find philosophers speaking of these three as the same thing. In the scheme I am proposing, however, they are to be distinguished, and an interpretation is to be conceived as a text composed of a text that is to be interpreted and of another text whose function, when taken together with the text under interpretation, is to produce understanding in an audience. Understandings, by contrast, are not conceived as texts, but rather as acts related to texts as their effects; an understanding is related to an interpretation as an effect is to a cause and should not be confused with it. Moreover, the process or activity whereby someone develops an understanding is not regarded as a text either, and thus must be kept distinct from the textual conception of interpretations I have presented here.

Also important to note is the need for interpretations. Interpretations that have the historical function are necessary for audiences other than historical authors and historical audiences because those audiences can seldom have understandings that are accurate without them; this I hope has become clear from what has been said concerning the function of interpretations and the Interpreter's Dilemma. It is not likely that contemporary audiences can effectively understand texts from which they are historically far removed without the help of interpretations. Moreover, interpretations that have either the meaning or implicative functions are also needed, because the understanding that historical authors and historical audiences have of texts frequently does not exhaust the meaning of those texts, and even if they do, it is often important for contemporary audiences to develop the implications of those meanings. The choice in most cases, then, is not whether one will produce or not produce interpretations, but whether the interpretations produced are good or bad.

We may ask, then, what are good and bad interpretations or, more precisely, what makes interpretations more or less effective or adequate? The effectiveness and adequacy of interpretations depends on how well they fulfill their function. That function, as we saw, could be to re-create in the contemporary audience the acts of understanding of the historical author and the historical audience, or the production in the contemporary audience of an understanding of the meaning of the text or the implications of that meaning. Thus, for example, an interpretation whose function it is to produce in the contemporary audience an understanding of the meaning of a text but fails to carry it out to some degree is, therefore, inadequate to that degree. Say that a text is ambiguous and the interpretation does not express the ambiguity, then the interpretation is inadequate. Consider the following text:

1.   Loosely wrapped in a newspaper he carried a book.

And consider the following interpretations of this text:

2.   'Loosely wrapped in a newspaper he carried a book' means he carried a book that was loosely wrapped in a newspaper.
3.   'Loosely wrapped in a newspaper he carried a book' means he was loosely wrapped in a newspaper while carrying a book.
4.   'Loosely wrapped in a newspaper he carried a book' means he carried a book that was loosely wrapped in a newspaper or he was loosely wrapped in a newspaper while carrying a book.

Interpretations 2 and 3 are obviously inadequate, because they do not capture the ambiguity expressed by 1. Interpretation 4, by contrast, appears to be a better interpretation for it preserves the ambiguity of 1.

But now let us suppose that the function of the interpretation is not to produce an understanding of the meaning of the text, as we had supposed, but rather to reproduce in the audience the acts of understanding that the historical author had. And let us further assume that, in addition to the text, the interpreter saw next to the text we have given as an example, another text from the historical author of the text in which he went on to condemn the loose morality of the man who was carrying the book because he did not cover himself properly. Then it would be clear that the adequate interpretation of 1 would be 3, for that would lead the contemporary audience to think as the author thought, namely, to think of a man who was loosely wrapped in a newspaper and carried a book.

The value, adequacy, or effectiveness of interpretations depends very much on how well they fulfill their specific function. In some cases, that function prescribes the preservation of textual ambiguities, but in other cases it prescribes the resolution of such ambiguities. No blanket indictment can be made against all interpretations that produce in contemporary audiences understandings different from those the historical author and the historical audience had. Nor does it make sense to put all interpretations on equal footing as far as value is concerned. Interpretations are more or less adequate and effective, and thus good or bad, depending on their specific function and how well they carry it out. To judge them, one must first determine that function.

The different functions of interpretations explain also the fact that there may be different interpretations of a text that are equally effective. Consider the example given earlier. If the function of one interpretation is to reproduce the acts of understanding of the historical author with respect to 1 and the historical author understood 1 in accordance with 3 and another interpretation seeks to produce an understanding of the meaning of 1, regardless of what the historical author thought it meant, then both 3 and 4 are effective interpretations, even though they conflict, as long as one keeps in mind their different specific functions. (For present purposes I am assuming, of course, that 4 correctly expresses the meaning of 1.) Likewise, it may turn out that the same interpretation carries out more than one function. Consider the case in which the historical author of 1 understood it in accordance with 4. In this case 4 would fulfill two functions: the re-creation in the contemporary audience of the acts of understanding the historical author had and also the production in this audience of acts of understanding that made the contemporary audience understand the meaning of 1.

In short, we may conclude that many of the puzzles raised in the contemporary literature concerned with the identity of texts and the possibility of conflicting interpretations vanish when one considers the nature of interpretations and their functions.[21] In this way we can resolve the vexing issue of whether interpretations involve construction or discovery, for example.[22] From what has been said it follows that all interpretations involve construction, namely, the production of a text that will produce acts of understanding in an audience. And they involve discovery to the degree that interpreters must search for the best means to produce those acts of understanding. But interpretations do not directly involve the construction or discovery of meaning. That task falls to understanding, although interpretations presuppose understanding of meaning.

III. Types of Interpretations: Textual versus Nontextual

Interpretations may be classified in all sorts of ways. For example, they may be classified as mental or physical, oral or written, personal or collective, and so on. None of these classifications, however, is particularly pertinent for the present discussion. One classification of interpretations, however, has important implications for us. It is the classification into textual and nontextual, and it is based on the cultural function of the interpretation in question.

We know from what was said earlier, that an interpretation is a text, and moreover, we know from Chapter 3 that texts have different cultural functions. An interpretation is, first and foremost, an attempt to produce acts of understanding in an audience in relation to a text. In some cases, such acts of understanding are intended to be closely related to the meaning of the text but in others they are not. Indeed, we often seek to produce acts of understanding in an audience vis-à-vis a text not simply to grasp its meaning, or the implications of its meaning, but for other reasons as well, such as making known the historical significance of past events, the character of other persons, and so on. These various purposes, which concur in general with the cultural functions of texts explored in Chapter 3, give rise to different sorts of interpretations.

Interpretations whose main or only purpose is to produce understandings of the meanings of texts (whether those meanings are taken to be determined by the acts of understanding of the historical author and the historical audience or not) and of the implications of those meanings may be distinguished from a second sort. That second sort are interpretations whose primary aim is not to produce such understandings, even in cases when such understandings are necessary for the fulfillment of the primary aim of the interpretations. I call the first *textual interpretations* and the second *nontextual interpretations*.[23]

A textual interpretation is precisely the sort of interpretation we have been discussing in this chapter. It is an interpretation of a text that adds to the text whatever is thought by the interpreter to be necessary to get certain results in contemporary minds in relation to the text, when those results are taken in one of three ways: First, as the re-creation of the acts of understanding of the historical author and the historical audience, that is, as the understanding of the meaning the historical author and the historical audience had; second, as the production of acts of understanding whereby the meaning of the text, regardless of what the historical author and historical audience thought, is understood by the contemporary audience; and third, as the production of acts of understanding whereby the implications of the meaning of the text are understood by the contemporary audience. A nontextual interpretation is one that, although it may be based on a textual interpretation, has something else as its primary aim even if such an aim involves or is a kind of understanding. In short, the functions of nontextual interpretations are different from the three functions textual interpretations have and are not primarily directed toward the meaning of the text or its implications.

The distinction between textual and nontextual interpretations may be easily illustrated by contrasting a textual interpretation with a historical interpretation, for historical interpretations constitute one type of nontextual interpretation. The significance of this example derives from the fact that the role of the interpreter who seeks to produce a textual interpretation is also usually a historical one; she wants to produce understandings in a contemporary audience, either understandings that the historical author and the historical audience also had or that they did not have but nonetheless are legitimate understandings of the meaning of the text, or to produce understandings of the implications of the meaning of the text. And this is achieved by finding out something about the past. The task of the historian who wishes to provide a historical interpretation, however, goes beyond that of the textual interpreter; the primary task here is not to produce a textual interpretation, but over and above that to provide a historical account of the past, and this account involves much more than a textual interpretation.

A historical interpretation is more than a textual interpretation because it seeks to reconstruct the intricate weave of thoughts and ideas and relations that were not recorded in the historical text and are neither part of its meaning nor of the implications of that meaning.[24] This is, indeed, what makes history appear more than just a series of atomically discrete events.[25] The ultimate aim of the historian is to produce an account of the past and that account includes not only textual interpretations, but also the reconstruction of the larger context in which the text was produced, the ideas that the historical author did not put down in writing or express in speech, the relations among various texts from the same author and from other authors, the causal connections among texts, and so on. The aim of the historian is more than the creation of an instrument that would cause the reproduction of the acts of understanding of the author and the historical audience when they were confronted with the text, or that would help the contemporary audience understand the meaning of the text in new ways, or to grasp better the implications of that meaning. The historian also wants to produce other acts of understanding in the audience that neither the author nor the historical audience had or could have had precisely because of their historical (i.e., temporal, cultural, and spatial) limitations and that are possible for the historian and his contemporary audience owing to their different historical location and perspective. These acts are not acts of understanding of just the meaning of the text or of the implications of that meaning, but go beyond them in significant ways.

In short, a textual interpretation is only the beginning and only one element of a historical interpretation. The task of historians is much larger than simply to offer textual interpretations of texts, although if they are going to get anywhere in their task they generally must begin with those types of interpretations. Qua textual interpreters, they need (1) to reproduce in the minds of their audience acts of understanding similar to those present in the minds of the authors and their contemporaneous audiences, (2) to produce in those audiences a better understanding of the texts in question by helping them understand parts of the meaning of the texts not understood by its historical authors and audiences, and (3) to help those audiences grasp some of the implications of that meaning. But this is not all they do. Qua historians their job is to go beyond this and provide an account of history that goes beyond the text. Historical interpretations, like other nontextual interpretations, aim to produce acts of understanding that involve more than the text, its meaning, and the implications of that meaning; they involve the relation of the text to other things.

Historical interpretations are just one sort of nontextual interpretations. There are many others, depending on the cultural functions interpretations may have. For example, there can be philosophical, inspirational, legal, political, scientific, and literary interpretations, among others. And within these there may be various subcategories as well. We have already spoken of psychological interpretations in which a text is seen as revealing something about the person who produced it in addition to whatever other meaning it has. This is a very popular type of interpretation among those literary critics who favor the Freudian scheme and are trying to apply it, sometimes indiscriminately, to every text they confront. But it should not be necessary to give more examples to illustrate the distinction between textual and nontextual interpretations.

Part of the significance of the distinction between textual and nontextual interpretations lies in that it may help us sort out some of the confusion surrounding interpretations, their function, and the task of interpreters. The confusion arises because most interpreters have given very little thought to the significance of what they do and as a result either misinterpret what they do or dismiss those who do something different. Consider, for example, the many literary critics who spend their time looking at texts through a Freudian schema. In this context, what these interpreters do is create texts that, added to historical texts, yield understandings in their audiences of the sort very different from what textual interpretations would yield. These audiences might conclude, for example, that a particular character of a play, written in the sixteenth century, acts in a certain way because he has certain sexual inclinations that are repressed in his unconscious. Now, this kind of Freudian interpretation may not tell us anything about what the historical author or the historical audience of the text actually understood when they attended a performance of the play or read a transcript of it. Nor can it be said to be implied by the meaning of the text. So, if this Freudian interpretation is presented as a textual interpretation, it can be regarded only as a misinterpretation, because it creates in the contemporary audience a misunderstanding of the meaning of the play or the implications of that meaning.

Yet, it would be too precipitous to conclude from this that this sort of interpretation is illegitimate or useless. The interpretation is, of course, illegitimate and useless if taken as textual. But if we take it as nontextual, then the picture changes drastically. For in that case the aim of the interpretation is none of the three aims we have associated with the three functions identified earlier. Rather, its aim might be precisely to provide a Freudian understanding of the text and, if the interpretation does so effectively, then it is not only legitimate but also successful—although its usefulness will still depend on the use which can be given to it.

It is very important to realize, however, that some nontextual interpretations presuppose an understanding of the text under interpretation by the interpreter. If, as is often the case, nontextual interpretations presuppose the understanding of texts but are based on misunderstandings of them, then such interpretations are at risk of not being legitimate, useful, valid, or effective, because they might lead contemporary audiences to misunderstandings and faulty inferences. The problem with many interpreters who produce nontextual interpretations is that they do not realize that often their interpretations require accurate understandings of the texts they seek to interpret before they can engage in the production of nontextual interpretations.

The question of which nontextual interpretations require understanding of the texts they interpret by the interpreters and which do not is not easy to answer. At first one is tempted to say that all interpretations, including nontextual ones, require such an understanding. But from what was said in Chapter 4 and earlier in this chapter, it is clear that this cannot be so. For understanding consists in grasping the meaning of a text, and not all interpretations presuppose grasping such a meaning on the part of interpreters. Indeed, even in the case of textual interpretations, only those whose function is the meaning or implicative functions make a strong case for requiring the understanding of the meaning of the text. The first because the meaning function entails precisely producing an understanding in a contemporary audience of the meaning of a text. The second because the implicative function entails producing an understanding of the implications of that meaning in a contemporary audience, and such an understanding presupposes in most instances an understanding of the meaning itself. The case of the historical function, however, is different. For the historical function aims to reproduce the acts of understanding in a contemporary audience of the acts of understanding of the historical author of the text and the historical audience, and such acts, as noted in Chapter 4, do not necessarily determine the meaning of the text. Only in cases where authorial understanding determines meaning could textual interpretations with a historical function be taken to presuppose, although not logically, an understanding of the text, if by that is meant, as I mean here, a grasp of the meaning of the text. Now, if the situation is not uniform with respect to textual interpretations, it should be expected that it will be even less uniform with respect to nontextual interpretations and therefore that not in all cases, or even in most, will they require understanding of the text in question. In which cases they do or do not will depend on the type of nontextual interpretation.

In short, then, contrary to what some philosophers think, there is nothing wrong with nontextual interpretations of texts as long as (1) they are not presented as textual, and (2) they are built on understanding, not misunderstanding, the texts under interpretation when such an understanding is a requirement of the interpretations. Freudians may have the interpretations they like as long as they do not misrepresent them as textual or construct them on misunderstandings that adversely affect the interpretations. And, like Freudians, we can also have Marxist, feminist, historical, literary, mystical, philosophical, sociological, and other interpretations. Indeed, the use of texts is to a great extent tied to these interpretations, for texts are useful only if they are put to a use beyond the conveyance of meaning.

Finally, it should not be assumed that nontextual interpretations conflict with textual ones or with each other. Because their function is to produce nontextual understandings of texts in audiences, which involve considering the text in different contexts and, as it were, under different lights, there is no necessity that these interpretations, or the understandings they produce, conflict. Thus, a Marxist interpretation and understanding of a text need not conflict with a Freudian one, for example. To think otherwise is not only unwarranted, but also the source of much unnecessary vexation among those who concern themselves with hermeneutics.

IV. Number, Truth Value, and Objectivity of Interpretations

Let us suppose that we accept what has been said so far concerning interpretations. Even then, we are still left with three puzzling questions: How many interpretations of a text are there? Can one interpretation be true and another false? And, what does it mean to say that interpretations are objective or subjective?

These three questions carry a different import, depending on whether they refer to textual or nontextual interpretations. Let us consider textual interpretations first and see how the questions apply to them.

A. Of Textual Interpretations

1. Number. The answer to the first question when applied to textual interpretations will depend on how many commentaries on a text have been done, and it would have to be determined on the basis of empirical evidence. If we asked, for example, whether there is one or many textual interpretations of Aristotle's *Metaphysics*, it is obvious from even a cursory review of the literature that there are many. But neither this type of answer nor the question that it answers is very interesting for the philosopher. What the philosopher would like to know is rather whether there is and can be only one *correct* interpretation of a text or whether there is room for more than one. Of course, if 'text' is taken to refer generically to all the texts discussed in Chapter 3, it is clear that there can be as many correct interpretations as there are texts. For the question to have any philosophical interest it has to refer either to a single historical text or to one of its contemporary versions. Understood in this sense, the issue that the question raises is at the heart of the hermeneutical inquiry and relates in many ways to similar issues that can be raised concerning science and philosophy. In the case of science, the question involves whether what physical scientists, for example, produce or seek to produce are more or less approximations to *the one correct* description of nature or whether what physical scientists produce or seek to produce are various versions of *equally correct* descriptions of nature. With philosophy, a similar question could be posed. Is there one correct philosophy or are there many? Note that the question of correctness approaches, but is not equivalent to, the question of truth, but I shall leave that aside for the moment.

One way of approaching the question of whether there is or can be only one or more than one correct textual interpretation of a text is by looking at the success of various interpretations. That, however, cannot give us an affirmative answer because there is so far no textual interpretation of any text of relatively substantial length and with a substantial degree of complexity whose success has proved unquestionable. The case with relatively simple texts, of course, may be altogether different. Nor do the extraordinary difficulties involved in providing textual interpretations, to which I pointed earlier, support optimistic predictions concerning future interpretations. Indeed, much philosophical effort since Kant has gone to show in one way or another that we have no way of arriving at final and definitive descriptions in science—or philosophy—and thus it would be presumptuous to assume that it is likely that we can arrive at final and definitive textual interpretations.

There is, however, another way of looking at this question that yields different results. If what I have argued concerning the nature and function of textual interpretations makes sense, then it is not possible to think that there can be one definitive interpretation of a text, even in the narrow case in which its function is to reproduce the acts of understanding of the historical author and historical audience of the text in a contemporary audience (let alone the other two). And this is so as long as there are cultural and conceptual differences between the historical author and the historical audience of the historical text on the one hand and the audience contemporary with the interpreter on the other.[26] Each new audience will require a new interpretation that will bridge the gaps between it and the historical author and the historical audience of the historical text if cultural, social, and other differences separate it from the historical author and historical audience. The only way in which there could be one definitive textual interpretation of a text would be if its audiences always had the same cultural and conceptual framework, but that, although not logically impossible, is not a realistic option.

Yet, there is no reason why there could not be a definitive interpretation of a text for a particular time and place, that is, an interpretation that best helps to bridge the gaps between the text and the audience of that time and place. And there is no reason either why there cannot be interpretations that are more enduring than others. Indeed, some interpretations may be such that they can bridge the gap between the historical text and several subsequent audiences rather than just one. Moreover, the notion of a possible, single, correct textual interpretation is methodologically significant, for this notion both propels ongoing efforts at interpretation, preventing complacency, and furthers the critical spirit that should animate any interpretative search.[27] Care should be taken, however, that the adherence to this notion be nondogmatic and nonideological. Its function, as that of the ideal text, is regulative rather than substantive, and, if kept at that level, its effects can be very beneficial.

If the function of a textual interpretation is not understood narrowly as referring only to the historical function, but broadly, as referring to the meaning and implicative functions as well, then it is even more clear that there can be many interpretations of a text. In that case the function of an interpretation is not the recreation in a contemporary audience of the acts of understanding of the historical author and the historical audience in relation to the text. Its function is rather (1) the production of acts of understanding that reveal the meaning of the text, even if the historical author and the historical audience did not have those acts, and (2) the production of acts that reveal the implications of that meaning. For the number of interpretations will depend on the breadth and implications of the meaning of the text. Moreover, in some cases the meaning of texts is openended, as determined by their cultural function, leaving open also the number of interpretations that may be given to them.

Before I leave the question of the number of textual interpretations we should consider a possible objection to the position presented here that is relevant at this point. According to that position, a textual interpretation is a text composed of a text that functions as *interpretandum* and a text that functions as *interpretans*. Moreover, I have indicated that interpretations change and must change with each new set of circumstances to make up for the differences between the conditions under which the historical text was produced and the conditions under which it is being considered. If this be so, then someone might object, first, that the understanding of texts through interpretations leads to an infinite regress in the following way: If for person P_1 to understand text T, produced by an author A, a text T_1 must be added to T so that together with T it makes up an interpretation I_1, then we are led into an infinite regress. To understand I_1, another text T_2 must be added to it, which together with it constitutes another interpretation I_2, and so on.[28] And this regress prevents anyone but the author of the text from understanding it.

This objection fails because it overlooks two important aspects of the view presented here. The first is that several persons can and often do understand texts without use of an interpretation. Indeed, we have noted earlier that an interpretation often presupposes understanding on the part of the interpreter. Not everyone who looks at the sign 'No smoking' needs to have it interpreted to understand it. This happens when the texts in question are historically contemporary with their audiences, but also can happen in cases in which the texts are not historically contemporary with their audiences but there are sufficient cultural bridges between the time and culture in which the texts were produced and the time and culture of the audience who is trying to understand it. And this applies to textual interpretations also, so it is not always necessary to interpret texts or interpretations to have them understood by an audience, leaving no fear of an infinite regress.

The second point is that what requires interpreting in an interpretation is the *interpretandum* of the interpretation and not the interpretation considered as a whole, unless the interpretation should become itself an *interpretandum*. Accordingly, it is not always necessary to go through other interpretations in order to interpret and understand a text, even though often, as we shall see later, that is a useful exercise and can increase the certainty concerning the effectiveness of textual interpretations.

The view presented here does not imply an infinite regress of interpretations. To understand T, P_n does not need to have an interpretation that looks like this: $I_1 + I_2 + I_3... + I_{\&}$. When P_n requires an interpretation, she only requires one that looks like: $I_1 = T + T_n$.

2. Truth Value. Now let us turn to the second question, concerned with truth and falsity of textual interpretations. We must begin by recalling that textual interpretations generally are texts in natural languages, and those texts are composed of sentences. In some cases they contain few sentences, but in other cases they contain many—as many as hundreds and thousands of them in very long texts. Indeed, it is difficult to think of an interpretation that contains only one simple sentence; for, as noted earlier, textual interpretations contain the *interpretandum* and the *interpretans*, and even if the *interpretandum* is composed of only one sentence, the interpretation will be composed of that sentence and whatever is added to it by the *interpretans*.

Consider the Spanish text, "Nadie fuma aquí." An interpretation of it for an English speaker, which boils down to a translation plus a semantic tie to the original text, could be something like: "'Nadie fuma aquí' means no one smokes here." This is obviously a complex sentence, composed of the original sentence and a predicate added to it, in which the truth table of the second sentence is more complicated than the truth table of the first. This example illustrates that textual interpretations are composed of complex sentences. So, when the texts under interpretation are each also composed of more than one sentence, the interpretations end up being composed of many sentences. And this, of course, poses difficulties for the determination of the truth value of the interpretation considered as a whole. Each of the sentences of which an interpretation is composed not only has its own truth value, but that truth value is no doubt related to the truth value of at least some other one of the sentences composing the interpretation. Moreover, because it is possible, indeed quite likely, that the sentences that compose an interpretation have different truth values, it becomes difficult, if not impossible, to speak of the truth value of the whole interpretation. Let me illustrate the point. Consider the following text:

> Nadie fuma aquí ahora. La última persona que fumó aquí fue condenada a muerte.

And let us have three interpretations of it for an English audience who does not understand Spanish:

Interpretation 1:   'Nadie fuma aquí ahora. La última persona que fumó aquí fue condenada a muerte.' means "No one smokes here now. The last person who smoked here was condemned to death."

Interpretation 2:   'Nadie fuma aquí ahora. La última persona que fumó aquí fue condenada a muerte.' means "Everyone smokes here now. The last person who smoked here was condemned to death."

Interpretation 3:   'Nadie fuma aquí ahora. La última persona que fumó aquí fue condenada a muerte." means "Everyone smokes here now. The last person who smoked here was given a prize."

In Interpretation 1, the *interpretans* correctly expresses the meaning of the *interpretandum*. In Interpretation 2, the second sentence of the *interpretans* correctly expresses the meaning of the second sentence of the *interpretandum*, but the first sentence does not. And in Interpretation 3, neither of the sentences of the *interpretans* correctly expresses the meaning of the sentences that make up the *interpretandum*. Now, the difficulty about which we have been speaking concerning the characterization of interpretations as true or false should be evident. For, even if we had no difficulty characterizing Interpretation 1 as true, and Interpretation 3 as false, what are we going to do with Interpretation 2? This difficulty compounds itself when *interpretanda* are very complex texts and when we take into account the truth value of the sentences that compose them, something which we have not done in the examples provided.

A more serious difficulty that needs to be brought up has to do with the function of interpretations. According to what was said earlier, their function is to produce acts of understanding in the contemporary audience. But, if that is so, their purpose is not to produce a perception of the truth and falsity of certain sentences, but rather to produce certain mental acts (unless, of course, such acts involve the perception of something as true or false), which means that the characterization of interpretations as true or false is irrelevant to their purpose. The point of interpretations is to produce an understanding of a text in a contemporary audience that, without the interpretation, would not be possible; it is not to produce an understanding of the truth value of what is understood. Consider the example given earlier. The function of the interpretation "'Nadie fuma aquí' means no one smokes here" is to make someone understand that the *interpretandum* means that no one smokes here, not that what the *interpretandum* means is true. The understanding of the truth of what the *interpretandum* means is actually the understanding of a different sentence, namely, "'Nadie fuma aquí' is true."

Finally, I have not yet referred to what is perhaps the most serious obstacle to speaking about the truth value of textual interpretations. This has to do with the fact that, as we saw earlier, textual interpretations have three different functions and these functions lead to different claims. It is one thing to claim that an interpretation is true because it reproduces in an audience acts of understanding similar to those of the historical author and the historical audience, another to claim that it is true because it causes in the contemporary audience acts of understanding of the meaning of the text, and still another to claim that it is true because it reproduces acts of understanding of the implications of the meaning of the text. It would make no sense to speak about the truth of textual interpretations without qualification, even if there were no other objections to it.

In spite of these difficulties, it does seem that, as mentioned earlier, we do wish to speak of interpretations as correct or incorrect and this may lead one to think that what is at stake is their truth and falsity.[29] From the view of textual interpretations presented here, however, it follows that truth and falsity is not what is at stake. What is at stake is the degree to which textual interpretations are effective in carrying out their functions. Truth and falsity apply rather to understandings. To reflect this sense, then, it would be better to speak of interpretations as more or less effective or more or less adequate.[30] This avoids the problems involved in judging the truth value of interpretations because, first of all, it reflects the function of interpretations, which is to produce certain kinds of understandings. Second, it is a matter of degree, so that an interpretation of a long text can be judged more or less adequate, depending on the degree to which its parts in turn cause accurate understandings of the parts of the *interpretandum* they interpret. It is not an all or none question, as is the case with truth, but rather a question of more or less.

3. Objectivity and Subjectivity. This brings us to the third question raised at the beginning of this section, concerned with the objectivity and subjectivity of interpretations. In the case of interpretations, as with understandings in Chapter 4, I will take the degree of subjectivity of an interpretation generally to refer to the degree to which an interpretation is a result of the interpreting subject independent of the interpreted object, that is, the text and whatever else determines its meaning.[31] Obviously, because the interpretations under consideration are textual interpretations, the object is always taken into account, and the subjectivity of the interpretation will always be influenced by that consideration.

Objectivity is the counterpart of subjectivity. In the case of interpretations, I take the degree of objectivity to refer to the degree to which an interpretation is a result of the interpreting subject's consideration of the object, and thus as dependent on that object, namely the text, and the factors outside the interpreting subject that determine its meaning. As with subjectivity, the objectivity of interpretations is a matter of degree, because all interpretations are to some extent the result of subjects and thus depend on them.

If we apply these considerations to textual interpretations, we can see that their degree of subjectivity and objectivity could depend on two factors. In the first place, because the *interpretandum* is a given, the subjectivity or objectivity of an interpretation will depend on the degree to which the *interpretans* is the product of the interpreting subject and subjective factors, rather than of the subject's consideration of the *interpretandum* and objective factors outside the interpreting subject. A highly subjective textual interpretation, then, is a text composed of textual additions to a historical text in whose production the interpreting subject took very little account of the historical text or the objective factors outside himself or herself that played a role in the determination of the meaning of the text. And a highly objective interpretation is one in which the historical text and the mentioned factors are given primary consideration by the interpreting subject.

In the second place, because one of the functions of textual interpretations is to produce in the contemporary audience acts of understanding similar to the acts that the historical author and the historical audience had, one may speak of the degree of subjectivity and objectivity of textual interpretations in reference to the degree that they fulfill that function. The more effective or adequate an interpretation is, the more objective it is, and the less effective and adequate, the more subjective it is.

This latter way of understanding the subjectivity and objectivity of textual interpretations, however, is out of line with the first sense discussed and, indeed, with the general understanding of subjectivity and objectivity given earlier. For it is perfectly possible for an interpretation in the first sense to be highly subjective and be at the same time highly objective in the second sense, and vice versa. Indeed, a historical interpretation produced with little regard for the text and the objective factors that play a role in the determination of the text's meaning may turn out to produce acts of understanding in the contemporary audience that are more similar to the acts which the text's author and the historical audience had than an interpretation whose production gave those factors primary importance. This understanding of subjectivity and objectivity confuses them with inaccuracy and accuracy, ineffectiveness or effectiveness. 'Subjectivity' and 'objectivity' are terms that describe the character of an interpretation in terms of its causes. Inaccuracy and accuracy, and ineffectiveness and effectiveness, on the other hand, describe an interpretation in terms of its effects. To avoid these confusions, it is more appropriate, when concerned with interpretations, to reserve the use of the terms 'subjective' and 'objective' for the first senses discussed.

B. Of Nontextual Interpretations

But what do we make of nontextual interpretations? Does what has been said about textual interpretations apply also to nontextual ones? As noted earlier, nontextual interpretations are interpretations in which there is a further and primary aim beyond the aims of understanding (1) the text as its historical author and contemporaneous audience did, (2) its meaning apart from what the historical author and the historical audience understood, and (3) the implications of the meaning of the text. In a psychological interpretation, for example, the aim is to understand the psychological state of mind of the author of the text, and similar things could be said, mutatis mutandis, about other types of nontextual interpretations. Now, the differences between textual and nontextual interpretations affect to some extent the issue concerned with the number of correct interpretations. For, indeed, it would seem quite clear that there can be not only as many nontextual correct interpretations as textual ones, but many more. Their number in excess of textual interpretations will depend on the functions that such interpretations are meant to carry out. The same text may yield correct religious, legal, historical, and psychological interpretations, among others, in addition to textual ones.

Indeed, one could argue that there may be, even within these parameters, many correct interpretations. Say that it is possible to give both Freudian and behavioral interpretations of a text. Under these conditions, perhaps it is better to drop the use of the term 'correct,' reserving it for cases where it is possible to disqualify some interpretations. The propriety of the use of the categories correct and incorrect may depend on the type of text in question, its function, and the purpose and nature of the interpretation.

With respect to truth and falsity, the differences between textual and nontextual interpretations have little effect on the issue insofar as, like textual interpretations, nontextual interpretations are texts composed of many sentences some of which are not subject to truth value. So, one could be led to conclude that nontextual interpretations have no truth value. However, nontextual interpretations have functions that go beyond textual interpretations and it is possible that some of those functions are precisely to provide descriptions or accounts that are subject to truth value. Consider the case of the psychological interpretation mentioned earlier. In such a case it is possible to argue that the aim of the psychologist is to offer as interpretation a description of the mental state of the historical author of a text and that, as such, it is subject to truth value: If the description adheres to what is the case, it is true, and if it does not, it is false. In short, we may conclude that, although the notion of truth value cannot be effectively applied to textual interpretations, it may be applied to nontextual interpretations depending on their cultural function.

When it comes to the subjectivity and objectivity of nontextual interpretations, the same principles applied to textual interpretations can be easily applied. Nontextual interpretations will be more or less subjective depending on the factors considered by the interpreting subject to produce the interpretation. And, as in the case of textual interpretations, this will apply in fact to the production of the *interpretans*, the text added to the *interpretandum* to fulfill the function of the interpretation. In this case it should be even more evident that the subjectivity or objectivity of the interpretation is independent from the degree to which the interpretation fulfills its function. Indeed, one psychologist, for example, may accurately describe the mental state of a person by chance, having paid little or no attention to the objective factors that played a role in the person's mental state, whereas another may describe it inaccurately in spite of having paid much attention to objective factors.

V. Understanding, Meaning, and Interpretation of Interpretations

In this chapter I have presented a conception of interpretations as texts. But if interpretations are texts, we can ask about them the same sorts of questions we have asked about texts throughout this book. There is no great difficulty in this, for I believe that the same answers I have given throughout to those questions apply also to interpretations as long as one keeps in mind the generic and specific functions of interpretations. Thus, if one were to ask whether one understanding of a particular interpretation is to be regarded as closed or openended, the answer would be, as in the case of other texts, that it depends very much on a variety of factors as determined by the cultural function of the interpretation. Some interpretations may have nontextual functions such that their understanding is not limited by, say, authorial understandings or even historical parameters. But there may be others in which this may not be so. Indeed, the freedom of understanding of textual interpretations with a historical function must necessarily be strictly limited to the production of acts of understanding that reproduce in the contemporary audience acts of understanding similar to those of the historical author and the historical audience of the historical text.

With respect to who or what determines the meaning of an interpretation, again the answer has to do with the cultural function. For the cultural function determines whether and to what extent the author of the interpretation, for example, determines the meaning.

Finally, the question arises as to whether interpretations require interpretation, and if they do, whether we do not fall into an infinite regress. The answer to the second part of the question was already provided earlier, in the context of an objection, so there is no need to repeat it here. With respect to the first part of the question, the answer follows from what has been said concerning texts and their cultural function. Some interpretations require textual interpretations to reveal what their authors and historical audiences understood by them, but others may not. It all depends on the cultural and historical gap between the historical and the contemporary audiences of the interpretations. And whether interpretations require other cultural interpretations will depend, as in the case of other texts, on their cultural function.

VI. Conclusion

Let me conclude by recalling what was said at the beginning of this chapter. There I pointed out that the interpretation of texts poses both serious and interesting problems for the philosopher and the historian. Texts are historical entities; they are produced at certain times and certain places by their authors. As such, texts are always part of the past and any time we turn to a text we are playing the role of the historian, trying to recover the past in some way. The problems originate in that we seldom have direct access to the meaning that texts are supposed to convey. We have access only to the entities that authors use to try to convey that meaning. Thus, the recovery of that meaning is a fundamental problem for hermeneutics and determines the nature and function of interpretations. In the discussion that followed, I tried to show how the solution to the problem posed by the recovery of the meaning of historical texts is to be found in the development of textual interpretations whose purpose is to bridge the gap between the circumstances under which the historical text was produced and the circumstances surrounding the contemporary audience that is trying to recover the meaning of the historical text or its implications.

Interpretations involve three factors: the text to be interpreted (*interpretandum*), the interpreter, and what is added to the text (*interpretans*) under interpretation. The *interpretandum* is a historical text or whatever approximations we have of it. The *interpretans* consists of the additions to the historical text made by the interpreter. The interpreter is the person whose job it is to modify the historical text by adding to it whatever is necessary to carry out the function of the interpretation. And the interpretation is the composite of *interpretandum* and *interpretans*.

The general function of interpretations is to produce in a contemporary audience acts of understanding related to the text under interpretation. This general function is further divided into three more specific functions: historical, meaning, and implicative. The first is to recreate in the contemporary audience the acts of understanding of the historical author and the historical audience of the text; the second is to produce in the contemporary audience acts of understanding whereby that audience grasps the meaning of the text, regardless of whether that was the meaning grasped by the historical author and the historical audience of the text; and the third is to produce acts of understanding in the contemporary audience that allow that audience to understand the implications of the meaning of the text. In all cases, however, an interpretation is a text composed of the text under interpretation and the interpretative additions added to it by the interpreter.

That interpretations include additions to the texts under interpretation generates the Interpreter's Dilemma in cases where the function of the interpretation is historical. This dilemma points out that either an interpreter adds something to a text to make the text understandable to an audience or does not. One who adds something to a text surely creates misunderstanding in the audience by distorting the historical text. But one who adds nothing cannot hope to make that audience understand a text far removed culturally and temporally from it.

The solution to the Interpreter's Dilemma lies in the Principle of Proportional Understanding. According to it the historical function of interpretations is to create the causal complex that can produce in a contemporary audience the same sort of result the text produced in the historical author and the historical audience. This is done by adding to the historical text elements that make up the contextual differences between the historical author and the historical audience, on the one hand, and the contemporary audience, on the other.

The understanding of interpretations and their function I have presented implies that interpretations are meant for audiences, not for interpreters (just as texts are meant for audiences, not for authors) and that understanding of the meaning of texts by interpreters is presupposed by the production of interpretations of those texts in most cases. How and to what extent that understanding is possible is the subject matter of part of the next chapter.

Apart from these general conclusions concerning the nature and function of interpretations, I also presented a classification of interpretations into textual and nontextual. Whether an interpretation is one or the other depends on whether its aim is simply to recover the meaning of historical texts and its implications or whether it has additional and more fundamental cultural functions besides.

The significance of this classification became clear when I subsequently discussed the much debated number, truth value, and objectivity of interpretations. For it turns out that such a debate is in part the result of a failure to distinguish between these two types of interpretations. In the case of textual interpretations, there may be as many of these interpretations as there are situations that require bridging gaps between the circumstances that surrounded the production of historical texts and the circumstances that surround the contemporary audience that seeks to understand them or situations in which the exploration of the meanings of texts and their implications are desirable. In the first of these cases, it is possible in principle to speak of one definitive interpretation for a particular set of circumstances, even though in practice this may never happen. The value of the notion of one, definitive interpretation is regulative, and thus can be of use in hermeneutics.

With respect to truth value, I concluded that it does not do to apply it to textual interpretations, both because of their complexity and because of their function. Indeed, their function suggests that it would be more appropriate to characterize them as effective or ineffective and adequate or inadequate rather than as true or false.

With respect to the objectivity and subjectivity of textual interpretations, I concluded that objectivity and subjectivity refer to the degree to which the interpreter, in developing the *interpretans*, takes into account the *interpretandum* and the objective or subjective factors that go into the determination of the meaning of a text. This makes the subjectivity and objectivity of textual interpretations independent of their effectiveness and adequacy.

Similar general principles were then applied to nontextual interpretations. Those interpretations were found to be multiple, indeed many more than textual ones, because at least in one case there is only one textual interpretation for every set of circumstances that require bridging the gap between the historical text and the contemporary audience, but there are many different cultural functions for which a textual interpretation may be used or that may be added to textual interpretations. Insofar as truth value is concerned, nontextual interpretations face the same difficulties as textual ones, but they may be assigned truth value if such value is prescribed by the cultural function they fulfill. Finally, the objectivity and subjectivity of nontextual interpretations depends again on the objective or subjective nature of the causes that produce them.

If the suggested distinctions between the two types of interpretations presented here are maintained, disagreements as to their number, truth value, and objectivity can be avoided. For it becomes clear that the disagreeing parties are often speaking of different types of interpretations and thus of different tasks.

In closing, I reiterated that interpretations are texts and as such the same questions asked earlier about the meaning, understanding, and interpretation of texts can be asked about them and the same answers follow. The limits of the meaning, understanding, and number of interpretations depend on their cultural functions.

In this chapter, I have presented a view of interpretations in which at least some of them are taken to presuppose understanding of the meaning of the texts under interpretation by the interpreter. But we have not discussed how that understanding is achieved. This is the subject matter of the next chapter, which deals with the discernibility of texts.

6

DISCERNIBILITY

To discern something, as any English dictionary will confirm, has to do with setting the thing apart from others in the context of knowledge; it is to know something as separate and distinct from other things. Many important questions can be raised concerning the discernibility of texts, but I shall discuss three here; they concern the discernibility of texts and their meaning considered in general: (1) How do I know that something is a text?, (2) How do I learn the meaning of a text? (3) How can I be certain that I know the meaning of a text?

All three of these questions pose problems because texts are entities with meaning but meaning is not a feature of the entities that constitute texts. Meanings are neither parts nor features of the entities that constitute texts and thus it does not seem possible, on the basis of considering those entities, to determine whether the entities have meaning attached to them, being thus texts, and what that meaning is. Yet, at the same time, we seem to know that at least some entities are texts, whereas others are not, and also to know the meaning of at least some of those that are. How can this happen, by what means does it happen, and how can we be sure that we do know what we think we know about texts and their meaning?

These questions address issues that are quite different from the issues raised in Chapter 1 of this book. In Chapter 1, we were concerned with the conditions of textuality, which is a fundamentally logical issue—although it may also be considered to have a metaphysical dimension because it involves the determination of the nature of textuality. The conditions we explored in Chapter 1 applied to the concept and nature of texts; in this chapter, however, I am concerned with conditions that apply to the knowledge we may have of texts. In Chapter 1, the central question addressed was: What makes X a text? And the answer to this question produced a series of conditions of textuality. The conditions apply to texts themselves apart from knowers. In this chapter, however, the fundamental questions have to do with conditions that apply to texts in relation to knowers considered qua knowers of texts. This is what makes the questions we shall take up here epistemic rather than logical or metaphysical; they concern the knowledge knowers have of texts rather than the concept or nature of texts.

The importance of the three questions mentioned cannot be underestimated, for indeed much of what has been said so far in this book depends to some extent, either directly or indirectly, on our ability to answer them with some degree of satisfaction. I have left their examination for last because the effort to answer them is a kind of reflection on what has been previously discussed. In this, I am going against standard modern practice, where epistemic issues take precedence over and are considered propaedeutic to any other kind of inquiry. The reversal of this order follows my conviction that epistemology is not a discipline concerned with the possibility of knowledge, but rather a reflection on the way we do know. As such, its place is not at the beginning of an inquiry, but at the end, after knowledge, or at least some knowledge, has been achieved. The reverse procedure produces paralysis, for the puzzles one encounters in epistemic inquiries have the power to ensnarl in a way that prevents substantive progress. Indeed, if physicists were to begin their inquiry with questions concerning whether and how they can know anything, they would have little time for discovery. Fortunately, they direct their efforts to the understanding of the world and only later, if they do it at all, to the understanding of how they have done it—I do not believe they ever really worry about whether knowledge about the physical world is possible. That is something that seems to concern only some philosophers.

Accordingly, I began this book with logic—the knowledge of our concepts—and only now, at the end, after I have established some parameters within which I feel some comfort, am I ready to ask questions about how I have established them. Moreover, because I believe I have made some progress, even though whatever results I have achieved are to be considered provisional and tentative, I shall dispense with the paralyzing question concerning the possibility of knowledge with respect to texts and concentrate rather on the more fruitful one of how progress in this area has been achieved.[1]

I shall divide the discussion into three parts, following the three questions we are addressing. This should not be taken as implying, however, that these three questions address clearly separable issues that can be resolved independent of each other. Indeed, as will become evident immediately, all three questions and their answers are closely related.

I. How Do I Know That Something Is a Text?

The answer to this question would seem prima facie quite easy. Having established the conditions of textuality in Chapter 1, it would seem that we need only to find out which entities fulfill those conditions to know if they are texts. Indeed, this question appears to be the epistemological counterpart of the logical question raised in Chapter 1 concerned with the definition of texts. The conditions were specified in the definition of a text as "a group of entities used as signs that are selected, arranged, and intended by an author in a certain context to convey some specific meaning to an audience." From this it would seem that to classify something as a text we must know that: first, there is an author; second, the author selected and arranged a group of entities used as signs in a particular way; and third, the selection and arrangement had as its aim to convey a specific meaning to an audience in a certain context. Unfortunately, it is not always possible to know these conditions and thus to know that something is a text.

In some cases, I can know that something is a text on the basis of observation or inference. For example, if I have seen and known something to be a text in the past I can always recognize it as a text when I see it again, even if I do not know its meaning; indeed, I can even recognize texts in languages other than the ones I know. But it is not always necessary for me to have seen and known something to be a text at some previous time to know that it is a text at a later time. If the signs of which a text is composed belong to a natural language I know, I often can recognize something as a text even when I have never encountered it before. This happens to us frequently; given the enormous flexibility of language, a day hardly goes by without encountering texts the likes of which we have never encountered before. Note, however, that if we do not know the language in which a text we have never seen before is presented to us, we can never be sure that it is a text even if we know the presumed text is composed of signs that belong to a language. We cannot be sure without knowing the signs and the rules according to which the signs have been arranged, whether the entities that constitute the signs are intended to mean something together or whether they have no meaning and are arranged without regard for any meaning. And note also that, in order to have certainty of textuality, we need to know that there is an author of the text who intended to convey meaning through it. If we have no knowledge of this we can never conclude with absolute certainty that the entities that constitute a text function as signs and are intended to convey meaning. Thus an arrangement of entities that looks like a token of a type text belonging to a natural language cannot be in all cases taken to be a text.

Texts can reveal their nature to us, but not in all circumstances and not in the same way; when we do not know the signs that compose a text, the rules that govern their arrangement, or the fact that they had an author we must look elsewhere for evidence of textuality. One place we can turn is to context. For example, if we are traveling by plane and go to the lavatory, we can easily identify as texts the designs painted on the door and various other parts of the lavatory even in cases where we have no knowledge of the language to which they belong. Their location helps us in this regard, for location suggests that someone put them there for the purpose of conveying certain meaning. But location is not a sufficient criterion of identification, because we could easily confuse a text with a decorative device. For those who do not know Arabic, for example, the textual designs commonly found in Moslem art do not appear to be texts.

Frequently we can get around this problem if next to the group of entities about whose nature we are unsure there is a text in a language we know. Thus, airplanes and airports frequently have signs in two or more languages and we infer, because of their proximity to each other, that they are all texts even though we may know the meaning of only one of them. In normal, daily life this mixture of contextual and textual evidence would be quite conclusive. However, unless the text we understand explicitly refers to the group of entities we do not understand, all we have is circumstantial evidence to conclude that the entities in question constitute a text; for they could still constitute merely some kind of decorative device.

One could also argue that there are other types of evidence. For example, someone might tell me that something is a text. This person could be someone who has already gone through the process of text identification or it could be the author or someone who is part of the audience of the text. This sort of evidence appears at first to be nontextual evidence, but upon reflection it turns out to be textual, because the communication between any two persons is generally carried out through a series of signs that would themselves constitute texts. This, of course, is not an objection against the procedure, but rather a better understanding of what it entails. This method is the most common method of first learning which things are texts and which are not; it is the method we all go through when we are learning to read and write. The way we learn to speak a language, on the other hand, is quite different, as I shall point out later. The most obvious objection against the conclusiveness of the procedure is that any person can lie or be mistaken and tell us that a group of entities constitute a text whereas in fact they do not.

Someone might object, however, that if texts are conventional, as I have argued in Chapter 1, the mere fact that someone identifies something as a text makes it a text and therefore in this instance lying or error is not possible. But this objection will not do, because, as noted earlier, for something to be a text certain conditions, in addition to authorial intent, must be met. Among these conditions is that the text have meaning; something cannot be a text unless a meaning be assigned to it. A group of entities without meaning, even if said to constitute a text, is not a text. And the same applies to the other conditions of textuality discussed in Chapter 1.

People can, directly or indirectly, reveal texts to us in another way also; namely, through their own behavior. By watching the reactions of people to certain objects we can sometimes determine that those objects are texts. Of course, to do this we must know what a text is and we must have observed, either in others or in ourselves, the type of behavior that is characteristic of those who come in contact with texts. And no less important is the context, for behavior can be faked. Here again we cannot be absolutely sure in all cases that something is a text.

In most circumstances, then, we know that something is a text on the basis of prior experience, because another text whose meaning we know makes it clear to us, because someone tells us, or because the behavior of persons reveals it to us. But what happens when we encounter a group of entities about which we have no prior experience, there are no texts that tell us whether it is a text, and there are no persons who know that it is a text and can tell us about it or can be observed while they are taking it in? What do we make of some stone carvings from a long lost culture about which we know nothing? Is it possible to determine that those carvings are texts?[2] The problem is difficult to resolve because what makes a group of entities a text is that they have been endowed with meaning by an author, and meaning is not something that is observably tied to a text. Thus, if we lack access to those who endowed a group of entities with meaning, or who understand their meaning, it would seem quite impossible to determine that such a group of entities constitute a text.

Contrary to this expectation, however, archeologists, palaeographers, and other scientists concerned with deciphering languages have concluded in various instances that certain designs and objects constitute texts, even if they did not succeed at the time in deciphering their meaning. And, what is more important, they have been proven to be right at a later time, when the meaning of those designs and objects has been deciphered.[3] Thus, even though it would not seem prima facie possible to identify entities as texts when we have no access to their meaning, there are cases in which such identification has successfully taken place. The question is: How can it be done or was it done?

We could answer this question by providing a detailed description of the procedure followed by the scientists who discovered the textuality of texts from ancient civilizations before they knew their meaning. But such an empirical description would reveal to us only the outward plumage of the process.[4] The philosopher is interested rather in the conceptual framework that makes such a process possible and effective, not in the particular empirical details associated with it.

I believe three factors, considered jointly, could help explain how the process of identification of texts takes place: similarity, cultural context, and human nature. Apart from the necessary and sufficient conditions of textuality identified in the definition of texts, all texts have some elements that are similar. At first this would seem contrary to some of the most important things that have been said about texts in this book. For example, it was stated in Chapter 1 that texts are conventional and also that anything whatsoever can function as a text. If that is the case, how can it be argued now that all texts share some similarity? Indeed, given the features mentioned, the only similarities among texts would seem to be that they have authors, audiences, meaning, and so on with the conditions contained in their definition. But, having access to none of these, how can we possibly argue that a group of entities constitute a text? To establish the similarity of a group of entities with other texts and thus conclude that the entities are a text, it would seem necessary precisely to have access to the factors to which we have stipulated we do not have access.

I believe this objection is misguided, however, and thus fails. The reason is that not only similarity in the stated ways is involved in the identification of texts.

Texts are similar in more ways than those. Their pertinent similarity is derived from the very function texts aim to fulfill (conveying specific meanings) and from the limitations that effectively carrying out that function imposes on them. There are many factors to which we could refer here, but I shall mention three to illustrate my point: organization, repetition, and abstraction. Let me begin with the last.

Abstraction is in many ways a most desirable characteristic of texts. The reason for its desirability is that the use of descriptive, say pictorial, signs in a text is more confusing than the use of abstract signs. A picture can get in the way of a concept, particularly if the concept that it represents is abstract. Moreover, abstract signs are more versatile than pictures and they are more economical as well. All these points are well illustrated in the history of writing, where abstract symbols came to take the place of pictographs. Whether this was the result of a conscious effort or not does not alter the fact that it was a move toward simplification, economy, and versatility.

Something similar can be said about repetition. Repetition seems to be a universal characteristic and, indeed, requirement of textuality. Again, the reasons seem simple enough. First is the fact that there are limited numbers of meanings that we wish to express and communicate, and thus it would seem natural that the signs used to communicate them would also be limited. Therefore, in extended texts one would expect to find a certain amount of repetition that would reflect the repetition of meanings themselves. In addition, it would not do to use a different sign every time a meaning is conveyed. That would preclude the possibility of communication altogether, unless there were some way of determining the meaning for the new signs, which seems quite impossible. The second reason is practical. A limited number of symbols and arrangements is more easily manageable than a large number of them. Economy thus dictates repetition.

Note that repetition should not be confused with regularity. Regularity is a kind of strict or mechanical repetition. For example, when every third entity in a series of entities is of the same sort, we have both regularity and repetition. However, we can have repetition without regularity when the entity in question, for instance, does not always occur after the same intervals and yet occurs at various places in a series. Regularity is typical of many nontextual designs, but is not characteristic of texts. The reason is that texts express meanings and meanings are seldom, if ever, regular. This does not imply that there are no cases of regularity in texts. Litanies and the like are texts in which regularity occurs, but these cases are relatively infrequent.

The third important element of similarity among texts to which I wish to bring attention is organization, and by this I do not mean just repetition but a certain discernible structure. Naturally, repetition suggests organization and structure, but it is not necessarily an indication of it. We can have repetition without structure if there is no pattern to the repetition in question. For example, the repetition of a white billiard ball after a black billiard ball in a long line of colored billiard balls indicates organization, but the repetition of white billiard balls at unexpected places and intervals in such a line does not indicate organization.

None of the three aspects in which texts are similar that have been mentioned, namely, abstraction, repetition, and organization, taken singly or together, is a sufficient condition of textual discernibility. And the necessity of at least the first two may be easily challenged. Let us take abstraction first.

The question we need to answer is whether abstraction is a necessary or sufficient condition of textuality. That it is not a sufficient condition should be quite obvious both from what has been said about texts throughout this book as well as from the many examples of abstract designs that can be cited that are not texts. If, as I argued in Chapter 1, art objects are not necessarily texts, and as we know there are many art objects that are nonrepresentational, then it is obvious that abstraction cannot be a sufficient condition of textuality. Pollock's drippings are abstract but they are not texts.

A more interesting question has to do with the necessity of abstraction for texts. Can there be texts that are not abstract in any way? My answer to this question is that I do not think so. In Chapter 1, I argued that texts must be composed of entities used as signs and that the meaning of those signs is not natural but conventional. Now, if that is the case, then we must also grant that what a sign means need not be anything naturally tied to it. And that seems to imply a kind of separation that is precisely what is involved in abstraction. This is quite obvious in the case of nonrepresentational signs. But, even in cases where a sign acts as a representation of something, abstraction is involved because the representation is never exactly like what it represents; always some features of the represented object are not present in the representation. A painting of a cat, for example, is quite unlike the cat—it does not have fur and it does not meow. If this is the case with so-called representational art, it is obviously much more so in the case of texts whose aim is not representational at all.

Still, although texts must be abstract in some way, for the epistemological purpose at hand it is not clear that their abstraction is always obvious. The problem is that, when the audience does not know whether a particular set of entities constitute a text, abstraction can play a role in the recognition of textuality only if it occurs in the ECTs apart from their relation to the meaning because the audience does not know whether there is a meaning or not. And the ECTs of a text can be anything, as noted in Chapter 1, and thus they need not be abstract. Therefore the abstraction of texts is necessary, but such abstraction is not necessarily, although nonetheless frequently, present in the ECTs of the text. Because of that, a lack of abstraction in a group of entities does not necessarily disqualify the group from being a text. Abstraction in ECTs, then, is not a necessary condition of textual discernibility.

With respect to repetition, again the answer to the question of sufficiency is rather obvious: Repetition is not a sufficient condition of textuality. Indeed, much nontextual design is repetitive. On the other hand, the question of whether repetition is a necessary condition of textuality is not so easily settled. In principle it would seem that repetition is not a necessary condition of textuality. Many short texts contain no repetition. The text 'Sit down' illustrates the point. And not only short texts, but considerably long ones could be composed in such a way that no repetition be involved. In fact, however, matters are quite different for, as noted earlier, practical considerations as well as the limitations of meanings that may be communicated make it a requirement, perhaps not of logic but of fact, that repetition be present in texts, particularly in very long ones.

With the third factor, organization, it would seem that organization alone cannot be a sufficient condition of textuality, but there can be no texts without some organization. That organization is not a sufficient condition should be obvious. Such things as organisms and intuitions display organization but it would be difficult to argue that in virtue of it they must be considered texts. On the other hand, some organization at least appears necessary to textuality, perhaps because the very meanings that texts convey are organized and thus require the entities used to express them also to be organized. Of course, the type of organization displayed by texts may vary widely, but there must be some of it for something to function as a text.

In short, even though at least two of the factors discussed appear to be necessary for textuality, even putting all three of them together does not yield a sufficient set of conditions of it. The problem is that, even if on the basis of similarities a system of rules is formulated according to which the entities that are taken to constitute the presumed text are put together, the results are purely formal and do not yield semantic information. Nonetheless, similarity on the basis of abstraction, repetition, and organization is, without a doubt, one of the factors that makes possible the identification of texts. As such it may be used as a criterion to construct conjectures as to the textuality or nontextuality of particular entities, even if not about their meaning.

Another and no less important factor is the cultural context in which the presumed text is found. There are certain places and circumstances where we would expect to find texts and there are others where we would not. Thus, it is to be expected that some type of record keeping and, therefore, texts be available in buildings where business transactions occur, where religious ceremonies take place, or where there is evidence of kingship and dynastic succession. If, under such conditions, we find objects that display marks that appear to be abstract, repeated, and organized in some fashion, we immediately suspect that we have a text. Of course, this is a suspicion at first. Archeologists would have to do much more work on the culture to increase probability, but similarity and context will play large roles in determining their conclusion one way or another.

Ultimately, however, the identification of texts relies on something more and deeper than similarity and context, for similarity and context are based on fundamental assumptions about the way human beings behave and communicate. The identification of texts in the last analysis rests on the belief that certain needs and aspirations are fundamental to all human beings and that there are more and less efficient ways of fulfilling them. Communication is one way. We identify something as a text because we can place ourselves in the cultural context where the presumed text is found and understand how the need for it arose and how it functions within that cultural context; we become the vicarious author or audience of the text.

The possibility of identifying something as a text rests, then, on the possibility of cultural transfer. Only if we are able to transfer from one culture to another can we expect to be able to discover textuality within a culture other than our own. But cultural transfer depends in turn on the fundamental identity of all members of the human species, that is, upon human nature.

None of this, however, seems to provide complete assurances that we will always and in all circumstances be able to know whether something is a text. For, first, there is the question of whether something is an artifact or has been produced by natural forces without input from subjects. And, second, even if it can be established that something is an artifact, the question whether it is intended to convey meaning is again a problematic matter. And finally, even if we know that something is an artifact with meaning, that is not sufficient to know it is a text unless we also know that its meaning is in part the result of the meaning of the signs that compose it. Does this entail, then, that we can never be certain that something is a text? For practical purposes the answer would seem to be negative. As we saw earlier, there are circumstances in which I can be pretty certain that something is a text, but, by the same token, there are others in which my certainty is very weak. The problem, of course, is that I cannot be absolutely certain that something is a text unless I know that it has meaning and its meaning is in part the result of the meaning of the signs of its components. Thus, the question of how I know that something is a text is closely related to the answer to the other two questions raised earlier, concerned, respectively, with the means whereby (1) I know the meaning of texts and (2) I achieve certainty concerning that meaning.

II. How Do I Learn the Meaning of a Text?

If the question concerned with how I know that something is a text is difficult to answer, the question concerned with how I learn the meaning of a text is even more difficult to answer. Indeed, this is a question that in one way or another has puzzled philosophers since the beginning of the discipline. It is particularly popular among contemporary philosophers, some of whom refer to the puzzle it poses as the *hermeneutic circle*.[5] But we find expressions of it in much earlier times. Augustine, following Plato, formulated a version of it in *De magistro* in the context of signs. He framed it as a dilemma about signs:

> If I am given a sign and I do not know the thing of which it is a sign, it can
> teach me nothing. If I know the thing, what do I learn from the sign?[6]

The dilemma, then, is quite simple: Either I know the meaning of a sign or
I do not. But, whether I know it or not, the consequence is the same: I cannot be
said to learn it from the sign. The same dilemma could apply to texts. Either I know
the meaning of a text or I do not. But, whether I know it or not, the consequence
is the same: I cannot be said to learn it from the text.[7]

Yet, our experience supports the notion that we can learn the meaning of
both signs and texts through signs and texts. Should we trust our experience, then,
or reject it on the basis of Augustine's notorious dilemma? Rather than try to
answer this question at the outset I would like to deal with the issue indirectly,
by asking instead about that on the basis of which we learn the meaning of texts.

Before I go on, let me point out that in what has been said the terms 'sign'
and 'text' have been used to mean the entities that constitute signs and texts, respectively. If the terms 'sign' and 'text' were used in the technical sense I have
given to them, namely, as ECTs related to a meaning, knowledge of signs and texts
would imply knowledge of their meaning. Only when one identifies signs and texts
with their ECTs considered apart from their meaning can one have knowledge
of the signs and texts without having knowledge of their meaning. Now let me
go back to the question that asks for the basis on which we learn the meaning
of texts.

The most obvious answer to this question is that we do learn the meaning
of texts on the basis of what others tell us. We can ask a child, for example, how
he or she knows that '2 + 2 = 4' means that two plus two equal four, and the child
will likely respond by saying: "My teacher told me so." Someone's telling is one
of the most common bases for learning the meaning of a text. But there are also
other ways. We know what some texts mean because someone has *shown* us what
they mean. This is particularly applicable to signs rather than texts but it can also
apply to texts. In the case of a sign, for example 'tree,' we may know that it means
"tree" because someone points to a tree after we ask, what does 'tree' mean? And
if we have a text that describes a complicated event, say running, the explanation
of what the text means could be achieved by pointing to someone who is running.
We may also know what a sign means on the basis of what the dictionary tells us,
and if the meaning we are searching for is that of a complex text with an involved
grammatical structure, we will need not only a dictionary but also a grammar.

It is not difficult, however, to punch holes through these explanations of
how we learn the meaning of texts. Indeed, philosophers have been doing that for
centuries. Augustine himself, for example, pointed out that ostensive definitions
are most inadequate to convey the meaning of signs, because they can never be

effectively tied to the object that is the meaning of the sign we wish to learn.[8] Take the case of 'tree.' Let us assume that I hear the sound that corresponds to the written sign and that, after asking what the sound means, someone points in a certain direction. And let us assume, to make matters simple, that we are in a prairie where only one object is to be seen on the horizon, a tree, and moreover that the pointing finger is directed quite clearly toward the tree. Would the ostensive sign be a sufficient condition for me to know that the meaning of the sign 'tree' is the tree toward which the finger is pointing? Prima facie nothing could seem more certain. Yet, when we look at the situation more carefully, the matter does not appear so simple. In the first place, pointing is a very vague sort of indicator, for indeed I could never be sure that the pointing referred to the tree and not to its color, shape, trunk, branches, a particular branch, leaves, a particular leaf, a bunch of leaves, some feature of the trunk, and so on. How could I know, then, that the pointing refers to the tree and not to one of its parts or features to the exclusion of others?

Another problem is that effective communication in this case assumes that I know what the act of pointing itself means, something that need not be so. It could very well be that in a certain society pointing means "I will think about it" and thus that the answer to my question, "What is the meaning of tree," was "I will think about it." This sounds odd to us, but it is certainly possible. Indeed, if, as I have argued in Chapter 1, signs are conventional, then there is no reason why we should be scandalized by the use of pointing as a sign for "I will think about it."

The purpose of this objection, then, is to bring up the difficulty posed by the fact that pointing itself is a sign and thus needs interpretation. Ostensive definition, in spite of prima facie appearances to the contrary, turns out to be a case of textual definition, that is, a case in which a text is used to specify the meaning of another text. In fact, the prima facie plausibility of ostensive definition to identify the meaning of signs disappears when it comes to texts, for it is difficult to imagine what one could point to even in the case of simple texts, let alone complex ones. What could I point to as the meaning of 'No smoking'? And what could I point to as the meaning of the text of *Don Quixote*?

It should be clear, then, that none of the examples provided uncovers ways on the basis of which learning the meaning of texts can be always efficiently achieved, even if in some cases it does take place. The reason has nothing to do with the idiosyncrasies of the examples; it has to do with the underlying factor common to all of them; namely, that they rely on texts to tell us the meaning of texts. What someone tells me is a text, what the dictionary has written on it is a text, and an ostensive definition is either a text or a sign, which for our purposes amounts to the same thing. The fundamental problem with having a text as the basis of our learning the meaning of another text is that either we engage in circularity or in an infinite regress. In the case of the infinite regress we have something like this: We are told what a text X means through another text

Y.[9] But, because Y is also a text, to learn what Y means we must be given another text Z that makes Y's meaning plain. But again, Z is a text, and to learn what Z means we must have recourse to another text W, and so on. We could express this infinite regress as follows:

'X' means Y.

'X' means Y and 'Y' means Z.

'X' means Y and 'Y' means Z and 'Z' means W.

And so on in infinitum.

One way to break this infinite regress is to come back to X at some point, in the following way:

'X' means Y and 'Y' means Z and 'Z' means W and 'W' means X.

That leads us back to where we started.[10] The upshot, then, is that knowledge about the meanings of texts cannot be based on knowledge of the meaning of texts even if those texts are other texts, for the ECTs that constitute texts are conventionally tied to the meanings of the texts and thus cannot unambiguously make them clear to us.

Reasonings similar to the one I have provided can be used by philosophers to support two sorts of views. According to one, there is no way to learn the meaning of texts.[11] This is the kind of skeptical conclusion that contradicts our experience. Such a contradiction, however, is not the view's main fault. Its main fault is that the conclusion is not supported by the reasonings given for it. The conclusion warranted by the reasoning is that we cannot learn the meaning of texts on the basis of other texts, *not* that we cannot learn the meaning of texts at all. There is in principle the possibility of learning the meaning of texts on some other basis than texts, even though we have seen objections to the commonly identified ways to do so.

This brings me to the second view; namely, that the meaning of texts is somehow innate to us.[12] And the main problem with this position is that, like the previous one, it contradicts our experience, for if the meaning of texts were to be innate, then texts themselves would have to be innate and, therefore, common to all human beings. Yet, our experience tells us that texts are neither innate—we all have to learn them—nor natural—they are the result of conventions. Experience, then, militates against this point of view.

Both of these positions share a common assumption: They set up standards that are not only unreasonable but inappropriate, as Aristotle accuses the skeptics of doing. Indeed he notes that their position is a result of having identified the criteria of all knowledge with the criteria for demonstrative knowledge.

As a result, they not only undermine forms of knowledge other than demonstrative, but also undermine demonstrative knowledge, for this knowledge is based on other forms of knowledge.[13] And a similar argument can be used to explain Plato's innatism. The adoption of unreasonable and inappropriate standards generates also the responses to the problem posed by the hermeneutic circle.[14]

Both skepticism and innatism must be rejected, but, if we do so, what alternative do we have left? We know that the skeptical point of view is unwarranted and experience tells us that in fact we do learn the meaning of at least some texts. Moreover, we have rejected the view that such meaning is somehow innate. Thus, if we know such meaning and it is not innate, then it must be learned through experience. But that learning cannot be through the experience of texts, for then we would end up in a circular argument or an infinite regress, as we saw earlier.

The alternative that I would like to propose is that ultimately the basis on which we learn the meaning of texts is expected behavior taken in context. Before I defend this view, however, let me turn to the next question in our agenda, for the answer to the question we have been discussing and the answer to that question are the same: that through which we ultimately learn the meaning of texts is also that through which we are certain of that meaning.

III. How Can I Be Certain That I Know the Meaning of a Text?

A. Expected Behavior and Certainty in Textual Understanding

A few years ago I was having a barbecue in my backyard for a group of philosophy graduate students, and as is likely to happen when philosophers get together, the conversation drifted toward philosophy. The topic that came up had to do with how communication can be effectively carried out. One of the students, Herbert Sitz, who since then gave up philosophy for sophistry (he became a lawyer) argued repeatedly that communication was not possible. He very skillfully repeated all the arguments that skeptics, going back to Gorgias, had given against the effectiveness of communication.[15] Finally, the question centered around a way of determining that communication has effectively taken place, in other words, on the criteria that could be used to determine so. It would not do, of course, to say that textual acknowledgment of understanding might serve this purpose, for one could always raise questions concerning the meaning of the acknowledging text. Indeed, one could always question whether the person who used the acknowledging text knew what had been said or written. In short, as we saw earlier, texts cannot serve as criteria for determining that communication has effectively taken place, at least prima facie. Sitz made this point effectively by asking for some nontextual proof that communication takes place.

We were drinking beer at the time and I had an unopened bottle in my hand. I proceeded to open it and managed to drop the cap in Sitz's way. I asked him to pick it up and throw it into the garbage can close by, which he did. I waited until he finished this action and then I pointed out to him that he had just proven that effective communication can take place because it just had. Moreover, I indicated that I knew so not through a text, but through his action, for he acted in accordance with the instructions I had given him through an oral text. His answer was to laugh and to say that what I had done was not fair, that I had tricked him. And my answer to that was that he had just offered further evidence that he understood the meaning of my words. Indeed, not only his response, but his laughter also corroborated the fact that he had understood me.

The point of this story is that the way we know someone else has understood a text we have used to communicate with that person is through behavior.[16] And the same point applies to a situation where we are trying to determine if we have properly understood a text used by another person. When we are learning a foreign language, we confirm that we have understood a word by pointing to the appropriate picture and watching the reaction of the teacher. And children seem to learn language in the same way, by mimicking the behavior of those who use it and watching their reactions to their use of the language. Consider the famous case of Helen Keller and how she came to realize that the meaning of a sign used to refer to water in English meant water. Ostension by itself does not seem to have worked, but repeated uses of the sign in a context that included certain behavioral patterns eventually led her to the connection between sign and meaning.[17] Once she understood that connection, then it was easy for her to learn other signs, which were again learned through behavior taken in context. Note that the questions "How do I know I have understood a text?" and "How do I know someone else has understood a text?" are two sides of the same question concerning the understanding of texts. And the answer I am proposing is that behavior taken in context constitutes the basis on which we can know that texts are understood.

Notice also that the question of how we know we have understood a text is closely related to the question of how we know we have misunderstood a text. For if we know we have understood a text, we also know we have not misunderstood it. And if we know we have misunderstood it, we also know we have not understood it. This is quite trivial, because the terms 'understood' and 'misunderstood' are complement terms. However, not knowing whether we have understood a text does not imply we have misunderstood it, just as not knowing whether we have misunderstood a text does not imply we have understood it. The way I know I understand a text may be different from the way I know I misunderstand a text, and thus what we have concluded here concerning understanding does not necessarily apply to misunderstanding. Behavior may, indeed, confirm misunderstanding but there may be other ways of knowing one has misunderstood a text. Our concern is not with misunderstanding, but with understanding, and so I shall not discuss how we know we misunderstand texts.

Not just any behavior, however, confirms understanding of the meaning of texts; it is expected behavior. That is, I know that what I have said has been understood because the behavior of those to whom I have said it fits my expectations. I knew that Sitz had understood me when he acted as I had expected he would act if he had understood me; that is, he picked up the bottle cap and threw it in the garbage can. Of course, it is possible that his picking up the bottle cap had nothing to do with what I had said, and it was mere coincidence that he did so at the time I had expected him to do it. So, taken by itself, his action was not sufficient for me to know that he had understood me. However, the context within which we were operating—the fact that there was no one else who asked him to pick up the bottle cap, the social expectations of the situation (that one abides by the host's directions), and the spatiotemporal proximity between my request and his action—all point in the same direction. Moreover, there was further confirming evidence: His remark, which indicated he had understood that I had tricked him, and his laughter were within the sorts of behavior that I would have expected of someone who had understood what I had said, and particularly what I would have expected of him.

Note, of course, that all along the context in which behavior occurs is essential to the effectiveness of both learning the meaning of texts and being certain of that meaning. In the case we have been examining, part of the confirmation I had concerning Sitz's meaning had to do precisely with the complex set of circumstances within which we found ourselves. The party, the character of the people present, the dialogue, the topics discussed, and so on. Behavior must be taken contextually.

The situation I have been describing is one in which a user of a text knows that the audience for which the user intends the text has understood it. The other side of this situation concerns how the audience of a text knows that it has understood the text. And the answer to this question, as already noted, follows along the same lines. In the case of Sitz, the question has to do with how he knew he had understood my request, which he did through my behavior. After he picked up the bottle cap, he heard me say something that fitted well within our overall conversation, namely, "You have proven my point." If I had said, "It looks like it will rain tomorrow," for example, his reasons for believing that he had understood me would not have been very strong. He could still think that he had understood me correctly based on the context of my remark. But the question would still be very much in doubt, particularly when in our culture it is expected that after a person carries out a request the one who made the request acknowledges the other's action by saying "Thank you." Now, I did not say "Thank you," but what I said suited even better the overall framework within which we were operating: the theoretical discussion of the possibility of effective communication.

The conclusion of this discussion, then, is that certainty concerning the understanding of texts is achieved on the basis of the occurrence of expected behavior in a particular context. We have two cases:

1. Text user U knows with certainty that the text he has used in context C has been understood by audience A if and only if A behaves in accordance with U's expectations concerning A's behavior in C.
2. Text audience A knows with certainty that it has understood the text that text user U has used in context C if and only if U behaves in accordance with A's expectations concerning U's behavior in C.

Cases 1 and 2 stipulate very strong conditions for certainty in the understanding of texts. Indeed, expected behavior is presented as the only necessary and sufficient condition of such certainty. Naturally, such a strong claim is open to challenge. Among the many objections that may be brought against it, six prima facie appear to be particularly effective and therefore must be discussed to determine whether 1 and 2 can stand as formulated or need modifications. The first three aim to show that behavior is not a sufficient condition of certainty in understanding; the last three that it is not a necessary condition of it.

Before I turn to these objections, however, let me add that for the sake of simplification I will assume a distinction between having certainty that an audience is acquainted with a text in use, on the one hand, and having certainty that the audience has understood it, on the other. I will also assume that in 1 the user knows the audience is acquainted with the text. The view I propose and the objections against it, then, are not concerned with how a user knows an audience is acquainted with a text, but with how a user knows an audience understands a text the user has used.

B. Objections

The first objection argues that this view ends up in the same kind of circularity or infinite regress to which attention was drawn earlier in this chapter, because what it does is to use behavior as a sign of understanding. U knows with certainty that A has understood the text he has used because A's behavior functions as a sign that U interprets to mean that A has understood the text U has given to A. Likewise, A knows with certainty that she has understood the text U has used because U's behavior functions as a sign which A interprets to mean that U knows that A has understood correctly the text U used. But, so the argument goes, if behavior functions as a sign, then we are back where we started, for we would need other signs to establish knowledge and this process is repeated again, ending up in an infinite regress or a vicious circle.

The answer to this objection goes back to something that was said in Chapter 1. The word 'sign' is used in many ways in English. In one way it applies to a term used to express a certain meaning. In this sense, terms such as 'cat' and 'table' are signs. In another way, the term is used to express a causal relation of some sort. In this sense lightning is a sign of thunder. The first use is semantic, whereas the second is not. Now, the objection that we are discussing profits from a confusion between these two usages of the term 'sign.' Indeed, the objection is effective only if 'sign' is used semantically, that is, if behavior is taken as a sign that expresses a certain meaning, which in this case is understanding, for then we are within the notorious hermeneutic circle. But if behavior is taken to be related to understanding causally, as an effect of understanding, then it is not a sign in the semantic sense and we are already outside the circle. We can say that U knows with certainty that A has understood what he has said because A's behavior is an effect of understanding. U knows this causal connection based on experience that has created certain expectations. The same could be applied mutatis mutandis to A's knowledge concerning her understanding of the text U has used to communicate with A.

Perhaps my point can be made more clear if we formulate the following argument, in which I claim to know that an audience A, to whom I spoke, understood me:

1. If A does Y, then A understood what I said.
2. A does Y.
   _____
3. Therefore, A understood what I said.

Now, my claim, expressed as 3, that is, as the conclusion of this argument, is that A understood what I said; or, in other words, that I know with certainty that A understood me when I told A something. This conclusion is reached because I observe, for instance, that A does what I ask her to do, and because I approach the situation with a hypothetical first premise 1 in which I establish a connection between A's action and A's understanding of what I say. It is, I believe, the status of 1 that is at stake. For those who adopt the objection I am trying to answer claim that 1 establishes a semantic connection between A's action and A's understanding of what I say. They claim that 1 means something like "A's action *means* that A understood me," and that the 'means' used here is no different from the one used when I say "'Rose' means rose." My claim, by contrast, is that it is not so. Indeed, even if we were to accept the translation of 1 into "A's action means that A understood me," something which I believe is incorrect, the 'means' of that sentence and the one in "'Rose' means rose" are not the same.

My reason for arguing this way is that the hypothetical first premise is not a semantic claim but a claim about two facts related causally. This claim is derived from the principle that all actions, including A's action, have causes and that the causes of A's action are either the fact that A understood what I said or some other cause. If, after an analysis of the circumstances, it makes no sense to conclude that such an action can be explained apart from understanding, as in fact happened with the example of Sitz given earlier, then we must conclude that understanding of what I said is at least part of what caused it. There is nothing semantic about the conditional or about the reasoning used to formulate it. Indeed, this conditional resembles other scientific claims such as "If an eclipse of the sun occurs, the moon is placed between the earth and the sun." There is nothing semantic about this claim, for to say that there is an eclipse of the sun does not mean, in a semantic way, that the moon is placed between the earth and the sun. Rather, it means that the location of the moon is causally related to the eclipse, just as A's understanding of what I say is causally related to A's action. So much, then, for the first objection.

The second objection is no less difficult to deal with. It points out that we cannot know with certainty that effective communication has taken place on the basis of expected behavior because behavior can be mechanical and thus not indicative of understanding.

Perhaps the best way to dramatize this objection is to refer to Searle's thought experiment known as the *Chinese-Room.*[18] The purpose of this experiment is the commendable aim of demonstrating that computers cannot be said to think or understand simply in virtue of a certain program.[19] Searle accomplishes this by showing through his experiment that the behavior associated with understanding can be explained in purely mechanical ways, without the implication that real understanding of the sort human beings have has taken place. Thus, although a computer, in accordance with a program, can provide the responses that one would associate with understanding, it cannot be considered an intelligent being and thus have achieved understanding merely on the basis of those responses.

The relevant point of the experiment for my purpose is that a respondent R can produce the right sort of responses to the queries of a questioner Q, and thus be said to be communicating effectively with Q, without having a clue as to what Q is asking or what he, R, is responding. But this contradicts what we said earlier, because we argued that expected behavior implies textual understanding and in the case of the Chinese-Room experiment expected behavior, namely, expected responses to Q's queries, takes place and yet R has no understanding of what Q is asking.

The seeming strength of this objection disappears, however, when one considers the situation more carefully, for one could still argue that expected responses indicate understanding, although in the case of the Chinese-Room experiment they certainly do not entail understanding by R. Whose understanding do they entail then? They entail understanding on the part of the person P who set up the mechanism for responding to Q's queries. So, although P may not have access to the particular questions asked by Q, P has access to the whole range of questions that Q may ask and, in setting up the response mechanism in the Chinese room, has taken all of them into consideration. In this sense, then, we can say that the expected responses, namely, a form of behavior, do imply textual understanding even if that textual understanding is not on the part of R. Indeed, Searle's conclusion that machines cannot think as we do supports my point, for R's mechanical behavior and lack of understanding indicate that someone else is responsible for the overall understanding of what Q asks.

The second point that can be made is that, in accordance with the experiment, Q would be going beyond the evidence he has if he were to conclude that R, or someone else present in the room, understands what he says. He cannot conclude that R understands him because he has no direct access to R's behavior. Moreover, he cannot conclude that someone in the room understands him because he does not know if there is anyone in the room—the only things he sees are pieces of papers with texts on them that are passed on to him. The only thing that Q is warranted in concluding is that someone understands his questions and, indeed, that is both true and in accordance with the position defended here. Indeed, the person who set up the response mechanism, that is, the programmer, understands the language Q uses and the questions he asks for she has set up possible responses to them.

A third objection argues that behavior is not a sufficiently specific criterion to account for certainty in understanding. Not all behavior confirms understanding, so to say that behavior confirms understanding is vacuous. Consider, for example, the case discussed at the beginning of this section. If, instead of picking up the bottle cap and so on, Sitz had looked around and said, "Boy, are we having fun today!" I could not have concluded with any degree of certainty that he had understood me. Of course, it would still be possible that he in fact had understood me. He could have understood not only what I had said, but the trick I was playing on him and, so, refused to play. Moreover, by answering as he did, he would have avoided falling into my hands while still planting a seed of doubt in my mind as to whether he had understood me. And, there is a third possibility; namely, he simply had not heard me. So his answer could be construed as supporting ignorance, misunderstanding, or understanding on his part. In short, I could not have certainty concerning whether Sitz had or had not understood me.

This objection has no merit against my position for two reasons. First, it has no merit because it is based on a consideration of behavior as criterion of certainty in understanding. But I have not argued that behavior confirms understanding, but rather *expected* behavior. It is not any behavior by Sitz that would have confirmed my belief that he understood me, only the behavior I expected.

Still, one may want to say that this reply does not quite answer the objection in the sense that I could certainly be mistaken as to the behavior I should expect as confirmation of Sitz's understanding, whence the charge of vacuity. Here the second reason alluded to plays a role. For I have not argued that all behavior confirms understanding and thus produces certainty nor that all expected behavior does so, because I have not been trying to develop criteria for the understanding of particular texts. My concern is only with generic criteria of certainty in understanding. Obviously, certainty in the understanding of particular texts will involve particular criteria that will have to do with the type and function of the texts in question as well as the context in which the texts are to be understood. That there is behavior that neither confirms nor disconfirms understanding does not mean that no behavior does. It is, of course, possible for a user to expect a kind of behavior in his or her audience as confirmation of understanding which actually constitutes confirmation of misunderstanding. But in such cases it is clear that the user is not familiar with the behavioral patterns of the culture in which he or she is using the text or even with the meaning of the text being used. Texts, as well as behavior, need to be taken in context.

So much, then, for the three objections that try to undermine the claim that expected behavior is not a sufficient condition of certainty in understanding. Now, we must deal with the objections that argue that it is not a necessary condition of understanding. I shall number these serially, following the three already discussed.

A fourth objection argues that there are texts that are not meant to elicit a behavioral response from their audience. Thus, if behavior were a necessary condition of certainty in the understanding of texts, there would be no way of telling whether the texts in question have been understood or not. But we know when we understand these texts, so behavior cannot be held as a necessary condition of certainty in understanding for all texts. Say that a person is in church, saying a prayer that consists in praising God. In a case like this, no response is required from God or anyone else listening to and understanding the person. But the person has certainty of God's understanding, for she believes that God is all powerful and all knowing and thus that he knows and understands everything that happens. So, behavior is not a necessary condition of certainty in the understanding of this text, and thus, it cannot be a necessary condition of the certainty of understanding texts, because it does not account for the certainty in understanding of at least some texts.

The answer to this objection is that, although some texts are not meant to elicit behavioral responses from their audiences, only when some expected response is given does one know the text has been understood by the audience. We know that God has understood us presumably because he behaves toward us in certain expected ways. If he is pleased with our praises, he showers us with gifts; and if he is not pleased, he sends us tribulations. Of course, this is an oversimplification of what is supposed to be an extremely complicated relationship. My point, however, is not about the relationship between God and his creatures, but about behavior and certainty in understanding. And this case does not undermine the view presented here. The certainty of the believer, who argues that she knows that God has understood her prayers, even though she has no evidence through God's behavior toward her, goes only so far as the belief she has in God. The certainty in question, then, is not of the same sort we have through behavior and cannot be used to undermine the view I have proposed.

A similar answer can be given if the objection is reformulated as arguing that some texts are not meant to elicit any particular behavioral response from their audiences. If no particular behavior can be expected, then it would seem that confirmation of understanding by an audience would escape the user.

Two points are in order as a response. First, it is difficult to imagine texts that, in context, do not point to some particular behavior or at least a range of behaviors as appropriate confirmation of understanding. Second, even if there were such texts, their existence does not militate against my view. I have argued that certainty in understanding is based on expected behavior, but I have not argued that such certainty is forthcoming with regard to every text. In view of this, to make the objection more compelling one would have to argue both that I have certainty of, say, the understanding an audience has of a text I use even though the text is not intended to or does not elicit particular forms of behavior. But on what basis could one then say one has such certainty? How can I know my audience understood the text I used? There seems to be no effective way to answer this question.

The case of how the audience knows it has understood the text I have used is slightly different, for it is arguable that the audience knows it has understood the text simply on the basis of the fact that it knows itself to be linguistically competent. If the text is in English, for example, and the audience knows that it understands English, that is, it has knowledge of certain signs and the arrrangements into which they can be meaningfully arranged, then the audience also knows that it has understood my text without needing to observe any behavior of mine. To this must be added, on the other hand, that the audience's linguistic competence is itself based on past behavior, namely, the observation and effective use of the language in question. Therefore it is true that an audience does not always need to have recourse to a user's behavior to understand the text in use. On the other hand, however, the audience cannot know if the user is using the text properly unless it knows the user to be linguistically competent or it observes confirming behavior in the user. But knowledge of the linguistic competence of the user again must be traced to behavior. In short, although this objection does not affect case 1, it does bring up the need to introduce a modification in 2 as follows:

2A.   Text audience A knows with certainty that it has understood the text that text user U has used in context C if and only if either U behaves in accordance with A's expectations concerning U's behavior in C or A knows itself to be linguistically competent in the language of the text in question.

The fifth objection argues against behavior as a necessary condition of certainty in the understanding of texts based on the fact that we understand all sorts of texts that are not accompanied by persons whose behavior is observable by us. How can we explain the certainty we have of our understanding of texts that are unaccompanied by persons whose behavior can help us decipher them? If expected behavior constitutes a necessary condition of the confirmation of the understanding of texts and texts themselves are not agents and thus cannot behave, how can we know with certainty when we have understood a text that is unaccompanied by an agent?

When we confront a text unaccompanied by a person, it is altogether possible that the text in question is one that we have encountered before or is at least very similar to one we have encountered before and that at the previous time the text was accompanied by a person. Under such conditions, provided that the contexts are also similar, we know the text means the same thing on the basis of past behavior. Thus, when I see a 'No Smoking' sign in a particular room where I had not seen it before, I conclude that smoking is not permitted because I have seen such signs before in similar contexts and their meaning has been made plain through behavior in those contexts. Hence, the behavior provides certainty even in cases when it is not connected to the immediate token of a text we encounter.

A more difficult case is one in which I have never encountered the text or a text similar to it before. However, if I am familiar with its parts and the rules that govern the arrangement of those parts, then understanding is also easily accounted for in terms of the knowledge of those parts and rules, although not directly on the basis of behavior. If I had never seen the sign 'No Smoking' but I know what 'No' and 'Smoking' mean and the rules that govern their association, I can conclude that the text means that smoking is not allowed. Note two things. The first is that my knowledge is traceable to behavior insofar as the parts and rules in question are expressions of behavior and themselves are the result of someone's behavior. The text has meaning because it has been written, or spoken by someone who regards it a meaningful. Hence, although I do not have direct access to the behavior that produced the text, I have access to the product of the behavior, and ultimately that behavior, the production and use of the text, that grounds my understanding. The second point to be noticed is that I have certainty of the meaning of the text because the text is in English and I know I am competent in that language. But, as noted earlier, I know my linguistic competency precisely on the basis of past behavior. Thus it is to behavior that we must trace certainty in textual understanding, for the meaning of texts is always given in the context of use. But, of course, as 2A makes clear, it is not always the behavior of the user that confirms certainty of understanding by audiences.

Both of these cases examined are simple, however, insofar as they concern simple texts. But do the same rules apply to more complicated texts and particularly to those that deal with abstract theoretical matters far removed from ordinary language and behavior? How can we be certain, for example, that we understand Francisco Suárez's *Disputationes metaphysicae* or Kant's *Critique of Pure Reason*?

Knowing with certainty involves testing, and indeed, that is what we have been dealing with all along. The thesis I have been defending amounts to the view that expected behavior is the test of understanding texts. The strength of the theory is that it provides an indirect way of determining the meaning of texts even if there is no way of observing the tie between the entities that constitute texts and the meanings of texts. I cannot have direct access to the meaning that the author intended to convey through a text by observing the entities that constitute the text, but by watching his actions I can infer, based on previous experiences, what that meaning is. However, in the case of texts to whose authors we have no access, we cannot expect behavior to reveal their meaning, and so the subject seeking certainty concerning their meaning must make up for that lack. She can do that in two ways: First by posing questions based on what she thinks she has understood of the text and, second, by anticipating the responses that the text should provide to those questions. The familiar exegetical claim that a text interprets itself is the key on this matter.[20] That the questions we pose and the answers we give to them are found in the text consitutes evidence that we have understood it. If they are not, then obviously we do not have evidence.

Of course, texts are limited in length and scope. Thus, not to find answers to questions we ask does not entail that we have misunderstood a text. But anticipating and finding those answers is confirmation that we either have understood the text or at least are on the right track toward understanding it. Lack of confirmation of this sort does not entail misunderstanding or lack of understanding, it entails only lack of confirmation. Again, this is not a simple and straightforward procedure. It is quite possible that we may think we have found an answer to a question we ask and it turns out that what we think is the answer is not an answer at all. I do not claim, then, that it is always possible to find answers to questions we pose or that the answers we think we find are in fact answers to those questions. Certainty in these matters is most often elusive, but even if elusive, it is nonetheless possible.

What happens, however, when I not only fail to find an answer I expected but in fact find an answer I did not expect, even one that contradicts what I expected to find or that contradicts what I understand the text to mean? Several possibilities suggest themselves: (1) I have misunderstood the text; (2) I have misunderstood the answer I found; (3) the author is inconsistent; or (4) the text I have is corrupt. Obviously, none of the last three possibilities implies that I have misunderstood the text, so barring further evidence, I am simply left in the dark as to whether I do or do not understand the text in question. The thesis I am defending is not about falsifiability, but about verifiability, if we may put it thus. How can I know that I have understood Francisco Suárez's *Disputationes metaphysicae*, then? If I ask questions about what it should say concerning this or that issue, and, after conjecturing what the answers ought to be, I find those answers in the text, I can assume I have understood it.

This view may not appear completely satisfactory to some who may argue further that, if the confirmation that we have understood a text comes from finding answers to questions we pose to the text, then we pretty well end up again in an infinite regress. Let me explain. According to what has been said, to be certain I understand T_1, I need to pose a question Q_1, and find an answer to Q_1. But the answer to Q_1 is a text, call if T_2, so presumably to be certain I understand T_2, I need to pose a question Q_2, and find an answer to Q_2. But the answer to Q_2 is also a text, call it T_3, and so the process goes on to infinity, which means I can never be certain I understand T_1.

The infinite regress is generated only if one accepts that the condition of understanding T_1 is *understanding* T_2. But that is not necessary. The confirmation of understanding T_1 does not come from understanding T_2, but from the fulfillment of an expectation that T_2 occur somewhere in the text under examination. To do otherwise implies indeed to fall into an infinite regress, but such regress is avoidable because T_2 is not taken as playing a semantic role. Of course, that I correctly predict T_2 does not only confirm that I understand T_1, but also that I understand T_2, so again the infinite regress is broken.

Finally, objection six argues that behavior cannot be a necessary condition of certainty in understanding because there are cases in which the user of a text is also its audience and in these cases no behavior mediates between user and audience. The audience knows directly and with certainty that she has understood the text without the intermediary agency of behavior. When I say to myself, "I have to get this chapter finished this month," I know what I have said without having to recur to behavior to confirm it.

At first it looks like this case is airtight, indeed, for how can it be argued that behavior is necessary for certainty in understanding when no behavior is involved other than the user's action of using the text? But upon reflection the matter looks quite different for various reasons. The first of these is that I have not argued in favor of a view in which all certainty in understanding texts requires to be mediated by behavior. My view concerns only certainty in understanding when the user and the audience are not one and the same. This should be clear from formulations 1 and 2 given previously, where I used different letters to represent the user and the audience.

Second, even if I had not restricted my view to the parameters specified, it is not clear that this objection is effective, for one may argue that in cases where the user and the audience are one, the very behavior of the user may count as evidence of understanding. After all, the user, like the author, selects a text with the intention of conveying a certain meaning and then uses the text to express that meaning. Indeed, the actions of selecting the text and using it is behavior that implies an understanding of its meaning. Hence the user, considered as audience, knows that he understands a text precisely because he has gone through the process of and activities involved in the use of the text.

But someone may still counterobject that if, as stated in Chapter 4, even an author may misunderstand a text he or she produces, the behavior in producing a text cannot ensure certainty as to its meaning. And the answer is that indeed it cannot in all cases. The author does have certainty of what the text means when that text is stipulative. But an author may be mistaken as to the meaning of the text when he or she is not the author of the signs and arrangements used to compose the text. Those signs and arrangements may have meanings of which the author is not aware. Under those conditions one can be mistaken, indeed, insofar as one is using already established materials. Even the behavior of authors, then, can fail to produce certainty. And when we come to users the case is even more evident, because users are more often mistaken than authors as to the meaning of the texts they use.

These remarks do not militate against the thesis that when we have certainty in understanding we have it through behavior and behavior is always necessary to achieve such certainty. The reason is the following: That the behavior of authors and users does not always produce certainty in understanding (in cases when those authors and users produce or use texts for no audiences other than themselves) does not entail that when such certainty is produced, it is not through behavior. Indeed, in such cases certainty must be achieved also through behavior, but the behavior must be that of persons other than the author or user. If an author or user is not sure of having used certain signs correctly to compose a text to express some meaning, the only recourse is to ask someone else whether that text means what he or she thinks it does. And that, of course, involves behavior, for what the author expects is to confirm or unconfirm his or her view on the basis of the behavior expected to be observed in the audience.

In short, the answer to the question, "How do I know with certainty that I have grasped the meaning of a text?" is that I know it either through the behavior I expect in the audience or users of the text or through the responses I anticipate the text will give to my questions. Indeed, the second is not very different from the first, for those responses are nothing but codified forms of expected behavior.[21]. Consider the case of my office neighbor. We belong to different cultural groups and initially different groups of language speakers. He is a third-generation Scots Irish from Texas; I am a first generation Hispanic from Cuba. He specializes in ethics and the philosophy of law; I do metaphysics and historiography. He is somewhat reserved; I am gregarious. He is an opera fan; I prefer orchestral music. He is crazy about early Italian Renaissance art; I go for medieval. And so on. I could make a long list of the things in which we differ and which separate us. Yet, we communicate effectively. How do we do it? Because we check each other out by raising questions about what we have said. Our dialogue is filled with inquiries and responses that are checked and rechecked with further inquiries and responses.[22] And the same applies when we deal with texts from the past. We can test our understanding of them by seeing whether we can anticipate their responses to our questions.

Of course, the view I have presented here involves a broad understanding of behavior in which the use of language and texts counts as behavior.[23] Moreover, it also includes cases in which texts are subjected to procedures in which certain responses are elicited from them. This "behavior" of texts may not be, strictly speaking, what is ordinarily taken as behavior, but it is vicariously based on the behavior of the authors and users (or audiences) of the text, because their responses to the questions posed would presumably be those contained in the text. I find no difficulty with this broad understanding of behavior but those who do may substitute it for something else in the formula presented earlier thus making room for texts for which the author, user, or an understanding audience is not available.

Now let me go back for a moment to the hermeneutic circle discussed in the preceding section. The problem posed by the circle is that it seems impossible to break it, for the understanding of texts seems to involve an infinite textual regress or a textual circle. I hope that what has been said shows, however, that the hermeneutic circle not only can be broken but is regularly broken in our everyday dialogue. Note that, to break the circle, we need only one case in which we can have certainty that a text has been understood on the basis of something that is not a text. A simple case in which we are certain that we have understood a text on the basis of something nontextual is sufficient because other cases can be generated through the same procedure and analogy. But in fact there is not just one case but many that could be cited.

Of course, someone might wish to dispute my examples in various ways, but I do not believe it would be difficult to come up with at least one example that indicates that behavior confirms understanding. Consider the case of two persons in the Sahara who have been without water for four days and reach a well. When the two persons see the well in the distance they rush toward it, desperate for water. But then one of them says to the other, "Stop, don't drink; the well is poisoned!" and the other person not only stops but bursts into tears (assume that his body still had enough water to produce them). Can we really say that the first person does not know with certainty that the second person has understood what he has said? Of course, he does not have apodictic certainty, but that is not the certainty at stake here. Like this there are many other examples. Indeed, they occur in our everyday interaction with others and thus illustrate how the hermeneutic circle is broken. Theoretically speaking, we need only one case to break it, for once it is broken, language can be used semantically for communication without fear of infinite regress or circularity. But the fact is that it is not broken only once but repeatedly by all those who use texts.

The conclusions I have reached depend, of course, on the conclusions reached in Chapter 4 concerning meaning and understanding. If, contrary to what I argued there, one holds that there are no limits to the meaning and, therefore, that also there are no limits to the understanding of texts, then it is obvious that there can be no way of achieving certainty concerning the meaning of any particular text. We cannot decide what its meaning is, and whether the understanding we have of it is correct or incorrect, true or false, for there is no way of determining whose understanding is canonical.[24] The answer to the question under discussion here, then, depends to some extent on the answer to the questions raised in Chapter 4, just as the answer to the question of the limits of understanding depends to some extent on the answer to the question of the limits of meaning. But they should not be confused. For it is altogether possible to argue that in principle there are limits to the meaning and understanding of texts and yet maintain that we have no way of determining them. In short, even if there are limits to the meaning and understanding of texts, it is possible that we have no way of knowing such limits and deciding the correctness and truth value of our understandings of them. My position, however, is that indeed, we have ways of doing so, as our everyday experience illustrates, and that those ways involve expected behavior taken in context.

That the meanings of some texts turn out to be broad or even openended because of the cultural function they have, does not entail that we cannot be certain concerning any meanings. Indeed, even of the meaning of openended texts we can have some certainty as long as we understand that the parameters of understanding those texts are openended. Nor should this openendedness cause scandal if we keep in mind the cultural functions of texts. These cultural functions are embedded in linguistic uses. In practice, cultural functions determine the expectations of audiences and users, and only when such cultural functions are ignored does frustration occurs as a result of misplaced expectations.

C. The Role of Tradition in the Discernibility of Texts

Even if we assume that the view I have presented here is correct, still another philosophical question needs to be answered; How do I know what behavior to expect in order to confirm my understanding? The basis for our expectations are to be found in both culture and nature.[25] Culture is whatever human beings add to nature. It contains everything from language to practices human beings devise in their responses to their environment. Nature is what results not from free human action, but from processes in which human beings have no role qua free agents. We are immersed in both of these worlds. We have created the world of culture in response to the challenges that our surroundings pose, and because those surroundings may differ from place to place and time to time, cultures tend to be idiosyncratic and reflect their origin and history. Nature, on the other hand, is supposed to be the common denominator underlying culture. For example, to use fork and knife instead of chopsticks for eating is a matter of culture, but eating itself is a matter of nature. Nature underlies culture and is in a sense an originator and promoter of culture. One should be careful to understand, however, that not all the needs and desires human beings have are the result of nature. Culture is not only a response to nature, but acquires a life of its own, so that often cultural developments are not the result of the attempt to fulfill natural needs, but rather are the result of responses to needs which are themselves culturally originated. The need to wash one's hands before dinner, the need to study for a test, the need to find a job are all cultural rather than natural needs and arise out of an attempt by human beings to respond to their cultural rather than natural environment.

The idea that human beings share a common nature is not popular today. It is frequent to find challenges in the literature to the view that human beings have characteristics that are not cultural. Indeed, features that for many centuries were regarded as part of nature are nowadays seen by many as cultural. Such are, for example, gender and race. But these challenges do not militate against the view I am proposing as long as they are not directed to the most basic features associated with human beings. When I speak of nature, I do not refer to notions that have evolved and developed in cultures. I do not speak of gender conceived in terms of what particular societies believe males and females should be and how they ought to behave. If gender is to be taken as a natural rather than a cultural phenomenon, it must refer to physiological differences and needs that are not the result of cultural development. Nor should it be assumed that the natural core of human beings is unchangeable. As long as there is continuity and authors and audiences share certain basic features, my view should work.

Human beings are products of natural processes and share much in common. To say that they are the product of culture alone and not of nature, or to divorce culture from nature, seems not only counterintuitive but also contrary to experience. This is not the place to develop a defense of natures, but it does seem that many of those who attack natures transform human beings into cultural entities divorced from their physical and biological foundation. Their view is somewhat similar to that of Plato, who identified each human being with a soul imprisoned in a body, except that for them the soul has become a cultural entity somewhat unrelated to the physical body.

The fact is that we share with other members of the human race certain needs, passions, tendencies, and ways of acting that establish bridges among us and help us communicate across times and cultures.[26] Indeed, the strong similarities among cultural phenomena developed independently by societies support this point. All societies have developed ceremonies and institutions surrounding religion, marriage, and death that share similarities and unite humankind.[27] A core of human nature binds us all and forms the basis of the variegated ideas and customs we develop, facilitating communication.[28]

In culture and nature human beings can find the basis for their effective communication through texts. Both culture and nature imply a baggage of shared practices. Nature implies a set of needs and responsive behaviors common to all human beings. Culture implies a set of practices common to the members of a group. In both cases we have a community, either natural or cultural, that shares patterns of behavior, or to use a Wittgensteinian expression, "a form of life."[29] And in these patterns of behavior the foundation of effective communication is found. When a pattern of behavior is passed down from generation to generation it is called *tradition*, so in tradition are found the causes of effective communication. Tradition ensures recognition and understanding; it ties together groups who live at different times or places, and it constitutes the basis of our expectations. We know what to look for through tradition.

Tradition itself may be understood in various ways. The Latin root of the term means a delivery, surrender, and teaching, and comes from the verb *trado*, to give up, hand over, deliver, transmit, and bequeath. The English term 'tradition,' and its counterparts in other modern European languages, are used frequently in connection with the transmission of beliefs and doctrines in oral as opposed to written form. Among Catholics, for example, the term is used to refer to the doctrines revealed by Christ or his disciples and not committed to writing. In this sense it contrasts with the Scriptures. And for Jews it refers to the unwritten code of law as opposed to the written one. If the term is understood in this way, as some kind of doctrine passed down from generation to generation in oral form, tradition would not be very helpful to us here, for as a text, even though an oral one, it would be subject to the same problems to which all texts are. For tradition to be of use to us, it would have to be interpreted nontextually. I propose to interpret it, then, as the set of practices and procedures that are passed down in a given culture. And my claim is that we learn what to expect from the understanding of texts through the set of practices and procedures that form part of a culture.

Note that there is no reason why the practices and procedures in question need not involve texts. They certainly can involve the use of texts, whose meaning is known, thus clarifying and explaining the meaning of other texts. But to avoid the hermeneutic circle we must fall back into a foundation that is not textual. Ultimately, tradition must be understood as practices and procedures, and even if those practices and procedure involve texts, those texts are not what ensure and found the transference of meaning but the uses, that is the practices and procedures, to which those texts are put.[30]

As I pointed out earlier, texts are conventionally tied to their meanings and those meanings are intended by authors to be communicated to audiences in particular contexts. To get at that meaning, then, we cannot approach texts directly; we must work as it were indirectly, through the cultural context, and that context is revealed to us through the practices of the communities in which the texts are produced. If we are not contemporaneous with the communities, it is through the practices that have been handed down and preserved that we can get to the meanings of the texts.

Consider the question of how we know, for example, that a sign such as 'cat' means cat. Obviously there is no natural connection between 'cat' and cat. That 'cat' means cat is the result, first, of some historical event, call it a baptism if you will, whereby one or more persons came to refer to individual cats as 'cat.'[31] This is, then, a conventional arrangement, regardless of whether it was the result of a conscious decision or not. But that does not explain why 'cat' means cat today. That it does depends not only on the baptismal event, but also on the tacit acceptance, maintained through practice, that 'cat' means cat. Thus 'cat' means cat because it was so established at some point in history and is currently accepted and used as such.

All this is metaphysical, if you will. Now, for the epistemological issue: How do I know that 'cat' means cat and that some text from the past that uses 'cat' means cat? The answer is that I know both things through the practices I have learned. I learned in school to write 'cat' when I meant cat, just as my teacher did before him, and so on back to the first person or group of persons who used 'cat' to mean cat. 'Cat' means cat because society uses it for cat, and I know that 'cat' means cat because I am part of that society and accept and use the rules of behavior of that society. Custom, then, codified in tradition, is the backbone of understanding texts not only from the past but even from the present.

Someone might object, however, that this is all very well in cases where we have access to those practices, but what do we do when we do not? Can we expect to learn the meaning of texts written in a dead language whose practices and customs have not survived either directly among its descendants or indirectly through its influence on other cultures?

We might still be able to decipher some of the texts if we can somehow reconstruct the customs and practices of the culture on the basis of the artifacts they left behind. The context of texts is very important for knowing both that they are texts and what those texts mean. Of course, if what we have is simply a text found in a place where no indication of any culture is present, it would be very difficult if not impossible to decipher it. Indeed, as noted in Section A, it might even be impossible to know it was a text.

Another objection might run as follows: Even when a text is found surrounded by artifacts, we still could not know the meaning of the text, for we would have no way of knowing the function of the artifacts in question. But, again, this I believe ignores that human practices respond to a limited number of fundamental needs, desires, and aims and that there are limited numbers of ways of fulfilling those needs, desires, and aims in determinate contexts. That body of needs, desires, and aims ultimately bridges the gaps among cultures and allows us to reconstruct the practices of people.

Our knowledge of the meaning of texts is based on the practices that have been passed down in connection with those texts; namely, on tradition. Or it is based on the practices that can be reconstructed from anthropological studies based in turn on the belief that there are certain fundamental needs, desires, and aims common to all human beings.

I do not mean to say that without tradition communication among human beings is impossible. For even without tradition nature still can form the basis of some communication among human beings. Sexual needs and desires can be made explicit to other human beings through the natural reactions of our bodies. But that is communication at a natural level and in terms of natural behavior. Putting food into one's mouth, chewing and swallowing it, some sexual activities, and so forth are good examples of natural behavior that communicate effectively one's state of mind and also the meaning of certain signs. But this always presumes presence. When we are confronted with texts produced in the past and we have no direct access to their authors, then nature cannot be the basis of efficient communication; tradition becomes indispensable.[32] This is the case because, as argued in Chapter 1, texts are not natural entities, but conventional ones and thus cannot be understood in terms of natural processes. They make sense only in the context of particular cultures and procedures.[33] A text outside a tradition, without a community that sustains it and preserves its meaning, is no more than a peculiar collection of entities.[34] The community and its practices are essential for the understanding of texts.[35]

The view that I have just presented is not revolutionary. Indeed, it is ingrained in the beliefs of many of our institutions, although there is by no means universal agreement on its validity. One institution whose claims are based on this view is the Roman Catholic Church. According to Roman Catholicism the Bible is indeed a sacred book in which God revealed his will to humanity. But to understand that book one must belong to a community that shares not only certain beliefs but also certain practices that have been passed on from generation to generation. Only in the context of these beliefs and practices—in other words, of these traditions—does the book make any sense.[36]

Luther's view, on the other hand, was that such a set of practices and beliefs was not needed. To know God's will we need only the Scriptures (*sola Scriptura*), which can be understood by the individual believer without help from any other human being. But this was possible because Luther believed God was there to help each individual person; so Luther also accepted the need for some external help, divine help, to know the meaning of the scriptural text. His view, by the way, is quite reminiscent of the Augustinian answer to the hermeneutic circle. In many ways, then, the Lutheran position grants the need for something other than the ECTs that constitute a text when we seek to understand the meaning of a text from the past, even if what is needed is not tradition. In the case of Sacred Scriptures, the author of the text, God himself, makes understanding possible.

The lesson we learn from both Catholics and Lutherans is that texts cannot speak for themselves. The need for a living community and a tradition for communication to take place is further illustrated in some religious stories and myths; for example, the Judaean story of the Tower of Babel, where lack of communication resulted in separation. Being a member of a community presupposes communication, and communication presupposes being a member of a community. If communication is interrupted, no community can survive;

and if the community breaks up, communication ceases.

On the other hand, the establishment of social ties results in enhanced understanding, and enhanced understanding results also in the strengthening or establishment of social ties. The biblical story of the reception of the Holy Spirit by Christ's apostles and disciples after his death illustrates how a social union enhances communication. According to the biblical story, the speech of the apostles was understood by all those who opened their hearts to it, presumably because they had become spiritual members of the new community of believers.

I do not want to emphasize the parallel between the philosophical point I am trying to make concerning the understanding of texts from the past and the lessons one can learn both from history and religion. But it seems appropriate to note that there is some background to what I have been saying that goes beyond mere philosophy.

Before I leave this topic I would like to emphasize, lest there be some lingering misunderstanding, the distinction between the issues I have discussed in this section of the chapter and questions involved in exegetical methodology. My concern has been with the determination of criteria on the basis of which I can (1) identify that something is a text, (2) learn the meaning of a text, and (3) be certain that I understand that meaning. Moreover, I have identified the foundations of those criteria with nature, culture, and particularly tradition. Exegetical methodology, that is, the study of the procedures that should be followed to get at the meaning of texts is an entirely different enterprise. It involves the formulation of rules that, if adhered to, will help in the understanding of texts. For example, the exegetical methodologist might conclude that the understanding of texts is helped by the consideration of what we know concerning the historical author, or that those who wish to understand texts should take into account the historical context in which they were produced. These rules might also indicate that understandings which turn out to be incoherent are suspect and that understanding is better achieved when certain careful procedures of textual analysis are followed. These are just examples of exegetical rules that may or may not be good and may or may not apply to the understanding of texts. But they do illustrate the differences between the questions that concern exegetical methodology and the epistemological questions with which we have been concerned thus far in this chapter. Naturally, exegetical methodology is an important field of study when it comes to texts and their understanding, but it is not one directly pertinent to our inquiry. For this reason I shall dispense with further reference to it.

IV. Conclusion

I began this chapter by raising the fundamental epistemic problem posed by texts, namely, that it is not clear how it is possible for us to know that something is a text or to know its meaning. This problem seems to follow from the fact that texts are entities with meaning but nothing in the entities themselves ostensibly reveals the meaning. This problem gave rise to three questions: How can I know that something is a text? How can I learn the meaning of a text? How can I be certain that I know the meaning of a text?

The answer to the first question was that there are various ways in which we know that something is a text. Other persons might tell us; we may remember the text from having experienced it before; we may know the language in which the text is presented; another text might tell us that the entities in question constitute a text; and so on. Moreover, even where these ways are not available to us, certain characteristics are common to most texts and, because of that, may serve to identify texts in most circumstances. These characteristics are abstraction, repetition, and organization. The existence of these characteristics acquires even more weight when they are combined with considerations of cultural context, for cultures tend to use texts in very specific ways. Finally, also certain fundamental human needs govern behavior and require communication which can give us clues as to whether something is or is not a text. Of course, not in all circumstances can we be certain of the textuality of a group of entities, but this is simply a corollary drawn from the very nature of texts. Unless we know that the entities in question have meaning, and thus by inference that they have an author or a user who intends to convey it through them, we cannot be certain they constitute a text. This leads naturally to the second question.

The second question, How can I learn the meaning of a text?, led us to an impasse in which we were confronted, on the one hand, with an infinite regress and on the other with a vicious circle. The reason is that the means we use to know the meaning of texts seem always to be texts. These alternatives in turn seem to lead either to a skeptical stance of a Gorgian character in which, contrary to our experience, it is claimed that we can never learn the meaning of a text, or to a Platonic conclusion that claims that the meaning of texts is innate.

The escape from this dilemma was made while attempting to answer the third question posed at the beginning of the chapter, which asked how I can be certain that I know the meaning of a text. The answer I defended is that, ultimately we know the meaning of texts and can acquire certainty concerning that knowledge through expected behavior taken in context. Expected behavior in context is what breaks the infinite regress and vicious circle into which we were led by the second question raised in this chapter. Moreover, we know what behavior to expect on the basis of nature and culture, the latter being codified and passed on through tradition. Indeed, behavior codified in tradition makes possible the understanding of texts to whose authors we do not have access, for these traditions are behavioral patterns in which users of texts engage and that they pass on to others.

This brings me to the end of the last chapter and second part of this study, concerned with the epistemology of texts. I add next a few remarks by way of conclusion, summarizing the main tenets of the part of the theory of textuality I have presented in this book.

CONCLUSION:
A THEORY OF TEXTUALITY —
LOGIC AND EPISTEMOLOGY

I began this book by posing some philosophical problems to which the consideration of texts give rise. In particular I indicated that the various things we call texts appear to have contradictory characteristics in such a way that the very notion of textuality seems to be threatened and undermined. To these initial problems others were added as I went along, considering various logical and epistemological dimensions of textuality. Most of these problems appear to be inherent in any philosophical investigation of textuality and therefore must be addressed by any theory of textuality which claims any kind of comprehensiveness or completeness. Other problems, however, surfaced only as a result of certain conceptual moves made to deal with other difficulties. Moreover, metaphysical issues related to textuality have been postponed for the following volume of this study.

Following the purpose I announced in the Preface, my strategy in dealing with the various problems that have surfaced has been to develop a theory that accommodates what I consider to be our most basic intuitions about texts and at the same time solves the problems that arise when those intuitions are subjected to critical examination. In formulating a theory of textuality, I have looked for a unifying and consistent conception of texts. Because of the length of the study and the many and diverse specific issues with which it deals it might appear that the theory is perhaps not as unified or consistent as I claim. For these reasons I devote this conclusion to the concise presentation of its main logical and epistemological tenets, so that its overall unity and consistency may become more apparent and that we may be better prepared to address the metaphysical issues to be explored in the volume that follows.

The two conceptual pillars on which the theory rests are, first, a conception of the nature of texts and, second, a particular understanding of the function of texts. On these the solution to the problems raised by texts presented in various parts of the book is found.

The conception of the nature of texts adopted in this book is expressed by the definition of texts as groups of entities, used as signs, that are selected, arranged, and intended by an author in a certain context to convey some specific meaning to an audience. The particular understanding of the function of texts posits them as playing diverse roles within a culture.

The definition of texts makes clear that texts are complex entities and thus composed of other entities. The entities of which texts are composed are signs, but signs are themselves constituted by entities used to convey meaning and therefore these entities can also be said to constitute texts. It is important to distinguish the entities that constitute texts, the signs that compose texts, and the texts themselves.

The entities that constitute texts can be of any sort; they can be physical or mental, for example, and within these categories they can vary considerably, depending on the entities in question. Moreover, these entities have meaning only if they are used as signs that in turn compose texts; they have no meaning when considered in themselves, but they acquire meaning when they are used as signs. Thus signs are those entities insofar as they are used to convey meaning.

Although signs, like texts, have meaning, they should not be confused with texts. The distinction between the two, however, does not rest in that texts are complex and signs are not, for in fact no sign is simple. Nor is the distinction based on the fact that texts are composed of signs whereas signs are not, for some signs are composed of other signs. Finally, the distinction is not a matter of complexity of meaning, for texts can have relatively simple meanings and signs can have highly complex ones. The distinction rests rather on the fact that the meaning of texts is in part the result of the meanings of the signs of which they are composed and the arrangement in which they are placed, whereas the meaning of signs is not the result in any way of the meanings of its components or their arrangement even in cases in which those components and arrangements are semantically significant.

This view entails a technical understanding of signs in which such things as publicly displayed notices are not signs. In this scheme, the latter are, properly speaking, texts. It also entails that the meaning of texts does not depend only on the independent meaning of the signs of which texts are composed, but also on their arrangement. For the same signs arranged in different ways can yield different meanings.

Textual meaning itself is conceived as what is understood when a text is understood and thus as related both to texts and to the act of understanding. This is a somewhat neutral conception of meaning that allows the meaning of texts to vary and include such things as physical objects and their physical features, mental entities, universal notions, and so on. It can accommodate the three most popular views of meaning, while avoiding their difficulties. These views are the referential, ideational, and functional. The first conceives meaning as reference; the second conceives it as ideas; and the third conceives it as use. Meaning, conceived in the suggested neutral way should be distinguished from significance. The significance of a text has to do with the relevance, importance, and consequences of it, and this relevance, importance, and consequences, although in part affected and resulting from its meaning, is related to factors other than meaning.

Significance is a relational notion that involves a text and its meaning, on one side, and other events, texts, phenomena, and so on, on the other.

The distinction among the entities that constitute texts, the signs that compose texts, the meaning of texts, and texts themselves makes it possible to understand how texts sometimes appear to have different and even incompatible features. For these features may be features of the entitites that constitute them, the signs that compose them, or the meaning of the texts rather than of the texts themselves. Thus, if a text is constituted by physical entities that are given non-physical meanings one may be tempted to think that something is wrong with the text if the features of both the entities and the meanings are predicated of the text. But if one understands that the predicates in question may apply strictly speaking only to the entities that constitute the text or to the meaning of the text and apply only in a manner of speaking to the text, then the difficulty disappears. Within the complexity of texts one can find answers to many of the puzzles that they pose.

That the primary function of texts is to convey meaning does not entail that it is their only function. Texts may and often do other things than produce understanding, but to do those other things they must also produce understanding. The production of understanding is a necessary condition for any other functions a text may have, even if those other functions are primary in the intention of the author or user.

The definition of texts makes clear another important point about texts, namely, that texts are always intended to convey meaning. The use of a text makes no sense unless this principle is accepted. But intention should not be confused with full awareness of what is intended or of the intention. One may not have full awareness of the meaning of a text and yet have the intention to communicate it. And one may not have full awareness of the intention to convey meaning and yet intend to do so.

An important corollary of the definition of texts is that texts are conventional entities. Their conventionality refers to the relation of their meaning to the entities that constitute them, for there is no natural semantic connection between the meaning of the signs that compose the text and those entities, or between the meaning of the text and those entities. The connection is the result of a convention developed by those who use the entitites that constitute texts as signs and as components of texts. Signs are never natural in the sense of having a natural connection to a meaning. This conventional character applies also to the semantic significance of the arrangement of those signs and the role of context.

Context is anything that, not being part of a text, can affect the meaning of the text. Hence, some contexts may depend to a great extent on the type of text in question, whereas others do not. The importance of context can be gathered from the fact that texts are intended by authors for certain audiences, thus assuming a language and so on. It is clear also from the fact that most texts are elliptical and, therefore, meant to be completed by additions that are not part of them and can be supplied only by an audience in a determinate context. The dependence of texts on context does not entail that all are equally dependent on context or depend on context in exactly the same way. Different texts will depend on context in different ways and in different degrees.

Contexts may be divided into two sorts: historical and contemporary. The first is the complete set of circumstances that affect the meaning of a text at the time of its production. The contemporary context, by contrast, consists of the complete set of circumstances that affect the understanding of the meaning of a text by an audience that is not contemporaneous with the text at the time of its production.

Finally, two other corollaries of the definition of texts become clear only upon reflection. If the connection between meaning and the entities that constitute texts is conventional, then the entities that function as signs in texts must be epistemically accessible, for no author can compose a text without having access to those entities.

The second corollary of the definition of texts I propose is that it narrows down the category of textuality considerably, ruling out all sorts of things that have been proposed as texts by recent hermeneuticists, literary critics, and philosophers of language. Texts constitute a narrow category of entities that have a very particular use, to convey meaning, and that are subject to strict conditions related to authorship, audiences, and contexts. At the same time, the conception of texts proposed in the definition allows complete freedom with respect to the choice of entities that are used as signs to make up texts. Indeed, the confusion between the two, namely, between texts and the entities that constitute them, is at least in part responsible for mistakenly extending the category of texts to entities that in fact are not texts.

The definition also makes possible the distinction between the category of texts and other categories sometimes confused with it, such as the categories of language, artifact, art object, and work. The confusion of texts and language is understandable, for most texts are composed of signs that belong to natural languages and those signs are arranged according to the rules of natural languages. Indeed, even texts that do not fit this description are composed of linguistic signs and arranged according to linguistic rules, thus sharing some characteristics with languages. But texts are not languages. Texts are not composed of rules, whereas languages are in part composed of rules. Texts have a definite structure, whereas languages do not. Texts are historically determined, whereas living languages are constantly changing. Texts logically presuppose languages, whereas languages do not logically presuppose texts. Texts have particular purposes, whereas languages, except for artificial ones, do not. Most texts have identifiable authors, whereas that is not so with natural languages. And, finally, texts have audiences, whereas languages do not.

The confusion of texts with language may lead to the conclusion that texts, like most languages, are flexible, have no very strict identity conditions, and are independent of authors and audiences. The fact is, however, that texts are less flexible than languages, having definite structures and generally identifiable authors and audiences. It is a mistake to conclude, then, that texts lack definition and determination. This is one of the reasons why it is important to understand the distinction between texts and language. Note, of course, that the distinction between texts and language does not imply that texts are not semantically flexible and that they are not dependent on their authors and audiences in various ways; it only implies that if they are so, it is not because they are languages or like languages.

The confusion of texts and artifacts is also understandable, for texts are always artifactual and thus share with artifacts some fundamental features. The conception of an artifact implicit in ordinary language suggests that artifacts are either inorganic or organic small objects that are either the products of intentional activity and design or are not the product of intentional activity and design but have undergone some change as a result of intentional activity and design. This conception, however, appears too restrictive and somewhat arbitrary. I substitute for it a broader conception of artifacts as entities that either are the product of intentional activity and design or, not being the product of intentional activity and design, have undergone some change or their context has undergone some change. This change in either case has to be the product of intentional activity and design and the artifactual entity is considered in the context where the change has occurred rather than apart from it.

This conception of artifacts is not completely satisfactory insofar as it does not clearly account for the status of some objects. These problematic cases, however, should not obscure the question of the artifactuality of texts. When artifacts are understood in the suggested way, texts can be classified as artifacts for two reasons. First, they are composed of signs and signs are artifacts because they are the product of intentional activity and design insofar as they are entities with meaning conventionally attached to them. Second, because for signs to make up texts they must be selected, arranged, and intended by an author to convey meaning and that entails intentional activity and design. However, the entities that constitute texts need not be artifacts—they can be natural objects to which artifactuality is conferred as a result of their use as signs. Nor are all artifacts texts, for most artifacts have no conventional connection with meaning and fail to meet the other conditions of textuality noted in the definition.

Something similar occurs with the category of art object. Although some art objects may be texts, not all art objects are texts and not all texts are art objects. For something to be an art object it must be an artifact and it must be capable of producing an artistic experience. The first condition ties together art objects and texts for, like art objects, all texts are artifacts. But not all texts are capable of producing an artistic experience. The conditions for objects to be capable of producing an artistic experience are two: that they be regarded as artifacts and as capable of producing an aesthetic experience. Thus the conditions of being an art object include being an artifact, being regarded as an artifact, and being regarded as capable of producing an aesthetic experience. Art objects are not required to be composed of signs, and even if their aim were to convey some meaning, their primary function has to do with the production of an artistic experience. Texts, by contrast, have no necessary connection to being regarded as capable of producing an artistic experience even if they share the condition of artifactuality with art objects. Nor does it make a difference that they also share having authors and audiences.

From all this it follows that texts and art objects are different and, therefore, that the attempt to reduce texts to art objects or art objects to texts is misguided. The distinction between art objects and texts in terms of, first, the character of the entities that compose them; second, the intended function of texts; and, third, the recognition of the capacity of art objects to produce an artistic experience allows us to understand, moreover, how the same object can be a text and an art object without the implication that to be one is the same as to be the other.

Although only recently has an explicit attempt been made to blur the distinction between texts and art objects, and only recently has the same explicit attempt been made with respect to texts and works, the confusion between texts and works is not a recent phenomenon. Indeed, in ordinary speech it is not clear that there is any sharp distinction between the two. The confusion between texts and works, however, leads to all sorts of problems, because, as in the case of the entities that constitute texts and the meaning of those entitites when they are used as signs, works and texts have different features.

In principle one can take five different positions with respect to the relation of the categories of text and work: the categories are identical, the category of text includes the category of work but not vice versa, the category of work includes the category of text but not vice versa, the categories overlap, and finally, the categories exclude each other. Only the last one can be taken as a point of departure for an adequate view of the relation of texts and works, for all the others encounter serious difficulties.

Recently, several versions of the last approach have been proposed. One identifies works with the acts in which authors engage when they produce texts; another identifies works with the entities that constitute texts; and the third regards works as a sui generis category. None of these views is satisfactory, however. The first because predicates normally applied to works cannot be applied to authorial acts; the second because the entities that constitute texts have no meaning and meaning is essential for works; and the third because it violates Ockham's razor.

My own position is that works are the meanings of certain texts. Not all texts have meanings that qualify as works; works are the meanings of those texts that a culture regards as works because they fulfill certain criteria developed by the culture. This entails that no general rules apply to what constitutes a work for all times and places. Not length, the degree of effort that it takes to produce a text, nor that it may be open to many and conflicting interpretations determines which texts have corresponding works. The notion of work is culturally conditioned and determined by the functions that particular cultures attach to certain texts.

Finally, let me add that my position is not to be confused with the view that works are interpretations of texts proposed by audiences. By *interpretation* in this context is usually meant "understanding." Thus an interpretation of a text is an understanding of it, that is, of what it means. The differences between this view and mine are that for me works are the meanings of certain texts, and therefore they cannot be identified with the understandings audiences may have of them. Audiences may understand texts in ways not warranted by their meaning, or they may understand only part of the meaning of texts. Moreover, understandings are acts in audiences, whereas meanings can be but need not be acts of any kind.

The introduction of the notion of cultural function leads naturally to the consideration of various types of texts depending on the function they have. The notion of function plays an important role not only in the determination of whether a text's meaning constitutes a work, but in the context of textual understanding and interpretation.

Function may be understood in various ways, two of which are particularly pertinent here. The first is the notion of linguistic function. Texts are linguistic in character and thus derive some of their functions from this. Like language, they can be used to inform, direct, express, evaluate, and perform. Less fundamental, but no less important, however, are the cultural functions a text may have that do not derive from their linguistic nature. They depend on various cultural phenomena and how they affect the uses to which texts are put. Thus texts may be classified as legal, literary, philosophical, scientific, religious, political, historical, pedagogical, confessional, entertaining, inspirational, pneumonic, and so on. None of the various functions identified is to be regarded as exclusionary. Texts may fulfill various functions at different times or at the same time, depending on a wide variety of factors. Nor are they exhaustive, because the functions of texts depend on a variety of factors that may change according to diverse circumstances.

That texts are constituted by entities of various sorts suggests other ways of classifying them in addition to those based on function. One of these is the modal classification of texts. According to it, texts are actual, intended, or ideal. The actual text is the text that exists outside the mind of an interpreter. It is either the historical text, the contemporary text, or the intermediary text. The historical text is the text the historical author actually produced, whether we have it or not. The contemporary text is the text available to us in the original language in which it was produced; sometimes, when the historical text has survived intact, the contemporary text is the same as the historical text. And the intermediary text is a text we do not actually have; it is not the historical text but nonetheless it is a text that existed at some time and functioned at the time as a contemporary text of an audience.

The intended text is supposed to be the text the author intended to produce, but did not produce. We are led to this notion because often authors believe that the texts they have produced are not the ones they intended to produce. I argue, however, that the notion of an intended text is incoherent if it is taken either (1) for anything other than a mental text that precedes a physical text, (2) for the historical text purged from any clerical mistakes, or (3) for the historical text the author produced. If it is none of these, it can be nothing other than (4) a set of ideas or intentions an author has concerning the text and its meaning. In this sense, intended texts are very much like intended art objects, for the latter also do not exist as intended prior to existing as actual, either in the mind or outside it.

Many factors influence authors while they compose texts, playing causal roles in various aspects of the composition. A text, just like an art object, is not caused by an author alone, but is rather a result of a causal complex that includes an author and a context where the author works.

The intended text exists only as a conjecture on the part of an interpreter or the author of the historical text after the historical text has been produced. At that point the author, or an interpreter, may say that what the author intended to write, for example, was such and such and not such and such. But this does not entail that there was an intended text before the historical text was produced; it entails only that the author may have had some ideas or intentions to which the historical text does or does not adhere.

The distinction between a historical text and an intended text derives from various assumptions. The first is taken from scriptural exegesis and assumes that a divine being reveals his perfect views through an imperfect medium. The second is that meanings are texts and thus that there is a set of meanings in the mind of the author that gets translated into a text either in the mind or outside it. The third is that the cause must explicitly and actually precontain everything that is present in the effect. The fourth is that the author is the sole cause of a text. And the last is that mental texts are the same thing as intended texts.

The ideal text may be understood in three different ways. First, it may be understood as an inaccurate version of a historical text produced and considered by an interpreter as an accurate copy of the historical text. Second, it may be understood as a text produced by an interpreter who considers that it expresses the view the historical text expressed imperfectly. Third, it may be taken as a text produced by an interpreter as the text that perfectly expresses the view the historical author should have expressed. In all three cases, the ideal text is a product of an interpreter and not of the historical author. The ideal text may be considered ideal because of one or more of the following reasons: the historical author did not produce it; it is not an accurate version of the historical text; it is a perfect model of the more or less imperfect copy that the historical author produced; and it is the more perfect text absolutely speaking.

The ideal text, considering both that it is not the historical text and that those who try to construct it accept it as such, functions in fact as a kind of regulative notion used by interpreters to understand, interpret, and evaluate a historical or contemporary text. It indicates where contemporary texts might be inaccurate or the authors of texts might have gone wrong and where they have not, by comparing what they did with what they should have done. It also serves to construe what authors may have wanted to say but failed to say adequately. The ideal text as such is a useful hermeneutical and historiographical tool, although its use can lead to abuses.

Having clarified the notion of text, how the notion of text is related to some other notions, and how texts may be classified, I turned to the epistemological issues of understanding, interpretation, and discernibility. To understand a text is to grasp its meaning. Textual understanding is a mental act or acts whose object is meaning. Thus meaning should not be confused with understanding. Nor should understanding taken in this way be confused with a faculty of the mind that sometimes is referred to with the same term. Because understanding is an act or acts of the subject or subjects who understand a text, there are as many numerically different understandings as acts performed by the author and audiences of texts. Acts of understanding are extensionally the same only if they are individually the same acts. They are extensionally different only if they are individually distinct acts. They are intensionally the same only if, having been prompted by the same type of ECTs, the meaning understood through them is the same. And they are intensionally different only if the meanings understood through them are different, even though they are prompted by the same type of ECTs. Thus, several persons can have the same act or acts of understanding, taken intensionally, and the same applies to a person at different times. Extensionally speaking, however, no person can have the same act of understanding as anyone else, nor can the same person have the same act of understanding at different times.

From this it follows that the identity of understandings when they are considered intensionally depends on textual identity. For the identity of understanding will depend on the sameness of meaning of certain ECTs. By contrast, textual identity is not dependent on identity of understanding.

Given the conditions of the identity of understanding and the identity of texts, misunderstanding cannot be construed as the understanding of meaning that does not belong to a text. Rather, misunderstanding is conceived as a confusion between two texts, so that one understands a text but thinks that one has understood another.

The most controversial issue concerning textual understanding today is the question of its limits. This issue can be posed in two different ways. In one way, it is the epistemological issue of whether there are limits to the understanding of texts such that an understanding that goes beyond those limits is no longer under-standing but becomes misunderstanding. The second issue is moral. It concerns the right of audiences to understand texts as they wish. Because understanding depends on meaning, we must first raise the question of the limits of meaning: Are there any limits to the meaning of texts? Some argue that there are no limits, texts are polysemous; others argue that there are strict and narrow limits so that every text has only one, narrowly understood meaning. Neither of these two positions, as stated, appears sound. To find a satisfactory middle ground between them I introduce three distinctions.

The first is a distinction between essential and accidental differences in meaning. Essential differences are those that establish also differences of identity among texts. Accidental differences are those that do not result in differences in textual identity.

Second, I distinguish between meaning and the implications of meaning. The implications of the meaning of a text are not part of that meaning but rather derivative from it. They are in fact the meaning of other texts that express such implications. Thus the identity of a text does not have to do directly with those implications, but only with the meaning from which those implications derive.

Finally, I distinguish between meanings and intentions. Textual meaning is what is understood when one is said to have understood a text, but intentions are neither what one understands when one is said to understand a text nor the act of understanding whereby one does so. Further, I reject the notion of a finished and complete intended textual meaning considered apart from the actual meaning of the produced text. The most that an intended textual meaning can be, apart from the meaning of the produced text, is either the meaning of another text of which the produced text is a translation or a set of vague ideas the author intends to convey.

From this it follows that meanings have limits, thus we must turn to the factors that establish such limits. Six of these are frequently mentioned in the lit-erature: author, audience, context, society, language, and the text itself. None of these, taken by itself, however, seems to fit the bill. The author cannot be the factor that exclusively establishes the limits of the meaning of a text because neither the author's intention nor the author's understanding can function in this way. Indeed, it is common to find that texts have meanings that their authors did not under-stand them to have.

The audience cannot be regarded as the factor that establishes the meaning of a text for several reasons. First, it cannot be the intention of the audience that establishes the meaning, for the audience has no particular semantic intention when it approaches a text beyond that of understanding (or misunderstanding) it. Nor can it be the audience's understanding, for that amounts to saying that there are no limits to the meaning of texts, because the number and type of audiences a text can have is potentially infinite. Moreover, that audiences should function in this way defeats the purpose of texts, which is precisely to convey meaning.

Context does not work because either it includes or amounts to the author and the audience, in which case the objections mentioned are effective. Or it neither includes nor amounts to the author and audience; but then it cannot establish meaning because context by itself cannot establish the conventional tie between ECTs and meaning that is essential to textuality.

Society cannot be considered to be the exclusive factor that establishes the meanings of texts because society is nothing but a group of individual persons, that is, authors or audiences. And we saw already that authors and audiences by themselves cannot function in this way. Moreover, not only is the text not the product of society at large, but there are substantial segments of society that have nothing to do with particular texts.

Language cannot function in this way because context plays a role in the determination of textual meaning and yet not all context is linguistic. Moreover, language contains virtually an infinite number of possible texts and meanings, but such an infinite number of possible texts and meanings does not entail any actual texts or meanings.

The text is the most recent candidate proposed to establish the limits of textual meaning, but by itself it fails, like the others considered. The view of the text as determinant of meaning can be understood in three ways. According to one the text is identified with the entities that constitute it, considered apart from any meaning that may be attached to them. This version of this position fails because it cannot explain how entities devoid of meaning can determine the limits of meaning.

A second version of this view considers a text as composed of entities endowed with meaning, that is signs, and arranged in syntactically significant ways. But if the entities that constitute texts have meaning, that meaning in turn must result from factors external to the text and thus this position is inconsistent.

Finally, some hold that a text does not preexist its understanding and, therefore, conclude that there are no limits to its meaning. The understanding of a text is a construct that is not preceded by the text or its meaning; the text and its meaning are the result of it rather than their cause. Obviously, this position amounts to one in which the audience is the determinant factor in the establishment of meaning. In this sense the view is no different from the one explored earlier. Moreover, even if the objections brought against that view were defeated, there must be something that precedes the audience's understanding, and this must be understood simply as ECTs or as ECTs with meaning. So this position amounts to one of the two already rejected.

In short, none of the factors discussed taken separately satisfactorily accounts for the limits of textual meaning. Nor does their combination do so, for a fundamental factor is missing from the list: the cultural function of the text. It is my contention that ultimately the cultural function of texts determines the role that the aforementioned factors play, and thus in turn determines the limits of textual meaning. Moreover, because cultural function varies from text to text and even for the same text, the limits of the meaning may vary accordingly. The culture, understood as a community of persons who share certain values and rules of behavior, establishes the rules according to which meaning is to be determined through the function they assign to a text.

Thus, contrary to what some believe, there are limits to the meaning of texts, but those limits are not always strict and narrow, because the cultural function of a text may prescribe limits that are broad, vague, or even openended. Moreover, often a culture does not directly determine the meaning, but delegates such a task to a person or group of persons in society who is considered authoritative. Nor is it helpful to speak of an author's meaning, an audience's meaning, a literal meaning, and so on. A text has one and only one meaning, but that meaning may not be as narrow and closed as some propose.

Because understanding depends on meaning, and meaning has limits, there must also be limits to understanding. Hence, I reject the view that there are no limits to understanding and, thus, that no misunderstanding is possible. And I reject the view that there are strict and narrow limits to the understanding of all texts and that such limits are imposed by the understanding of authors. In my view the limits of understanding are imposed by the limits of meaning which are in turn established by a variety of factors whose role is determined by cultural function.

Misunderstanding occurs when a text is confused with another text that has similar ECTs but whose meaning is essentially different. This may happen, for example, when the implications of the meaning of a text are confused with the meaning. Whether a text is misunderstood, then, depends very much on its cultural function and not on whether the understanding duplicates the understanding the author of the text had, for the author of a text may not only understand its meaning partially, but may in fact misunderstand it.

This leads to the moral question of whether it is legitimate for audiences to understand texts differently than their historical authors. The issue is particularly important because it concerns such texts as constitutions, about whose understanding there is wide disagreement. Two views are prevalent. One, assuming that it is authors who determine textual meaning and thus cannot be conceived to misunderstand the texts they create, argues that it is not legitimate to understand texts differently from the way their historical authors understood them. At the opposite extreme are those who claim that it is legitimate to understand all texts differently than their historical authors. The problem with both of these positions is that social practices supply plenty of counterexamples to them. Moreover, they are based on the faulty assumption that the historical author always has a definite and complete understanding of the meaning of a text prior to the production of the text. Both positions, then, are untenable. The view I defend holds that the legitimacy of understanding texts differently from the way in which their historical authors understood them depends on the cultural function of the texts. For some texts this is not acceptable, but for others it is.

Having concluded that texts may be understood in different ways by their historical authors and their audiences, we need to turn to the question of the truth value and objectivity of such understandings. With respect to truth value, we might say that understandings are true when they accurately grasp the meaning of texts and they are false when they do not. Truth value, then, does not depend on similarity with authorial understanding. With respect to objectivity we might say that the degree of objectivity of understanding depends on the degree to which a subject considers the object and thus depends on that object; namely, the text and the factors outside the understanding subject that determine its meaning. The degree of subjectivity will depend, accordingly, on the degree that the subject considers factors other than the text. Naturally, because all texts are products of subjects but are themselves objects, it follows that objectivity and subjectivity in understanding are matters of degree.

Frequently, understandings are not distinguished from interpretations. Interpretations, however, may be taken in various ways in addition to simply meaning understandings. An interpretation may also be taken to refer to the process or activity whereby one develops an understanding of a text. Moreover, the term 'interpretation' is also used to refer to texts that are added to other texts to make possible their understanding by certain audiences. This third sense is the pertinent one for our discussion. In this sense an interpretation, like a definition, is composed of two parts: the text under interpretation, or *interpretandum*, and the text added to that text to help with understanding, that is, the *interpretans*.

Any historical text can be the object of an interpretation, although often what is available to an interpreter is only a contemporary text that is not identical with the historical text. The intended and ideal texts have only regulative and instrumental functions in interpretations. The intermediary text has little to do with interpretations beyond helping to explain disparities and what appear to be gaps in contemporary texts.

The *interpretans* should not be confused with the ideal text, for the ideal text is the text an interpreter believes should have been produced as the historical text. The ideal text is not a text added to the historical text to make it understandable to an audience that otherwise would not be able to understand it.

Because interpretations are texts, they can also be considered historical texts composed by historical authors. But they are not the historical texts that they aim to interpret, and their authors are not the historical authors of those texts.

That an interpretation adds to a historical text another text poses the question of how an interpretation can help to understand the historical text. For any addition to a text appears to imply a distortion of it and thus to stand in the way of its accurate understanding. But if no interpretation is provided, how can a historical text be understood by a contemporary audience that in most cases is removed linguistically, temporally, and culturally from the text? This is what I call the Interpreter's Dilemma. From this some hermeneuticists have concluded that the understanding of texts from the past is not possible, because all interpretations are anachronistic. This inference, however, is unwarranted.

The reason for this mistake is that the inference does not take into account that interpretations have different functions depending on their aims. The overall, generic function of interpretations is to produce understandings in a contemporary audience in relation to a particular text. But in addition to this generic function interpretations may have at least three other different functions. The historical function aims to re-create in the contemporary audience the acts of understanding of the historical author and the historical audience of the historical text. The meaning function aims to produce in contemporary audiences acts of understanding that may go beyond the acts of understanding of the historical author and the historical audience of the text, revealing aspects of the meaning of the text with which their historical authors and the historical audiences may not have been acquainted. Finally, the implicative function aims to produce in contemporary audiences acts of understanding whereby those audiences understand the implications of the meanings of texts, regardless of whether the historical authors and the historical audiences were aware of those implications. Naturally, these three functions are not mutually exclusive, but it is important to keep in mind which of these three functions is intended to judge its success. Moreover, which of these functions is preeminent depends to an extent on the cultural function of the text. And note that the Interpreter's Dilemma applies only to the first.

The solution to the Interpreter's Dilemma is found in the Principle of Proportional Understanding. According to this principle, an interpretation of a text (composed of a historical text and the interpretative textual additions of an interpreter), taken in a contemporary context, should be related to the contemporary audience with respect to the production of their contemporary acts of understanding as the historical text, taken in the historical context, is related to the historical author and the historical audience with respect to the acts of understanding of the historical author and the historical audience. The foundation of this principle is that texts cause understanding and two different texts can produce the same understanding. Thus, an interpretation is a text that produces in the contemporary audience an understanding similar to that had by the historical author and the historical audience by adding elements to the historical text without which a contemporary audience could not have such an understanding because of its cultural and temporal distance from the historical text.

Note, of course, that a successful historical interpretation generally, if not logically, presupposes that the interpreter has an accurate historical understanding of the text. Whether this accurate historical understanding is possible or not is another question to which I shall turn later. For the present what is important to keep in mind is that interpreters prepare the causal framework that allows someone else to reach the kind of understanding of a text the historical author and historical audience had.

As noted, not all interpretations have a historical aim or have primarily a historical aim. The meaning and implicative functions of interpretations fulfill other aims. We should not expect to measure the effectiveness or adequacy of interpretations in the same way. The value, adequacy, or effectiveness of interpretations depends very much on how well they fulfill their specific functions. In some cases that function prescribes the preservation of textual ambiguities, but in other cases it prescribes the resolution of such ambiguities. No blanket indictment can be made against all interpretations that produce in contemporary audiences understandings different from those the historical author and the historical audience had. Nor does it make sense to put all interpretations on equal footing as far as value is concerned. Interpretations are more or less adequate or effective, and thus good or bad, depending on their specific function and how well they carry it out. To judge them, one must first determine that function.

Many of the puzzles raised in the contemporary literature concerned with the identity of texts and the possibility of conflicting interpretations vanish when one considers the nature of interpretations and their functions. In this way also we can resolve the vexing issue of whether interpretations involve construction or discovery. From what has been said it follows that all interpretations involve construction; namely, the production of a text that will produce acts of understanding in an audience. And they involve discovery to the degree that interpreters must search for the best means to produce those acts of understanding. But interpretations do not directly involve construction or discovery of meaning.

Interpretations may be classified in a variety of ways. Indeed, as texts their classification could follow the classification of texts we saw earlier. However, the most significant classification of interpretations is one, based on their function, into textual and nontextual. A textual interpretation adds to a text whatever is thought by the interpreter to be necessary to produce certain results in contemporary minds in relation to the text, when those results are taken as (1) the re-creation of the acts of understanding of the historical author and the contemporaneous audience or (2) the production of acts of understanding whereby the meaning of the text or the implications of that meaning are understood by the audience.

By contrast, a nontextual interpretation is one that, although it may be based on a textual interpretation, has something else as its primary aim. In the latter case, the interpreter is after much more than the understanding of the text and its implications, whether based on the understanding the historical author and the historical audience had or not. Thus a historical interpretation, for example, seeks to produce a historical understanding of the text, meaning much more than what the text means, implies, or was taken to mean by its historical author and historical audience, to include its relation to other events, and so on.

It is a mistake, then, to rule out, as is frequently done, nontextual interpretations as inaccurate or anachronistic simply because they do not do what textual interpretations are supposed to do. And it is also a mistake to present nontextual interpretations as textual ones or to measure one against the other. On the other hand, it must be kept in mind that nontextual interpretations pressuppose, at least in most cases, textual ones and thus rely on the understanding of texts.

From what has been said follow the answers to the questions of the number, truth value, and objectivity of interpretations, although the answers will depend on whether the interpretations in question are textual or nontextual. In the case of textual interpretations there can be no single definitive interpretation for all audiences. Those audiences and the individual persons who compose them will vary in ways that require changes in what is added to the *interpretandum* to create the proper understanding of the text. There can be, at least in principle, definitive interpretations for a particular audience at a particular time and place, and there can be interpretations that are more enduring than others. But all that will depend on the text in question and the conditions that surround its audience. The search for definitive and enduring interpretations is methodologically significant, however, even if in practice there is little hope of producing them. The reason is that such an idea propels the attempt to produce interpretations that will reach the ideal, thus promoting effort and often improvements.

With respect to truth value, it must be noted, first, that interpretations are texts usually composed of many sentences whose truth value may vary and may even contain sentences that do not have truth value at all. Thus it would be difficult to make a judgment concerning the truth value of interpretations considered as a whole. Moreover, the function of textual interpretations is not to establish truth but to produce understanding of *interpretanda* in audiences. Therefore it is not their truth that is at stake, but whether they are effective or not in carrying out that task. Interpretations should not be judged in terms of truth value, but in terms of their degree of effectiveness.

With respect to subjectivity and objectivity, an interpretation will be more or less subjective depending on the degree to which it is the result of the interpreting subject independent of the interpreted object; that is, the text and whatever determines it meaning. Naturally, in textual interpretations the object is always taken into account to some degree, for the interpretation always includes the *interpretandum*. Still there are degrees of consideration of that object, and this accounts for degrees of objectivity and subjectivity.

In the case of nontextual interpretations it is clear that if what has been said concerning the variety of their aims is true, there can be not only as many as there are textual interpretations but many more. Thus, there may be, for example, psychological interpretations, historical interpretations, and so on.

With respect to truth value two points are in order. The first is that, like textual interpretations, nontextual interpretations are composed of many sentences, whose truth value may differ. So it is difficult, if not impossible, to make a judgment as to the overall truth value of a nontextual interpretation. The second point is that the function of a nontextual interpretation may or may not have to do with making truth value claims. Thus, whether a nontextual interpretation can be subject to truth value judgments will ultimately depend on the function it has.

The answer to the question of subjectivity and objectivity of nontextual interpretation follows along the lines of the answer provided for textual interpretations. The objectivity or subjectivity of a nontextual interpretation will depend on the degree that objective or subjective factors are considered in its production.

Some interpretations presuppose the understanding of the texts they interpret. But it is not clear how textual understanding is possible, for it is not clear which factors produce such an understanding if it indeed occurs, or whether there can be any certainty concerning such an understanding. More fundamentally still, it is not clear that one can have certainty that something is a text at all. Three questions suggest themselves in this context, then: How do I know that something is a text? How do I learn the meaning of a text? How can I be certain of the meaning of text?

There appear to be all sorts of ways in which I can know that something is a text. I can do so, for example, on the basis of observation, inference, and past experience. Testimony or behavior from other persons can also reveal to us that something is a text. However, in some cases none of these factors is available. In such cases other factors may help us infer textuality. Three of these are particularly effective: similarity, cultural context, and human nature.

Similarity is based on the general function of texts, namely, to convey specific meanings. At least three pertinent characteristics of texts derive from this function: organization, repetition, and abstraction. These characteristics do not form a core of necessary and sufficient conditions, however. Abstraction and organization are necessary conditions of textuality but repetition is not. And abstraction cannot be a necessary condition even of textual discernibility. Moreover, none of these considered singly or together with the others provides sufficient conditions of textual discernibility. A stronger case can be made on the basis of these factors taken together with cultural context, for the cultural context can suggest to us sometimes that something must have functioned as a text. Ultimately, however, the identification of something as a text relies on the view that all human beings behave and communicate in similar ways, for this view underlines the inferences about the significance of the features mentioned and cultural context. We identify something as a text because we vicariously become its author or audience. None of this, however, is sufficient to conclude that we can always and in all cases be certain that a particular set of entities constitute a text. For that we need to know that the entities have meaning and, thus, have been intended by someone to convey it.

If there are difficulties identifying textuality, there are even more difficulties identifying the meaning of texts. This is so because it appears that any attempt to learn the meaning of a text is mediated through texts. Thus we end up either in an infinite textual regress or in a vicious textual circle. This is often referred to as the *hermeneutic circle*—we can never escape textuality and thus can never claim to have reached meaning. This conclusion has been used by philosophers as evidence to support two different views. According to one, texts are beyond understanding—we can never learn their meaning. According to the second, the meaning of texts is innate—it does not derive from our acquaintance with texts. Both of these positions are unacceptable. The first is unacceptable because our experience supports the view that in fact we do learn the meaning of at least some texts. The second is unacceptable because it goes contrary to the view assumed in this book that all our knowledge begins in experience and thus does not antecede it.

To present an alternative to these views I turn to the third question mentioned earlier, for the way to support that we can know the meaning of texts and that such a meaning is not innate is to establish how we can learn with certainty such a meaning. My proposal in this direction is that certainty of meaning is achieved only through the observation of expected behavior. Thus the author or user of a text knows with certainty that the text he or she has created or used in a particular context has been understood by an audience when the audience behaves in accordance with the expectations concerning the audience's behavior in that context which the author or user has. The case with an audience is slightly different but nonetheless dependent on expected behavior. An audience knows with certainty that it has understood the text an author has created or a user has used in a particular context either because the author or user behaves in accordance with the audience's expectations concerning the author's or user's behavior in the context in question or because the audience knows it is competent in the language of the text, that is, it knows that it knows the meaning of certain signs and the arrangements into which they can be meaningfully put. Expected behavior turns out to be, then, directly or indirectly and taken in context, both a necessary and sufficient condition of certainty in understanding. This view requires a broad conception of behavior in which the use of language and texts count as behavior, for most of the behavior we expect, when we use or are audiences of a text, is linguistic.

With this proposal we can get away from the dilemma posed by the hermeneutic circle. We are not trapped in texts, for the confirmation of our effective understanding of texts is not based on texts, but on a certain behavior, taken in context, which consists most often in the use of certain texts.

Even if we accept this solution to the problem posed by the hermeneutic circle, we still need to answer the question of how it is possible to be certain about the meaning of texts from the past for which we have no access to the behavior of the authors or users. How do I know I have understood correctly a recorded or a written message?

The answer to this is to be found, first, in the need of such texts to be seen as contemporary texts are, namely, as forms of behavior. It makes no difference whether those texts are our contemporaries or whether we have access to their authors or users. We must look at them, as it were, as frozen instances of behavior, which can be thawed under appropriate conditions. But even this is not sufficient, for we also have to know that we are privy to the rules that govern them; that is, we must know that we are linguistically competent. In short, how do we know which behavior to expect and which frozen items will confirm that we have understood a text or not?

The answer to this question is to be found in an elaboration of what was said before concerning the role of culture and nature in the discernibility of texts. Culture and nature provide us with the reasons why something can be considered a text. Likewise, they provide us with the parameters of what we should expect to find in a text. For both culture and nature imply a baggage of shared practices. Nature implies a set of needs and responsive behavior common to all human beings. Culture implies a set of practices common to the members of a group. In both cases we have a community, whether natural or cultural, that shares patterns of behavior. And in these patterns of behavior the foundation of effective communication is to be found. When a pattern of behavior is passed from generation to generation it is called a *tradition*, thus tradition ensures recognition and understanding, forming the basis of effective communication. Indeed, texts plucked from the tradition within which they were produced are silent; they speak to us only within the forms of life that made them possible.

With this last point I have completed the general exposition of the logical and epistemological dimensions of the theory of textuality I set out to develop. I hope those who have stayed with me until now have not been disappointed. I regard the theory as a beginning rather than an end. For those who see flaws in it, it is the beginning of a critical appraisal and the formulation of the theory that should take its place; for those who agree with its fundamental aspects but find it incomplete it is the beginning of the process of completion. For me it is both, for no serious philosopher is ever satisfied with what he or she has accomplished. Indeed, to do so and become an apologist for one's own work is a clear indication that one has ceased being a philosopher altogether.

NOTES

Preface

1. Cf., for example, Kripke, *Naming and Necessity*, p. 64. Even though some Wittgenstenians have tried to portray Wittgenstein himself as a theorist of sorts, others have come to his "rescue." See Rorty, "Cavell on Skepticism."

2. Cf., for example, Rosen, "The Limits of Interpretation," p. 214.

3. For a vigorous defense of theory building in this spirit, see Abrams, "What's the Use of Theorizing About the Arts?"

4. *Philosophy and Its History*, ch. 1.

Introduction

1. I say "very often," because there are cases in which the meaning does seem to have something to do with the nature of the object in question. For example, the meaning of 'A' seems to have to do with A. I shall return to this point in Chapter 1.

2. Legibility may be considered to apply to a physical object because it concerns the recognition of a physical shape. Thus, when I read, I perceive and recognize certain shapes. That something be illegible entails that it is such that it does not allow the recognition of such shapes.

3. There are other types of issues as well, such as semantic and axiological ones. But my plan is to discuss only logical and epistemological.

4. For post-Kantians this relation seems to be reversed—reality becomes a reflection of thought. Cf. Castañeda, "Philosophy as a Science and as Worldview," p. 37.

5. Consider the extended argument Rorty presented in *Philosophy and the Mirror of Nature*.

6. Elsewhere I have claimed that much of the confusion that surrounds the problem of individuation is due precisely to a confusion between epistemology and metaphysics. *Individuality*, Prolegomena.

7. Here are included Thomists, Aristotelians, and others who continue working as if Kant had never existed. Among these are neo-Thomists like Etienne Gilson and Jacques Maritain, for example. This kind of approach is evident in Gilson's *Being and Some Philosophers* and Maritain's *The Degrees of Knowledge.*

8. In this group fall logical positivists like A. J. Ayer. See *Language, Truth, and Logic.*

9. Most analysts of one sort or another could be interpreted in this way. See P. F. Strawson's *Analysis and Metaphysics* and Michael Dummett's *The Logical Basis of Metaphysics.* Some Continental philosophers, like Jacques Derrida, appear to reject both metaphysics and logic and thus occupy a place by themselves. See Derrida's *Of Grammatology.* Something similar may be said about neo-pragmatists, not because they reject logic or metaphysics, but because they have very idiosyncratic views of them. See Rorty, "Philosophy as Science, as Metaphor, and as Politics."

10. We also speak of interpreting actions, physical features, facial expressions, and so on. Some of these uses of 'interpretation' can be explained in the same way I explain its use in relation to events. Others can be explained by pointing out that 'interpretation' is often used to mean understanding, as I shall point out in Chapter 5. And still others fit in with the notion of interpretation as applicable to texts, as is the case with the interpretation of certain facial expressions.

Chapter 1. Intension

1. Some philosophers would claim that a definition of texts is impossible. This view originates in two sources primarily. The first is Wittgenstein's comments about language games and family resemblance. See *Philosophical Investigations*, secs. 65–67, pp. 31–32, and *The Blue and Brown Books*, p. 17. The second is Aristotle's views concerning artifacts. See *Physics* II, ch. 1, 192b20, p. 236. For my purposes, let it suffice to say that, in accordance with what I have stated in the Preface, the definition I offer is to be taken as propaedeutic and instrumental rather than as dogmatic, legislative, or revelatory of a "real essence." It is to be taken as what Abrams has called a "speculative instrument." "What's the Use of Theorizing About the Arts," p. 25.

2. See also Gracia, "Can There Be Texts Without Historical Authors?" and "Can There Be Texts Without Audiences?"

3. This distinction should not be confused with the distinction between "marks" and "inscriptions" introduced by Goodman and Elgin. Marks become inscriptions when they are treated as having a syntactic role. "Interpretation and Identity," p. 60. Contrary to this, I believe that syntactic role or function is not enough for textual or sign identity. The identity of a text and the identity of the entities that constitute it are necessarily linked, but they are not the same. This distinction is roughly analogous to the distinction Danto draws between a work of art and the "mere" thing of which it consists. See *The Transfiguration of*

the Commonplace, ch. 1, pp. 1 ff., and *The Philosophical Disenfranchisement of Art*, p. 42. See also Margolis, "Works of Art as Physically Embodied and Culturally Emergent Entities," p. 189, and "The Ontological Peculiarity of Works of Art," pp. 47–48. Some deconstructionists speak as if the distinction between texts and signs, on the one hand, and the entities that constitute them, on the other, were not possible, thus effectively reducing signs to "marks on a page." Derrida, for example, separates a sign from a referent, a meaning, and the intention to signify. "Signature Event Context," p. 183. More on this in Chapter 4.

4. The view that signs are entities of any sort used to convey meaning is not universally accepted by any means. Some authors argue that signs are not entities considered in relation to meaning via use, but actually relations themselves. See, for example, John Poinsot (i.e., John of St. Thomas), *Tractatus De signis* I, 1, p. 120, and Gadamer, *Truth and Method*, pp. 262 and 267. More on this in Chapter 4.

5. Not everyone accepts the distinction between texts and signs. For Goodman and Elgin, signs are nothing but short texts. "Interpretation and Identity," p. 58. The literature on signs is very extensive; suffice it to say that it goes back to the Greeks and the medievals, although the first major treatise on signs produced by the scholastics is found in the *Corpus Conimbricensis*. See Doyle, "The *Conimbricenses* on the Relations Involved in Signs," p. 568. Nor does everyone's view fit within those I discuss. For example, Eco states that texts are characterized by the capacity "of generating multiple readings . . . and interpretations," whereas signs do not have that capacity. *Semiotics and the Philosophy of Language*, p. 24. For others, however, this capacity attaches to works. See the section on works in Chapter 2 of this book.

6. That it is not complex might be contested by pointing to the fact that a color used as a sign needs to be extended in some sense and also to have a certain shade. Indeed, it may be that there are no cases of completely simple signs. But one could always answer that extension is not a characteristic of the sign in question, but of the entity that constitutes the sign because it has no semantic significance in itself. Moreover, with respect to shade, it might be argued that a certain shade of the color is significant and that such a shade is nothing complex.

7. For other arguments against the view that texts can be composed of only one sign, see Ricoeur, "On Interpretation," p. 359.

8. Perhaps Goodman and Elgin would, since they do not distinguish between texts and signs. See note 3.

9. Cf. the case of 'slab!' discussed by Wittgenstein in *Philosophical Investigations* 19–20, pp. 8–10.

10. Cf. Aristotle, *On Interpretation*, ch. 4, 16b25–35, pp. 41–42.

11. Apart from the difficulties I will mention, there are the difficulties involved in

explaining how exactly the meaning of texts are related to the meaning of the signs that compose them. See Davidson, *Inquiries into Truth and Interpretation,* ch. 2.

12. As Aristotle notes, even if the parts of a sign are meaningful (*Poetics* 1457a30, p. 1476), when we use them we do not think of those parts as having meaning by themselves (1457a10, p. 1475).

13. This is what has led Frege, Ricoeur, Rorty, and others to argue that signs have meaning only within sentences (or propositions). For Frege, see *Foundations of Arithmetic,* p. x; for Ricoeur, see "Creativity in Language," p. 124; and for Rorty, see *Philosophy and the Mirror of Nature,* p. 303. See also Wallace, "Only in the Context of a Sentence Do Words Have Any Meaning." It seems to me that this view is not beyond doubt. In first place, because not all signs are used in sentences, and yet they appear to have meaning in those contexts. Many of them are used in nonsentential expressions (e.g., "My goodness!") and some of them are used by themselves (e.g., pointing). In second place, when a sign is mentioned and not used, it still appears to have meaning; dictionaries are full of these.

14. I am assuming that "text" is a generic category that includes sentences, but not everyone agrees with that. Among those who do not agree are Danto, *The Philosophical Disenfranchisement of Art,* p. 76, and Eco, "Texts and Encyclopedia," p. 585.

15. Much of the discussion of meaning in some contemporary circles is intended to prove just the opposite; namely, that there is no distinction between signs and texts on the one hand, and meanings, on the other, as Derrida puts it, "between the signifier and the signified." "Structure, Sign, and Play in the Discourse of the Human Sciences," p. 251. The reasons for this view have to do with the so-called hermeneutic circle. I discuss the circle and the way to break it in Chapter 6.

16. One could argue that (3) and (4) do not mean exactly the same thing because 'and' and 'plus' and 'make' and 'equal' are not in fact synonymous. But this is an objection against an example and does not affect the point I am making as long as it is granted that at least on some occassions texts composed of different signs can mean exactly the same thing, that is, that there is such a thing as textual synonymity. That there is seems to me obvious if one compares the other texts given as examples.

17. I am using 'reference' as roughly equivalent to extension. Thus the reference of 'human' is its extension; namely, all the things that are human or, put in another way, all the things of which 'human' can be truly predicated. The referential view of meaning is widespread throughout the history of philosophy. Indeed, even Quine feels he has to argue against it in "On What There Is." It was the primary motive behind discussions of "nothing" and "what is not" in the ancient and medieval worlds. See Plato, *Sophist* 237c ff., pp. 980 ff., and Augustine, *De magistro* II, 3, p. 577.

18. Actually, even this is controversial, as is clear from the so-called paradox of reference. As is well known, Frege's solution to it was to argue precisely that there is a

distinction between meaning and reference. See "On Sense and Reference."

19. Plato, of course, is believed to have thought so, but his view has been the subject of intense criticism, beginning with Aristotle, ever since. See Aristotle's *Metaphysics* I, 9, 990b1–993a28, pp. 706–12.

20. The standard objections raised by philosophers are well known. Recently, however, this view has been attacked by literary critics as well. See, for example, Miller, "Steven's Rock and Criticism as Cure," p. 29.

21. Cf. Putnam, "The Meaning of 'Meaning,'" p. 217.

22. This mentalistic or psychologistic conception of meaning was very prevalent before Frege and Carnap. See, for example, Locke, *An Essay Concerning Human Understanding*, Introduction, 8, and Bk. 3, 2, 2, vol. 1, p. 32, and vol. 2, p. 9. There are, however, some who adopt this view while opposing psychologism. Ingarden, for example, speaks of nonpsychological "ideal concepts" in *The Literary Work of Art*, p. 364.

23. Cartesian innatism seems unavoidable for supporters of this position.

24. How the idea of cat is unpacked is not very important. What is important is that its unpacking will always contain something more than the unpacking of cat, as happens also with dog and the idea of dog. See Quine, "On What There Is," p. 2.

25. For other criticisms of the psychologism entailed by this view, see Putnam, "The Meaning of 'Meaning,'" pp. 219 ff. See also my *Individuality*, ch. 6, for issues related to the meaning of proper names and definite descriptions.

26. Cf. Austin, *How to Do Things with Words*, pp. 98 ff. The view of meaning as use has spread beyond the confines of Anglo-American philosophy. See, for example, Günther Buck, "The Structure of Hermeneutic Experience and the Problem of Tradition," p. 36.

27. This is in line with Austin's view that the performance of these acts requires that the locution have meaning understood as sense and reference. *How To Do Things with Words*, p. 94. It is also in line with Searle's view that an illocutionary act is a function of the meaning of a sentence uttered. *Expression and Meaning*, p. 64. For Searle, a meaningful sentence, and we could without distortion say "a meaningful text," is "just a standing possibility of the corresponding (intentional) speech act." "Reiterating the Differences," p. 202. I should note, however, that not all locutionary acts involve the performance of illocutionary acts. This is obvious in the case of signs that compose texts. When I say, "Peter, open the door," I have performed a locutionary act of uttering the sentence and the illocutionary act of ordering Peter to open the door. But the utterance of each of the words in the sentence does not imply a performance of illocutionary acts even though they are locutionary ones. This distinction is not important for my purposes, however, for I am concerned only with textual meaning, not with

sign meaning. Note also that not everyone agrees with Searle. Strawson, for example, holds that an illocutionary act is a function of the speaker's meaning. "Intention and Convention in Speech Acts." Moreover, the most common view of meaning as use is contrary to the view presented here. For Searle's convincing arguments against the view of meaning as use, see "Meaning and Speech Acts," particularly pp. 32 ff.

28. One could in fact translate such acts as writing into the locutionary language while preserving the oral character of that language. One could say, for example, that the act of writing is the act corresponding to the locutionary act one would perform if one were to utter the text being written.

29. Barthes has gone so far as to say that writing is performative. "The Death of the Author," p. 145.

30. This entails that 'to mean' is precisely to produce or cause or to be capable of producing or causing understanding. This view formed part of various medieval theories of signification. See Spade, "The Semantics of Terms," p. 188. Contemporary authors are divided as to whether the use of language entails the purpose of communication. For example, Davidson believes it does, but Black and Chomsky disagree. See Davidson, *Inquiries into Truth and Interpretation*, pp. 272–73, where he quotes Black and Chomsky.

31. For a different, but related, view on the distinction between meaning and significance, see Hirsch, "Objective Interpretation," and *Validity in Interpretation*, p. 62. For Hirsch, in these texts, meaning was simply the meaning the author understood the text to have, whereas everything else came under significance. Later, in "Three Dimensions of Hermeneutics," pp. 249–50, he changed his view, holding that meaning "is that which a text is taken to represent" whereas significance "is meaning-as-related-to-something-else." Hirsch's most recent view of significance has points of similarity with the one I propose here, although there are important differences between the two because his notion of meaning is quite different from mine. For another view of significance, see Jones, *Philosophy and the Novel*, p. 183.

32. This is a much debated point. Among the views which differ most radically from the one I present is Eco's. Eco argues that the function of texts is "to produce" what he calls "a model reader." *The Limits of Interpretation*, pp. 58 ff.

33. In this sense Abrams goes too far when he suggests that authors, even those poets he cites, write in order to be understood. "Rationality and Imagination," p. 457.

34. Ayer, *Language, Truth, and Logic*, p. 109 and elsewhere in ch. 6. Notice that Ayer insists he does not claim that ethical statements are statements *about* the feelings of those who utter them. If that were so, they could be true or false and thus have meaning, that is, express propositions. Rather, his view is that ethical statements are expressions *of* feeling and thus nonpropositional.

35. See my "Can There Be Texts Without Audiences?" Among those who reject

the need for audiences are structuralists and practitioners of the *nouveau roman*. As Eco states, "in a structuralist framework, to take into account the role of the addressee looked like a disturbing intrusion." *The Limits of Interpretation*, p. 44. Black and Chomsky also believe that audiences are not required. Black, "Meaning and Intention: An Examination of Grice's Views," p. 264; Chomsky, *Problems of Knowledge and Freedom*, p. 19.

36. Austin, I believe, made this point clearly. *How To Do Things with Words*, p. 121.

37. Obviously, if they are misunderstood, they may also produce results, although those results, such as actions and emotions, may not be the ones intended by the author. In either case it is necessary that some kind of understanding, whether correct or incorrect, be produced before other results follow. Cf. Austin, *How To Do Things with Words*, pp. 115–16.

38. For my purposes here I do not need to use a strong conception of *cognitive meaning*. It suffices to say that cognitive meaning pertains to the understanding and that such meaning involves criteria of validation. See Meiland, "Interpretation as a Cognitive Discipline," p. 31.

39. Schiffer argues in *Meaning*, p. 49, that to mean something is to have a particular kind of intention and that the meaning in question can be specified in terms of the intention. See also Knapp and Michaels, "Against Theory 2," p. 49.

40. Of course, the audience may in fact understand what I am trying to do through body language. But that proves my point, for it is not the Spanish text that causes understanding, but rather a different text composed of the signs I produced through bodily movements and the like.

41. Or, as is frequently put, "interpretations." See Fish, "Interpreting the *Variorum*," p. 482.

42. Cf. Searle, "Reiterating the Differences," p. 202.

43. If Frege and others, who have argued that meaning is always a function of a sentence and thus that no signs have meaning apart from it, are right, then this distinction becomes useless. See also note 13.

44. One could, of course, argue that in cases of syncategorematic terms they have meaning apart from the use and that such a meaning consists in the rules of their proper use. But even in such a case one would have to distinguish between the meaning apart from use and the meaning in use.

45. There are contexts, however, where 'man,' 'a man,' and 'the man,' may have the same meaning. For example, in the sentences 'Man is a rational animal' and 'A man

is a rational animal,' both 'man' and 'a man' mean the same thing. In cases such as these, the contexts of the sentences where the terms occur need to be considered.

46. Of course, not all terms belonging to natural languages have well-established meanings. Many terms are vague and can be used in many different ways, some of which may not accord to any established pattern.

47. I do not intend by this that meanings are features of texts. I intend to discuss the ontological status of meanings and their relations to texts in the volume of this study devoted to metaphysics.

48. One could argue that an exception to this rule would be a text in a language in which syntactical function was not a matter of arrangement but of features. Say that the subject function were expressed by the color red, the object function by blue, and the verb function by white. In such a language one could disregard the arrangement of signs as long as signs were color coded. But even in this case matters are not so clear. For it could be argued that, although no physical arrangement of signs is required, there is still a requirement of a logical arrangement expressed by color.

49. Indeed, the author may choose not to choose, seeking some arrangement determined by factors other than himself. But in doing so the author is in fact a vicarious cause of the arrangement and thus a controlling factor of the text.

50. At least one of the defenders of literal meaning holds that such a meaning is absolutely context free. Katz, *Propositional Structure and Illocutionary Force*, p. 14. For critical analyses of this view, see Gazdar, *Pragmatics*, pp. 3–4, Dascal, *Pragmatics and the Philosophy of Mind*, p. 168, n. 26, and Searle, *Expression and Meaning*, pp. 117 ff.

51. Cf. Tolhurst, "On What a Text Is and How It Means," pp. 4 ff. Perhaps the most radical use of context is to be found in Wittgenstein's appeal to the relation of language to "forms of life." *Philosophical Investigations*, secs. 19–27, pp. 8–13. Recently, some deconstructionists use the importance and indeterminacy of context to argue that no text can have a univocal meaning. Cf. Miller, "Ariachne's Broken Woof," p. 59. More on this in Chapter 4.

52. Borges, "Pierre Menard, Author of the Quixote."

53. This example is used by Walton in "Style and the Products and Processes of Art," p. 94.

54. Context is thus understood very broadly, as any of the many systems that can affect meaning. Cf. Putnam, "Realism and Reason," pp. 123–40.

55. There are taxonomies of context that do not depend on the type of text in question, such as, for example, the division into specific, shallow, and background contexts. Dascal and Weizman, "Contextual Exploitation of Interpretation in Text Understand-

ing." See also Weizman and Dascal, "On Clues and Cues."

56. Not everyone puts such different things under one label. For example, Searle draws a distinction between context and background in "The Background of Meaning." For a criticism of Searle, see Gibbs, "Literal Meaning and Psychological Theory," pp. 285 ff.

57. Ricoeur, "Creativity in Language," p. 125.

58. See Derrida, "Signature Event Context," p. 192, and *Of Grammatology*, p. 185. I return to this issue in Chapter 4. But, as we saw in note 50, it is not only deconstructionists who argue against contextual semantic determination.

59. This assumes a very strict notion of literal meaning as context free, such as that defended by Katz (see note 50). Literal meaning has been attacked not only by literary critics, such as Miller ("Steven's Rock and Criticism as Cure"), but also by others such as Gibbs ("Literal Meaning and Psychological Theory"). For a recent defense of literal meaning, see Dascal, "Defending Literal Meaning."

60. Dascal has explored some of these other senses in ibid.

61. Dickie has pointed out, for example, that literary texts do not ordinarily seem to have nonlinguistic contexts. *Aesthetics*, pp. 118–19.

62. Strictly speaking, *convention* seems to imply some kind of agreement, but this is not always so clear. For, first, conventions can be established by single persons who determine they will abide by certain rules, and, second, it is possible to develop, as Lewis has done, accounts of convention that do not involve agreement. Whether conventions require agreement or not, however, is immaterial for my purposes as long as it is clear that they presuppose input and design by persons. For Lewis, see *Conventions*, p. 42. For a dissenting opinion, see Davidson, *Inquiries into Truth and Interpretation*, ch. 18.

63. As some semioticians acknowledge, any entity can be used as a sign of some other entity. Deely, *Basics of Semiotics*, p. 55, and Morris, *Foundations of a Theory of Signs*, p. 20.

64. This is a popular position in the history of philosophy. See, for example, Aristotle, *On Interpretation*, chs. 2 and 4, 16a20ff. and 17a1–2, pp. 40–41 and 42, and Thomas Compton Carleton, *Logica* 42, 3, p. 157. Most authors influenced by Aristotle in the Middle Ages adhered to this view, a fact particularly evident in commentaries on Aristotle's *On Interpretation*. See, for example, Aquinas's *Commentary on Aristotle's "On Interpretation"* (completed by Cajetan), Lesson 4, par. 6, p. 39. A few Aristotelian authors of the period showed awareness of the contrary position, but serious consideration of it took place only in the sixteenth and seventeenth centuries. See Ashworth, "Traditional Logic," pp. 155-56.

65. For Augustine, see *On the Teacher;* and for a later statement of the Augustinian position, see Bonaventure, *Retracing the Arts to Theology.*

66. Peirce seems to have room in his theory for such a view. Cf. Greenlee's *Peirce's Concept of Sign*, pp. 70 ff. See also Jakobson's discussion of this issue in *Language and Literature*, ch. 22.

67. The first case is the one used by John Poinsot (i.e., John of St. Thomas) to justify the notion of natural sign. For him a natural sign is a sign that has some natural connection to what it signifies, whereas an artificial one lacks that connection. See Poinsot, *Tractatus de signis* I, 2, p. 147.

68. Cf. Currie, *The Nature of Fiction*, p. 114.

69. Cf. Ockham, *Summa totius logicae* I, ch. 1, p. 48. This position has textual support in Aristotle's *On Interpretation*, ch. 1, 16a3–7, p. 40.

70. The only way to arrange the signs in question to convey the meaning that no smoking is permitted seems to be 'No smoking is permitted.' One could, of course, say, "Smoking is not permitted" or "Is smoking permitted? No!" But in both of these cases changes have been introduced in the signs ('not' for 'no' in the first) or in the number of signs (the addition of '?' and '!' in the second).

71. I have given references to this point of view, adopted by many deconstructionists, in Chapter 5.

Chapter 2. Extension

1. I assume that intension determines extension, although this position has come under fire recently. For a discussion of this issue, see Putnam, "The Meaning of "Meaning,'" pp. 219 ff.

2. Cf. Ricoeur, "Structure, Word, Event," p. 113.

3. The question of what constitutes a "whole" or "complete" language is difficult to answer and beyond the limits of this discussion.

4. Ricoeur, "Structure, Word, Event,", p. 114.

5. Chomsky, *Current Issues in Linguistic Theory*, pp. 7–8.

6. Cf. Ricoeur, "Creativity in Language," pp. 122–3. But note that for Ricoeur, language is more akin to discourse, and therefore it is the system of signs, not discourse, to which he attaches anonimity of author and audience.

7. I refer to pertinent authors and their texts in Chapter 4.

8. Artifacts have not been extensively discussed among philosophers. For some recent discussions, see Dipert, "Art, Artifacts, and Regarded Intentions"; Dickie, *Aesthetics;* Carter, "Salmon on Artifact Origins and Lost Possibilities"; Iseminger, "The Work of Art as Artifact"; Kornblyth, "Referring to Artifacts"; Schwartz, "Putnam on Artifacts"; Stalker, "The Importance of Being an Artifact"; and Losonsky, "The Nature of Artifacts." One of the issues under discussion is whether artifacts are to be distinguished from natural objects in that the first have essences or natures, whereas the second do not. Losonsky lays out the controversy clearly. For my purposes the issue is not pertinent.

9. The category of tool is closely related to that of artifact. Indeed, Dipert has argued that all artifacts fall into this category, although his understanding of 'tool' is technical. See *Artifacts, Art Works, and Agency*, p. 28.

10. For a defense of the physicality of artifacts, see Fletcher, "Artifactuality Broadly and Narrowly Speaking," particularly pp. 45–46 and 49.

11. Perhaps this is what Aristotle has in mind in *Nicomachean Ethics* 1140a11–16, p. 1025, when he speaks of the role of reasoning in the making that art involves. See also Dickie, *Art and the Aesthetic*, p. 46, who argues that "art is a concept which necessarily involves human intentionality," and Dipert, *Artifacts, Art Works, and Agency,* pp. 29–30.

12. I take it this is what Dickie means in *Art and the Aesthetic*, p. 44. Fletcher has argued against this view in "Artifactuality Broadly and Narrowly Speaking," pp. 44 and *statim*. For him artifactuality presupposes a change in an object itself and not just in its relation to something else. The same position is taken by Demeraux in "Artifacts, Natural Objects and Works of Art," p. 135, and Sankowski in "Free Action, Social Institutions, and the Definition of 'Art,'" pp. 69 ff.

13. Because my concern here is not with art as such, I shall ignore the complications that may arise from the distinction between art that consists of actions, such as performances, and art that consists of physical objects, such as sculptures. For present purposes I shall consider all art, including performances, as objects, where *object* is understood in a very general sense.

14. Various sorts of distinctions have been proposed between the aesthetic and the artistic. See Korsmeyer, "On Distinguishing 'Aesthetic' from 'Artistic,'" Dickie, *Art and the Aesthetic,* particularly ch. 8, pp. 182–200, and Beardsley, "Aesthetic Experience Regained."

15. Dickie has defended the artifactuality of "art works" in *Aesthetics,* ch. 11, and also in *Art and the Aesthetic,* pp. 25, 34, and 38. Dewey has done so also in *Art as Experience,* pp. 48–49. Indeed, artifactuality is widely accepted as a requirement of art and some authors appear to make it a sufficient condition of it. Dipert, for example, has argued that "the artifactuality condition alone, properly understood and slightly aug-

mented, might suffice for a definition of 'art work'. . . ." in "Art, Artifacts, and Regarded Intentions," pp. 401 ff. For attacks on the condition of artifactuality, see Glickman, "Creativity in the Arts," pp. 143–44; Weitz, "The Role of Theory in Aesthetics," pp. 27–35; and Sclafani, "'Art' and Artifactuality," pp. 403 ff. For a response to some of the arguments against the artifactuality of art, see Margolis, "The Ontological Peculiarity of Works of Art."

16. Because of the difficulties in the determination of what constitutes artistic and aesthetic experiences, many aestheticians have abandoned the attempt to use these notions for the understanding of art and instead have turned to other criteria. Dickie, for example, defines an *art work* as an artifact that has certain relationships to a social institution. *Aesthetics*, pp. 98–108.

17. Panofsky recognizes the connection between art objects, artifactuality, and aesthetic experience, but comes up with a view very different from mine when he defines "a work of art as a man-made object demanding to be experienced aesthetically." "The History of Art as a Humanistic Discipline," p. 14.

18. Walton has argued that the category of aesthetic is given too much emphasis when it comes to art, because not all art is meant to be observed and thus to be aesthetically experienced. Art is more a matter of action and performance than of reception and observation. "Style and the Products and Processes of Art."

19. Dipert explores the notion of "being regarded" with respect to artifacts and art objects but, contrary to my proposal, ties it to the intention of the author. Thus an art object is one regarded by an audience as having been produced with certain intentions. This raises the issue of the so-called intentional fallacy. More on this in Chapter 4. For Dipert, see "Art, Artifacts, and Regarded Intentions."

20. I have not raised the question of forgeries because I believe it to be largely irrelevant here. Let it suffice to say that I do not regard the notions of artistic value and aesthetic value as equivalent and that I consider artistic value to be socially conditioned and historically determined. See my "Falsificación y valor artístico." For a different approach, see Koestler, "The Aesthetics of Snobbery."

21. Often the category of art is used honorifically to mean good art. But the conditions of art and good art should be kept separate, because there are degrees of "goodness" in art and some art, even when created by the best artists, is quite bad. The confusion between the categories of art and good art is responsible for many theories of art that exclude from the category of art many objects considered by others to be included in it.

22. Panofsky, "The History of Art as a Humanistic Discipline," p. 11.

23. For some the aesthetic has to do with the "delectable," but for others it does not. Poussin seems to have been the first to have proposed "delectation" as the end of art, although the medievals had held long before him that *delectatio* was the mark of the

beautiful. See Blunt, "Poussin's Notes on Painting." The whole notion of aesthetic experience and its use to characterize art is frequently contested. For example, Dutton, in "Artistic Crimes," raises important questions about it in the context of forgeries; see also the article by Walton cited earlier.

24. Note that the artifactuality condition makes possible, contrary to Dickie, for one to be mistaken in conferring the status of art object ("work" for Dickie). Thus, this view avoids some of the objections raised against Dickie's theory. For Dickie, see *Art and the Aesthetic,* p. 50.

25. I noted in the Preface that the production of a theory carries with it an aesthetic dimension and to that extent perhaps one could argue that Kant may have experienced an aesthetic experience from producing the theory proposed in the *Critique of Pure Reason.* If this is so, perhaps one could also argue that the readers of the book can also have a vicarious aesthetic experience. However, the aesthetic experience in this case is not produced by the text as such but by the theory, which is the meaning of the text—the aesthetic object is not the text but what I shall call in the next section of this book, *the work.*

26. I have not seen anyone actually defend this point of view. I mention it as a logical possibility and because some of the language used by contemporary literary critics and deconstructionists occassionally suggests it.

27. This is a logical consequence of the view that holds that anything subject to interpretation is a text. See the references to Derrida, Miller, and others in Chapter 4, and to Nehamas in this chapter.

28. This view has been recently called *textualism* by Currie in "Work and Text," p. 325. Among supporters of the view are Goodman and Elgin. See their "Interpretation and Identity."

29. Nehamas, "What an Author Is," p. 688.

30. Nehamas, "What an Author Is," pp. 687–88, and "Writer, Text, Work, Author," pp. 281 ff.

31. Of course, some authors might readily assent because they hold that translation is impossible; e.g., Quine, "On the Reasons for Indeterminacy of Translation."

32. That we predicate very different predicates of works and texts can be traced to different identity conditions. For a view of the identity conditions of works, see Wilsmore, "The Literary Text Is Not Its Work."

33. There are also many nonobvious ones. For an example, see Barthes, "From Work to Text."

34. Cf. Nehamas, "What an Author Is," pp. 687 ff. For a critical discussion of this

view, see Currie, "Work and Text," p. 336; see also *The Nature of Fiction,* ch. 3. A version of this view identifies the work with the experiences of the author. This view is discussed and effectively rejected by Ingarden in *The Literary Work of Art,* pp. 12–16.

35. See the works by Currie cited in the previous note. Even if one were to accept speech-act theory, it would not follow from it that a text is an act. Consider the case of the command "Peter, open the door." In this case the sounds uttered considered together with their meaning, that is the text, are neither the locutionary act of uttering them, the illocutionary act of ordering Peter to open the door, or the perlocutionary act of getting Peter to open the door.

36. As Barthes points out, a work is something "concrete, occupying a portion of book-space . . . the text, on the other hand, is a methodological field." "From Work to Text," p. 74. Currie reverses the categories when he describes texts as word sequences. "Work and Text," p. 338. Ingarden argues against this position in *The Literary Work of Art,* p. 14.

37. Currie seems to suggest such a view in "Work and Text," pp. 337–8. As he puts it, "Why not simply say that there are works, and that they are distinct from texts?"

38. For this and other objections against these views, see Currie, "Work and Text," pp. 336–37.

39. Ingarden comes close to adopting this position but bypasses it when he identifies the work with an ideal concept (or concepts); it is a mistake to consider meaning always as a concept or something ideal. Ingarden, *The Literary Work of Art,* pp. 16–19 and 364.

40. The view that identifies works with understandings poses serious difficulties for the identity of texts, as Goodman and Elgin have indicated in "Interpretation and Identity," pp. 53 ff. Note that they call "interpretation" what I call "understanding." For the distinction between interpretation and understanding, see Chapters 4 and 5.

41. Cf. Iser, *Prospecting,* pp. 6 ff., and Eco, *The Open Work,* p. 3.

42. The cultural dimension of works has been brought out by Margolis in "Works of Art as Physically Embodied and Culturally Emergent Entities," p. 193.

43. Lists of legal principles, such as the ten commandments, for example, may constitute works, if legal codes are considered types of works.

44. I agree, then, with Nehamas's position that there is no such a thing as a theory of the work. For, indeed, there is no identifiable set of necessary and sufficient conditions for all works at all times. But my reasons are quite different from his. Indeed, in terms of my reasons, he does after all have a theory of the work, because he identifies as the necessary and sufficient conditions of works that they be texts that generate authors. See

his "Writer, Text, Author, Work," pp. 282 and 284.

45. For some of these objections, see Goodman and Elgin, "Interpretation and Identity," p. 56, and Currie, "Work and Texts," pp. 335–36.

Chapter 3. Taxonomy

1. Fish, for example, distinguishes between a document and a text. "Interpreting 'Interpreting the *Variorum*,'" in *Is There a Text in This Class*? p. 175. Rorty has drawn attention to the attempt in certain quarters to look at philosophy and science as literary genres, an attempt to treat texts in these disciplines as literary. "Nineteenth-Century Idealism and Twentieth-Century Textualism," pp. 141 ff. Note that the differences between different types of texts do not preclude similarities. Indeed, it is as much a mistake to emphasize differences and ignore similarities as to emphasize similarities and ignore differences. Ingarden, *The Literary Work of Art*, p. 358.

2. Moreover, some of the classifications that are used for signs apply also to texts. For example, the classification between direct (v.g., gestures, speech) and indirect (v.g., writing) signs. Ricoeur makes this distinction in "Explanation and Understanding," p. 150. Texts could also be classified according to styles. Style, particularly in art, is a subject that has received considerable attention in recent years. See, for example, Berel Lang, ed., *The Concept of Style*.

3. The historical author may actually be more than one person, as it happened, for example, with the American Declaration of Independence. See my "Texts and Their Interpretation."

4. The autograph is the copy of the text produced by the author. The term is used primarily in connection with manuscripts handwritten by authors, but can be extended to texts produced by them that are not handwritten.

5. Weisheipl, *Friar Thomas D'Aquino*, p. 362.

6. For the notion of copy-text and its implications, see Tanselle, "Greg's Theory of the Copy-Text and the Editing of American Literature," pp. 167–229.

7. For an example of someone who appears to use this notion, see Tanselle, "Textual Criticism and Deconstruction," p. 5. Currie speaks of a text as "the text the author intended," in *The Nature of Fiction*, p. 119.

8. See Nehamas, "What an Author Is," p. 689.

9. Cf. Wilsmore, "The Literary Work Is Not Its Text," p. 310.

10. Tomas, *Creativity in the Arts*, p. 98. There are cases, of course, where the idea

is quite preci. and the resulting object exemplifies it closely. But even in such cases differences always creep in as a result of the process of production.

11. This is in part the reason why, as we shall see in Chapter 4, the meaning of a text cannot be reduced to the author's intentions, as Hirsch and others argue.

12. The opp site view, namely, that God so assisted his human instruments that they accurately produced the text he wished, is also widespread. See Brown, "Hermeneutics," p. 606.

13. Cf. Beardsley, *Aesthetics*, pp. 17–29, and Searle, "Reiterating the Differences," p. 202.

14. Greetham claims that the notion of an ideal text goes back to the ancients and, as we shall see, there are some ways to understand this notion that indeed echo Plato. "[Textual] Criticism and Deconstruction," p. 17.

15. Truth may not be the ultimate criterion of perfection in all cases, of course, because not all texts have as function the expression of truth. Texts may also express emotion, for example. Moreover, there are degrees in this position. Some may be content with the notion of a "better" rather than a "perfect" view.

16. See, for example, Copi, *Introduction to Logic*, ch. 2.

17. Questions have often been given a separate category, being classified under an interrogative function.

18. Cf. Ayer, *Language, Truth, and Logic*, pp. 107–9.

19. See Pound, *An Introduction to the Philosophy of Law*, pp. 31–32.

20. Iser speaks of literary texts as "fictional" and as being characterized by "indeterminacy." *Prospecting*, pp. 6 ff. The conception of literary texts as texts subject to multiple interpretations is similar to the view of art works as works that permit multiple interpretations. See Eco, *The Open Work*, p. 3. Stegmüller has argued against the view that any of the humanities can be distinguished from the sciences on the basis of the potential for multiple, equally unfalsifiable interpretations in "Walther von der Vogelweide's Lyric of Dream-Love and Quasar 3C 274," pp. 119 ff.

21. Jakobson has drawn attention to the dominant aesthetic function of poetry. *Language and Literature*, p. 43.

22. I discuss this distinction in *Philosophy and Its History*, pp. 121–22 and 165–66. Intensional historicity refers to what the text expresses, its meaning; extensional historicity refers to the historical circumstances under which a text was produced.

23. Cf. Gracia, *Philosophy and Its History,* pp. 93–98, and Mandelbaum, "The History of Ideas, Intellectual History, and the History of Philosophy," pp. 44–45.

Chapter 4. Understanding

1. For a dissenting opinion, see Stegmüller, "Wolter von der Vogelweide's Lyric of Dream-Love and Quasar 3C 273," p. 109. For analogies among understanding texts (specifically novels), persons, and arguments, see Jones, *Philosophy and the Novel,* pp. 196 ff.

2. The understanding of the author may help explain something about the text, such as why and how it was produced. But understanding and explanation are not the same, as Eliot and others make clear. See Eliot, "The Frontiers of Criticism," p. 121.

3. Cf. Nehamas, "Writer, Text, Author, Work," p. 288. See also my "Can There Be Texts Without Authors?"

4. I speak of persons here for the sake of convenience but, as noted earlier in the book, there is no reason why only persons should be able to understand texts.

5. Against this some philosophers have argued that no two persons can ever have what I have called *intensionally* the same acts of understanding, although the language they use to make this point differs. Whether this is to be taken as factual or logical impossibility is not clear. In most cases it seems to be a logical impossibility. This appears to be so, for example, with perspectivists like Nietzsche and Ortega and with historicists like Hegel and Charles Taylor. The point they make is that no two persons can ever have the same understanding based on the same ECTs because those understandings depend on context (perspective or historical coordinates) and no two contexts are the same. I am not at this point making a judgment as to whether this is possible. My answer to this issue will be contained in the second volume of this study.

6. According to Gadamer, for example, the meaning of a text is never determinate, for it always depends on what the audience brings to it. *Truth and Method,* pp. 262–63 and 274. As he puts it (p. 264), "one understands differently when one understands at all." See also Warnke, *Gadamer,* p. 67, and Wachterhauser, "Interpreting Texts," pp. 440 ff. Miller criticizes the "metaphysical reading" of texts that assumes a "univocal meaning." "The Critic as Host," pp. 219, 222, 225, *et statim.* And Plato notes on the meaning of poems in particular, that "nobody can produce a conclusive argument." *Protagoras* 347e, p. 340.

7. Some, however, speak as if it were so. See, for example, Miller, "The Critic as Host," p. 8, where he states that "a text has no meaning in itself." What the critic must ask is about its effects on the critic. "Walter Pater: A Partial Portrait," pp. 97 and 100. See also Foucault, "Nietzsche, Freud, Marx," p. 65. The attack on meaning is not restricted to postmodernists. Some interpreters argue that Wittgenstein entertained a kind

of skepticism about meaning. See Kripke, *Wittgenstein on Rules and Private Language,* p. 55.

8. Some, however, go further and explicitly argue that texts have no meaning. As Derrida puts it, there is no "transcendental signified." "Structure, Sign, and Play," p. 249.

9. This case is made by Derrida in most of his writings. See, for example, *Of Grammatology,* p. 69 and "Structure, Sign, and Play," p. 249. The case for unlimited semiosis is frequently boosted with references to the broad meaning of most signs. But, as we saw in Chapter 1, texts and signs differ substantially. So, even if one were to accept that signs have no determinate meaning, that does not necessarily apply to texts as well. The constraints on the meanings of texts is much greater than on the meanings of signs because texts are composed of more than one sign and those signs are arranged in syntactically prescribed and semantically significant ways.

10. Cf. Jones, *Philosophy and the Novel,* pp. 181–82. Jones claims that all attempts at making sense of a text are "aspectival." An aspect is "the point of view from which something is seen." This looks very much like Heidegger's *Vorsicht* and Ortega y Gasset's *perspectiva* applied to texts. For Heidegger, see *Being and Time,* sect. 32, pp. 191-2. For Ortega, see *El tema de nuestro tiempo,* p. 202. The recent background of this view is found in Nietzsche (see "Interpretation," pp. 47 ff.), but it goes all the way back to the Stoic-influenced School of Pergamum (see Bloom, "The Breaking of Form," p. 13).

11. This position is more frequently assumed than explicitly defended. Indeed, it is implied by much of what critics and scholars do. For an explicit defender, see Hirsch, *Validity in Interpretation,* pp. 25, 27, and 46. Some trace this position back to the Aristotelian-influenced School of Alexandria. See Bloom, "The Breaking of Form," p. 13.

12. Specht cites the case of Stefan George. "Literary-Critical Interpretations—Psychoanalytic Interpretations," p. 159.

13. Jones argues that the implications of a text are properties of the text, by which I take him to mean, contrary to my view, that the implications of the meaning of a text are part of that meaning. *Philosophy and the Novel,* p. 182. Wachterhauser attributes to Gadamer the view that the logical implications of what authors say are included in the meaning of what they say. "Interpreting Texts," p. 448.

14. Very frequently, the issues raised by the meaning of texts are put in terms of intentions. See Eco, *The Limits of Interpretation,* pp. 50 ff. Some go so far as to identify meaning with authorial intentions. See Hirsch, *Validity in Interpretation,* pp. 209 ff., and Tolhurst's discussion of Hirsch's view in "On What a Text Is and How It Means," p. 3.

15. Likewise, they should not be confused with beliefs. See Dworkin, *A Matter of Principle,* pp. 157–58. For a different opinion, see Knapp and Michaels, "Against Theory."

16. This is a point that Hirsch seems to grant. See Warnke, *Gadamer*, p. 43.

17. Fish argues against a literal meaning in *Is There a Text in This Class?* pp. 338 ff., but Eco defends it in *The Limits of Interpretation*, pp. 5 ff., 42, n. 1, and 53–54, and so does Tolhurst in "On What a Text Is and How It Means," pp. 4 ff. According to my position, I need not adopt the controversial view that all texts have a literal meaning. For a survey of the recent literature on this topic, see Dascal, "Defending Literal Meaning."

18. Cf. Hirsch, *Validity in Interpretation*, p. 25: "the meaning of a text is the author's meaning." Juhl has argued that "to appeal to the text . . . as evidence for an interpretation *is* to appeal to the author's (likely) intention." "The Appeal to the Text," p. 285. And Knapp and Michaels explicitly identify the meaning of a text with the author's intended meaning in "Against Theory," pp. 724 ff., and "Against Theory 2," p. 49. Wolterstorff's view that the artist determines what constitutes correctness of performance, if applied, mutatis mutandis, to authors and texts, would seem to yield a position similar to this one. "Toward an Ontology of Art Works," p. 136. Panofsky's emphasis on the original intention and the past seems to line him up here as well, but he tempers his remarks with references to the content of a work, which he understands as "the basic attitude of a nation, a period, a class...[as] unconsciously qualified by one personality" "The History of Art as a Humanistic Discipline," pp. 14 and 17. Meiland has recently argued that Hirsch's view is more subtle than the one generally attributed to him. For he holds not that the meaning of a text is the author's meaning, but that for purposes of interpretation, when interpretation is considered a cognitive process, the author's meaning is the only one that counts. "Interpretation as Cognitive Discipline," p. 27. The origin of the view that textual meaning is determined by the author is to a great extent to be found in the Catholic exegetical tradition, in which God's intention determines the true meaning of the Scriptures. See Connolly and Keutner, *Hermeneutics versus Science?* p. 6, and Brown, "Hermeneutics," p. 607, who identifies the literal meaning with the author's meaning. The literal meaning must be contrasted with the fuller sense (*sensus plenior*, an expression coined by A. Fernández in 1925), which is the deeper meaning of Scriptures intended by God. See Brown, pp. 615–16. There are, however, antecedents in passages of Plato; see *Phaedrus* 275e, p. 521.

19. The view that it is the author's "intention" has been explicitly defended by Hirsch and Juhl. See the previous note. Among those who oppose this view are Dickie, *Aesthetics*, pp. 112 ff.; Beardsley, *Aesthetics*, pp. 17 ff.; Wimsatt and Beardsley, "The Intentional Fallacy," in *The Verbal Icon*, p. 3; and Stevenson, "On the Reasons That Can Be Given for the Interpretation of a Poem," pp. 125–26.

20. This view is closer to what Schleiermacher, Wolf, and Collingwood held. See Connolly and Keutner, *Hermeneutics versus Science?*, pp. 9–10. See also Collingwood, *The Idea of History*, pp. 282–83, and Schleiermacher, *Hermeneutics*, pp. 188 and 183. Redpath criticizes I. A. Richards for holding a view of this sort, in *Principles of Literary Criticism*. Redpath, "Some Problems in Modern Aesthetics," pp. 371–72. For Dickie, see *Aesthetics*, pp. 117 and 119. Dickie argues, for example, that meaning is always public and thus not up to the author.

21. See note 12 and Tolhurst, "On What a Text Is and How It Means," p. 9. As we

shall see later, however, not everyone who accepts that authors may know less about the meaning of a text they created than others accepts Jones's "aspectivism" or Ortega's "perspectivism." See for example, Stegmüller, "Walther von der Vogelweide's Lyric of Dream-Love and Quasar 3C 273," pp. 113, 116 ff. For Jones and Ortega, see note 10. Mulhern draws a sharp distinction between what an author believes a text means and what the text means. "Treatises, Dialogues, and Interpretation," p. 639.

22. For the emphasis on the audience, exclusively or in conjunction with other factors, see Eco, *A Theory of Semiotics*, pp. 66–68; and Miller, "Tradition and Difference," p. 12. Along these lines, Fish goes so far as to argue that the "reader" is actually responsible for the text; the reader writes the text. So there is no text, and therefore no meaning, independent of the reader. "Interpreting the *Variorum*," p. 482, and *Is There a Text in This Class?* p. vii. Fish's view echoes Gadamer, "Text and Interpretation," p. 388. Of course, because texts may have many audiences, the question arises as to which of these is the one that determines meaning. Historically minded hermeneuticists favor the contemporaneous audience, but others think differently. For different types of audiences, see my "Can There Be Texts Without Audiences?"

23. The talk about the audience's intentions is not rare in the pertinent literature. See Eco, *The Limits of Interpretation*, p. 50.

24. Jones, *Philosophy and the Novel*, p. 185.

25. This is a standard objection not very popular these days. For its supporters, see Beardsley, "The Affective Fallacy."

26. Eco seems to subscribe to this view in *The Limits of Interpretation*, pp. 21, 37 ff.

27. Cf. Tolhurst, "On What a Text Is and How It Means," and Helen Lang, "Philosophy as Text and Context," pp. 158–70. Hampshire, moreover, has noted the impossibility of evaluation outside of context, in *Innocence and Experience*, p. 91.

28. Borges, "Pierre Menard, Author of the *Quixote*," p. 43. See also Walton's discussion of the passage in "Style and the Products and Processes of Art," pp. 89–90.

29. Other objections raised against context in the literature have to do with its apparent indeterminacy. See Dascal, "Defending Literal Meaning," p. 276. Indeed, some deconstructionists trace the limitlessness of textual meaning to the importance of context for meaning and its "undecidability." See Miller, "Ariachne's Broken Woof," p. 59, and Derrida, "Signature Event Context," pp. 174, 182, and 192.

30. Cf. Putnam, "The Meaning of 'Meaning,'" p. 228.

31. Putnam recognizes this and thus introduces the notion of a "division of linguistic labor." Loosely, his view is that in all linguistic communities there are some members

who have the burden of determining whether some things are or are not what they are called. "The Meaning of 'Meaning,'" p. 228.

32. Schleiermacher appears to subscribe to this view, but rather than speaking about language in general, he refers to the linguistic domain common to the authors and what I have called their contemporaneous audiences in "Can There Be Texts Without Audiences?" *Hermeneutics*, pp. 183 ff. Barthes, at the beginning of "The Death of the Author," writes as if the only reality in a text (i.e., some writing, for him) were its language, a view he attributes to Mallarmé, although later in the article he appears to make the audience (i.e., the reader, for him) responsible for giving unity to a text. See pp. 143 and 148. And Miller, in "Ariachne's Broken Woof," p. 49, suggests that language coercively models minds rather than the reverse. See also the pertinent remarks of Dennett in *Consciousness Explained*, pp. 227–52, concerning the relation of language to minds.

33. The view that language determines meaning can be understood as claiming that it is the linguistic conventions that do so. Understood in this way, the position may be attributed to Wimsatt and Beardsley among many others. See "The Intentional Fallacy." The view has been recently opposed from very different camps. See, for example, Knapp and Michaels, "Against Theory 2," and Pradham, "Minimalist Semantics."

34. There are different varieties of this view. See Beardsley, "The Authority of the Text," p. 37; Derrida, "Signature Event Context," p. 9, and also *Of Grammatology*, p. 158; and Meiland, "Interpretation as a Cognitive Discipline," pp. 30 ff. Some authors speak of the *intentio operis*, but do not explain how a text, or a work, can have an intention other than the intention of the author or the audience, because it is not a subject. See Eco, *The Limits of Interpretation*, pp. 50 ff.

35. As Derrida puts it, "noir sur blanc." "La double séance," p. 203. A text consists of marks interspersed with blank spaces, margins, and so on. See also "Signature Event Context," pp. 181 ff.

36. Some deconstructionists reject the charge that meaning is indeterminate; their point is that meaning is not determined by the historical author or the historical context. See Slinn, "Deconstruction and Meaning," pp. 80 ff. For someone who accuses deconstructionists of holding that meaning is indeterminate, see Louch, "Critical Discussion," pp. 325–33. Rorty describes a critic who adopts this position as one who "beats the text into a shape which will serve his own purpose." "Nineteenth-Century Idealism and Twentieth-Century Textualism," p. 151.

37. For someone who argues in favor of consistency, see Eco, *The Limits of Interpretation*, p. 60. Wachterhauser attributes this view to Gadamer in "Interpreting Texts," p. 450. For someone who attacks it as insufficient, see Juhl, "The Appeal to the Text," pp. 281. See also Said, "Roads Taken and Not Taken in Contemporary Criticism," p. 337.

38. There are others, of course. For example, Ricoeur seems to think that a text is composed of polysemous signs and has a meaning that is autonomous with respect to the intention of the author, the initial situation in which the text was produced, and the

audience for which it was produced. This seems to be a position somewhere in between the first and the second I will list later. I do not discuss this and other variations and combinations of the views I discuss both because of lack of space and because the arguments used against the ones I discuss are effective against the others. For Ricoeur, see *Hermeneutics and the Human Sciences* (1989), p. 108.

39. Some of Derrida's statements suggest this radical position. See the references in notes 34 and 35. This position may itself be subdivided according to two possible interpretations. According to one, the text is, strictly speaking, just marks and blanks without meaning. According to the other, the text consists of these marks and blanks considered as signs without determinate meaning whose syntactical arrangements are themselves semantically nonsignificant. In this case, the signs are considered to be so because they can be endowed with meaning by interpreters. The bases of these interpretations are the so-called traces, remains, simulacra, of past interpretations often detected through the free play of etymology and differences. For passages that support these views, never quite clearly delineated among deconstructionists, see Derrida, "La différance," pp. 9–14, 23–25, and "La structure, le signe et le jeu dans le discourse des sciences humaines," pp. 411 and 427; and Miller, "Walter Pater: A Partial Portrait," p. 107.

40. Slinn, "Deconstruction and Meaning," p. 86, and Miller, "Theory and Practice," p. 611. If the view is not taken as the most radical but as the second version described in note 42, then there is no license because one can go only by the traces and it may be that 3, 4 and 5 cannot be justified in those terms. But according to this understanding no rules can justify selecting some meanings and rejecting others, as Abrams has pointed out in "The Deconstructive Angel," p. 433. To this Fish has responded with the notion of interpretative communities whose members function within certain conventions and canons. *Is There a Texts in This Class?* pp. 174 and 180.

41. See Louch, "Critical Discussion"; Ellis, *Against Deconstruction;* Hirsch, *The Aims of Interpretation;* Abrams, "Rationality and Imagination in Cultural History" and "The Deconstructive Angel"; and White, "The Absurdist Moment in Contemporary Literary Theory."

42. This appears to be what Wimsatt and Beardsley had in mind in "The Intentional Fallacy," in *The Verbal Icon*, p. 10. See also Beardsley's "The Authority of the Text.". See also Meiland, "Interpretation as a Cognitive Discipline," p. 38.

43. As Fish argues against Norman Holland. See Fish, *Is There a Text in This Class?* pp. 345 ff. Internalists themselves in fact are often forced to grant the point. See Wimsatt and Beardsley, "The Intentional Fallacy," in *The Verbal Icon*, p. 10. Their critics do not lose time pointing this fact. See, for example, Currie, *The Nature of Fiction*, p. 110. Juhl attacks the internalist position from another point of view in "The Appeal to the Text," bringing in the need for consideration of the author's intentions. For some of the sources of the internalist-externalist controversy, see the entries by Wimsatt and Beardsley in the Bibliography.

44. Cf. Eliot, "The Function of Criticism," p. 19.

45. Krauss, "Postmodernism and the Paraliterary," pp. 292–93; Fish, "Interpreting the *Variorum*, p. 482; and Bloom, "The Breaking of Form," p. 7.

46. Margolis has expressed this criticism by pointing out that, even if texts have no fixed natures, they must have some stable properties to be the referents of discourse. "Reinterpreting Interpretation," p. 242.

47. Slinn, "Deconstruction and Meaning," p. 85.

48. Stern, "Factual Constraints on Interpreting," pp. 205–21.

49. For a recent defense of the need to take several of these factors into account rather than just one, see Phelan, "Validity Redux."

50. Louch sees the point clearly in "Critical Discussion," p. 329.

51. Logical positivists see texts as expressing conceptual relations or as expressing empirically verifiable matters of fact; see Ayer, *Language, Truth, and Logic*, ch. 1. Derrida's program appears to imply that all texts are poetic; see Fischer, *Does Deconstruction Make Any Difference?* p. 104.

52. Cf. Putnam, "The Meaning of 'Meaning.'" This is explicitly acknowledged in legal literature. Cf., for example, *Planned Parenthood of South Eastern Pennsylvania vs. Casey*, 112 sct., p. 2814.

53. Wittgenstein, *Philosophical Investigations* 66 ff., pp. 31 ff.

54. The point has been recently made by Gadamer, Fish, and Hirsch, although they use it for different purposes. See Warnke, *Gadamer*, pp. 49–50; Fish, *Is There a Text in This Class?* p. 44; and Hirsch, "Three Dimensions of Hermeneutics," pp. 259 ff. But the notion that there is a normative, even a "moral" element in the rules of linguistic usage goes back a long way. It is present, for example, in the seventeenth century. See Doyle, "Thomas Compton Carleton, S. J." p. 6.

55. The distinction between my view and that of Gadamer is precisely that for him the limits of the meaning of texts are *never* strict, for the meaning of a text is nothing but the history of its effects. *Truth and Method*, p. 267.

56. For someone who opposes the notion of "one meaning" of a text, even, I assume, in the restricted way I present it here, see Ellis, *Against Deconstruction*, pp. 124 ff.

57. Abrams has used the notion of a "central core" in "Rationality and Imagination," p. 457, but his view is that such a core applies to what authors undertake to communicate and, thus, we must infer, is determined by authors. Meiland, who mentions a

"common core" of meaning and defends the notion of textual meaning as distinct from significance, literary meaning, and interpretations (i.e., understandings in my terminology) does not hold the author to be the determiner of that meaning, but the basic structure of the text and its relation to impersonal social linguistic conventions. "Interpretation as a Cognitive Discipline," pp. 42, 30, 35–36, and 38.

58. This is probably what Goodman and Elgin have in mind in "Interpretation and Identity," p. 56.

59. Cf. Wolterstorff, "Toward an Ontology of Art Works," p. 141.

60. Most of the literature to which I shall be referring in the notes in this section uses the term 'interpretation' to refer to what I call understanding or interchanges the terms 'interpretation' and 'understanding.' See, for example, Nehamas, "The Postulated Author," pp. 143, 145, and 148–49.

61. This seems to be what Hirsch had in mind when he argued that the author's understanding—he uses 'interpretation'—of a text must be taken as canonical. See *Validity in Interpretation*, p. 5. Later, however, he seems to have modified his view in "Three Dimensions of Hermeneutics," p. 246. Hirsch's view goes back to Schleiermacher, although it differs from Schleiermacher's view in some important respects. For Schleiermacher, see *Hermeneutics*, pp. 183 f. See also Warnke, *Gadamer*, pp. 43–44. Some authors recognize that some understandings are intended to recover the author's understanding of a text, but they also accept other types of understandings. Specht calls the first *hypothetical interpretations* and the second *constructive interpretations*. "Literary-Critical Interpretations—Psychoanalytical Interpretations," p. 155. See also Redpath, "Some Problems in Modern Aesthetics," pp. 360–75, and Stevenson, "On the Reasons that Can Be Given for the Interpretation of a Poem," pp. 124–30.

62. The argument is often and explicitly formulated in ethical terms. See, for example, Hirsch, "Three Dimensions of Hermeneutics," pp. 259–60, and *The Aims of Interpretation*, pp. 90–91. Hirsch goes so far as to say, in a Kantian spirit: "To treat an author's words merely as grist for one's own mill is ethically analogous to using another man merely for one's own purposes." And, then, in an Augustinian fashion (see Augustine's *Contra Academicos*), he accuses those who wish to open the gates to unlimited understanding while they complain when their texts are understood differently from the way they themselves do. Such *tu quoque* arguments have never proven convincing to those to whom they have been directed and it is naive to think they will do so in this case. For a criticism, see Meiland, "Interpretation as a Cognitive Discipline," pp. 43–44. Juhl puts up a vigorous defense of the only one understanding (i.e., interpretation) view in *Interpretation*, ch. 8, pp. 198 ff. in particular.

63. For the details of this controversy, see Slinn, "Deconstruction and Meaning," and Louch, "Critical Discussion," mentioned earlier. The view that the meaning of a text is not restricted to its historical meaning as understood by the author of the text and his or her contemporaneous audience was generally accepted in the medieval period. This atti-

tude was essential to the task they identified for themselves of bringing harmony to the various authoritative texts they had at their disposal. But they distinguished among various meanings of texts. For example, Origen identified literal meaning with the meaning of words considered independent of the authors's intent, and Thomas Aquinas distinguished between the literal *significatio*—when the words signify things—and the spiritual *significatio*—when the things that the words signify are used as "figures" of other things. For Origen, see Brown, "Hermeneutics"; for Aquinas, see *Quaestiones Quodlibetales* 7, q. 6, a. 14, p. 155. For the details of the scholastic method, see Gracia, "Scholasticism." The immediate source of this view for contemporary authors, however, is Nietzsche. See *The Will to Power*, sects 602 and 606, pp. 326 and 327, among other places.

64. It is no surprise, then, that the challenges to the view that emphasizes the author have come from intellectuals who have investigated power structures. See, for example, Foucault, "Prison Talk," and "Nietzsche, Freud, Marx," p. 65.

65. Miller, "Tradition and Difference," p. 12.

66. See Foucault, "Nietzsche, Freud, Marx," who speaks of "interpretations" but often means understandings. Foucault gets his cue from Nietzsche, of course, to whose *On the Genealogy of Morals* he explicitly refers. See also Miller, "The Critic as Host," p. 226. This does not mean, however, that we can avoid thinking of texts as having univocal meanings. Miller acknowledges that this notion is embedded in our language. "Tradition and Difference," p. 12.

67. Bloom, *The Anxiety of Influence*, p. 95, where he states that every interpretation (i.e., understanding) is a misinterpretation (i.e., misunderstanding). This view echoes Gadamer's position, already noted, according to which "one understands differently if one understands at all." *Truth and Method*, p. 264. For a criticism of Gadamer's view, see Warnke, *Gadamer*, p. 70, and Juhl, *Interpretation*, pp. 7–8. Miller subscribes to a similar view when he states that "all reading is misreading" in "Walter Pater: A Partial Portrait," p. 98. Recently, Ellis has argued that this position is no position at all. *Against Deconstruction*, p. 112.

68. Ricoeur has argued that these positions seem to be driven by concerns for the objectivity of the text and the subjectivity of the audience. "Explanation and Understanding," p. 152. And Miller finds a justification of the techniques of deconstruction not only in that it works, revealing "hitherto unidentified meanings and ways of having meaning in major literary texts," but also in its resistance "to the totalizing and totalitarian tendencies of [nondeconstructionist] criticism." See "The Critic as Host," p. 252. Barthes's language of "capitalist ideology" and "liberation" suggests the same. See "The Death of the Author," pp. 143 and 147.

69. See, for example, Abrams, "A Note on Wittgenstein and Literary Criticism," "Rationality and Imagination in Cultural History," "What's the Use of Theorizing About the Arts?" and "The Deconstructive Angel"; Jones, *Philosophy and the Novel*, ch. 5;

Meiland, "Interpretation as a Cognitive Discipline," pp. 29 ff.; and Eco, *The Limits of Interpretation,* ch. 2. As Nehamas points out in "The Postulated Author," these critics find some constraints for understanding in a variety of sources, including the rules of language.

70. This issue has been a matter of dispute for centuries. For example, Suárez, Hurtado de Mendoza, and Arriaga, among others, held that hearers could not understand the meaning of what they hear more clearly than the speakers, whereas Molina, Vázquez, and Thomas Compton Carleton thought they could. See Doyle, "Thomas Compton Carleton," pp. 13–15. More recently, the position I have been describing has gained widespread support. Kant, for example, says that "it is by no means unusual, upon comparing the thoughts which an author has expressed in regard to his subject, whether in ordinary conversation or in writing, to find that we understand him better than he understood himself." *Critique of Pure Reason,* ch. 1, sec. 1, p. 310. Both Schleiermacher and Dilthey developed this insight. See Makkreel, *Dilthey,* p. 271, and *Imagination and Interpretation in Kant,* pp. 160–63. And Unamuno, with his characteristic wit, asks, "Since when is the author of a book the person to understand it best?" "On the Reading and Interpretation of *Don Quijote,*" p. 974. But it is Plato perhaps who first chastised poets for not knowing the meaning of their poems. *Apology* 22b, p. 8, and *Protagoras* 347e, p. 340. See also Goodman and Elgin, "Interpretation and Identity," p. 55; Stallman, "Intentions," p. 399; and Eliot, "The Frontiers of Criticism," p. 126.

71. On how audiences can be more clear in their understanding than authors, see Thomas Compton Carleton, *Logica* 42, 7, nn. 3–5. Texts quoted by Doyle, "Thomas Compton Carleton," p. 22.

72. Cf. Beardsley, *The Possibility of Criticism,* p. 19.

73. Meiland, "Interpretation as a Cognitive Discipline," p. 26.

74. Cf. Putnam, "Meaning and Reference," pp. 119-32.

75. For Popper, see *The Logic of Scientific Discovery,* pp. 40–41. Eco makes this connection when he says that a text "can mean many things, but there are senses that would be preposterous to suggest." *The Limits of Interpretation,* p. 5. See also pp. 42 and 60–61.

76. Cf. Cain's comments about the development of the New Criticism, in "Authors and Authority in Interpretation," pp. 617-34, and Eliot's in "The Frontiers of Criticism," p. 114.

77. Berger argued for this position on the basis of the framers' "intentions." *Government by Judiciary,* pp. 363–73, and "Academe vs. The Founding Fathers," pp. 468–71. And Bork argues for a similar position in *The Tempting of America,* chs. 7–12. This position and its opposite are not the only ones currently under discussion in legal circles. For a sampler of opinion, see Garvey and Aleinikoff, *Modern Constitutional Theory.*

78. Cf. Arthur S. Miller, "Do the Founding Fathers Know Best?" *Washington Post,* Nov. 13, 1977, pp. E5 and E8; and Brest, "Berger vs. Brown et al.," *New York Times,* Dec. 11, 1977, p. 44. Dworkin argues that "interpretations" are political. *A Matter of Principle,* pp. 162 ff. Note that the arguments of Berger, Miller, Brest, and Dworkin are framed in terms of intentions rather than understandings. I have formulated the issue in terms of understanding for reasons already explained, but I shall come back to intentions later. For a recent discussion of the issues involved in the position of those who favor intent, see Pannier, "An Analysis of the Theory of Original Intent." The discussion of this issue has been taken up by philosophers outside legal circles. Gadamer proposes a similar position to the one I am describing in *Truth and Method,* p. 305.

79. This is in fact Arthur Miller's view. See "Do the Founding Fathers Know Best?" p. E5.

80. Connolly and Keutner, *Hermeneutics versus Science?* pp. 4 ff.

81. Augustine and other Church Fathers believed that the divine intention was at least partly unknown to the human authors of Scriptures. See Brown, "Hermeneutics," p. 610.

82. In *Conflict of the Faculties,* p. 123, Kant writes: "the God Who speaks through our own (morally practical) reason is an infallible interpreter of His words in the Scriptures, whom everyone can understand." See also Makkreel's discussion of this text in *Imagination and Interpretation in Kant,* pp. 146–48.

83. Rorty has pointed out that what he calls *textualism,* the view that there is nothing but texts, wants to place literature at the center of culture and to treat science and philosophy as literary genres. "Nineteenth-Century Idealism and Twentieth-Century Textualism," p. 141.

84. For those who reject that there are limits to the meaning of texts, there can be no true or false, correct or incorrect understandings. Nietzsche, *Gesammelte Werke,* p. 64. But even avowed deconstructionists accept the notion that readings (which I assume means understandings) of texts can be challenged and shown to be inadequate. See Miller, "Theory and Practice," p. 611.

85. In recent secondary literature on this topic one area of particular concern has to do with truth in understanding of fiction. The problem arises because a fictional text would seem to mean something that is not true and that, if properly understood, is understood as not being true. This is a complicated issue, which requires more discussion than I can give it and whose solution hinges also on the nature of fiction itself. I might suggest in passing, however, that truth in understanding does not entail that one must understand something to be true. For some recent discussions of this and related problems, see Beardsley, "Aesthetic Intentions and Fictive Illocutions"; Currie, *The Nature of Fiction,* particularly Ch. 2; and Juhl, *Interpretation,* particularly ch. 7.

Chapter 5. Interpretation

1. Apart from the three senses of 'interpretation' I discuss, there are others that are not so obvious or clear, but that are nevertheless frequently present in hermeneutical discussions. For example, the expression 'there is still room for interpretation' suggests that an interpretation is a certain type of understanding different from one expected or canonical. Cf. Ricoeur, "Creativity in Language," p. 128. Along somewhat similar lines, an interpretation can be taken as an understanding that goes beyond what is warranted by directly observable phenomena. See my *Philosophy and Its History*, p. 48. Sometimes 'interpretation' is used as a synonym of 'meaning.' Meiland, "Interpretation as a Cognitive Discipline," p. 25. And at other times it is used to mean explanation (see Weitz, *Hamlet and the Philosophy of Literary Criticism*, ch. 15), or as the explanation of the meaning (see Stevenson, "On the Reasons that Can Be Given for the Interpretation of a Poem," p. 127).

2. Cf. Hirsch, "Three Dimensions of Hermeneutics," p. 246. The conception of interpretation as understanding is widespread. On this, particularly among Continental philosophers, see Descombes, "Le moment français de Nietzsche."

3. Cf. Specht, "Literary-Critical Interpretation—Psychoanalytic Interpretation," p. 154.

4. Ricoeur, "Creativity in Language," p. 125, and Meiland, "Interpretation as a Cognitive Discipline," pp. 23 ff.

5. As we shall see in Section II, these texts aim to make other texts understandable. A version of the distinction between understanding and making understandable is found in Schleiermacher, *Hermeneutics*, p. 96. This distinction is rejected by Gadamer in *Truth and Method*, pp. 274 ff. See Wachterhauser's discussion of this issue in "Interpreting Texts," p. 443. I should mention that those who subscribe to a speech-act theory hold that interpretations are speech acts. Wolterstorff, "Evidence, Entitled Beliefs, and the Gospels," p. 431.

6. Some postmodernists reject the idea of a text that antecedes, is the referent of, or is separate from an interpretation, just as they reject the view of such a text anteceding, being the referent of, or being separate from an understanding. I have discussed these views in Chapter 4 in the context of understanding and what has been said there concerning these views and understanding applies, mutatis mutandis, to interpretation. The notion that an interpretation involves an addition to an original text, modifying it in some ways, is suggested by Abrams in "The Deconstructive Angel," p. 426, but he does not distinguish clearly between interpretation as understanding and interpretation properly speaking.

7. Boethius, *De Trinitate* I, p. 6.

8. I discuss different types of audiences in "Can There Be Texts Without Audi-

ences?" The intended audience is the person(s) the historical author had in mind when composing the historical text; the contemporaneous audience is the person(s), contemporary with the historical author, who can in principle understand the text; the intermediary audience is the person(s) who has or may become acquainted with the text, but who is neither contemporaneous with the author nor contemporary(ies) of those who are trying to understand the text; the contemporary audience is the person(s) who has or may become acquainted with the text and is not the author, his contemporaries, or the intermediary audience; the author considered as audience is the author in his or her role as audience; the historical audience is another name for the contemporaneous one.

9. Borges, "Pierre Menard, Author of the *Quixote*."

10. Gracia, *Philosophy and Its History,* p. 214.

11. I discuss anachronism and antiquarianism in *Philosophy and Its History*, pp. 66–72.

12. For a dissenting opinion, see Currie, "Work and Text," pp. 338–39, where he argues that only works are subject to interpretations. The causal function of interpretations was recognized by Stevenson in "Interpretation and Evaluation in Aesthetics."

13. In some cases it would be impossible. For example, if the divinity in question is infinite, it would be impossible for a finite being to have acts of understanding that are of the same sorts in relation to a text as those the divinity has.

14. This position appears to be the one rejected by Nehamas, according to which "to understand a text is to recreate someone else's state of mind," and which he rejects because "authors have no states that we can recreate at all." His statement is plausible because he conceives the author as what I have called, in "Can There Be Texts Without Historical Authors?", the *pseudo-historical author;* that is, as a construct in the mind of audiences, and not as the historical author in the sense I use here. For the historical author surely did have mental states when he or she considered the text, qua audience. Still, Nehamas does reject the view that, even though the historical author had mental states, it is the job of interpreters to help re-create them. My view is, of course, that this is one, among several, legitimate functions of interpreters. For Nehamas, see "What an Author Is," p. 690, and "Writer, Text, Work, Author," pp. 275 ff. For others who also reject the historical function, see the references in Chapter 4 to those who reject limits to the meanings and interpretations of texts. For supporters of the historical function, see Hirsch, *Validity in Interpretation*, pp. 46–47; Steiner, *After Babel*, pp. 26 ff.; and Panofsky, "The History of Art as a Humanistic Discipline," p. 14. I argued for this position in *Philosophy and Its History*, pp. 211 ff., precisely because in a historical context this function becomes preeminent. See also Collingwood, *The Idea of History*, p. 283.

15. This is the answer, then, to the question raised in Chapter 4 concerning the possibility of two or more persons having intensionally the same acts of understanding in relation to the same ECTs. It is possible provided the causal framework that elicits the

acts of understanding makes up for the differences that separate the persons in question.

16. I first formulated this principle in "Texts and Their Interpretation," p. 539. The only change I have made on it is that here I call *historical audience* what I previously called *contemporaneous audience.* I do this to avoid confusions with the contemporary audience.

17. Goodman and Elgin appear to suggest that translations never have the same meaning as the original they translate. This is so, of course, in cases where the work, i.e. the meaning, is essentially tied to the ECTs of the text as is the case in some literary works. But it need not be the case with the translation of many scientific or ordinary language texts, where the meaning is not essentially tied to the ECTs of the text.

18. Some postmodernists would have to reject this function because they do not see interpretations as capturing meaning at all. See Barthes, *S/Z*, pp. 11–12.

19. Whether the activity of getting at those meanings is described as uncovering deep and hidden meanings or expanding and broadening the meaning is a question much disputed in the literature but whose answer does not affect my position. For opposing views on this, see Nehamas, "Writer, Text, Work, Author," pp. 276 ff., and Horton, *Interpreting Interpreting,* p. 7. See also Foucault, "Nietzsche, Freud, Marx," p. 59.

20. See Nehamas, "What an Author Is," p. 686.

21. For some of the puzzles, see, for example, Currie, "Work and Text," pp. 330–1.

22. There has been much discussion of this issue in the literature. See, for example, Stern "Factual Constraints on Interpreting," pp. 205–21.

23. Abram's notion of "linguistic interpretation," which he contrasts with "historical interpretation," may appear to be similar to my notion of "textual interpretation." It cannot be taken as equivalent, however, because his view of interpretation is closer to understanding than to the view I have presented here. "The Deconstructive Angel," p. 426.

24. For a different view of historical and nonhistorical interpretations, see Jones, *Philosophy and the Novel,* p. 184.

25. Gracia, *Philosophy and Its History,* pp. 42 ff.

26. This point has been well understood by deconstructionists, although for different reasons than I give here. See Miller, "Steven's Rock and Criticism as Cure," p. 331, and Foucault, "Nietzsche, Freud, Marx." Foucault argues that interpretation is an endless task (p. 63). Peirce anticipates this view in various ways. See, for example, *Collected Papers*, vol. 6, p. 170. For my analysis of this claim, see "Can There Be Definitive Interpretations?" Among those who disagree with Foucault is Juhl, *Interpretation,* p. 198.

27. Indeed, some deconstructionists grant that it is unavoidable. See Miller, "Tradition and Difference," p. 12.

28. The point of this objection seems to me to be accepted by those who think that understandings and interpretations of texts *can never* have closure. See Miller, "Steven's Rock and Criticism as Cure, II," p. 333. The recent source of this sort of objection is to be found in Foucault's "Nietzsche, Freud, Marx."

29. Not everyone identifies correctness with truth and incorrectness with falsity. Hirsch considers correctness or incorrectness to pertain to "validation," whereas truth and falsity pertain to "verification." For him "to verify is to show that a conclusion is true; to validate is to show that a conclusion is probably true on the basis of what is known." *Validity in Interpretation*, p. 171.

30. This point has been made by Weitz in the context of art and literary criticism, although for not quite the same reasons. "The Philosophy of Criticism," pp. 207–16, and *Hamlet and the Philosophy of Literary Criticism*, ch. 15, particularly pp. 261 ff., although Weitz understands interpretations as explanations.

31. For a different approach to the objectivity and subjectivity of interpretations, see Jones, *Philosophy and the Novel*, pp. 191 ff. See also Currie, *The Nature of Fiction*, pp. 107–8.

Chapter 6. Discernibility

1. For the question of progress in philosophy, see Gracia, *Philosophy and Its History*, ch. 6.

2. Although sometimes the case of Maya glyphs is brought up in this context, this case is quite different, for the Spaniards were told by Mayans not only that there was meaning to them, but also the meaning of key glyphs. This is why scholars have been able to decipher them. See Landa, *Yucatán*, p. 105; and Coe, *The Maya*, pp. 190 ff.

3. The epistemic issues raised by these activities and the questionable significance of some of the conclusions reached through them have been discussed in detail by philosophers of social sciences. See, for example, Wylie, "Archeological Cables and Tacking."

4. The most well known case of something considered to be textual whose meaning was discovered only later are Egyptian hieroglyphs, for only after the Rosetta Stone was found and Champollion deciphered it was their meaning known. See Budge, *The Rosetta Stone in the British Museum*. And the same can be said about Minoan Linear B, for only on the assumption that it was a text did scholars set out to decipher it. See Chadwick, *The Decipherment of Linear B*, pp. 55 ff. There are other scripts that scientists take to constitute texts and whose meaning we do not know, such as Minoan Linear

A and Elamite. In some cases some results have been achieved based on certain conjectures about the languages on which the texts appear to be rendered and their relations to other languages, but these results can be regarded only as having the force of the conjectures on which they are based. See, for example, Fairservis's efforts with respect to Harappan. "The Script of the Indus Valley Civilization."

5. Rosen, "The Limits of Interpretation," p. 224, and Connolly and Keutner, *Hermeneutics Versus Science?* p. 7. The formulation of the hermeneutic circle is a matter much disputed today. For example, Stegmüller examines six different formulations of it, arguing that no single phenomenon is at stake, that it does not concern understanding, and that it is not a circle at all. "Walther von der Vogelweide's Lyric of Dream-Love and Quasar 3C 273," pp. 104 and 110 ff. The origin of the circle is found in Schleiermacher, *Hermeneutics*, pp. 175 ff., although it was taken up and broadened by Dilthey. Indeed, Dilthey opened the circle by allowing it to go beyond the text and encompass the historical context. See Makkreel, *Dilthey*, pp. 270–72. The contemporary author who perhaps more widely used the hermeneutic circle is Heidegger, but he reinterpreted it in such a way that it applies not just to texts, but to all knowledge. His argument, in *Being and Time*, is that the object of knowledge is either a part or a whole, but knowledge of the part requires knowledge of the whole and knowledge of the whole requires knowledge of the part, so that no knowledge is ever independent. This mereological argument is given in a historicist context, making it impossible to break the circle. This is the point of departure of much of Gadamer's thought. See "On the Circle of Understanding," pp. 68 ff. The same point is applied to texts by Günther Buck in "The Structure of Hermeneutic Experience and the Problem of Tradition," p. 32. It is arguable that even Quine's ontological relativism is a version of the hermeneutic circle. *Ontological Relativity and Other Essays*, pp. 50–21. See also Rorty, *Philosophy and the Mirror of Nature*, p. 319; Bloom, "The Breaking of Form," p. 9; and Derrida, "Structure, Sign, and Play," p. 250.

6. Augustine, *De magistro*, ch. 10, 33, pp. 623–24. For an antecedent, see Plato, *Meno* 80e, p. 363, and *Theaetetus* 147b, p. 852.

7. Stegmüller also sees the various formulations of the hermeneutic circle as dilemmas, although in fact his formulations look more like circles than dilemmas. See "Walther von der Vogelweide's Lyric of Dream-Love and Quasar 3C 273," pp. 110, 112, and 113.

8. Augustine, *De magistro*, ch. 10, 34, pp. 624–25.

9. This infinite regress is readily accepted by Barthes and others. See Barthes, "The Death of the Author," p. 146; and Miller, "Steven's Rock and Criticism as Cure," p. 333.

10. I take it this is Nehamas's point in "The Postulated Author," p. 139. Postmodernists openly acknowledge circularity. See Derrida, *Of Grammatology*, p. 158; Foucault, "Nietzsche, Freud, Marx," p. 64; and Slinn, "Deconstruction and Meaning," p. 83. See also Panofsky, "The History of Art as a Humanistic Discipline," p. 9.

11. This is the sort of position that drives most deconstructionists. The pertinent texts have been noted in Chapter 4 and the previous note.

12. This is in fact the kind of solution Augustine proposed to the problem, except that he identified the source of the meaning in question—which he took to be ideas—with God. *De magistro*, ch. 16, 45–46, pp. 635–87. Augustine is the source of the innatism of Descartes, Malebranche, and other early modern philosophers.

13. Aristotle, *Posterior Analytics,* ch. 3, 72b5 ff., pp. 113–15.

14. Abrams has noted the high standards used by Derrida, for example, in "How to Do Things with Texts," p. 571.

15. For Gorgias's arguments, see Sextus's account in Robinson, *An Introduction to Early Greek Philosophy,* pp. 295–98. The view that we can never understand a text as someone else understands it, and particularly its historical author and historical audience, is defended or assumed by much of the recent literature on textuality. See, for example, Jones, *Philosophy and the Novel,* pp. 181–82, and Nehamas, "The Postulated Author," p. 148. I have given other pertinent references in Chapter 4.

16. This is implicit in Wittgenstein's view of language as "a practice" which is part of a common "form of life." See Abrams, "How To Do Things with Texts," pp. 570–71

17. Gibson, *The Miracle Worker,* pp. 117 ff.

18. Searle, "Minds, Brains, and Programs," pp. 417–18.

19. Ibid., p. 417.

20. Augustine, *De doctrina christiana*, III, 2–3, p. 79.

21. Some philosophers extend the notion of response beyond the parameters I have designated for it. But this seems to me to weaken rather than strengthen the view, because one may argue that what is at stake is precisely whether a certain behavior constitutes a response or not. For someone who uses the notion of response, see Schiffer, *Meaning*, ch. 3.

22. Cf. Ricoeur, "Creativity in Language," p. 127.

23. This is not an unusual assumption; see Quine, "Indeterminacy of Translation Again," p. 5.

24. This appears to be the conclusion reached by deconstructionists like Derrida and Miller and by other postmodernists such as Gadamer and Fish. The pertinent texts are cited in Chapter 4.

25. Ignoring these is what leads Rorty and others to reject the view that we can know that past authors talk about some of the things we talk about. *Philosophy and the Mirror of Nature,* p. 267.

26. Winch, "Understanding a Primitive Society," pp. 307–24.

27. Vico, *The New Science,* pars. 332–33, p. 53.

28. Even some radical Newreaders accept this. Fish notes, for example, that "The ability to interpret is not acquired; it is constitutive of being human." *Is There a Text in This Class?* p. 172.

29. Again, even some radical Newreaders have come around to this view to explain agreement in understanding. For Fish the agreement is found in the canons and conventions of "interpretative communities." Ibid., pp. 171 ff.

30. Ibid., p. 303.

31. Kripke, *Naming and Necessity,* pp. 96 and 59, n. 22.

32. This is perhaps part of what Quine means by saying that empathy is not sufficient for radical translation. "Indeterminacy of Translation Again," p. 7.

33. Cf. Wittgenstein, *Zettel,* p. 173.

34. Quine is right, then, to say that we can never be sure we have the correct translation (read understanding) of a text from a culture with which we have not had any contacts. Tradition is necessary for this certainty because only within a tradition can we know what behavior to expect in what circumstances and in connection with which texts. But he is wrong, in my view, to extend this conclusion to texts within a culture. Quine, "On the Reasons for Indeterminacy of Translation" and "Indeterminacy of Translation Again."

35. This is the second part of my response to the historicist and perspectival view that no two persons can ever have intensionally the same understandings of a text.

SELECT BIBLIOGRAPHY

This bibliography contains only items that have been consulted in the preparation of this book.

Abrams, M. H. "How to Do Things with Texts." *Partisan Review* 46 (1979): 566–88.

"The Deconstructive Angel." *Critical Inquiry* 3 (1977): 425–438.

"Rationality and Imagination in Cultural History: A Reply to Wayne Booth." *Critical Inquiry* 2 (1976): 447–464.

"A Note on Wittgenstein and Literary Criticism." *ELH* 41 (1974): 541–54.

"What's the Use of Theorizing About the Arts?" In Morton W. Bloomfield, ed. *In Search of Literary Theory,* pp. 3–54. Ithaca, NY: Cornell University Press, 1972.

Natural Supernaturalism: Tradition and Revolution in Romantic Literature. New York: W. W. Norton, 1971.

Aldrich, V. *Philosophy of Art.* Englewood Cliffs, NJ: Prentice-Hall, 1963.

Allaire, Edwin B. "Berkeley's Idealism Revisited." In Colin M. Turbayne, ed., *Berkeley: Critical and Interpretative Essays*, pp. 197–206. Minneapolis: University of Minnesota Press, 1982.

Alston, William P. "Sign and Symbol." In Paul Edwards, ed., *Encyclopedia of Philosophy,* vol. 7, pp. 437-41. New York: Macmillan, 1967.

Aquinas, Thomas. *Commentary on Aristotle's "On Interpretation",* trans. Jean Oesterle. Milwaukee: Marquette University Press, 1962.

Quaestiones quodlibetales, ed. R. Spiazzi. Rome: Marietti, 1949.

Summa theologicae, ed. De Rubeis, Billuart et al., 4 vols. Turin: Marietti, 1926–27.

Aristotle. *Basic Works,* ed. Richard McKeon. New York: Random House, 1941.

Categories. In Richard McKeon, ed., *The Basic Works of Aristotle,* pp. 3–37. New York: Random House, 1941.

Metaphysics. In Richard McKeon, ed., *The Basic Works of Aristotle*, pp. 681–926. New York: Random House, 1941.

Nicomachean Ethics. In Richard McKeon, ed., *The Basic Works of Aristotle,* pp. 927–1112. New York: Random House, 1941.

On Interpretation. In Richard McKeon, ed., *The Basic Works of Aristotle,* pp. 38–61. New York: Random House, 1941.

Physics. In Richard McKeon, ed., *The Basic Works of Aristotle,* pp. 213–394. New York: Random House, 1941.

Posterior Analytics. In Richard McKeon, ed., *The Basic Works of Aristotle*, pp. 108-186. New York: Random House, 1941.

Armstrong, D. M. *Nominalism and Realism,* 2 vols. Cambridge: Cambridge University Press, 1980.

"Meaning and Communication." *Philosophical Review* 80, no. 4 (1971): 427–47.

Ashworth, E. J. "Traditional Logic." In Charles B. Schmitt et al., eds., *The Cambridge History of Renaissance Philosophy*, pp. 143-72. Cambridge: Cambridge University Press, 1988.

"'Do Words Signify Ideas or Things?' The Scholastic Sources of Locke's Theory of Language." *Journal of the History of Philosophy* 19 (1981): 299–326.

Augustine. *Contra academicos,* ed. V. Capanaga et al. In *Obras Completas de San Agustín,* vol 3, pp. 70–191. Madrid: Biblioteca de Autores Cristianos, 1971.

De magistro, ed. V. Capanaga et al. In *Obras Completas de San Agustín,* vol. 3. pp. 573–637. Madrid: Biblioteca de Autores Cristianos, 1971.

De libero arbitrio, ed. V. Capanaga et al. In *Obras Completas de San Agustín,* vol. 3. pp. 213–437. Madrid: Biblioteca de Autores Cristianos, 1971.

De doctrina christiana, ed. W. M. Green. *Corpus scriptorum ecclesiasticorum latinorum,* vol. 80. Vienna: Tempsky, 1963.

On the Teacher, trans. J. H. S. Burleigh. In John Baillie et al., eds., *Augustine: Earlier Writings,* pp. 69–101, vol. 6 of the Library of Christian Classics. Philadelphia: Westminster Press, 1953.

Austin, J. L. *How To Do Things with Words,* ed., J. O. Urmson. Cambridge, MA: Harvard University Press, 1962.

Averroes. *On the Harmony of Religion and Philosophy,* trans. G. F. Hourani. London: Luzac and Co., 1961.

Ayer, A. J. *Language, Truth, and Logic.* New York: Dover Publications, 1936.

Barthes, Roland. "From Work to Text," trans. Josué V. Harari. In Josué V. Harari, ed., *Textual Strategies: Perspectives in Post-Structuralist Criticism,* pp. 73–81. Ithaca, NY: Cornell University Press, 1979.

"The Death of the Author." In *Image, Music, Text,* trans. Stephen Heath, pp. 142–48. New York: Hill and Wang, 1977.

The Pleasure of the Text, trans. Richard Miller. New York: Hill and Wang, 1975.

S/Z. Paris: Editions du Seuil, 1970.

Beardsley, Monroe C. "Intentions and Interpretations: A Fallacy Revived." In Michael Wreen and Donald Callen, eds., *The Aesthetic Point of View: Selected Essays.* pp. 188–207. Ithaca, NY: Cornell University Press, 1982.

"Fiction as Representation." *Synthese* 46, no. 3 (1981): 291–311.

Aesthetics: Problems in the Philosophy of Criticism, rev. ed., New York: Macmillan, 1980.

"Aesthetic Intentions and Fictive Illocutions." In P. Hernadi, ed., *What Is Literature?* pp. 161–77. Bloomington: Indiana University Press, 1978.

"The Authority of the Text." In *The Possibility of Criticism,* pp. 16–37. Detroit: Wayne State University Press, 1970.

The Possibility of Criticism. Detroit: Wayne State University Press: 1970.

"Aesthetic Experience Regained." *Journal of Aesthetics and Art Criticism* 28 (1969): 3–11.

Aesthetics: Problems in the Philosophy of Criticism. New York: Harcourt, Brace and Co., 1958.

Beckett, Samuel. *Texts for Nothing,* trans. Samuel Beckett. London: Carder and Boyars, 1974.

Bellarmine, Robert. *Disputationes de controversiis Christianae fidei adversus huius temporis haereticos*, 4 vols. Venice, 1596.

Berger, Raoul. "Academe vs. the Founding Fathers." *The National Review* 30 (1978): 468–71.

   Government by Judiciary: The Transformation of the Fourteenth Amendment. Cambridge, MA: Harvard University Press, 1977.

Black, M. "Meaning and Intention: An Examination of Grice's Views." *New Literary History* 4 (1972-1973): 257–79.

Blondel, Eric. "Interpreting Texts with or without Nietzsche." In G. L. Ormiston and A. D. Schrift, eds., *Transforming the Hermeneutic Context: From Nietzsche to Nancy*, pp. 69-88. Albany: SUNY Press, 1990.

Bloom, Harold. "The Breaking of Form." In Harold Bloom et al., *Deconstruction and Criticism*, pp. 1–37. New York: Seabury Press, 1979.

   Poetry and Repression. New Haven, CT: Yale University Press, 1976.

   A Map of Misreading. New York: Oxford University Press, 1975.

   Kabbalah and Criticism. New York: Seabury Press, 1975.

   The Anxiety of Influence: A Theory of Poetry. New York: Oxford University Press, 1973.

   et al. *Deconstruction and Criticism.* New York: Seabury Press, 1979.

Blunt, A. "Poussin's Notes on Painting." *Journal of the Warburg Institute* 1 (1937): 344–51.

Boeckh, August. *Enzyklopädie und Methodenlehre der philologischen Wissenschaften*, ed. Ernst Bratuschek. Stuttgart: Teubner, 1966.

Boethius. *De Trinitate.* In *The Theological Tractates*, trans. H. F. Stewart and E. K. Rand. Cambridge, MA: Harvard University Press, 1968.

Bonaventure. *Retracing the Arts to Theology.* In Sister Emma Thérèse Healy, *St. Bonaventure's "De reductione artium ad theologiam," A Commentary with an Introduction and Translation.* St. Bonaventure, NY: Saint Bonaventure College Press, 1939.

Booth, Wayne. *The Rhetoric of Fiction.* Chicago: University of Chicago Press, 1961.

Borges, Jorge Luis. "Pierre Menard, Author of the *Quixote*," trans. James E. Irby. In Donald A. Yates and James E. Irby, eds., *Labyrinths,* pp. 36–44. Norfolk, Conn.: New Directions, 1962.

Bork, R. *The Tempting of America: The Political Seduction of the Law.* New York: The Free Press, 1991.

Brest, Paul. "Review of Raoul Berger's *Government by Judiciary." New York Times,* 11 December, 1977.

Brown, R. "Hermeneutics." In R. Brown et al., *The Jerome Biblical Commentary,* pp. 603–23. Englewood Cliffs, NJ: Prentice Hall, Inc., 1968.

Buck, Günther. "The Structure of Hermeneutic Experience and the Problem of Tradition." *New Literary History* 10 (1978): 31–47.

Budge, E. A. Wallis. *The Rosetta Stone in the British Museum.* London: Religious Tract Society, 1929.

Cain, William E. "Authors and Authority in Interpretation." *Georgia Review* 34 (1980): 617–34.

        "Authority, 'Cognitive Atheism,' and the Aims of Interpretation: The Literary Theory of E. D. Hirsch." *College English* 39 (1977): 333–45.

Carleton, Thomas Compton. *De signo.* In *Philosophia universa* (*Logica, Disputatio* 42), pp. 156–63. Antwerp, 1649.

Carter, William R. "Salmon on Artifact Origins and Lost Possibilities." *Philosophical Review* 92 (1983): 223–32.

Castañeda, Héctor-Neri. "Philosophy as a Science and as a Worldview." In Avner Cohen and Marcelo Dascal, eds., *The Institution of Philosophy: A Discipline in Crisis?* pp. 35-60. La Salle, IL.: Open Court Press, 1989.

Chadwick, John. *The Decipherment of Linear B.* Cambridge: Cambridge University Press, 1967.

Chappell, V. C. "Particulars Re-Clothed." *Philosophical Studies* 15 (1964): 60–64.

Child, Arthur. *Interpretation: A General Theory.* Berkeley: University of California Press, 1965.

Chomsky, Noam. *Problems of Knowledge and Freedom.* New York: Pantheon Books, 1971.

Current Issues in Linguistic Theory. London: Mouton, 1964.

Cioffi, F. "Intention and Interpretation in Criticism." In Cyril Barret, ed., *Collected Papers in Aesthetics,* pp. 161–83. Oxford: Oxford University Press, 1965.

Clark, H. and T. Carlson "Context for Comprehension." In J. Long and A. Baddeley, eds.,*Attention and Performance,* pp. 313–33. Hillsdale, NJ: Lawrence Erlbaum, 1981.

Close, A. J. "Don Quixote and the 'Intentionalist Fallacy.'" *The British Journal of Aesthetics* 12 (1972): 19–39.

Coe, Michael D. *The Maya.* New York: Thames and Hudson, 1993.

Cohen, Avner, and Marcelo Dascal, eds. *The Institution of Philosophy: A Discipline in Crisis?* La Salle, IL: Open Court Press, 1989.

Collingwood, Robin George. *The Idea of History.* Oxford: Clarendon Press, 1946.

Conimbricenses. *De signo.* In *Commentarii Collegii Conimbricensis et Societatis Jesu. In Universam Dialecticam Aristotelis Stagiritae,* Secunda pars, pp. 4–67. Lyons: Horatius Cardon, 1606.

Connolly, John M. and Thomas Keutner, trans. and eds. *Hermeneutics versus Science? Three German Views: Essays by H. G. Gadamer, E. K. Specht, W. Stegmüller.* Notre Dame, IN: University of Notre Dame Press, 1988.

Cooper, C. J. *"Stare Decisis:* Precedent and Principle in Constitutional Adjudication." *Cornell Law Review* 73 (1988): 401–46.

Copi, Irving M. *Introduction to Logic.* New York: Macmillan, 1986.

"Essence and Accident." *The Journal of Philosophy* 51 (1954): 706–19.

Coulmas, Florian. *Writing Systems of the World.* Oxford: Basil Blackwell, 1989.

Cover, R. *"Nomos* and Narrative." *Harvard Law Review* 97 (1983): 4–68.

Cruttwell, Patrick. "Makers and Persons." *Hudson Review* 12 (1959–60): 481–507.

Culler, Jonathan. *The Pursuit of Signs.* Ithaca, NY: Cornell University Press, 1982.

Structuralist Poetics: Structuralism, Linguistics, and the Study of Literature. Ithaca, NY: Cornell University Press, 1975.

Currie, Gregory. "Work and Text." *Mind* 100 (1991): 325–39.

The Nature of Fiction. Cambridge: Cambridge University Press, 1990.

An Ontology of Art. London: Macmillan, 1989.

"What Is Fiction?" *The Journal of Aesthetics and Art Criticism* 43, no. 4 (1985): 385–92.

Danto, Arthur C. *The Philosophical Disenfranchisement of Art.* New York: Columbia University Press, 1986.

The Transfiguration of the Commonplace: A Philosophy of Art. Cambridge, MA: Harvard University Press, 1981.

"The Artworld." *Journal of Philosophy* 61 (1964): 571–84.

Dascal, Marcelo. "The Limits of Interpretation," In press.

"Defending Literal Meaning." *Cognitive Science* 11 (1987): 259–81.

Pragmatics and the Philosophy of Mind. Vol. 1: *Thought in Language.* Amsterdam: John Benjamins, 1983.

"Language and Money: A Simile and Its Meaning in Seventheenth Century Philosophy of Language." *Studia Leibnitiana* 8, no. 2 (1976): 187–218.

and E. Weizman. "Contextual Exploitation of Interpretation in Text Understanding: An Integrated Model." In M. Papi and J. Versdrueren, eds., *The Pragmatic Perspective*, pp. 31–46. Amsterdam: John Benjamins, 1985.

Davidson, Donald. "Radical Interpretation." In *Inquiries into Truth and Interpretation,* pp. 125–39. Oxford: Oxford University Press, 1984.

Inquiries into Truth and Interpretation. Oxford: Oxford University Press, 1984.

Essays on Actions and Events. Oxford: Clarendon Press, 1980.

and J. Hintikka, eds., *Words and Objections.* Dordrecht: Reidel, 1968.

Davis, Stephen. *Definitions of Art.* Ithaca, NY: Cornell University Press, 1991.

Deely, John. *Basics of Semiotics.* Bloomington: Indiana University Press, 1990.

Deleuze, Gilles. *Qu'est-ce que la philosophie?* Paris: Minuit, 1991.

Demeraux, David. "Artifacts, Natural Objects and Works of Art." *Analysis* 37 (1977): 134–44.

Dennett, Daniel C. *Consciousness Explained.* Boston: Little, Brown & Co., 1991.

Derrida, Jacques. *Limited Inc.* Evanston, IL Northwestern University Press, 1988.

    Positions, trans. Alan Bass. Chicago: University of Chicago Press, 1987.

    Glas, trans. John P. Leavey, Jr., and Richard Rand. Lincoln: University of Nebraska Press, 1986.

    Writing and Difference, trans. Alan Bass. Chicago: University of Chicago Press, 1978.

    "Signature Event Context." *Glyph* 1 (1977): 172–97.

    Of Grammatology, trans. Gayatri Chakravorty Spivak. Baltimore, MD: Johns Hopkins University Press, 1976.

    Speech and Phenomena and Other Essays on Husserl's Theory of Signs, trans. David B. Allison. Evanston, IL: Northwestern University Press, 1973.

    "La double séance." In *La dissémination,* pp. 199–317. Paris: Editions du Seuil, 1972.

    "La différance." In *Marges de la philosophie,* pp. 3–29. Paris: Editions de Minuit, 1972.

    "Structure, Sign, and Play in the Discourse of the Human Sciences." In R. Macksay and E. Donato, eds., *The Structuralist Controversy: The Languages of Criticism and the Sciences of Man,* pp. 247–72. Baltimore: Johns Hopkins University Press, 1970.

    "La structure, le signe et le jeu dans le discourse des sciences humaines." In *L'écriture et la différence,* pp. 409–28. Paris: Editions du Seuil, 1967.

Descombes, V. "Le moment français de Nietzsche." In L. Ferry and A. Renant, eds., *Pourquoi nous ne sommes pas nietzschéens,* pp. 101–28. Paris: Grasset, 1991.

Dewey, John. *Art as Experience: An Introduction.* New York: G.P. Putnam's Sons, 1980.

Dickie, George. *Art and the Aesthetic: An Institutional Analysis.* Ithaca, N.Y.: Cornell University Press, 1974.

    Aesthetics: An Introduction. Indianapolis: Bobbs-Merrill, 1971.

Dijk, T. A. van. *Text and Context.* New York: Longman, 1977.

Dilthey, W. *Selected Writings*, ed. and trans. H. P. Rickman. Cambridge: Cambridge University Press, 1976.

Dipert, Randall R. *Artifacts, Art Works, and Agency.* Philadelphia: Temple University Press, 1993.

"Art, Artifacts, and Regarded Intentions." *American Philosophical Quarterly* 23, no. 4 (1986): 401–8.

"The Composer's Intentions: An Examination of Their Relevance for Performance." *Musical Quarterly* 66 (1980): 205–18.

"Types and Tokens: A Reply to Sharpe." *Mind* 89 (1980): 587–8.

Doepke, F. "The Structure of Persons and Artifacts." *Ratio* 29 (1987): 36–51.

Doyle, John P. "Thomas Compton Carleton, S.J.: On Words Signifying More Than Their Speakers or Makers Know or Intend." *The Modern Schoolman* 66 (1988): 1–28.

"Peter John Olivi on Right, Dominion, and Voluntary Signs." In John Deely and Jonathan Evans, eds., *Semiotics 1986*, pp. 419–29. New York: Plenum Press, 1987.

"The *Conimbricenses* on the Relations Involved in Signs." *Semiotics* (1984): 567–76.

Dummett, Michael. *The Logical Basis of Metaphysics.* Cambridge, MA: Harvard University Press, 1991.

"What Does the Appeal to Use Do for the Theory of Meaning?" In A. Margalit, ed., *Meaning and Use*, pp. 123–35. Dordrecht: Reidel, 1976.

Dutton, D. "Artistic Crimes." In D. Dutton, ed., *The Forger's Art: Forgery and the Philosophy of Art*, pp. 172–87. Berkeley and Los Angeles: University of California Press, 1983.

Dworkin, Ronald. *A Matter of Principle.* Cambridge, MA: Harvard University Press, 1985.

Eaton, Marcia. *Aesthetic and the Good Life.* London and Toronto: Associated University Press, 1989.

"Art, Artifacts, and Intentions." *American Philosophical Quarterly* 6 (1969): 165–9.

Eco, Umberto. *The Limits of Interpretation.* Bloomington and Indianapolis: Indiana University Press, 1990.

The Open Work, trans. Anna Cancogni. Cambridge, Mass.: Harvard University Press, 1989.

Semiotics and the Philosophy of Language. London: Macmillan Press, 1984.

"Text and Encyclopedia." In J. S. Petöfi, ed., *Text vs. Sentence*, pp. 585–94. Hamburg: Buske, 1979.

The Role of the Reader. Bloomington: Indiana University Press, 1979.

A Theory of Semiotics. Bloomington: Indiana University Press, 1976.

Eliot, T. S. "The Frontiers of Criticism." In *On Poetry and Poets*, pp. 113–31. New York: Octagon Books, 1957.

"The Function of Criticism." In *Selected Essays 1917–1932*, pp. 12–22. London: Faber and Faber, 1932.

Ellis, J. M. *Against Deconstruction*. Princeton, NJ: Princeton University Press, 1989.

The Theory of Literary Criticism: A Logical Analysis. Berkeley: University of California Press, 1974.

Engel, Pascal. "The Decline and Fall of French Nietzscheostructuralism." In B. Smith ed., *European Philosophy and the American Academy*. La Salle, IL: Hegeler Institute, 1994.

"Interpretation without Hermeneutics." *Topoi* 10 (1991): 137–46.

Fairservis, Walter A., Jr. "The Script of the Indus Valley Civilization." *Scientific American* 248 (1983): 58-66.

Ferry, L., and A. Renant, eds. *Pourquoi nous ne sommes pas nietzschéens*. Paris: Grasset, 1991.

Fischer, Michael. *Does Deconstruction Make Any Difference? Poststructuralism and the Defense of Poetry in Modern Criticism*. Bloomington: Indiana University Press, 1985.

Fish, Stanley. *Is There a Text in This Class? The Authority of Interpretive Communities*. Cambridge, MA: Harvard University Press, 1980.

"Interpreting 'Interpreting the *Variorum*.'" *Critical Inquiry* 3 (1977): 191–98.

"Interpreting the *Variorum*." *Critical Inquiry* 2 (1976): 465–85.

"Facts and Fictions: A Reply to Ralph Rader." *Critical Inquiry* 1 (1975): 883–91.

"What Is Stylistics and Why Are They Saying Such Terrible Things About It?" In Seymour Chatman, ed., *Approaches to Poetics*, pp. 109–52. New York: Columbia University Press, 1973.

"Literature in the Reader: Affective Stylistics." In *Self-Consuming Artifacts,* pp. 383–427. Berkeley: University of California Press, 1972.

Fletcher C. E., III. "Principalist Models in the Analysis of Constitutional and Statutory Texts." *Iowa Law Review* 72 (1987): 891-941

Fletcher, James J. "Artifactuality Broadly and Narrowly Speaking." *Southern Journal of Philosophy* 20 (1982): 41–52.

Foucault, Michel. "Nietzsche, Freud, Marx." In G. L. Ormiston and A. D. Schrift, eds., *Transforming the Hermeneutic Context: From Nietzsche to Nancy*, pp. 59–68. Albany: SUNY Press, 1990. Original French text in *Nietzsche,* in Cahiers de Royaumont, Philosophie No. VI, VIIe colloque—4–8 juillet 1964, pp. 183–92. Paris: Les Editions de Minuit, 1967.

"Prison Talk." In Colin Gordon, ed., *Power/Knowledge*, pp. 37–54. New York: Pantheon Books, 1980.

"What Is an Author?" trans. Donald F. Bouchard and Sherry Simon. In Donald F. Bouchard, ed., *Language, Counter-Memory, Practice: Selected Essays and Interviews*, pp. 113–38. Ithaca, NY: Cornell University Press, 1977.

The Order of Things: An Archeology of the Human Sciences, trans. of *Les Mots et les choses.* New York: Vintage Books, 1973.

The Archeology of Knowledge, trans. A. M. Sheridan. New York: Harper and Row, 1972.

Frank, Manfred. "The Interpretation of a Text." In G. L. Ormiston and A. D. Schrift, eds., *Transforming the Hermeneutic Context: From Nietzsche to Nancy*, pp. 145–176. Albany: SUNY Press, 1990.

Frege, Gottlob. "On Sense and Reference." In P. Geach and M. Black, eds. and trans. *Translations from the Philosophical Writings of Gottlob Frege,* pp. 56-78. Oxford: Blackwell, 1952.

Foundations of Arithmetic, trans. J. L. Austin. Oxford: Blackwell, 1950.
Frye, Northrop. *Anatomy of Criticism.* Princeton, NJ: Princeton University Press, 1957.

Gadamer, Hans-Georg. "Mythopoetic Inversion in Rilke's *Duino Elegies,*" trans. John M. Connolly and Thomas Keutner. In John M. Connolly and Thomas Keutner, eds., *Hermeneutics Versus Science? Three German Views*, pp. 79–101. Notre Dame, IN: University of Notre Dame Press, 1988.

"On the Circle of Understanding," trans. John M. Connolly and Thomas Keutner. In John M. Connolly and Thomas Keutner, eds., *Hermeneutics Versus Science? Three German Views*, pp. 68–78. Notre Dame, IN: University of Notre Dame Press, 1988.

"Text and Interpretation." Trans. Dennis J. Schmidt. In Brice R. Wachterhauser, ed., *Hermeneutics and Modern Philosophy*, pp 377-96. Albany, NY: State University Press, 1986.

Philosophical Hermeneutics, ed. and trans. David Linge. Berkeley: University of California Press, 1976.

Truth and Method, 2nd ed., trans. Garrett Barden and Robert Cumming. New York: Crossroad, 1975.

Gallie, W. D. "Essentially Contested Concepts." In *Philosophy and Historical Understanding*, pp. 157–91. New York: Schocken Books, 1964.

Garvey, J. H. and T. A. Aleinikoff. *Modern Constitutional Theory: A Reader*, 2d. ed. St. Paul, MN: West Publishing, 1991.

Gasché, Rodolphe. *The Tain of the Mirror: Derrida and the Philosophy of Reflection.* Cambridge, MA: Harvard University Press, 1986.

"Deconstruction as Criticism." *Glyph* 6 (1979): 177-215.

Gazdar, G. *Pragmatics: Implicature, Presupposition, and Logical Form.* New York: Academic Press, 1979.

Geertz, Clifford. *The Interpretation of Cultures: Selected Essays.* New York: Basic Books, 1973.

Gibbs, R. "Literal Meaning and Psychological Theory." *Cognitive Science* 8 (1984): 275–304.

"Do People Always Process the Literal Meanings of Indirect Requests?" *Journal of Experimental Psychology* 9 (1983): 524–33.

Gibson, William. *The Miracle Worker.* New York: Bantam Books, 1962.

Gilson, Etienne. *Being and Some Philosophers*, 2nd ed. corrected and enlarged. Toronto: Pontifical Institute of Mediaeval Studies, 1952.

Glickman, Jack. "Creativity in the Arts." In Lars Aagaard-Mogensen, ed., *Culture in Art*, pp. 130–46. Atlantic Highlands, NJ: Humanities Press, 1976.

Glucksberg, S., P. Gildea, and H. Bookin. "On Understanding Nonliteral Speech: Can People Ignore Metaphors?" *Journal of Verbal Learning and Verbal Behavior* 21 (1982): 85–98.

Goodenough, Ward H. *Culture, Language and Society*. Menlo Park, CA: The Benjamin Cummings Publishing Co., 1981.

Goodman, Nelson. *Languages of Art: An Approach to a Theory of Symbols*. London: Oxford University Press, 1968.

——. *The Structure of Appearance*, 2nd ed. Indianapolis: The Bobbs-Merrill Company, 1966.

—— and Catherine Z. Elgin. *Reconceptions in Philosophy and Other Arts and Sciences*. London: Routledge, 1988.

—— and Catherine Z. Elgin. "Interpretation and Identity." In *Reconceptions in Philosophy and Other Arts and Sciences*, pp. 49–65. London: Routledge, 1988.

Gracia, Jorge J. E. "Can There Be Texts Without Historical Authors?" *American Philosophical Quarterly* 31, no.3 (1994): 248–53.

——. "Can There Be Texts Without Audiences? The Identity and Function of Audiences." *Review of Metaphysics* 47, no.4 (1994): 711–34.

——. "Autor y represión," *Cuadernos de Etica* forthcoming.

——. "La legitimidad en la interpretación." Volume in honor of Ricardo Maliandi. Buenos Aires: Universidad de Río Cuarto, 1995.

——. "Can There Be Definitive Interpretations? An Interpretation of Foucault in Response to Engel." In B. Smith, ed., *European Philosophy and the American Academy*, pp. 41–51. La Salle, IL: Hegeler Institute, 1994.

——. "Las interpretaciones definitivas." *Revista Latinoamericana de Filosofía* 19 (1993): 203–12.

——. *Philosophy and Its History: Issues in Philosophical Historiography*. Albany: SUNY Press, 1992.

"Texts and Their Interpretation." *Review of Metaphysics* 43 (1990): 495–542

Individuality: An Essay on the Foundations of Metaphysics Albany: SUNY Press, 1988.

Introduction to the Problem of Individuation in the Early Middle Ages, 2nd rev. ed. Munich and Vienna: Philosophia Verlag, 1988.

"Scholasticism." In Joseph Strayer, ed., *Dictionary of the Middle Ages*, vol. 11., pp. 55–58. New York: Charles Scribner's Sons, 1982.

"Falsificación y valor artístico." *Revista de Ideas Estéticas* 116 (1971): 327–33.

Graff, Gerald. *Literature Against Itself.* Chicago: University of Chicago Press, 1979.

Greenlee, Douglas. *Peirce's Concept of Sign.* The Hague and Paris: Mouton, 1973.

Greetham, D. C. "[Textual] Criticism and Deconstruction." *Studies in Bibliography* 44 (1990): 1–30.

Grey, T. C. "Do We Have an Unwritten Constitution?" *Stanford Law Review* 27 (1975).

Grice, H. P. "Utterer's Meaning and Intentions." *Philosophical Review* 78, no. 2 (1969): 147–77.

"Utterer's Meaning, Sentence Meaning and Word Meaning." *Foundations of Language* 4, no. 3 (1968): 225–42.

"Meaning." *Philosophical Review* 66, no. 3 (1957): 377–88.

Griffin, D. R. and D. W. Sherburne. "Editor's Preface." In Alfred North Whitehead, *Process and Reality*, pp. v–x. New York: The Free Press, 1988.

Haack, Susan. "Surprising Noises: Rorty and Hesse on Metaphor." *Proceedings of the Aristotelian Society,* New Series 88 (1987–88): 179–87.

Hacking, Ian. "All Kinds of Possibility." *The Philosophical Review* 84 (1975): 321–37.

Hallowell, Alfred. *Culture and Experience.* New York: Schocken Books, 1967.

Hamacher, Werner. "Hermeneutic Ellipses: Writing the Hermeneutical Circle in Schleiermacher." In G. L. Ormiston and A. D. Schrift, eds., *Transforming the Hermeneutic Context: From Nietzsche to Nancy*, pp. 177–210. Albany: SUNY Press, 1990.

Hampshire, Stuart. *Innocence and Experience*. Cambridge, MA: Harvard University Press, 1989.

Harman, Gilbert. "An Introduction to Translation and Meaning." In D. Davidson and J. Hintikka, eds., *Words and Objections*, pp. 14–27. Dordrecht: Reidel, 1968.

Harris, Marvin. *Cultural Materialism*. New York: Random House, 1979.

Hartman, Geoffrey. *Deconstruction and Criticism*. New York: Seabury Press, 1979.

Heidegger, Martin. *Being and Time*, trans. John Macquarrie and Edward Robinson. New York: Harper Books, 1962.

Hirsch, E. D., Jr. *The Aims of Interpretation*. Chicago: University of Chicago Press, 1976.

"Three Dimensions of Hermeneutics." *New Literary History* 3 (1972): 245–61.

Validity in Interpretation. New Haven, Conn.: Yale University Press, 1967.

"Objective Interpretation." *PMLA* 75 (1960): 463–79.

Hobbes, Thomas. *Leviathan. On the Matter, Forme and Power of a Commonwealth Ecclesiastical and Civil*, ed. Michael Oakshott. New York: Collier Books, 1962.

Holland, Norman. *Readers Reading*. New Haven: Yale University Press, 1975.

Horton, Susan. *Interpreting Interpreting: Interpreting Dicken's "Dombey."* Baltimore: Johns Hopkins University Press, 1979.

Hurtado de Mendoza, Pedro. *Logica*. Lyon, 1624.

Husserl, Edmund. *Formal and Transcendental Logic*, trans. Dorian Cairns. The Hague: Nijhoff, 1978.

Ingarden, R. *The Literary Work of Art: An Investigation on the Borderlines of Ontology, Logic, and Theory of Literature*, trans. with an Introduction by George G. Grabonicz. Evanston, IL: Northwestern University Press, 1973.

Iseminger, Gary. "The Work of Art as Artifact." *British Journal of Aesthetics* 13 (1973): 3–15.

Iser, Wolfgang. *Prospecting: From Reader-Response to Literary Anthropology*. Baltimore: Johns Hopkins University Press, 1989.

"The reading process: A Phenomenological Approach." In Jane P. Tompkins, ed., *Reader Response Criticism*, pp. 50–69. Baltimore: Johns Hopkins University Press, 1980.

Jakobson, Roman. "Questions of Literary Theory." In *Language and Literature*, pp. 19–120. Cambridge, MA: Harvard University Press, 1987.

———. *Language and Literature*. Cambridge, MA: Harvard University Press, 1987.

Jones, Peter. *Philosophy and the Novel: Philosophical Aspects of "Middlemarch," "Anna Karenina," "The Brothers Karamazov," "A la recherche du temps perdu," and of the Methods of Criticism.* Oxford: Clarendon Press, 1975.

Juhl, P. D. *Interpretation: An Essay in the Philosophy of Literary Criticism.* Princeton, NJ: Princeton University Press, 1980.

———. "The Appeal to the Text: What Are We Appealing To?" *Journal of Aesthetics and Art Criticism* 36, no. 3 (1978): 277–87.

———. "The Doctrine of 'Verstehen' and the Objectivity of Literary Interpretations." *Deutsche Vierteljahrsschrift für Literaturwissenschaft und Geistesgeschichte* 49 (1975): 381–424.

Kahn, S. J. "What Does a Critic Analyze?" *Philosophy and Phenomenological Research* 13 (1952–53): 237–45.

Kaminsky, J., and R. Nelson. "Scientific Statements about Humanly Created Objects." *Journal of Philosophy* 55 (1958): 641–7.

Kant, Immanuel. *Conflict of the Faculties,* Introduction by Mary J. Gregor, trans. M. Gregor and Robert E. Anchor. New York: Abaris Press, 1979.

———. *Critique of Pure Reason.* Trans. Norman Kemp Smith. London: Macmillan, 1963.

Katz, Jerrold J. *Propositional Structure and Illocutionary Force: A Study of the Contribution of Sentence Meaning to Speech Acts.* New York: Thomas Y. Crowell, 1977.

———. *Semantic Theory.* New York: Harper and Row, 1972.

Kearney, Richard. "Paul Ricoeur and the Hermeneutic Imagination." *Philosophy and Social Criticism* 14, no. 2 (1988): 115–45.

Kemp, J. "The Work of Art and the Artist's Intentions." *British Journal of Aesthetics* 4 (1964): 146–54.

Knapp, S., and W. B. Michaels. "Against Theory 2." *Critical Inquiry* 14 (1988): 49–68.

"Against Theory." *Critical Inquiry* 8 (1982): 723–42.

Koestler, Arthur. "The Aesthetics of Snobbery." *Horizon* 7 (1965): 80–3.

Kornblyth, Hilary. "Referring to Artifacts." *Philosophical Review* 89 (1980): 109–14.

Korsmeyer, Carolyn. "On Distinguishing 'Aesthetic' from 'Artistic.'" *The Journal of Aesthetic Education* 11, no. 4 (1977): 45–57.

Krauss, Rosalind, E. "Postmodernism and the Paraliterary." In *The Originality of the Avant-Garde and Other Myths*, pp. 291–95. Cambrige, MA: MIT Press, 1983.

Kripke, Saul A. *Naming and Necessity.* Cambridge, MA: Harvard University Press, 1987. Reprint of 1980 edition.

Wittgenstein on Rules and Private Language. Oxford: Basil Blackwell, 1982.

Landa, Friar Diego de. *Yucatán: Before and After the Conquest*, trans. with notes W. Gates. Mexico: San Fernando, 1993.

Lang, Berel, ed. *The Concept of Style.* Ithaca, NY: Cornell University Press, 1987.

Lang, Helen. "Philosophy as Text and Context." *Philosophy and Rhetoric* 18 (1985): 158–70.

LePore, E., ed. *Truth and Interpretation: Perspectives on the Philosophy of Donald Davidson.* Oxford: Basil Blackwell, 1985.

Lessing, Alfred. "What Is Wrong with a Forgery?" *Journal of Aesthetics and Art Criticism* 23 (1964): 461–71.

Lewis, Charlton T., and Charles Short. *A Latin Dictionary.* Oxford: Clarendon Press, 1966.

Lewis, David. *Convention.* Cambridge, MA: Harvard University Press, 1969.

Locke, John. *An Essay Concerning Human Understanding,* 2 vols. New York: Dover Publications, 1959.

Losoncy, Thomas A. "The Being of the Work of Art: Aristotle on His Predecessors." *Diotima* 15 (1987): 60–5.

Losonsky, Michael. "The Nature of Artifacts." *Philosophy* 65 (1990): 81–88.

Lottman, Jury. *The Structure of the Artistic Text.* Ann Arbor: University of Michigan Press, 1977.

Louch, Alfred. "Critical Discussion." *Philosophy and Literature* 10 (1986): 325–33.

Lowe, E. J. "On the Identity of Artifacts." *Journal of Philosophy* 80 (1983): 220–31.

Luther, Martin. *Selections,* ed. J. Dillenberger. Garden City, NY: Doubleday, 1961.

Lyons, John. *Semantics.* Cambridge: Cambridge University Press, 1977.

Lyotard, Jean-François. *The Postmodern Condition: A Report on Knowledge,* trans. Geoff Bennington and Brian Massumi. Minneapolis: University of Minnesota Press, 1984.

MacIntyre, Alasdair. *Three Versions of Moral Inquiry: Encyclopedia, Genealogy, and Tradition.* Notre Dame, IN: University of Notre Dame Press, 1990.

——— *Whose Justice: Which Rationality?* Notre Dame, IN: University of Notre Dame Press, 1988.

——— "Contexts of Interpretation." *Boston University Journal* 24 (1976): 41–6.

Makkreel, Rudolf A. *Imagination and Interpretation in Kant: The Hermeneutical Import of the "Critique of Judgment".* Chicago: University of Chicago Press, 1990.

——— *Dilthey: Philosopher of the Human Studies.* Princeton, NJ: Princeton University Press, 1975.

Man, Paul de. *Blindness and Insight: Essays in the Rhetoric of Contemporary Criteria.* New York: Oxford University Press, 1971.

Mandelbaum, Maurice H. "The History of Ideas, Intellectual History, and the History of Philosophy." *History and Theory,* Beiheft 5 (1965): 33–66.

Margolis, Joseph. "Reinterpreting Interpretation." *Journal of Aesthetics and Art Criticism* 47, no. 3 (1989): 237–51.

——— *Art and Philosophy.* Brighton, Sussex: Harvester Press, 1980.

——— "The Ontological Peculiarity of Works of Arts." *Journal of Aesthetics and Art Criticism* 36, no. 1 (1977): 45–50.

——— "Robust Relativism." *Journal of Aesthetics and Art Criticism* 35 (1976): 37–46.

"Works of Art as Physically Embodied and Culturally Emergent Entities." *British Journal of Aesthetics* 14, no. 3 (1974): 187–96.

"Critics and Literature." *The British Journal of Aesthetics* 11 (1971): 369–84.

"Numerical Identity and Reference in the Arts." *British Journal of Aesthetics* 10 (1970): 138–46.

"On Disputes about the Ontological Status of a Work of Art." *The British Journal of Aesthetics* 8 (1968): 147–54.

The Language of Art Criticism. Detroit: Wayne State University Press, 1965.

"The Logic of Interpretation." In Joseph Margolis, ed., *Philosophy Looks at the Arts,* pp. 108–18. New York: Scribner Publishers, 1962.

ed. *Philosophy Looks at the Arts.* New York: Scribner Publishers, 1962.

Maritain, Jacques. *The Degrees of Knowledge,* trans. Gerald B. Phelan. New York: Charles Scribner's Sons, 1959.

"Sign and Symbol." *Journal of the Warburg Institute* 1 (1937): 1–11.

Meiland, J. W. "Interpretation as a Cognitive Discipline." *Philosophy and Literature* 2 (1978): 23–45.

Merrell, Floyd. *Deconstruction Reframed.* West Lafayette, OH: Purdue University Press, 1988.

Mill, John Stuart. *A System of Logic, Ratiocinative and Inductive; Being a Connected View of the Principles of Evidence and the Methods of Scientific Investigation.* New York: Harper and Brothers, 1850.

Miller, Arthur S. "Review of Raoul Berger's *Government by Judiciary. Washington Post,* 13 November 1977.

Miller, J. Hillis. "Theory and Practice: Response to Vincent Leitch." *Critical Inquiry* 6 (1980): 609–14.

"The Critic as Host." In Harold Bloom et al., *Deconstruction and Criticism.* pp. 217–53. New York: The Seabury Press, 1979.

"Ariachne's Broken Woof." *Georgia Review* 31 (1977): 44–60.

"Walter Peter: A Partial Portrait." *Daedalus* 105 (1976): 97–113.

"Stevens' Rock and Criticism as Cure, I and II." *Georgia Review* 30 (1976): 5–31 and 330–48.

"Tradition and Difference" *Diacritics* 2 (1972): 6–13.

Mills, Charles W. "Comment on John Pittman's 'MacIntyre on Tradition.'" *APA Newsletter* 91, no. 1 (1992): 22–26.

Molina, D. Newton de, ed. *On Literary Intention.* Edinburgh: University of Edinburgh Press, 1976.

Morris, Charles. *Signs, Language, and Behavior.* New York: Prentice-Hall, 1946.

Foundations of a Theory of Signs. Chicago: University of Chicago Press, 1938.

Mulhern, J. J. "Treatises, Dialogues, and Interpretation." *The Monist* 53, no. 4 (1969): 631–41.

Murphey, Murray. *Philosophical Foundations of Historical Knowledge.* Albany: SUNY Press, 1994.

Nagel, Thomas. *Mortal Questions.* New York: Cambridge University Press, 1979.

Nehamas, Alexander. "Writer, Text, Work, Author." In Anthony J. Cascardi, ed., *Literature and the Question of Philosophy,* pp. 267–91. Baltimore: Johns Hopkins University Press, 1987.

"What an Author Is." *The Journal of Philosophy* 83 (1986): 685–91.

"The Postulated Author: Critical Monism as a Regulative Ideal." *Critical Inquiry* 8 (1981–1982): 133–49.

Nietzsche, Friedrich. "Interpretation." In G. L. Ormiston and A. D. Schrift, eds., *Transforming the Hermeneutic Context: From Nietzsche to Nancy,* pp. 43–58. Albany: SUNY Press, 1990.

The Will to Power, trans. Walter Kaufmann and R. J. Hollingdale. New York: Random House, 1967.

On the Genealogy of Morals, trans. Walter Kaufmann and R. J. Hollingdale. New York: Vintage Books, 1969.

Gesammelte Werke, vol. 16. Munich: Musarion Verlag, 1920.

Norris, Christopher. *The Deconstructive Turn: Essays in the Rhetoric of Philosophy.* London: Methuen, 1983.

Deconstruction: Theory and Practice. London: Methuen, 1982.

Ockham, William of. *Summa totius logicae, selections.* In Philotheus Boehner, ed. and trans., *Ockham: Philosophical Writings,* pp. 35–43 and 50–106. London: Nelson, 1957.

Ogden, C.K., and I. A. Richards. *The Meaning of Meaning.* New York: Harcourt, Brace and Co., 1941.

Ohmann, Richard. "Speech Acts and the Definition of Literature." *Philosophy and Rhetoric* 4, 1 (1971): 1–19.

Ormiston, G. L., and A. D. Schrift. eds. *Transforming the Hermeneutic Context: From Nietzsche to Nancy.* Albany: SUNY Press, 1990.

Ortega y Gasset, José. *El tema de nuestro tiempo.* In *Obras completas,* vol. 3, pp. 143–242. Madrid: Revista de Occidente, 1947.

Palmer, R. *Hermeneutics.* Evanston, IL: Northwestern University Press, 1969.

Pannier, Russell. "An Analysis of the Theory of Original Intent." *William Mitchell Law Review* 18 no. 3 (1992): 695–729.

Panofsky, Erwin. "The History of Art as a Humanistic Discipline." In *Meaning in the Visual Arts: Papers in and on Art History,* pp. 1–25. Garden City, NY: Doubleday, 1955.

Patterson, Dennis M. "Authorial Intent and Hermeneutics." *Canadian Journal of Law and Jurisprudence* 2 (1989): 79–83.

"Interpretation in Law: Toward a Reconstruction of the Current Debate." *Villanova Law Review* 29 (1984): 671–94.

Peirce, Charles Sanders. *Collected Papers,* ed. Charles Hartshorne and Paul Weiss. vol. 6. Cambridge, MA: Harvard University Press, 1931.

Peña, Lorenzo. *Hallazgos filosóficos.* Salamanca: Publicaciones Universidad Pontificia, 1992.

Petöfi, J. S. "A Frame for Frames." *Proceedings of the Second Annual Meeting of the Berkley Linguistic Society* 2 (1976): 319–29.

Phelan, James. "Validity Redux: The Relation of Author, Reader, and Text in the Act of Interpretation." *Papers in Comparative Studies* 1 (1981): 80–111.

Pittman, John. "MacIntyre on Tradition." *APA Newsletter* 91, no. 1 (1992): 19–22.

Planned Parenthood of Southeastern Pennsylvania v. Casey, 112 S.Ct. 2791 (U.S. June 29, 1992).

Plato. *Apology.* In Edith Hamilton and Huntington Cairns, eds., *The Collected Dialogues of Plato, Including the Letters,* pp. 3–26. New York: Pantheon Books, 1961.

Meno. In Edith Hamilton and Huntington Cairns, eds., *The Collected Dialogues of Plato, Including the Letters.* New York: Pantheon Books, 1961, pp. 353-84.

Phaedrus. In Edith Hamilton and Huntington Cairns, eds., *The Collected Dialogues of Plato, Including the Letters,* pp. 475–525. New York: Pantheon Books, 1961.

Protagoras. In Edith Hamilton and Huntington Cairns, ed., *The Collected Dialogues of Plato, Including the Letters,* pp. 308–352. New York: Pantheon Books, 1961.

Sophist. In Edith Hamilton and Huntington Cairns, eds., *The Collected Dialogues of Plato, Including the Letters,* pp. 957–1017. New York: Pantheon Books, 1961.

Theaetetus. In Edith Hamilton and Huntington Cairns, eds., *The Collected Dialogues of Plato, Including the Letters,* pp. 845–919. New York: Pantheon Books, 1961.

Poinsot, John (John of St. Thomas). *Tractatus de signis,* interpretative arrangement by John Deely in consultation with Ralph Austin Powell. Berkeley: University of California Press, 1985.

Pollard, P., and J. St. B. T. Evans. "The Effect of Prior Beliefs in Reasoning: An Associational Interpretation." *British Journal of Psychology* 72 (1981): 73–82.

Popper, Karl, R. *The Logic of Scientific Discovery.* New York: Harper and Row Publishers, 1968.

Pound, R. *An Introduction to the Philosophy of Law.* New Haven, CT: Yale University Press, 1959.

Porphyry. *Isagoge,* trans. Edward W. Warren. Toronto: Pontifical Institute of Mediaeval Studies, 1975.

Pradham, S. "Minimalist Semantics: Davidson and Derrida on Meaning, Use, an Convention." *Diacritics* 16 (1986): 66–77.

Pugliatti, Paola. *Lo sguardo nel racconto.* Bologna: Lanichelli, 1985.

Putnam, Hilary. *Reason, Truth and History.* Cambridge: Cambridge University Press, 1981.

"Realism and Reason." In *Meaning and the Moral Sciences,* pp. 123–40. London: Routledge & Kegan Paul, 1978.

"Meaning and Reference." In Stephen Schwartz, ed., *Naming, Necessity and Natural Kinds*, pp. 119–132. Ithaca, NY: Cornell University Press, 1977.

"The Meaning of 'Meaning.'" In *Mind, Language, and Reality.* Philosophical Papers, vol. 2, pp. 215–77. Cambridge: Cambridge University Press, 1975.

"Language and Reality." In *Mind, Language and Reality,* pp. 272–90. Philosophical Papers, vol. 2. Cambridge, MA: Cambridge University Press, 1975.

Quine, W. V. O. "Indeterminacy of Translation Again." *Journal of Philosophy* 84 (1987): 5–10.

"On the Reasons for Indeterminacy of Translation." *Journal of Philosophy* 67 (1970): 178–83.

Ontological Relativity and Other Essays. New York: Columbia University Press, 1969.

Word and Object. Cambridge, MA: MIT Press, 1960.

"Two Dogmas of Empiricism." In *From a Logical Point of View*, pp. 20–46. Cambridge, MA: Harvard University Press, 1953.

"On What There Is." *In From a Logical Point of View,* pp. 1–19. Cambridge, MA: Harvard University Press, 1953.

Rabinowitz, Peter J. *Before Reading: Narrative Conventions and the Politics of Interpretation.* Ithaca, NY: Cornell University Press, 1987.

Redpath, T. "The Meaning of a Poem." In C. A. Mace, ed., *British Philosophy in Mid-Century,* pp. 361–75. London: Allen and Unwin, 1957.

"Some Problems in Modern Aesthetics." In C.A. Mace, ed., *British Philosophy in the Mid-Century*, pp. 361–90. London: Allen and Unwin, 1957.

Richards, I. A. *Principles of Literary Criticism.* London: Routledge and Kegan Paul, 1966.

"Toward a Theory of Translating." In Arthur F. Wright, ed., *Studies in Chinese Thought,* pp. 247–62. Chicago: University of Chicago Press, 1953.

Ricoeur, Paul. "On Interpretation." In Kenneth Baynes et al., eds,. *After Philosophy: End or Transformation?* pp. 357–80. Cambridge, MA: MIT Press, 1988.

Hermeneutics and the Human Sciences, ed. J. Thompson. Cambridge: Cambridge University Press, 1987.

Time and Narrativity, 3 vols, trans. K. McLaughlin and D. Pellauer. Chicago: University of Chicago Press, 1984.

"Structure, Word, Event." In Charles E. Reagan and David Stewart, eds., *The Philosophy of Paul Ricoeur: An Anthology of His Work,* pp. 120–33. Boston: Beacon Press, 1978.

"Creativity in Language: Word, Polysemy, Metaphor." In Charles E. Reagan and David Stewart, eds., *The Philosophy of Paul Ricoeur: An Anthology of His Work,* pp. 109–33. Boston: Beacon Press, 1978.

"Explanation and Understanding: On Some Remarkable Connections Among the Theory of the Text, Theory of Action, and Theory of History." In Charles E. Reagan and David Stewart, eds., *The Philosophy of Paul Ricoeur,* pp. 149–66. Boston: Beacon Press, 1978.

Interpretation Theory: Discourse and the Surplus of Meaning. Austin: University of Texas Press, 1976.

"The Model of the Text: Meaning and Action Considered as a Text." *Social Research* 38 (1971): 529–62.

Robinson, John Mansley. *An Introduction to Early Greek Philosophy.* Boston: Houghton Mifflin Co., 1968.

Rorty, Amélie Oksenberg, ed. *The Identities of Persons.* Berkeley: University of California Press, 1976.

Rorty, Richard. "Philosophy as Science, as Metaphor, and as Politics." In Avner Cohen and Marcelo Dascal, eds., *The Institution of Philosophy: A Discipline in Crisis?* pp. 13–33. La Salle, IL: Open Court, 1989.

"Nineteenth-Century Idealism and Twentieth-Century Textualism." In *Consequences of Pragmatism (Essays, 1972–1980),* pp. 139–59. Minneapolis: University of Minnesota Press, 1982.

"Cavell on Skepticism." In *Consequences of Pragmatism (Essays: 1972–1980).* pp. 176–90. Minneapolis: University of Minnesota Press, 1982.

Philosophy and the Mirror of Nature. Princeton, NJ: Princeton University Press, 1979.

Rosen, Stanley, "The Limits of Interpretation." In Anthony J. Cascardi, ed., *Literature and the Question of Philosophy,* pp. 213–41. Baltimore: Johns Hopkins University Press, 1987.

Rosenblatt, Louise M. *The Reader, the Text, the Poem: The Transactional Theory of the Literary Work.* Carbondale and Edwardville: Southern Illinois University Press, 1978.

Rumelhart, D. E. "Some Problems with the Notion of Literal Meanings." In A. Ortony, ed., *Metaphor and Thought,* pp. 78–90. London: Cambridge University Press, 1979.

Russell, Bertrand. *Logic and Knowledge, Essays 1901-1950.* ed. R. C. Marsh. London: Allen and Unwin, 1956.

    An Inquiry into Meaning and Truth. London: Allen and Unwin, 1940.

Said, Edward. "Roads Taken and Not Taken in Contemporary Criticism." *Contemporary Literature* 17 (1976): 327–48.

Sankowski, Edward. "Free Action, Social Institutions, and the Definition of Art." *Philosophical Studies* 37 (1980): 67–79.

Saunders, John Turk, and Donald F. Henze. *The Private Language Problem.* New York: Random House, 1967.

Saussure, Ferdinand de. *Course in General Linguistics,* trans. Wade Baskin. New York: Philosophical Library, 1959.

Saville, Anthony. *The Test of Time.* Oxford: Clarendon Press, 1982.

    "The Place of Intention in the Concept of Art." In H. Osborne, ed., *Aesthetics,* pp. 158–76. London: Oxford University Press, 1972.

Schank, Robert C. *Conceptual Information Processing.* Amsterdam and New York: North-Holland and Elsevier, 1975.

Schauer, F. "Precedent." *Stanford Law Review* 39 (1987): 571–605.

    "1787: The Constitution in Perspective: 'We Ordain and Establish': The Constitution as Literary Text: The Constitution as Text and Rule." *William and Mary Law Review* 29 (1987): 41–51.

Schiffer, S. R. *Meaning.* Oxford: Clarendon Press, 1972.

Schleiermacher, F. D. E. *Hermeneutics: The Handwritten Manuscripts,* ed. Heinz Kimmerle, trans. James Duke and Jack Forstman. Missoula, MT: Scholars Press, 1977.

Hermeneutik, ed. Heinz Kimmerle. Heidelberg: Carl Winter, 1959.

Scholes, Robert. *Protocols of Reading.* New Haven, CT: Yale University Press, 1989.

Schwartz, Stephen. "Putnam on Artifacts." *Philosophical Review* 87 (1978): 566–74.

Sclafani, R. J. "'Art' and Artifactuality." *Southwestern Journal of Philosophy* 1, no. 3 (1970): 103–10.

Searle, John R. *Intentionality: An Essay in the Philosophy of Mind.* Cambridge: Cambridge University Press, 1984.

"Minds, Brains, and Programs." *The Behavioral and Brain Sciences* 3 (1980): 417–24.

"The Background of Meaning." In John R. Searle et al., eds., *Speech Act Theory and Pragmatics,* pp. 221–32. Dordrecht: Reidel, 1980.

Expression and Meaning: Studies in the Theory of Speech Acts. Cambridge: Cambridge University Press, 1979.

"Literal Meaning." *Erkenntnis* 13 (1978): 207–24.

"Reiterating the Differences: A Reply to Derrida." *Glyph* 1 (1977): 198–208.

"The Logical Status of Fictional Discourse." *New Literary History* 5 (1975): 319–32.

"A Taxonomy of Illocutionary Acts." *Minnesota Studies in Philosophy of Science* 6 (1975): 344–69.

Speech Acts: An Essay in the Philosophy of Language. Cambridge: Cambridge University Press, 1969.

"Austin on Locutionary and Illocutionary Acts." *Philosophical Review* 77 (1968): 405–24.

"Meaning and Speech Acts." In C. D. Rollins, ed., *Knowledge and Experience.* pp. 28–37. Pittsburgh, PA: University of Pittsburgh Press, 1962.

Skinner, Q. "Motives, Intentions and the Interpretation of Texts." *New Literary History* 3 (1971–72): 393–408.

Slinn, E. Warwick. "Deconstruction and Meaning: The Textuality Game." *Philosophy and Literature* 12 (1988): 80–87.

Smith, Barry. "Textual Deference." *American Philosophical Quarterly* 28, no. 1 (1991): 1–12.

"Practices of the Arts." In J. C. Nyiri and Barry Smith, eds., *Practical Knowledge: Outlines of a Theory of Traditions and Skills,* pp. 172-209. London: Croom Helm, 1988.

Sontag, Susan. *Against Interpretation.* New York: Fallar, Steams and Giroux, 1961.

Sosa, Ernest. "Serious Philosophy and the Freedom of Spirit." *Journal of Philosophy* 84 (1987): 707–26.

Spade, Paul Vincent. "The Semantics of Terms." In Norman Kretzmann et al., eds., *The Cambridge History of Later Medieval Philosophy,* pp. 188-210. Cambridge: Cambridge University Press, 1982.

Specht, Ernst Konrad. "Literary-Critical Interpretation—Psychoanalytic Interpretation," trans. John M. Connolly and Thomas Keutner. In John M. Connolly and Thomas Keutner, eds., *Hermeneutics versus Science? Three German Views,* pp. 153–69. Notre Dame, IN: University of Notre Dame Press, 1988.

Spingarn, J. E. "The New Criticism." In *Creative Criticism in America,* pp. 3–38. New York: Harcourt, 1931.

Stalker, Douglas. "The Importance of Being an Artifact." *Philosophia* 8 (1979): 701–1?

Stallman, Robert W. "Intentions." In Alex Preminger et al., eds., *Princeton Encyclopdia of Poetry and Poetics,* pp. 398–400. Princeton, NJ: Princeton Universit Press, 1974.

Stegmüller, Wolfgang. "Walther von der Vogelweide's Lyric of Dream-Love and Quas. 3C 273: Reflections on the So-Called 'Circle of Understanding' and on the S(Called 'Theory-Ladenness of Observation,'" trans. John M. Connolly and Th(mas Keutner. In John M. Connolly and Thomas Keutner, eds., *Hermeneuti(Versus Science? Three German Views,* pp. 102–52. Notre Dame, IN: Universit of Notre Dame Press, 1988.

Steiner, George. *After Babel: Aspects of Language and Translation.* New York: Oxfor(University Press, 1975.

Stern, Laurent. "Factual Constraints on Interpreting." *Monist* 73 (1990): 205-21.

Stevenson, C. L. "On the Reasons That Can Be Given for the Interpretation of a Poem." In J. Margolis, ed., *Philosophy Looks at the Arts,* pp. 121–39. New York: Scribner Publs., 1962.

"Interpretation and Evaluation in Aesthetics." In Max Black, ed., *Philosophical Analysis*, pp. 319–58. Ithaca, NY: Cornell University Press, 1950.

Stock, Brian. *Listening for the Text: On the Uses of the Past.* Baltimore: The Johns Hopkins University Press, 1990.

Strawson, P. F. "Intention and Convention in Speech Acts." *Philosophical Review* 73, no. 4 (1964): 439–60.

    Analysis and Metaphysics: An Introduction to Philosophy. Oxford: Oxford University Press, 1992.

Suárez, Francisco. *Disputationes metaphysicae*. In Carolo Berton, ed., *Opera omnia*, vols 25 and 26. Paris: Vivès, 1981.

Sulreman, Susan R., and Inge Crossman, eds. *The Reader in the Text: Essays on Audience and Interpretation*. Princeton, NJ: Princeton University Press, 1980.

Tanselle, G. T. "Textual Criticism and Literary Sociology." *Studies in Bibliography* 44 (1991): 83–143.

    "Textual Criticism and Deconstruction." *Studies in Bibliography* 43 (1990): 1–33.

    A Rationale of Textual Criticism. Philadelphia: University of Pennsylvania Press, 1989.

    "Greg's Theory of the Copy-Text and the Editing of American Literature." *Studies in Bibliography* 28 (1975): 167–229.

Tolhurst, W. E. "On What a Text Is and How It Means." *British Journal of Aesthetics* 19 (1979): 3–14.

    and Wheeler, S. C. "On Textual Individuation." *Philosophical Studies* 35 (1979): 187–97.

Tomas, Vincent, ed. *Creativity in the Arts*. Englewood Cliffs, NJ: Prentice-Hall, 1964.

Tompkins, Jane P., ed. *Reader-Response Criticism: From Formalism to Post-Structuralism*. Baltimore: Johns Hopkins University Press, 1980.

Trilling, L. *The Liberal Imagination*. Garden City, NY: Doubleday, 1950.

Unamuno, Miguel de. "On the Reading and Interpretation of *Don Quixote*." In J. R. Jones and K. Douglas, eds., *Miguel de Cervantes, Don Quijote*, pp. 974–79. New York: W. W. Norton, 1981.

Van Dijk, Teun A. *Text and Context: Explorations in the Semantics and Pragmatics of Discourse.* London: Longman, 1977.

Vico, Giovanni Battista. *The New Science,* trans. from 3rd ed. (1744) Thomas Goddard Bergin and Max Harold Fisch. Garden City, NY: Anchor Books, 1961.

Wachterhauser, Brice. "Interpreting Texts: Objectivity or Participation?" *Man and World* 19 (1986): 439–57.

Wallace, J. "Only in the Context of a Sentence Do Words Have Any Meaning." *Midwest Studies in Philosophy, 2: Studies in the Philosophy of Language,* ed. P. A. French, T. E. Uehling, Jr., and H. K. Wettstein. Morris, MN: University of Minnesota Press, 1977.

Walton, Kendall L. "Style and the Products and Processes of Art." In Berel Lang, ed. *The Concept of Style,* pp. 72–103. Ithaca, NY: Cornell University Press, 1987.

Warnke, Georgia. *Gadamer: Hermeneutics, Tradition and Reason.* Stanford, CA: Stanford University Press, 1987.

Wasserstrom, R. *The Judicial Decision: Toward a Theory of Legal Justification.* Stanford, CA: Stanford University Press, 1961.

Weisheipl, James A. *Friar Thomas D'Aquino: His Life, Thought and Work.* Garden City, NY: Doubleday and Co., 1974.

Weitz, Morris. *Problems in Aesthetics.* New York: Macmillan, 1970.

Hamlet and the Philosophy of Literary Criticism. Chicago: University of Chicago Press, 1964.

"The Philosophy of Criticism." *Proceedings of the Third International Congress on Aesthetics,* Venice, Sept. 3–5, pp. 207–16. Turin: Edizioni della Rivista di Estetica, Instituto di Estetica dell'Universitá di Torino, 1957.

"The Role of Theory in Aesthetics." *Journal of Aesthetics and Art Criticism* 15 (1956): 27–35.

Weizman, Elda, and Marcelo Dascal. "On Clues and Cues: Strategies of Text-Understanding." *Journal of Literary Semantics* 20, no. 1 (1991): 18–30.

Wellek, R., and A. Warren. *Theory of Literature.* New York: Harcourt, Brace, and World, 1956.

Wheeler, S., III. "The Indeterminacy of French Interpretation." In E. LePore, *Truth and Interpretation.* Oxford: Blackwell, 1985.

White, Hayden. "The Absurdist Moment in Contemporary Literary Theory." *Contemporary Literature* 17 (1976): 378–403.

Wilsmore, Susan. "The Literary Work Is not Its Text." *Philosophy and Literature* 11 (1987): 307–16.

Wimsatt, W. K. "Genesis: A Fallacy Revisited." In P. Demetz et al., eds., *The Disciplines of Criticism: Essays in Literary Theory, Interpretation, and History,* pp. 193–225. New Haven, CT: Yale University Press, 1968.

and Monroe C. Beardsley. "The Intentional Fallacy." In *The Verbal Icon: Studies in the Meaning of Poetry,* pp. 3–18. Lexington: University of Kentucky Press, 1954.

and Monroe C. Beardsley. "The Intentional Fallacy." *The Sewanee Review* 54 (1946): 468–88.

Winch, Peter. "Understanding a Primitive Society." *American Philosophical Quarterly* 1 (1964): 307–24.

Winston, P. H. *Artificial Intelligence.* Reading, MA: Addison-Wesley, 1977.

Wittgenstein, Ludwig. *Tractatus Logico-Philosophicus,* trans. C. K. Ogden. London: Routledge and Kegan Paul, 1981.

Zettel, ed. G. E. M. Anscombe and G. H. von Wright. Berkeley: University of California Press, 1967.

Philosophical Investigations, trans. by G. E. M. Anscombe. New York: Macmillan, 1965.

The Blue and Brown Books. New York: Harper and Row, 1965.

Wolterstorff, Nicholas. "Evidence, Entitled Belief, and the Gospels." *Faith and Philosophy* 6, no. 4 (1989): 429–59.

Art in Action. Grand Rapids, MI: Eerdmans Publishing Co., 1980.

Works and Worlds of Art. Oxford: Oxford University Press, 1980.

"Toward an Ontology of Art Works." *Nous* 9, no. 2 (1975): 115–42.

"Are Properties Meanings?" *The Journal of Philosophy* 67 (1960): 277–81.

Wylie, Alison. "Archaeological Cables and Tacking: The Implications of Practice for Bernstein's *Options Beyond Objectivism and Relativism.*" *Philosophy of Social Sciences* 19 (1989): 1–18.

Zemach, E. M. "Nesting: The Ontology of Interpretation." *The Monist* 73 (1990): 296–311.

INDEX OF AUTHORS

This index includes only authors mentioned in the main text of the book or in the notes. It was prepared by Kenneth Shockley.

Abrams, M.H., 235, 236, 240, 256, 257, 259, 262, 264, 267
Aleinikoff, T.A., 260
Aquinas, Thomas, 75, 91, 93, 243, 259
Aristotle, 17, 22, 90, 148, 149, 168, 192, 236, 237, 238, 239, 243, 244, 245, 267
Arriaga, Roderigo de, 260
Ashworth, E.J., 243
Augustine, 32, 93, 110, 189, 190, 238, 244, 258, 261, 266, 267
Austin, J.L., 239, 241
Averroes, 148, 149
Ayer, A.J., 236, 240, 250, 257

Barthes, Roland, 240, 247, 248, 255, 259, 264, 266
Beardsley, Monroe C., 245, 250, 253, 254, 255, 256, 260, 261
Beethoven, 58
Berger, Raoul, 260, 261
Black, M., 240, 241
Bloom, Harold, 252, 257, 259
Blunt, A., 247
Boethius, Anicius Manlius Severiuns, 149, 262
Bonaventure, 244
Borges, Jorge Luis, 117, 242, 254, 263
Bork, R., 260
Bosch, Hieronymus, 56
Boticelli, Sandro, 54
Brest, Paul, 261
Brown, R., 250, 253, 259, 261

Buck, Günther, 239, 266
Budge, E.A. Wallis, 265

Cain, William E., 260
Cajetan (Thomas de Vio), 243
Carleton, Thomas Compton, 243, 260
Carnap, Rudolf, 239
Carter, William R., 245
Castañeda, Héctor-Neri, 235
Cervantes, Miguel de, 16, 27, 60, 61, 65, 117
Chadwick, John, 265
Champollion, Jean François, 265
Chomsky, Noam, 240, 241, 244
Cicero, Marcus Tullius, xix
Coe, Michael D., 265
Collingwood, Robin George, 253, 263
Connolly, John M., 253, 261, 266
Copi, Irving, 250
Currie, Gregory, 244, 247, 248, 249, 256, 261, 263, 264, 265

Danto, Arthur C., 236, 238
Dascal, Marcelo, 242, 243, 253, 254
Davidson, Donald, 238, 240, 243
Deely, John, 243
Demeraux, David, 245
Dennett, Daniel C., 255
Derrida, Jacques, 236, 237, 238, 243, 247, 252, 254, 255, 256, 257, 266, 267
Descartes, René, 267

Descombes, V., 262
Dewey, John, 245
Dickie, George, 243, 245, 246, 247, 253
Dilthey, W., 260, 266
Dipert, Randall R., xviii, 245, 246
Doyle, John P., 237, 257, 260
Duchamp, Marcel, 53
Dummett, Michael, 236
Duns Scotus, John, 74
Dworkin, Ronald, 252, 261

Eco, Umberto, 237, 238, 240, 241, 248, 250, 252, 253, 254, 255, 260
Elgin, Catherine Z., 236, 237, 247, 248, 249, 258, 260, 264
Eliot, T.S., 56, 251, 257, 260
Ellis, J.M., 256, 257, 259
Euclid, 67, 69

Fairservis, Walter, A., Jr., 266
Fernández, A., 253
Fischer, Michael, 257
Fish, Stanley, 241, 249, 253, 254, 256, 257, 268
Fletcher, James J., 245
Foucault, Michel, 251, 259, 264, 265, 267
Frege, Gottlob, 238, 239, 241

Gadamer, Hans-Georg, 237, 251, 252, 254, 255, 257, 259, 261, 262, 266, 268
Garvey, J.H., 260
Gaudí, Antoni, 80
Gazdar, G., 242
George, Stefan, 252
Gibbon, Edward, 15
Gibbs, R., 243
Gibson, William, 267
Gilson, Etienne, 236
Glickman, Jack, 246
Góngora, Luis de, 66
Goodman, Nelson, 236, 237, 247, 248, 249, 258, 260, 264

Gracia, Jorge J.E., 236, 251, 259, 263, 264, 265
Gratian, 89
Greenlee, Douglas, 244
Greetham, D.C., 250

Hammurabi, 89
Hampshire, Stuart, 254
Hegel, G.W.F., 251
Heidegger, Martin, 252, 266
Hirsch, E.D., Jr., 240, 250, 252, 253, 256, 257, 258, 262, 263, 265
Holland, Norman, 256
Horton, Susan, 264
Hurtado de Mendoza, 260

Ingarden, Roman, 239, 248, 249
Iseminger, Gary, 245
Iser, Wolfgang, 248, 250

Jakobson, Roman, 244, 250
Jerome, vii
Jones, Peter, 240, 251, 252, 254, 259, 264, 265, 267
Juhl, P.D., 253, 255, 256, 258, 261, 264
Justinian, 89

Kant, Immanuel, xxiv, 55, 56, 57, 90, 169, 202, 247, 260, 261
Katz, Jerrold J., 242, 243
Keutner, Thomas, 253, 261, 266
Knapp, S., 241, 252, 253, 255
Koestler, Arthur, 246
Kornblyth, Hilary, 245
Korsmeyer, Carolyn, 245
Krauss, Rosalind E., 257
Kripke, Saul, 235, 252, 268

Landa, Friar Diego de, 265
Lang, Berel, 249
Lang, Helen, 254
Leibniz, Gottfried Wilhelm, 96

Lewis, David, 243
Locke, John, 239
Losonsky, Michael, 245
Louch, Alfred, 255, 256, 257
Luther, Martin, 211

Makkreel, Rudolf, xviii, 260, 261, 266
Malebranche, Nicolas, 267
Mallarmé, Etienne Stéphane, 66, 255
Mandelbaum, Maurice H., 251
Margolis, Joseph, 237, 246, 248, 257
Maritain, Jacques, 236
Meiland, J.W., 241, 253, 255, 256, 257, 258, 260, 262
Michaels, W.B., 241, 252, 253, 255
Mill, John Stuart, 84
Miller, Arthur S., 261
Miller, J. Hillis, 239, 242, 243, 247, 251, 254, 255, 256, 259, 264, 265, 266, 268
Molina, D. Newton, 260
Morris, Charles, 243
Mozart, Wolfgang Amadeus, 81
Mulhern, J.J., 254

Nehamas, Alexander, 247, 248, 249, 251, 258, 260, 263, 264, 266, 267
Nietzsche, Friedrich, 251, 252, 259, 261

Ockham, William of, 244
Origen, 259
Ortega y Gassett, José, 289

Pannier, Russell, 261
Panofsky, Erwin, 246, 253, 263, 267
Peirce, Charles Sanders, 244, 264
Phelan, James, 257
Plato, 16, 91, 103, 190, 208, 238, 239, 250, 251, 253, 260, 266
Poinsot, John (John of St. Thomas), 237, 244
Pollock, Jackson, 56, 187
Popper, Karl R., 135, 260
Pound, R., 250

Poussin, Nicolas, 246
Pradham, S., 255
Putnam, Hilary, 239, 242, 244, 254, 257, 260

Quine, W.V.O., 238, 239, 247, 266, 267, 268

Redpath, T., 253, 258
Richards, I.A., 253
Ricoeur, Paul, 237, 238, 243, 244, 249, 255, 259, 262, 267
Robinson, John Mansley, 267
Rorty, Richard, 235, 236, 238, 249, 255, 261, 266, 268
Rosen, Stanley, 235, 266
Russell, Bertrand, 81

St. John of the Cross, 58, 58
St. Paul, 96
Sankowski, Edward, 245
Schiffer, S.R., 241, 267
Schleiermacher, F.D.E. 253, 255, 258, 260, 262, 266
Schwartz, Stephen, 245
Sclafani, R.J., 246
Searle, John R., 198, 199, 239, 240, 241, 242, 243, 250, 267
Sextus Empiricus, 267
Shakespeare, William, 18, 69
Sitz, Herbert, 193, 195, 199
Slinn, E. Warwick, 255, 256, 257, 258, 267
Socrates, vii, 15, 18, 103
Spade, Paul Vincent, 240
Specht, Ernst Konrad, 252, 258, 262
Stalker, Douglas, 245
Stallman, Robert W., 260
Stegmüller, Wolfgang, 250, 251, 254, 266
Steiner, George, 263
Stern, Laurent, 257, 264
Stevenson, C.L., 253, 258, 262, 263
Strawson, P.F., 236, 239

Suárez, Francisco, 60, 63, 91, 202, 203,
   260

Tanselle, G.T., 249
Taylor, Charles, 251
Tolhurst, W.E., 242, 252, 253, 254
Tomas, Vincent, 250

Unamuno, Miguel de, 260

Vázquez, Gabriel, 260
Velázquez, Diego Rodríguez da Silva y,
   62, 69
Vico, Giovanni Battista, 268
Voltaire, François Marie Arouet de, 96

Wachterhauser, Brice, 252, 255, 262
Wallace, J., 238
Walton, Kendall L., 242, 246, 247, 254
Warnke, Georgia, 251, 253, 257, 258,
   259
Weisheipl, James A., 249
Weitz, Morris, 246, 262, 265
Weizman, Elda, 242
White, Hayden, 256
Wilsmore, Susan, 247, 249
Wimsatt, W.K., 253, 255, 258
Winch, Peter, 268
Wittgenstein, Ludwig, 60, 124, 236, 237,
   242, 257, 268
Wolf, F.A., 253
Wolterstorff, Nicholas, 253, 258, 262
Wylie, Alison, 265

INDEX OF SUBJECTS

This index is intended as a guide to readers who wish to find the main places where key topics and terms are discussed. No attempt has been made to record all the places where those topics and terms are discussed.

abstraction, 186, 231
act(s): locutionary, illocutionary, and perlocutionary, 17, 21-22, 239, 240, 248; mental, 22, 103, 112; of understanding, 103-107, 127, 161, 223
actual texts(s), 74-76, 97, 221
aesthetic experience(s) vs. artistic experience(s), 53-59, 73, 219-220, 246, 247; and literary text(s), 90
aesthetic object(s), 52-55
aesthetic value vs. artistic value, 246
Analysis, xvii
Anglo-American philosophy, xiv
arrangement(s), 25-26, 242; conventional vs. natural, 33
artifact(s): vs. art object(s), 52-59, 71, 72-73, 246, 247; and design(s), 44-52, 219; vs. intention(s), 44-52, 219, 245; vs. text(s), 44-52, 70, 71, 219, 245; vs. work(s), 62, 68, 247
artistic experience. See aesthetic experience vs. artistic experience
artist(s) vs. author(s), 77-79
art object(s), 52-59, 71, 72-73, 79, 219-220, 246; vs. aesthetic object(s), 52-55; vs. artifact(s), 52-59, 71, 72-73; 246, 247, and design(s), 55-56; vs. cognitive meaning, 69; vs. meaning, 56-57, 69; vs. text(s), 52-59, 219; religious, 92-93; vs. work(s), 62, 68
art work(s). See work(s)
audience(s): contemporaneous, 129, 255,

263, 264; contemporary, 142, 152-164, 263, 264; function of, 160; historical, 129, 151-160, 263, 264; intended, 263; intention(s) of, 116-117; intermediary, 263; and meaning, 116-117, 125; rights of, 136-141; and understanding(s), 116-117, 136-141, 224
author(s): vs. artist(s), 77-79; intention of, 28, 29, 82, 112, 115, 119, 137, 224, 246, 249, 255, 256, 260, 261; and meaning, 72, 114-116, 125, 134, 253; pseudo-historical, 263; real vs. instrumental, 139; rights of, 130

Chinese Room, 198-199
civilization(s) vs. culture(s), xiii
contemporary text, 75-76, 97, 128, 221-222
context(s): 26-30, 242, 243; historical vs. contemporary, 30, 129, 218; indeterminacy of, 242; and knowledge of texts, 183, 184, 188-189, 195; vs. meaning(s), 28, 117, 118, 218, 225, 242; of signs, 13; of texts, 13, 218; taxonomies of, 242
Continental philosophy, xiv, xvii, 236
convention(s), 243; and design(s), 243; and sign(s), 31-33, 217, 244; and text(s), 30-34, 209-210, 217, 219
cultural function: of texts, 86-87, 89-98, 111, 123-127, 131, 135, 138, 144,

145, 155, 159, 170, 207, 221; of interpretations, 164, 166, 176, 177, 179; and meaning, 123-127, 138-141; and limits of meaning and understanding, 107-145, 225-226; and works, 67-68
culture(s): vs. civilization(s), xiii; vs. nature, 207-209

design(s), 44-52; Mabstract, 187; and artifacts, 44-52, 219; and art objects, 55-56; vs. convention(s), 243; and works, 67, 69, 70
discernibility, xxvii-xxviii, 181-214

ECTs. *See* entities that constitute texts
entities that constitute texts: vs. meaning, 14-15; vs. texts, 4-7, 119-120, 216, 237; vs. works, 63-64
epistemology, xxii-xxiv, 182; of texts, xxvii-xxviii, 99-214
exegetical methodology, 212-213
expected behavior, 189-213
extension of 'text', xxvi, 41-72, 244-251

falsifiability, 57, 203
form(s) of life, 209, 233, 242, 267
function(s) of interpretation(s), 152-164, 167, 170; historical, 153-160, 170, 178, 228; implicative, 154-155, 161, 170, 178, 228; meaning, 154, 160, 170, 178, 228
function(s) of texts:
confessional, 94-95; cultural, 86-87, 89-98, 111, 123-127, 131, 135, 138, 144, 145, 155, 159, 170, 207, 221; directive, 87-88; entertaining, 95; evaluative, 88; expressive, 88; historical, 93-94; informative, 87; inspirational, 95; legal, 89-90, 124; linguistic, 86-89, 98, 221; literary, 90; pedagogical, 94; performative, 88; philosophical, 90-91; pneumonic, 95; political, 94; psychologi-

cal, 138; primary, 19-22, 217; religious, 92-93, 124; scientific, 91-92, 124
hermeneutic circle, 189-193, 209, 211, 232, 238, 266
historical text(s), 74-75, 79, 84-85, 93-94, 97, 128, 138, 221-222
historicity: intensional vs. extensional, 250
history of philosophy and texts, xiii

ideal text(s), 83-86, 97, 170, 221-223; vs. historical text(s), 84-85
illocutionary act(s). *See* act(s)
innatism, 192-193, 239, 267
intended text(s), 76-83, 97, 113, 221-222, 249; and meaning(s), 81; vs. mental text(s), 80-81
intension of 'text': xxv-xxvi, 1-39, 236-244
intention(s), 23-24; and artifact(s), 44-52, 219, 245; and art object(s), 55-56; of audience(s), 116-117; of the author, 28, 29, 82, 112, 115, 119, 137, 224, 246, 249, 255, 256, 260, 261; and meaning(s), 112-114, 137, 144, 224, 250; and text(s), 23-24, 72, 76-83, 114; vs. understanding(s), 112-114; and work(s), 67, 69, 70, 255
intentional fallacy, 246
intermediary text, 76, 97, 221
interpretandum, 149, 150, 151, 152, 158, 161, 170, 171, 174, 176, 177, 179, 227, 229
interpretans, 149, 150, 151, 152, 158, 161, 170, 171, 174, 176, 177, 179, 227
interpretation(s), xxvii-xviii, 147-180, 221, 262-265; adequacy and effectiveness of, 162, 163, 173, 179, 229; constructive vs. hypothetical, 258; and contemporary audience(s), 152-164; and contemporary text(s), 150, 151; correct vs. incorrect, 169;

cultural function of, 164, 166, 176, 177, 179; definition of, 149; definitive, 169-170, 179; etymology of, 147; function of, 152-164, 173, 178; generic function of, 159, 228; historical, 164-168, 228, 229-230, 264; and historical audience(s), 151-160; and historical author(s), 152-160; historical function of, 153-160, 170, 178, 228; and historical text(s), 150; implicative function of, 154-155, 161, 170, 178, 228; and intended text(s), 150-151; and intermediary text(s), 151; interpretation of, 177; and Interpreter's Dilemma, 152-164, 228; limits of, 127; linguistic, 264; as meaning(s), 262; meaning of, 176-177; meaning function of, 154, 160, 170, 178, 228; mental, spoken, or written, 150; and misinterpretation(s), 166-167; and misunderstanding(s), 158, 160, 167, 168; and natural languages, 171; nature and ontological status of, 147-152; nontextual, 164-168, 178, 229-230; number of nontextual, 175, 178-179; number of textual, 168-171, 178-179; objectivity and subjectivity of nontextual, 176, 178-179, 231, 265; objectivity and subjectivity of textual, 174-175, 178-179, 230; of texts, xxvii-xviii, 147-180; textual, 164-168, 178, 229-230, 264; truth value of nontextual, 175-176, 231; truth value of textual, 171-173, 231; types of, 164-168, 178; understanding of, 176; as understanding(s), 148, 221, 236, 248, 258, 262; and understandings of texts, 152-164; validity of, 66-67; vs. work(s), 70
Interpreter's Dilemma, 152-164, 228

language(s): artificial, 42-44, 71, 218; and meaning, 118-119, 132, 225; natural, 25, 26, 37, 42-44, 116, 139, 140, 171, 183, 218, 242; vs. sign(s), 43-44; vs. text(s), 41-44, 70, 71, 218, 244
linguistic competence, 201-202
locutionary act(s). See act(s)
logic, xxii-xxiv, 182, 236; of texts, xxv-xxvi, 1-98

meaning(s), 14-23, 252-261; and art objects, 56-57, 69; and audience(s), 116-117, 125; authorial, 72, 125, 253; and author(s), 114-116, 134; cognitive, 20-23, 56, 57, 59, 69, 72, 241; complexity of, 10-11, 216; constructed by audiences, 126; and context(s), 28, 117, 118, 125, 218, 225, 242; core of, 125-126, 135, 257, 258; and cultural function, 123-127, 138-141;vs. entities that constitute texts, 14-15; essential and accidental differences in, 110-111, 130-131, 144, 160, 224; and falsifiability, 57, 203; functional view, 17, 216; historical, 152, 258; ideational view of, 16, 216, 248; implications of, 111-112, 118, 130, 144, 224; implicit vs. apparent, 62; and intended text(s), 81; and intention(s), 112-114, 137, 144, 224, 250; and interpretation(s), 262; and language, 118-119, 132, 225; limits of, 22, 23, 24, 108-127, 225-226, 252, 254, 261; literal, 29, 125, 242, 243, 253, 259; referential view of, 15-16, 216, 238; vs. significance, 18-19, 216-217; of signs, 13, 126, 187, 190-191, 196-197, 216, 238, 239; simple, 10, 216; and society, 117-118, 225; specific, 14-23, 109; vs. understanding, 14-23, 103-104, 107, 240; as use, 17-18, 239, 240, 241; and verifiability, 57, 203; vs. work(s), 65-70, 126, 220-221

metaphysics, xxii-xxiv, 236
misunderstanding(s). *See*
    understanding(s)

organization, 186, 231

perlocutionary act(s). *See* act(s)
philosophy: Anglo-American, xiv;
    conception of, xiv; Continental, xiv,
    xvii, 236; history of, xiii; and
    theory, xiv, 235
Principle of Contextual Relevance, 29
Principle of Epistemic Accessibility, 34-
    36, 218
Principle of Proportional Understanding,
    156-157, 178, 228

reference: vs. meaning, 15-16; paradox
    of, 238
repetition, 186-188, 231

significance vs. meaning, 18-19, 216-217

sign(s): abstract, 186; context of, 13; vs.
    entities that constitute signs, 5-6; vs.
    languages, 43-44; meaning of, 13,
    126, 187, 190-191, 196-197, 216,
    238, 239; natural vs. conventional,
    31-33, 217, 244; as displayed
    notices, 11; syncategorematic, 25;
    vs. texts, 7-14, 70, 216, 237, 238;
    vs. works, 237
skepticism, 192-193
society and meaning(s), 117-118, 225
style, 64, 249

text(s):
    actual, 74-76, 97, 221; vs.
    artifact(s), 44-52, 70, 71, 219, 245;
    artistic, 72; vs. art object(s), 52-59,
    219; complexity of, 7-14, 60; as
    concept(s), xx-xxi; confessional, 94-

95; contemporary, 75-76, 97, 128,
150, 151, 221-222; context of, 13,
218; conventionality of, 30-34, 209-
210, 217, 219; definition of, 1-4,
215-216; directive, 87-88;
discernibility of, xxvii-xxviii, 181-
214; vs. ECTs, 4-7, 119-120, 216,
237; entertaining, 95; epistemology
of, xxvii-xxviii, 99-214; ethical, 19;
etymology of, 7; evaluative, 88;
expressive, 88; extension of, xxvi,
41-72; functional classification of,
86-98; historical, 74-75, 79, 93-94,
97, 128, 138, 150, 221-222;
historicity of, 28-29; ideal, 83-86,
150, 151, 170, 221-223; informative, 87; inspirational, 95; intended,
76-83, 97, 113, 150, 151, 221-222,
249; intension of, xxv-xxvi, 1-39;
and intentions, 23-24, 72, 76-83,
114; intermediary, 76, 97, 151, 221;
interpretation of, xxvii-xviii, 147-
180; knowledge of, 182-189, 195;
vs. language(s), 41-44, 70, 71, 218,
244; legal, 89-90, 111; and limits of
meaning, 119-123; literary, xvi, 36,
67, 69, 72, 73, 90, 110, 135, 138,
243, 250; logical, epistemological,
and metaphysical issues about, xxii-
xxiv; logic of, xxv-xxvi, 1-98;
mental, 35, 80, 81, 113, 133, 222;
modal classification of, 74-86, 221-
223; natural vs. conventional, 31-
34; as nonphysical objects, xx-xxi,
6; oral, xiii, 17, 115, 194; pedagogical, 94; performative, 20, 88;
philosophical, xvi, 19, 67, 90-91;
as physical object(s), xx-xxi, 6, 55,
80, 83, 113, 222; pneumonic, 95;
psychological, 138; poetic, 119,
120; political, 94; purpose of, 19-22;
religious, 92-93, 111, 138; revealed,
81, 82, 139; scientific, xvi, 91-92,
123, 124; vs. sign(s), 7-14, 70, 216,
237, 238; specific meaning of, 14-
23, 109; taxonomy (classification)

of, xxvi, 73-98, 221-223; understanding of, xxvii, 99-145, 152-164,
194-213, 217; vs. works, 59-70,
220-221; written, xiii, 6, 14, 17, 73,
76, 115, 133, 202
textualism, 247, 261
tradition(s): and discernibility of texts,
207-213, 233, 268; interpretative,
137
translation, 62-63, 65, 68, 69, 72, 81,
115, 147, 149, 152, 158-159, 247,
264, 268

understanding(s), xxvii, 99-145, 189-213,
251-261; as act(s), 103-107, 127,
161, 223; and audiences, 116-117,
136-141, 224; of the author, 115,
135, 136-141, 145, 224; certainty in
textual, 193-213, 232; complexity
of, 104; vs. explanation, 147, 251;
intended, 113; vs. intention(s), 112-
114; and interpretation(s), 148, 152-
164, 176, 221, 227, 236, 248, 258,
262; limits of, 107-145, 223-226;
logical, epistemological, and
metaphysical, xxii-xxiv; vs.
meaning(s), 14-23, 103-104, 107,
240; as mental act(s), 103, 112;
vs. misunderstanding(s), 101-102,
105, 106, 108, 127-145, 194-195,
223-226; number of, 104-105;
objectivity and subjectivity of, 142,
145, 227; sameness and difference
of, 104-105, 223; of texts, xxvii, 99-
145, 152-164, 194-213, 217; and
textual identity, 106-107; truth value
of, 141-142, 145, 261; vs. works,
65, 70, 248

verifiability, 57, 203

work(s): of art, 36, 61, 68, 126, 236, 245,
246, 247, 250; vs. art object(s), 62,
68, 247; vs. artifact(s), 62, 68, 247;

and design(s), 67, 69, 70; vs. ECTs,
63-64; and cultural function(s), 67-
68; and design, 67, 69, 70; as
experience(s) of authors, 248;
fictional, 15; vs. intention(s), 67, 69,
70, 255; vs. interpretation(s), 70;
literary, xx, 64, 69, 126, 264; as
meaning(s), 65-70, 126, 220-221; of
nature, 61; of philosophy, 67; of
science, 67; vs. sign(s), 237; vs.
text(s), 59-70, 220-221; vs.
understanding(s), 65, 70, 248